P9-AFQ-967

"He who knows not the world,

knows not his own place in it."

MARCUS AURELIUS

The Unicorn
BOOK of
1952

Prepared under the Editorial Direction of

JOSEPH LAFFAN MORSE, Sc.B.,LL.B.

Editor in Chief

THE NEW FUNK & WAGNALLS ENCYCLOPEDIA

UNICORN BOOKS, INC., NEW YORK

STAFF

Joseph L. Morse, Editor in Chief
Richard M. Gordon, Executive Editor
Clayton Rawson, Art Director
Homer Cable, Picture Research
John Hackett, Consultant

WRITERS: Val Adams • George A. W. Boehm • Patricia Coffin
David Dempsey • Stanley W. Page • Terry Ferrer • Harrison Forman
Lewis Funke • Roland Gammon • Gordon C. Hamilton • Karl Hess
Ned Kenworthy • Joseph Roddy • Stephen White • Robert Whalen
Samuel T. Williamson • Harry B. Murkland • Nancy G. Wilbur
Martin Fass • Al B. Perlman • Morris Weeks, Jr. • Barbara Yuncker

PRODUCTION: James Allen • Richard Davy • Kathleen Lester
Annabelle Nemser • Ruth Renz • Marjorie Rose • Sheldon Rose

Copyright, 1953,
Unicorn Books, Inc.

Copyright Under the Articles of the Copyright Convention of the Pan-American Republics and the United
States. Manufactured in the United States of America.

Preface

TO SUMMARIZE THE OUTSTANDING EVENTS during a single year of a world in turmoil was no easy task. Further, to recreate these events, breathing life into dead statistics and stale news, relating single developments to a vast complex of past history and future consequences, and then integrating the whole into a single vivid picture—this was a job of greater magnitude than the reader will imagine.

That we have succeeded in some degree in our object is due almost wholly to the faithful and hardworking group of writer-scholars whose names appear on the opposite page, and particularly to Richard M. Gordon, who carried the work through from my first bare outline and statement of style to the finished book you see here. Further special commendation must go to John Hackett, whose assistance to Mr. Gordon on editorial content was invaluable, to Clayton Rawson, whose artistic eye and hand made these pages so attractive to read, and to Homer Cable, whose taste and ingenuity have yielded the finest news pictures of the year to make our book a prize to be treasured.

By these special mentions I wish to take no credit from any other of those whose labor produced the completed work. The reader will understand, I am sure, that only loving, skillful, and cooperative endeavor could have made the volume possible.

We are really proud of it. As the first in an indefinite, continuing series of such books it represents more than our best effort. It is a promise of still better books to come, since now we have learned our problem in every aspect, and are better equipped to improve on it for future years.

We—all of us on the staff—hope the reader will enjoy our book, will refer to it frequently as time goes on, and, twenty or more years from now, will gain even greater pleasure from a rereading in detail of what happened to everyone on the planet in this great year 1952.

Here is the stuff of history—living history, or as living as history can be, because it happened only yesterday.

JOSEPH LAFFAN MORSE
Editor in Chief

Contents

THE UNICORN

BOOK OF 1952

End of an Era

THE DAYS OF OUR YEARS MULTIPLY; THE seasons pass. But occasionally the wheel of time seems to pause before rolling forward. Men look at one another and say: "We have seen the end of an era." So they spoke in the final days of 1952.

In the United States, in 1952, the greatest outpouring of voters in American history turned the nation's government over to Dwight D. Eisenhower and the Republican Party. Thus came to a close the era of Franklin D. Roosevelt and Harry S. Truman.

In this twenty-year era, the U. S. staged a peaceful revolution, fought a global war against Tojo, Hitler, Mussolini, and emerged from its traditional peacetime isolation to lead the free world against Soviet Communism.

In the U.S.S.R., doctors watched the failing health of Yosif Vissarionovich Djugashvili, 73. Within a four-room apartment behind the Kremlin's thirteen-foot-thick walls, the era of Joseph Stalin was about to be closed by death. In thirty years he had completed a revolution of violence, made the Soviet Union the world's second-strongest power, brought eight hundred million people under his sway.

In London, Dowager Queen Mary looked out over the Thames from her window in Marlborough House. What changes she had seen! Fifty-five years before, at Queen Victoria's Diamond Jubilee—Mary was 30 and just married—the British Empire was at the height of its power. Now India was gone, and Britain was hard put to pay its way in the world. In six months her granddaughter Elizabeth would be crowned. But she would not live to see the great event.

In the British crown colony of Kenya, bearded Jomo ("Burning Spear") Kenyatta, schooled in England and married to a white Londoner, faced trial. He was chieftain of tribal (Mau Mau) terrorists bound by blood oath to butcher Englishmen. In terrible form, the Mau Maus dramatized the world-wide revolt of the colored races against colonialism.

In Korea, G.I. Joe, the pupil of Jefferson, Lincoln, and Wilson, warred against the servants of Marx, Stalin, and China's new dictator, Mao Tse-tung.

The greatest of all these portents of change occurred on the barren atoll of Eniwetok in the mid-Pacific. There the U.S. successfully tested a hydrogen bomb, and brought to earth some of the majesty and frightfulness of the light of the stars.

Yet, in momentous 1952, and especially in the United States, there was much to be thankful for. The American people had more jobs than ever before, more money, more luxuries, more leisure. Biologists were conquering disease. More American children were being educated. The American press was free. The courts dealt out justice within the democratic rule of law.

All in all, those ideals which had seemed so important to the signers of the Declaration of Independence—life, liberty, and the pursuit of happiness — were still, after 176 years, the ideals of the nation.

NATIONAL AFFAIRS

HER TRUSTY BROWNIE focused on President Truman, young lady in Middletown, Conn., waits patiently to take a picture. Margaret Truman seems amused

Truman's Last Year

ON A THURSDAY EVENING IN APRIL, 1945, a phone call came into an office in the Capitol in Washington. It was for the Vice-President of the United States. Harry Truman listened, paled, grabbed his hat and dashed out, saying, "I've got to go to the White House."

Franklin Roosevelt was dead; Truman was President. As he took the oath of office two hours later in the Cabinet Room of the White House, Mrs. Truman quietly wept. Next day the new President said to newsmen: "Boys, if you ever pray, pray for me now. I don't know whether you fellows ever had a load of hay fall on you."

Thus began Harry Truman's seven years and nine months in the White House. During those years he wrote history in the grand style. It was he who ordered the world's first atomic bomb dropped (on Hiroshima), helped to guide World War II to a close, rallied the free world in the cold war against Communism, gave the go-ahead for the Marshall Plan of U.S. aid to Europe and for the North Atlantic alliance of fourteen nations for defense against aggression, sent U.S.

PRESIDENT HARRY TRUMAN delights his audience in New Britain, Conn., with an unscheduled piano concert following a campaign talk. The singer in the family, daughter Margaret, is leaning over to offer a few words of encouragement

troops into battle against the Reds in Korea.

For Harry Truman, they were years of sharp ups and downs. The plucky ex-farmer and ex-haberdasher from the Mid-western heartland stood high with the voters in those first few months in 1945. He stood high with them again in 1948, when he astounded political experts by winning the Presidency in his own right. But at some other times Truman's stock was low. Many said he "wasn't big enough" for the Presidency. In general that was how it was during 1952. "Tru-manism" became practically a cuss-word in politics.

The temper of the times was evident early in the year when the President de-livered his annual State of the Union mes-sage to Congress. Democrats applauded him politely, but not often. Republicans clapped once—when he said corruption in government must be cleaned up.

These were some of the reasons why Truman was in hot water.

Inflation. Prices were high—and Tru-man got much of the blame. The prob-lem came to a head in a long, complicated struggle over wages in steel. At stake was far more than the steelworkers' pay. Higher steel wages could mean higher steel prices, and these in turn could set off a surge of inflation that might hit everyone's pocketbook.

Truman became embattled with steel management, Congress, the Supreme Court. The upshot was a two-month steel strike—and anticlimax. Steel wages and prices went up, but in the meantime U.S. business generally had leveled off. The dread of inflation faded. Nevertheless, the Republicans made political capital of the charge that Truman had botched the anti-inflation program.

The Red Hunt. Truman was on the defensive over charges of "Communist infiltration" in government. The main target was the State Department, headed by Secretary Dean Acheson. Republicans cried that Acheson was "soft on Communism", that his policies had helped bring on the Communist conquest of China and the Korean war. They ridiculed his waxed mustache and polished manners. The attack on him reached a climax when the State Department admitted it had failed to keep American Communists off the staff of U.N. headquarters in New York.

Scandals. There was white-hot controversy over graft among Federal tax collectors. Investigators in Congress brought out stories of big pay-offs and smaller favors—including mink coats—taken by officials from men in trouble over taxes. Mink coats became a bitter political joke. Taxpayers showed their anger when the Treasury Department sent them notices to make sure their tax returns were correct. Many replied, in effect: *Watch your own mistakes!*

MRS. DWIGHT D. EISENHOWER, the nation's next First Lady, calls at White House, Washington, D.C., where she and the President-elect will be living for the next four years. Welcoming her is Mrs. Truman

In Congress the anti-Truman trend was decisive. The Democrats had majorities in both House and Senate, but the President could not hold his party in line. Real power was in the hands of a coalition of conservative Southern Democrats and Republicans who fought the President to a standstill. Much of the story of national government in 1952 was the story of crackling conflict between the White House and the great domed Capitol a mile distant up Pennsylvania Avenue.

Congress pigeonholed most of what Truman packaged under the label Fair Deal—national health insurance, the Brannan farm plan, repeal of the Taft-Hartley labor law, new civil-rights laws. It ignored his call for higher taxes, universal military training for 18-year-olds, and admission of Alaska and Hawaii to Statehood.

Congress weakened the inflation-control law. It passed a new immigration act over Truman's veto. It cut—from $7.9 billion to $6 billion—the amount he wanted for aid to allies. It cut U.S. defense funds from $51.4 billion to $46.6 billion.

President Truman fought hard, but he could not stem the tide. And it kept running against him all during the 1952 election campaign. It was a far cry from '48, when the crowds yelled "Pour it on, Harry!" This time, here and there on the whistle stops, people threw eggs and tomatoes at him.

It was not that many people really hated Truman. Many still felt affection for him and his family. People cheered warmly whenever his smiling daughter Margaret stood beside him on the back platform of the campaign train. But the voters did not seem to be listening any more to what Truman had to say.

President Truman himself took it all in stride. The Presidency is a lonely job and only one man at a time can know what it is like. In his final year, Harry Truman often was philosophical. He was thinking of himself as the thirty-third in the line of Presidents, and anticipating how his chapter would look in the history books. He did not think he had done so badly. At various times in 1952 he said:

"I have had a most happy and I guess as full a life as any man of this age."

"No one man can really fill the Presidency. The President has too many and too great responsibilities. All a man can do is try and meet them."

"There are a great many people, probably a million people, who could have done the job better than I did it, but I had the job and I had to do it."

"[It is] an all-day and nearly all-night job. Between you and me and the gatepost, I like it."

"It does not make any difference what is said about [a President] while he is alive. The Presidents who have done things, who were not afraid to act, have been the most abused."

Many Americans—summing up what Truman meant for America in the great scheme of world history—felt that, for all his faults, much of his record would be vindicated by the judgment of posterity.

Truman neared the end of his Presidency in full physical vigor, his smile bright, his stride jaunty.

When he turned 68 on May 8, he said he felt 28—and "no bragging". Wryly he declared he was sure many people would like to tie a rock to ex-Presidents and throw them into the Potomac. But he was going to have a good time and do just as he pleased. The betting was that in private life he would still be in there pitching for the Democrats.

In any event, there was no quarrel over Truman's right eventually to have an epitaph like one in Arizona he called the best a man could have. It read:

HERE LIES JACK WILLIAMS
HE DONE HIS DAMNDEST

DEFENSE

BEFORE CALVIN COOLIDGE (A CLOSE MAN with a dollar) left the White House in 1929, he complained that the military budget was becoming "stupendous". The figure that alarmed him was $668 million a year.

In 1952, the United States spent on defense about $42 billion. In addition it spent over $5 billion for aid to our allies —most of it for military assistance.

The difference between $668 million and $47,000 million measures the change

HELICOPTER HOVERS over "bombed" building as civil-defense worker descends via rope in demonstration of new rescue technique

that had taken place in American thinking in twenty-five years. It measures also America's new world leadership in the struggle to contain Communist aggression.

Actually, despite the huge sums spent, the year 1952 saw a lag in arms production. In January, President Truman announced that there would have to be a "stretch-out" of the defense build-up, that the planned peak would have to be deferred from mid-1953 to mid-1954. But the complexity of modern weapons made it impossible to meet even the revised schedules. The peak probably would not be reached until the end of 1954.

Nevertheless, in 1952 the nation made great strides toward its cold-war goal of 21 army divisions and 18 regimental combat teams, 3 marine divisions, a navy of 408 combatant ships with air support, and an air force of 143 wings. (A wing has up to 75 planes.)

Moreover, the procurement offices of the army, navy, and air force had ordered some $80 billion worth of arms for these projected forces. The tooling up of defense plants was well in hand. Large stockpiles of critical raw materials (tin, rubber, copper, manganese) had been accumulated. At the White Sands Proving Ground in New Mexico, tests went forward on guided missiles and atomic artillery. On June 14 at Groton, Conn., the President laid the keel of the *Nautilus*—the first atomic-powered submarine. And it was announced that in five years the navy probably would have an atomic-powered aircraft carrier.

While it was supplying its own troops in Korea, in Europe, in the Mediterranean, in the continental United States, the nation was also sending arms to its allies under the Mutual Security Program.

The President announced that from the beginning of the Program in August, 1951, to November, 1952, the U.S. had shipped over $3 billion in weapons and equipment to Britain, France, Italy, the Netherlands, Belgium, the Middle East, and Indochina, including 17,230 tanks and combat vehicles, 92,700 military transport vehicles, 432 naval vessels, 2673 aircraft, 19,843 artillery pieces, and 1,403,213 small arms and machine guns. ·

Since Hiroshima, these have come to be called "conventional weapons". Their production was overshadowed by a terse announcement from the Atomic Energy Commission on Sunday, Nov. 16. It said:

"Joint Task Force 132 [comprising the Atomic Energy Commission, army, navy, and air force] . . . has completed . . . weapons development tests at Eniwetok atoll in the Marshall Islands. . . . The test program included experiments contributing to thermonuclear weapons research."

The key word was "thermonuclear". The H-bomb had arrived.

In three years, the scientists of the A.E.C. had found a way to reproduce the sun's life-giving force. But they had reproduced it in a weapon with unparalleled death-dealing potentialities.

Scientists have long known that the sun's light and heat come from a seemingly endless process called "fusion", which generates enormous energy. In fusion the lightest element, hydrogen, is transformed into the second-lightest element, helium. Thus fusion is the opposite of fission—the process that takes place in the A-bomb. In fission, atoms of uranium or plutonium are split into lighter elements.

Once the scientists had mastered the A-bomb, they knew that they might be able to duplicate solar fusion. In the tremendous heat and pressure developed by the A-bomb's explosion, they thought they might have "the trigger" to change hydrogen atoms into helium.

This is what the scientists did. The actual structure of the H-bomb is, of course, secret. But the theory is common knowledge. It has two basic parts.

First, there is the A-bomb trigger. Second, there is the super-explosive charge composed of two isotopes (variants) of hydrogen—deuterium and tritium. Deuterium is fairly easy to produce; it is found in water at the ratio of 1 part to 5000. Tritium, however, must be produced slowly and at great cost.

The H-bomb announced on Nov. 16 had been set off at 7:15 A.M. Eniwetok time on Nov. 1. It was supposed to be super-hush-hush. But there was a slip-up. The mail of enlisted men was not censored. Soon letters began arriving in the United States describing "the bomb" shipped to Eniwetok in a welded compartment of a navy vessel and the awesome morning when, from a distance of 30 miles, the men of Task Force 132 saw a sheet of flame 2 miles wide shoot 5 miles into the air.

Yet this H-bomb was believed to be only a "baby", a "test-tube" model. The terrifying thing about the H-bomb is that it can be made of any desired power. Scientists believe it possible to produce an H-bomb equal to 1000 A-bombs, which would have an explosive force of 50 million tons of TNT.

Such a bomb would devastate an area

of more than 300 square miles by blast, and 1200 square miles by fire. If it were placed in a cobalt casing (cobalt is highly receptive to radioactivity), the explosion might produce a radioactive cloud, equal in potency to 5,000,000 pounds of radium, which could spread death over thousands of miles.

But that is not all. The explosion of the H-bomb releases fairly large amounts of what scientists call "Carbon 14"—a radioactive isotope of carbon which requires 5600 years to lose half its radio-activity. This carbon would make its way into the human body. Thus, scientists foresee that the end result of an H-bomb war might be a world in which both the victor and the vanquished would be sterile or would produce monstrous offspring.

In the terrible light produced by the flash over Eniwetok, Harry S. Truman, as 1952 ended, sat down to write his last State of the Union message, sent to Congress on Jan. 7, 1953. In that message he said:

ARMY'S NEWEST death-dealing tank, the "Patton 48", boasting a score of major improvements over present combat models, makes its devastating debut. Government has ordered nearly $2-billion worth

"War today between the Soviet empire and the free nations might dig the grave, not only of our Stalinist opponents, but of our own society, our world as well as theirs. . . . The war of the future would . . . destroy the very structure of a civilization that has been slowly and painfully built up through hundreds of generations."

Then he turned to the Kremlin with an awful warning:

"There is something I would say to Stalin: You claim belief in Lenin's prophecy that one stage in the development of Communist society would be war between your world and ours. But Lenin was a pre-atomic man. . . . War . . . cannot now be a stage in the development of anything save ruin for your regime and your homeland."

As 1953 began, the statesmen of the free world, and the people of the whole world, prayed that Stalin would read the President's words in the light of the flash over Eniwetok on the morning of Nov. 1, 1952.

HARRY TRUMAN seized steel plants when C.I.O.'s Philip Murray (center) and U.S. Steel's Benjamin Fairless (below) couldn't agree

INFLATION

IN 1952, MR. AND MRS. JOHN J. CITIZEN enjoyed good times. Business boomed. Unemployment was low. True, prices were high. A dollar put less than half as much food in Mrs. Citizen's market basket as before World War II. Taxes hurt, too. But Mr. and Mrs. Citizen had dollars to spend and some to save.

Yet 1952 saw fierce economic struggle in the U.S. It was waged by labor, management, and the government. Inside the government, the President, Congress, and the Supreme Court came into collision.

The controversy raged on month after month. The stakes, it seemed, were enormous. Upon the outcome, economists said, hinged the question of whether an inflationary spiral was to hit every American pocketbook and seriously damage the U.S. economic system.

Then, when it was all over, the realization dawned that the danger of serious inflation was past. Some even feared '53 or '54 might bring a slump.

Inflation is often a result of war and of mobilization for defense against war. When the government spends vast sums on armaments, it buys steel, aluminum, and other materials that ordinarily would go to civilian consumers. Factories turn out tanks, for instance, instead of cars. Goods for consumers grow scarce. People bid against each other for the goods, and prices go up.

With millions of workers producing for defense, labor also grows scarce. Companies offer higher pay to get the men they need. At the same time, the unions, with the prices going up, demand higher wages to protect the workers' standard of living.

Higher wages mean that the companies have to charge higher prices for their output. Thus prices and wages chase each other up in a spiral. Even union members who win raises gain little headway. People with fixed incomes—pensioners, for example—lose out. Savings and life insurance policies decline in value. If the inflation proceeds far enough, the end is economic chaos and collapse.

To avoid such a calamity, to "hold the line" against inflation, the U.S. had set up a complex system of controls. In charge was the top government agency for the defense build-up, the Office of Defense Mobilization (O.D.M.). Its boss was big, blunt Charles Edward ("Electric Charlie") Wilson, ex-president of General Electric, and no relation to Charles Erwin ("Engine Charlie") Wilson, president of General Motors, later to be Eisenhower's secretary of defense.

Under Electric Charlie Wilson stood the Economic Stabilization Agency (E.S.A.), supervising government controls on prices and wages. Under E.S.A. stood two agencies. One, the Office of Price Stabilization (O.P.S.), had clamped ceilings on the prices that could be charged for millions of items. The other, the eighteen-man Wage Stabilization Board (W.S.B.), set limits on how high wages could go. Sometimes, when companies and unions deadlocked and strikes threatened, W.S.B. stepped in to recommend settlements.

As 1952 began, these agencies were hard put to hold the line. Most important, a great struggle was shaping up in the giant steel industry. Biggest steel producer on earth (100,000,000 tons a year), the industry supplied the metal for everything from bobby pins to warships. It was the backbone of U.S. defense. It was led by United States Steel (Big Steel).

Against steel management was ranged steel labor, represented by the United Steelworkers, one of the biggest unions in the Congress of Industrial Organizations (C.I.O.). The union had 650,000 members in steel. Its leader, soft-spoken but determined Philip Murray, also headed the C.I.O.

MEMBERS of steelworkers' union cheer headline announcing end of 53-day strike

Steel management and steel labor started their struggle with a dispute over wages. The steelworkers were talking strike unless they got a raise; they were averaging $1.88 an hour, and the W.S.B. indicated there was room for a raise in steel under its wage ceilings. But management steadfastly refused to grant a raise— unless O.P.S., at the same time, allowed higher price ceilings for steel. And O.P.S. turned down the price boost requested by management, declaring that the companies were making enough profit to pay higher wages without charging higher prices.

Even by itself, the controversy looked ominous for U.S. defense. A long stoppage in steel would hurt arms production badly. More than that, hikes in steel prices and wages might set off boosts in prices for all the goods that steel goes into, and a wave of wage demands by other unions. A new turn in the inflation spiral could weaken the whole anti-inflation program.

President Truman had already warded off a strike by phoning Phil Murray and telling him: "Phil, you will get fair treatment." Murray kept the men on the job, while Truman ordered the W.S.B. to step in and try to find a compromise. Thereafter the struggle unfolded in three phases.

1. In March, events moved swiftly. The W.S.B. came up with its compromise—a wage hike of about 26.1 cents an hour. The union accepted. Industry still said no —not without higher prices. Benjamin Fairless, head of Big Steel, insisted: "We're not going to borrow from Peter to pay Phil." In a stormy White House session, Electric Charlie Wilson told Truman that, if steel wages went up, steel prices would have to go up too. Truman disagreed and Wilson quit.

On April 3, Murray wired the steel companies: "You are hereby notified that . . . a strike has been called . . . effective 12:01 A.M. April 9." The eyes of the nation turned to President Truman to see what he would do. Ninety minutes before the deadline, he went on radio and TV, backed the union against the companies, and announced to a stunned nation: "At midnight the government will take over the steel plants."

Secretary of Commerce Charles Sawyer wired the companies that he was in charge and told them to raise the American flag over their mills. Murray called off the strike.

The struggle now resembled a hurricane. At the center—in the argument over steel wages and prices—there was dead

GONE FISHIN': Defense Mobilizer Charles E. Wilson, who quit after differences with Truman, told newsmen his only plans were to take vacation

NEWLY ELECTED President Walter Reuther of C.I.O. gets big hand from Vice-President Allan Haywood (l.) and Clothing Workers' chief Jacob Potofsky. He succeeded late Philip Murray

calm. All around it swirled gales of controversy.

Congress was in an uproar against Truman. Clarence Randall, head of Inland Steel, went on radio and TV to declare:

"This evil deed . . . discharges a political debt to the C.I.O." Senator Taft said Truman had "usurped power which he does not have". Industry launched a huge publicity drive against Truman.

The President protested: "I am a constitutional President." He and his supporters argued that he had to seize steel in order to keep the industry producing for defense. But most of the press assailed him bitterly—more so when he maintained that he could seize the press too if need be, though he saw no need. Press editorials charged "dictatorship" and "socialism". The staid *New York Times* warned: "That way lies slavery to Government edict . . ."

The steelworkers were with Truman, but they grumbled. One complained: "All we know is, we still haven't got that raise."

2. The arena of struggle now was the courts. The companies mobilized battalions of lawyers to get the courts to say that the seizure of steel was unconstitutional. The government and the unions sent in their own lawyers to counterattack. A historic legal case was in the making, a major test of the basic structure of the U.S. government—the system of checks and balances by which the branches of the government keep each other in line.

The first round was fought in the Federal District (lower) Court in Washington, D.C., before Judge David A. Pine, 60, graying, studious, never before in the national spotlight.

Company lawyers contended that the President had no power to seize steel; to stop the strike he should have sought an injunction under the Taft-Hartley Act. Government lawyers retorted that Taft-Hartley would be unfair because the union already had held off the strike for months. They cited precedents for Truman's order: Jefferson bought Louisiana without legal authority; Lincoln freed the slaves in the Emancipation Proclamation although no law said he could.

Judge Pine's questions indicated that he was skeptical of the government's contentions. He asked a government attorney:

"You mean, if the government seized you, you couldn't stop it?" The attorney, taken aback, replied: "I'll have to think that one over." Judge Pine ruled the seizure unconstitutional.

The last round was fought in the white-marble, templelike building of the Supreme Court—highest court in the land. The lawyers worked far into the night over their briefs—175 pages for the government, 150 pages for the companies. Then the nine black-robed justices heard the case before a packed courtroom.

In May, they rendered their decision. The majority (six of the nine justices) ruled: "This seizure order cannot stand."

It was the first time in history that the Supreme Court had drawn a strict line on the power of the President. On steel seizure, it was the last word. As the late chief justice Charles Evans Hughes once said: "The Constitution is what the judges say it is."

3. Steel management had full charge of its plants once more. But, minutes after the court ruling, it also had a strike. In the steel towns—many of them clustered in the great industrial belt across Pennsylvania, Ohio, and Indiana—steelworkers dropped their tools and set up pickets outside the plant gates. The steelmaking furnaces and hearths went cold.

In June, Truman went before Congress. He got no applause and one loud boo. He put it to Congress: Either enact legislation "authorizing . . . [me] to seek an injunction . . ." or give me power to seize steel. Senator Taft called the idea "childish" and Congress did nothing about steel. Instead, it ordered the W.S.B. reorganized and stripped of its power to step into labor-management disputes.

Now industry began to starve for steel. For eight long weeks, paralysis slowly crept through the economic system. At the bargaining table, steel union and management spokesmen made some headway, but neither side would give the last half inch that would spell peace.

Then, late in July, the normally unruffled secretary of defense, Robert A. Lovett, a big businessman himself, warned that something had to be done—and fast. He called the strike a "catastrophe", said it had hurt U.S. defense production more than the worst enemy air raid could have done. Truman called Fairless and Murray to the White House, declared that he wanted an agreement within twenty-four hours—"or else".

Suddenly the end came. Murray and Fairless sat alone in a room in the White House for three and a half hours. Fairless said, in effect: "Phil, we've got to do things differently. We've got to learn to get along together. Don't think the companies are trying to break the union. We are not." Murray assured Fairless that the workers knew they had a stake in the industry's welfare.

They settled on a raise of about 21 cents an hour for the steelworkers, bringing the average wage up to about $2.10.

O.P.S., in turn, later lifted steel price ceilings about $5.65 a ton above the previous average of $110. Murray and Fairless also agreed to go through the steel towns together, making harmony speeches.

But this was not to be. On Nov. 9, a San Francisco hotel telephone operator rang Phil Murray's room with the 6:30 A.M. wake-up call he had requested. When the room failed to answer, a hotel employe unlocked the door and found Murray on the floor between the twin beds, dead of a heart attack. Mrs. Murray, asleep in her bed, had not heard the phone; her hearing aid was turned off.

One final act remained in the 1952 inflation story. In the fall, John L. Lewis, the hard-boiled old chieftain of the United Mine Workers, negotiated a raise of $1.90 a day for the coal miners. But when the W.S.B. said its policy would allow them only $1.50, the miners walked out of the pits.

Again Truman stepped in, calling Lewis to the White House and asking him, pointblank, to call off the strike while the W.S.B. ruling was reconsidered. Lewis agreed. The President then said: "Come on, I want to show you something. If that fellow Eisenhower is elected, you'll never see the inside of this place." He took Lewis on a thirty-minute tour of the White House.

Over the years, the two men had clashed hard and often. But now observers saw politics at work. Lewis had just come out for Stevenson for President.

Truman ordered the coal miners given their $1.90—and thus set off a new furor. Industry members on W.S.B. quit. W.S.B. never was able to operate again.

In fact, the whole anti-inflation program was now coming apart at the seams. U.S. production, rapidly regaining stride after the stoppages in steel and coal, zoomed to the astonishing rate of one third of a trillion dollars a year—an average of more than $20,000 for every man, woman, and child in America.

Where scarcities had been feared, surpluses appeared. There were more automobiles, television sets, refrigerators, and hundreds of other items in the stores and salesrooms than consumers wanted to buy. Food prices were sliding. Although rents were inching upward, the cost of living changed but little all during the year.

Thus economists at year's end were talking, not of inflation, but of its opposite, deflation.

Republicans now demanded that all price and wage controls be junked. They declared that the "whole bottom" had fallen out of the control program. But Truman insisted that the anti-inflation machinery must stand. He was leaving the decision on what to do next to his successor, Dwight Eisenhower.

MRS. T. LAMAR CAUDLE (seated right), wife of former assistant attorney general (center), wears mink coat which was later object of probe by House committee. Caudle, shown again on opposite page answering committee's questions, was ousted by President Truman

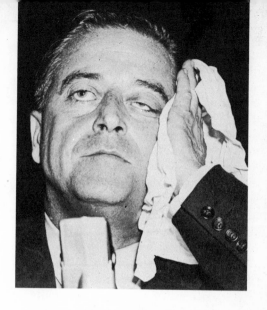

The "Mess" in Washington

EARLY IN 1952, A REPUBLICAN CONGRESS-man, watching the Truman administration struggling with the corruption issue, exulted:

"Those Democrats are going to investigate the Democrats right out of office."

That's just about what happened. The Republicans had a made-to-order situation for a campaign year. For two years, scandal had succeeded scandal. The forms of corruption varied widely. Officials in the Reconstruction Finance Corporation had smoothed the way for government loans to firms that did not really qualify for them. Officials in the Internal Revenue Bureau had fixed tax-fraud cases.

The Republican strategy was to cry "Mess!" The Democrats were damned if they did and damned if they didn't.

If the President tried to clean house, the Republicans could shout "Whitewash!" If Democrats in Congress went after the dirt to prove their honesty, the Republicans could say: "See! What did we tell you!"

The Democrats were never able to shake off the charges. Early in the year President Truman tried to take the offensive. The result was the Morris-McGrath fiasco, which gave the Republicans added ammunition.

The story had its beginnings in late 1951 in the case of T. Lamar Caudle, the assistant attorney general in charge of the Tax Division of the Justice Department.

Caudle's history is the story of a small-town North Carolina lawyer who came up the ladder—county prosecuting attorney, U.S. district attorney appointed by Franklin D. Roosevelt, then a big jump under Truman to assistant attorney general in charge of the Criminal Division of the Justice Department, and, finally, in 1947, to assistant attorney general in command of the Tax Division.

In this last job, it was Caudle's responsibility to prosecute cases of tax fraud.

In 1951, a Congressional committee found that Caudle had been chummy with businessmen and lawyers who had tax cases pending before the Department of Justice. One of these businessmen had got Mrs. Caudle a mink coat at a "bargain". Another had given Caudle $5000 for being "middleman" in a second-hand airplane sale.

In November, 1951, Mr. Truman fired Caudle for activities "incompatible with official duties". But shortly afterward peppery, dapper Attorney General Howard McGrath, who had helped mastermind Truman's '48 victory, told a Con-

gressional committee he had no idea why the President had given Caudle the sack. McGrath said his assistant might have been indiscreet, but he couldn't see that he had done anything wrong.

At this, President Truman went through the roof. There were rumors that he would dismiss McGrath. Then, as he cooled off, the President decided to appoint a bipartisan commission to investigate corruption. He chose as its head Federal Judge Thomas F. Murphy, the gruff, 6-foot, mustached legal mastiff who, as district attorney, had secured the conviction of Alger Hiss.

Murphy at first told the President he would take the job, then evidently concluded that there was no future in it. He decided to remain a judge.

The Republicans chortled. The President then told McGrath to go and get himself an assistant to do the cleanup.

At the end of January, McGrath picked his man—Newbold Morris, a New York

ENRAGED at Senate subcommittee's attempt to prove him unqualified as corruption hunter, Newbold Morris holds press conference, accuses committee member Sen. McCarthy of "character destruction"

OUSTED after two months by Attorney General McGrath, who resented questionnaires on personal finances, Morris relaxes on Washington park bench

lawyer, independent Republican who had worked with New York City's reform mayor Fiorello La Guardia back in the thirties and forties.

Morris immediately ran into trouble. First, he went to Congress and asked for powers to subpoena witnesses and grant them immunity for telling what they knew about corruption in the Federal government. Congress said no. Some legislators said such powers could be abused and should be reserved for courts and Congressional investigations. But since an investigator can get nowhere without these powers, observers in Washington thought there were other reasons behind the refusal. Some Republicans said frankly they feared Morris would use the subpoena power to tie up witnesses so that Congressional committees could not get at them. And some Congressmen feared Morris would use the power of immunity to protect, against later prosecution, government officials who talked.

Morris ran into more trouble when he came up for Senate confirmation. It was revealed that his law firm had reaped rich fees in a sale of surplus government oil tankers. Morris himself had had no part in the deal, but, as a member of the firm, he had shared in the profits.

Finally Morris, the amateur, got in a snarl with McGrath, the old political pro. Morris wanted to have 25,000 top government employees fill out a questionnaire listing their sources of outside income and all holdings of stock and real estate. He first sent the questionnaires to 596 employees in the Justice Department, including McGrath himself. McGrath was furious.

In the first week of April, McGrath testified before a House Judiciary Committee. He was in a belligerent mood. He said he had not filled out the questionnaire, didn't know whether he would or not, and didn't know whether or not he would let any member of his department fill it out. That was on a Monday.

On Tuesday, the President called for a transcript of McGrath's remarks to the Committee—a sign of trouble brewing. On Wednesday, McGrath went to the White House. He told the President he regarded the questionnaire as an infringement of personal rights. He said he would quit unless it were withdrawn.

Later that afternoon, while waiting to welcome Queen Juliana of the Netherlands at the airport, the President and McGrath got in an open row just out of earshot of reporters. They shouted angrily and waved their arms at each other.

Thursday morning, McGrath sent Morris a letter: "Your appointment . . . is hereby terminated." That afternoon, shortly before his press conference, President Truman called McGrath, asked for his resignation. McGrath said: "You have it, Mr. President."

A few minutes later, the President told reporters there was a new attorney general, James P. McGranery, a Federal judge in Philadelphia. McGrath wired him congratulations and advised, "Bring a pair of asbestos trousers with you."

The Republicans were gleeful. Although they had been attacking Morris, they now defended him. They turned their fire on McGranery, again crying "Whitewash!"

As a matter of fact, McGranery managed to take some of the heat out of the corruption issue. From the moment he assumed office, he co-operated fully with Congressional committees, and many Republicans privately admitted he did a good job.

But it was too late. It mattered little that a Democrat—Senator Estes Kefauver —in 1950–51 had uncovered the tie-up of Democratic city machines with organized crime. Or that a Democrat—Senator J. William Fulbright—in 1950–51 had uncovered influence-peddling in the Reconstruction Finance Corporation, and that the Truman administration had reorganized the R.F.C., and got rid of the offenders. Or that Democrats headed the committee investigating the Tax Division of the Justice Department and the King Committee investigating the Internal Revenue Bureau of the Treasury Department.

The thing that mattered was that the corruption took place in a Democratic administration. After twenty years in office the Democrats (like Republican regimes in the past which had held power so long) appeared to have grown morally lax. And the voters rose up and smote them.

MRS. OLGA KONOW told Senate committee she netted $300,000 for part in surplus-tanker deal

A number of years ago, the Baltimore journalist Frank Kent, one of the shrewdest of political observers, wrote of the Teapot Dome oil-steal scandal in the Harding administration: "It had been generally believed that the American people instinctively revolted against crookedness . . . that any political party caught red-handed in corruption would inevitably be swept out of power. . . . It is so no longer."

Kent was referring to the fact that the voters, after the Teapot Dome scandal, did not sweep the Republicans out of office.

Political observers gave three reasons why corruption was such a big issue in 1952.

First, they believed there had been a transformation in the American electorate. They agreed that the voters are more sensitive to corruption than in the past, quicker to take revenge on politicians and bureaucrats who betray the public trust.

Second, they thought that the comparative pettiness of some of the corruption had made it more dramatic. A woman voter who might get lost in the financial

JAMES P. McGRANERY (left) succeeded J. Howard McGrath (right) as attorney general. President Truman demanded McGrath's resignation after McGrath ousted Newbold Morris

maze of a Teapot Dome scandal could easily get indignant over a mink coat because she could visualize the coat on a government official's wife.

Third, voters were aroused because so much of the corruption involved the Internal Revenue Bureau. People might have hazy ideas about some government agencies, but they know they have a date each March 15 with Uncle Sam's tax collector. They know they have to keep that date and they don't see why some bigwig should avoid it because he has a smart lawyer who knows his way around Washington.

Take the case of Joseph D. Nunan Jr. For many years, Nunan had been an internal revenue collector in New York City —in one of the biggest tax districts in the country. From 1944 to 1947 he had been commissioner of the Internal Revenue Bureau in Washington—the top tax-collecting job. Then Nunan resigned and went back to his law firm.

His firm represented many companies with tax-fraud cases pending before the government. Nunan himself was the attorney in some of these cases. A Senate committee revealed that, after he left his Commissioner's job, Nunan represented the Indianapolis Brewing Company, against which the government had a tax claim of $812,000. This claim was settled for $4500.

In 1951 Nunan had refused to tell a House Ways and Means subcommittee anything about his finances on the ground that he might incriminate himself. He was asked if there were "any specific crimes for which you could be indicted?" Nunan said: "Yes, sir, there are."

In December, 1952, Nunan was indicted for filing false income-tax returns and cheating the government out of $91,086 between 1946 and 1950. Part of this time, Revenue Collector Nunan was the top man responsible for collecting taxes from all U.S. citizens.

It was this kind of thing, political observers believed, that made 1952 the exception to the rule that corruption switches few votes. Even the Democratic candidate for President, Adlai Stevenson, when asked whether the word "mess" expressed his own feelings, said: "It has been proved, hasn't it?"

ALGER HISS, onetime State Department official, begins five-year sentence in Federal prison for perjury. Republicans made him 1952 campaign issue

EARL BROWDER arrested, once America's No. 1 Communist

COMMUNISM

AT RUN-DOWN 25TH STREET AND SEVENTH Avenue in lower Manhattan stands a shabby, four-story building. It has a down-at-heel look. And down-at-heel were the fortunes of the party that makes the building its national headquarters—the Communist Party in the U.S.A.

Major blows had befallen the party.

Eight of its national leaders were in jail, convicted of conspiring to advocate the violent overthrow of the government. Three others were fugitives. Fourteen "second string" leaders were convicted in Los Angeles. Some were on trial in New York City. Others faced trial in Hawaii.

The Justice Department was moving in on the party every time it chose substitute leaders—chopping off its head whenever it grew a new one.

Even the Communists' ex-chief, aging Earl Browder, scratching a bare living as a printer after being booted out of the party for wartime "collaboration" with the U.S. government, got into trouble. He and his Russian-born wife were indicted for perjury in connection with her U.S. naturalization.

In politics, the U.S. Communists were pariahs. Their power at the polls had dropped sharply in the four years between Presidential elections.

In 1948 the Progressives, the leftist "third party" backed by the Communists, had rolled up more than 1,100,000 votes

ESPIONAGE AGENTS Julius and Ethel Rosenberg, who supplied Russia with atomic-bomb secrets, were sentenced in April, 1951, to die in electric chair. At end of 1952 they were still alive and pleading for clemency. Trial judge called crime "worse than murder"

for the fuzzy-voiced former Democrat Henry A. Wallace. In 1952 the Progressives, abandoned by nearly all but the Communists, got only about 150,000 votes for a frenetic lawyer named Vincent Hallinan who, during most of the campaign, had been in jail for contempt of court.

The party membership was down to about 30,000 (from 70,000 before Korea). Court trials had revealed that the party ranks were riddled with undercover government agents. *The Daily Worker*, the Communist newspaper, appealed frantically for donations to keep it going.

Despite the party's hard times, there still were plenty of things an individual American Communist could do. He could join the party, attend meetings, picket, protest, read *The Daily Worker*, travel anywhere in the country. He could vote, run for office, campaign.

But he could not conspire to advocate violent overthrow of the government without risking jail. He could not, as a known Communist, be hired by the government. He could not get a defense job

in which secrets might come under his eye. He could not obtain a passport to travel abroad. If foreign-born, he could be deported.

The American people, however, were worried not only about avowed, aboveground Communists. They were worried about underground Communists, too—those who hid their Communist sympathies while doing the work of the party. Three big cases supplied reasons why.

Alger Hiss, tall, slim, now 48, had been in jail since 1951 for swearing falsely that he had never given secret State Department documents to the self-admitted Communist courier Whittaker Chambers. A "model prisoner", he worked as a clerk in the Federal prison at Lewisburg, Pa. In the fall of 1952, he applied for parole. The government said no.

Judith Coplon, dark and petite, ex-Justice Department worker who had secret rendezvous with the Russian Valentin Gubitchev, still was free. Now married and a mother, she had been convicted as a spy. But she had won appeals on technicalities and, at year's end, it was uncertain whether she would be retried.

Julius and Ethel Rosenberg were in the death house at Sing Sing. While their lawyer tried every legal stratagem to save them, the drab couple awaited electrocution as "brains" in an atomic spy ring.

All over the world, Communists waged a "free the Rosenbergs" propaganda drive. They laid wreaths at Sing Sing gates. They cried "Anti-Semitism!" Irving Kaufman, the judge who sentenced them, said "I feel that their crime was worse than murder."

The spy cases drove home to the U.S. the danger of Communist plotting. But the big question was how to spot the plotters. Some people in the U.S. hunted Reds relentlessly. Others said the hunters were hurting the innocent as well as the guilty and threatening U.S. liberties.

A few citizens owned up to hobnobbing with Communists in the past, but denied they themselves were Communists.

Judy Holliday—the actress with a high I.Q. who played dumb blondes—told a Congressional committee she had unwittingly let her name be used by Communist fronts. "I have been slightly—more than slightly—stupid," she said.

Abe Burrows—the comic and coauthor of the Broadway hit *Guys and Dolls*—said: "I'll say I was downright stupid."

All in all, it was a good year for the hunters. Chief among them were two "Macs"—both Senators, one a Republican, the other a Democrat.

The Republican was square-jawed Joseph R. McCarthy of Wisconsin, who dropped bombshells in a low, slow voice. His assault on "Communism in the State Department" was in its third year. He began 1952 with one trophy in hand and another just out of reach. Both trophies were

PICKET LINE parading near White House in "Save the Rosenbergs" campaign is itself picketed by young man with a somewhat misspelled sign

"old China hands". They were veterans of Far East diplomacy, closely identified with Secretary of State Dean Acheson's policies, and charged by McCarthy with helping to engineer the Communist conquest of China.

The trophy McCarthy got was John Stewart Service, son of American missionaries in the Orient. He had been cleared earlier after six loyalty investigations. The State Department fired him after a seventh because in 1945 he allegedly let pro-Communists see confidential papers on the Orient.

The trophy McCarthy didn't quite get was John Carter Vincent, who had been in the Far Eastern service for twenty-eight of his fifty-three years. The ex-Communist editor Louis Budenz, now a Roman Catholic professor at Fordham University, had sworn that Vincent was "under Communist discipline". Late in the year, the Loyalty Review Board, top agency for screening out disloyal government employees, decided that Vincent should be fired. But at Acheson's behest Truman set up a special board to look into the case again.

McCarthy himself, symbol of the Red hunt, had many foes whose loyalty was above reproach. They called him a dangerous man who blackened reputations with wild charges. They pointed out that he often made his accusations in the Senate, where he was immune to lawsuit.

McCarthy's most persistent challenger was Senator William Benton, ex-advertising man and New Deal Democrat from Connecticut. Benton urged McCarthy's expulsion from the Senate for "calculated deceit and falsehood".

But McCarthy in 1952 reached a new peak of political power. In the election campaign he moved boldly. He charged that Democratic Presidential candidate Stevenson himself was "soft" on Communism, said he'd "put some Americanism"

in Stevenson if he could get on the Democrat's campaign train with a club. Democrats retorted that McCarthy was talking like a Nazi storm trooper.

Nevertheless, many Americans evidently were strong for him. A Wisconsin voter summed it up: "Sure, McCarthy's rough. But he's doing something about the Communists, isn't he?"

Wisconsin re-elected McCarthy. In the U.S. Senate, a committee investigating Benton's charges reported that it had "questions" about McCarthy. Why, for instance, did he take $10,000 from a housing concern when he was on a Senate Committee dealing with housing? Where did he get the $172,000 he deposited in a Washington bank?

The committee gave no answers.

The other "Mac" in the Red hunt was white-haired, ponderous Pat McCarran of Nevada, head of the Senate Internal Security Subcommittee. A major McCarthy target had been eloquent, peppery Owen Lattimore, professor, Far Eastern expert, sometime consultant to the State Department, denounced by McCarthy as an "architect" of Communist victory in China.

McCarran had Lattimore on the witness stand thirteen days—the longest grilling in Washington memory. They wrangled furiously. McCarran charged Lattimore with "evasion" and "significant untruth". Lattimore called Budenz a "glib liar" and McCarthy a "witch burner".

What they wrangled over seemed, as Lattimore said, "trivial". Example: Did Lattimore lunch with the Russian ambassador in Washington before or after the Nazi invasion of Russia in 1941? Lattimore said it was after the invasion—which put Russia in the Allied camp in World War II. McCarran insisted that it was before, and that Lattimore lied in order to hide his "pro-Communism".

At the end, the committee called Lattimore an "instrument" of "the Soviet conspiracy". It suggested that he be tried for perjury.

Lattimore invited prosecution. In December, a grand jury indicted him. He shouted his plea: "Not guilty!" His trial in '53 promised to be sensational.

McCarran's other main target was the United Nations. The U.N. was locked in a bitter debate over Korea, but McCarran gradually stole the headlines. His line of attack was that the U.N. Secretariat was "harboring" American Communists.

Whittaker Chambers, who had been the jowly nemesis of Alger Hiss, came from his Maryland farm to tell about a man in the Secretariat he knew as a Communist. A parade of U.N. employees filed past the committee. Most refused to say whether or not they were Communists; it might incriminate them. The senators spluttered with indignation. One said, and McCarran agreed: "[If the U.N. will not] help us purge it of spies and saboteurs . . . the U.N. ought not to be allowed to sit in America."

The heat was on the portly Norwegian U.N. secretary general, Trygve Lie. The U.N. was a world body. Communist countries were members, and so Communists had to be in the Secretariat. But the U.S. was the U.N.'s "host", and Lie had to reckon with American political tempers.

He fired the suspect American employees. Then he complained that the U.S. State Department had promised to help him keep American Communists off his staff but had not given him enough information.

When Dean Acheson testified for the State Department he seemed weary, glad his regime was ending. He admitted the screening of U.N. employees hadn't worked, but said: "My associates did the best they could." He announced that Truman was setting up a new system for U.N. loyalty checks by the F.B.I.

Acheson was sardonic. Asked about policy decisions made years back, he remarked: "My hindsight is sore at this point." About loyalty in the State Department, he said: "It is harder to get into the State Department than it is into the Union League Club."

After years of attack from Capitol Hill, Acheson had taken his last going-over.

TIRELESS FOE of alleged Communists in government was Senator McCarthy. His aggressive tactics made him one of year's controversial figures. Wisconsin voters re-elected him after bitterly fought contest

NBC
RADIO
MBS
T·V
ALL THE PEOPLE
DEMOCRATIC
NATIONAL CONVENTION
OHIO

DEMOCRATS' FIRST TEAM:
Adlai Stevenson and John J. Sparkman

Democratic Convention

THE FIGHT FOR THE DEMOCRATIC NOMINA-
tion for President began and ended in
scenes of drama involving two men.

One was Harry Truman of Missouri,
fourth Democratic President since the
Civil War (after Cleveland, Wilson, and
Franklin D. Roosevelt). The other was
Governor Adlai (*ad'-lay*) E. Stevenson of
Illinois, who would try to become the fifth
—and fail.

The two men enacted the first scene
on an evening in January, 1952, in Washington. Stevenson dropped in at Blair
House, where the Trumans were living
while the White House across the street
was being renovated. What he and Truman said was secret. But when word of

the meeting got around, the political
dopesters guessed the truth; the President
of the U.S. was sizing up a possible successor for the most powerful job on earth.

The second scene took place on a hectic
night in July in Chicago. The Democratic
convention had just made its choice—
Stevenson for President. In an atmosphere
charged with emotion, Truman, full of
bounce, introduced Stevenson to the roaring delegates. Millions had stayed up into
the small hours to watch on TV. Many
were seeing Stevenson in action for the
first time. Flashing his quick smile, he
held up his fingers in a V for victory and
said: "I will fight to win . . . with all my
heart and soul."

This man on whom the Democrats pinned their hopes had been born well-to-do. Schooled as a lawyer, he had spent most of his career in government. He had served in the State Department and in the U.S. delegation to the United Nations. In 1948 he had run for office for the first time —for the governorship of Illinois.

Even in his own State, he was little known. Professional politicians had asked one another, "Who *is* this fellow Ad-lye?"

Nevertheless, in Illinois in 1948, Stevenson won with a huge plurality of 572,000 while Truman was squeaking through with only a 34,000 edge. In his four years in Springfield, the State capital, Stevenson had made what most observers considered a good record

Now, at 52, he was in the prime of life. He was partly bald and, despite frequent tennis, rather plump. He had three sons. He was divorced; his wife got the decree, it was said, because he had entered politics against her wishes. He loved jokes and told them often.

In his approach to government, Stevenson, a scholar, reminded many of Woodrow Wilson. He was liberal, but not all-out for Truman's Fair Deal. He had a literary gift, and applied it painstakingly in his speeches. He kept a notebook full of quotations and quips to use. In U.S. politics, his was a new, ringing voice.

The events in 1952 that led to Stevenson's nomination made a strange story, full of surprises. As the campaign year opened, the great question was: What will Truman do?

The candidate then getting most of the headlines was Senator Estes Kefauver (*ess'-tess kee-foh'-ver*), tall and good-looking, and with a soft Tennessee drawl. Millions had seen him and liked him on TV as his Senate Crime Investigating Committee in 1951 exposed shady dealings between gamblers and politicians. Kefauver's trade-mark was a coonskin cap, and it was in the ring.

Kefauver started running early and hard. In February and March, he and his pretty wife Nancy tramped up and down the village streets of New Hampshire, scene of the nation's first Presidential primaries. He used the folksy approach. Stopping the townspeople, he would say: "Afternoon, ma'am, I'm Senator Kefauver and I'm running for President. I certainly would appreciate your support."

Kefauver won New Hampshire, beating Truman, then considered unbeatable. Later he entered thirteen primaries from coast to coast—and captured eleven. In popular vote appeal, Kefauver at all stages was unmatched.

COONSKIN CAP symbolized Senator Estes Kefauver's campaign for nomination. Tennessean achieved fame via televised 1951 crime hearings

SHAKE HANDS AND COME OUT FIGHTING: Aspirants for Democratic Presidential nomination fraternize—(l. to r.) Averell Harriman, Mutual Security Administrator; Vice-President Alben Barkley; Senators Estes Kefauver (Tenn.); Robert S. Kerr (Okla.); Richard B. Russell (Ga.)

But the odds were against him. Democratic leaders considered him unqualified to occupy the White House. Some resented the Kefauver Committee's probing into racketeering in Democratic strongholds. Tom Connally, the flamboyant, white-maned senator from Texas, said he didn't see why Estes "should be allowed to parlay a case against crapshooters into a Presidential nomination".

Truman didn't think much of Kefauver, either, and politicos recalled a remark by plain-spoken old John Nance Garner of Texas, former Democratic Vice-President. Anyone who ran without the President's okay, Garner said, had about as much chance "as a can of stale beer".

But Senator Paul Douglas of Illinois wrote to Kefauver: "Some of the politicians, bureaucrats, and kingmakers may not want you, because they know they cannot control you. But the people are for you. Let the voice of the people be heard."

The first surprise came on March 29. The Democrats had a big party dinner in Washington. Truman, tanned and rested after a Florida vacation, was the star speaker. The press had advance copies of his speech, but it said nothing about whether he would run and everyone was relaxed as he read it. Then the President came to an extra sheet he had inserted, with a few sentences written in his own hand. Without pause, he read on:

"I shall not be a candidate. . . . I shall not accept a renomination."

There was a stunned silence, then a chorus of "No! No!" In a few moments, Harry and Bess Truman were in their limousine headed for the White House. The President brushed away a tear.

Back in the hotel dining room, all eyes were on one of the diners, Adlai Stevenson. His face was expressionless.

LIGHTLY CLAD MODEL (left) poses atop Chicago fire escape to publicize Senator Richard Russell's candidacy. Stunt won newspaper space, but nomination eluded the conservative Georgian

Now the race was wide open and the candidates multiplied. The trouble was that most of them, like Kefauver, had drawbacks. Besides Kefauver, there were three main contenders:

Bachelor Senator Richard B. Russell of Georgia, able, well-liked, a powerful figure in the Senate, and champion of the South. But many Democrats feared that if they nominated Dick Russell they would drive away Negro and liberal votes.

Tall, slender Averell Harriman, immensely wealthy, ardent New Dealer, veteran of twenty years in administrative jobs under Roosevelt and Truman, now mutual security director in charge of aid to the Allies. But he was shy, ill at ease as a speaker, short on political experience. "No glamour," party leaders said.

Vice-President Alben W. Barkley, 74, married for the second time only three years before, famous teller of stories and thundering orator, probably the most widely beloved of all the contenders. But the politicians said he was too old.

That left Stevenson. He wouldn't say *Yes*, and when he said *No* it would not stick. It was not that he was being coy. He evidently couldn't make up his mind.

Late in April, he sounded as if he had decided. In a formal statement he declared: "I could not accept the nomination for any other office [than governor of Illinois] this summer."

Soon afterward, Stevenson met Truman at the Omaha airport, during a Midwestern flood crisis. "Adlai," Truman said,

PIG FARMER Henry Krajewski, 40, (right) was Presidential candidate of Poor Man's Party. There were 14 candidates, including Prohibition and Vegetarian nominees

"I don't believe it." Many other politicos were skeptical, too.

In May, Stevenson switched again. When Illinois Democrats asked him to "make himself available", he said he agreed with the "spirit" of the idea.

In June, he declared: "This subject is getting mighty tiresome." But party leaders saw nothing tiresome in it. They had to have a candidate. And many felt that no one else in sight could fill the bill as well as Stevenson.

Came July and convention time in the cavernous auditorium out by the Chicago stockyards. The other contenders kept beating the drums and claiming victory. But all watched Stevenson.

Just before the first bang of the convention gavel, he had a showdown with the Illinois delegation. The scene was a hotel ballroom; the press was barred. But behind drapes at one end of the room, newsmen crouched, hearing every word.

Stevenson said earnestly: "I couldn't, wouldn't, did not wish to be a candidate for President." All he wanted to do, he insisted, was run for re-election as governor. He told a story of a man who was asked whether he wanted to go to heaven or hell and replied: "I don't want to go to either place. I want to stay right here." The Illinois delegates decided party and country were bigger than Stevenson. They voted to back him for President.

The convention was a real scrap. The Democrats' hopes were high. They got a lift from the bitter Eisenhower-Taft struggle the Republicans had just waged in this same Chicago arena. No one was overconfident about the prospect of beating the general. But the Democratic hopefuls eyed the nomination as a prize that could well lead to the White House.

The big Democratic fight was between the New Dealers and the South. In general, the New Dealers were backing Harriman. Most were young. One, Representative Franklin D. Roosevelt Jr. of New York, much like his father in looks and voice, was making his first bid for national leadership.

The New Dealers set out to exact a pledge of loyalty from the Southerners—a promise to use "all honorable means" to place convention nominees on the State ballots. Some Southerners balked.

Most fiercely opposed to a firm pledge was shrewd, wiry James F. Byrnes, who had been in turn U.S. senator, Supreme Court justice, top Presidential assistant, secretary of state, and now governor of South Carolina. Despite his eloquence and the heated opposition of other Southern delegates, the loyalty-pledge resolution was carried by voice vote. The delegations from South Carolina, Virginia, and Louisiana refused to sign the pledge. Sam Rayburn of Texas, permanent chairman of the convention, then ruled they had forfeited their seats. Rayburn's ruling, along with a motion to seat Virginia regardless of its stand on the loyalty pledge, brought the New Deal-Dixiecrat stew again to the boiling point. While the vote on the motion to seat Virginia was in progress, several States, including Illinois, abandoned their pro-New Deal position, and the motion carried 615 to 529. The convention restored the seats of South Carolina and Louisiana the next day.

At the height of the battle, disaster almost struck the convention. Jimmy Byrnes had the floor when a fire broke out in some litter nearby. A man from Boston grabbed the microphone and shouted over and over, "It's only a newspaper!" When the fire was out, Byrnes remarked: "I want to announce that I did not set the place on fire." The realization that a panic had been narrowly averted snapped the tension over the loyalty pledge.

At last the balloting for the nomination got under way. Kefauver started strong. So did Stevenson and Russell.

One little-known Democrat had a moment of glory. He was heavy-set Tom Gavin, Kansas City brewer serving as alternate to one of the regular delegates from Missouri, Harry Truman. Gavin had the President's instructions on how to vote. He had kept the secret well. For days he had played hide-and-seek with reporters and had given them no clue to Truman's choice.

Then came Gavin's turn to cast his vote. He stood and read a letter to him from the President: "I hope you can see your way clear to vote for Adlai Stevenson . . ." The rest of the letter was drowned out by cheers and boos.

The band wagon began to roll. On the second ballot, Kefauver, Russell, and Stevenson gained. Truman flew in from Washington, ready to do the honors when the nominee was chosen. When the convention recessed for dinner, the President talked with Harriman people at a swank restaurant next door to the auditorium. The word went out: Harriman was throwing his votes to Stevenson.

It was all over but the counting. After the third ballot, Kefauver went to the rostrum, looking utterly exhausted after his long, hopeful, and now barren quest for the big prize. He thanked his supporters for all they had done, adding wearily: "I, and I know all my friends, will join to . . . elect Governor Stevenson as President of the United States."

Stevenson had won without lifting a finger. It was the first genuine draft of a Presidential nominee in more than half a century. Now it was up to Stevenson to answer in the campaign the question millions of voters still were asking: "Who *is* this fellow Adlai?"

''FIRST LADY OF THE WORLD'', in opinion of millions, Mrs. Eleanor Roosevelt stands under portrait of her late husband while addressing convention. She received 15-minute ovation

"IKE WILL RUN!" Senator Henry Cabot Lodge tells newsmen on Jan. 6, 1952, and Eisenhower band wagon is on its way. Announcement was first official indication general was "interested" in Presidency

Republican Convention

IT WAS OCTOBER, 1951. ON THE THIRD FLOOR of the Senate Office Building, Senator Robert A. Taft, Republican, of Ohio, sat in his inner office, reflecting on his past and future.

The senator, 62, balding, a little paunchy now, was known to colleagues as "Mr. Republican" and he deserved the title. When he walked into the Senate chamber in the midst of a big debate, the galleries immediately sensed his authority in his party. His thirteen years in the Senate had given him stature, but they had not mellowed him. He still had a mind like a steel trap, a sense of rectitude as unbending as a thorn stick, a disposition—at times—like a chestnut burr. Nor

had the thirteen years softened his ambition. Senator Taft wanted to be President.

Twice he had been a candidate for the nomination—in 1940 and 1948. And twice the "Eastern internationalists" of the party —people whom Senator Taft called the "Republican me-tooers"—had thwarted his ambition. In 1940 they had beaten him with Wendell Willkie, the political amateur with the tousled hair and the infectious grin. In 1948 they had beaten him with Governor Thomas E. Dewey of New York, whose slicked-down hair covers one of the toughest, sharpest political minds in the country.

The year 1952, Senator Taft knew, was his last chance. He also knew that the

Dewey wing was determined to beat him again. Unable to win the Presidency himself, Dewey now had cast himself in the role of President-maker. The man he had chosen was General Dwight D. Eisenhower, America's foremost military hero.

In 1945, fresh from his triumphs as supreme commander of the Allied forces that toppled Hitler's "1000-year Reich", General Eisenhower had said that anybody who thought of him as a President "ought to have his head examined". In 1948 Ike had been wooed by both parties and had said *No!*

But Ike wasn't saying *No* in the autumn of 1951. In fact, he wasn't saying anything for publication. But all summer, scouts from the Dewey camp had been dropping in on Ike at his North Atlantic Treaty headquarters in Rocquencourt, France, just outside Paris. The word they brought back was: "Ike's a Republican. He's available. But he doesn't want to fight for the nomination. He wants to be drafted."

All this was well known to Senator Taft. The one thing he feared was the kind of draft—skillfully engineered—that

had put Willkie over in 1940. The only way to kill off a draft, the senator figured, was to start early and sew up enough delegates to the Republican National Convention to win a first-ballot nomination. If Ike wanted the nomination he would have to fight for it. Taft was determined on that.

And so, on the afternoon of Oct. 16, 1951, Senator Taft called in reporters and threw his hat into the ring. Then he took off on a seven-week tour of fifteen States.

The Eisenhower forces began to worry. They dropped all idea of a draft. On Nov. 5, 1951, the general came from France to Washington to discuss N.A.T.O. affairs with President Truman.

When he left, he told reporters: "Now if I have friends that have been my friends so long they believe they know how I would act and react under given situations, that's their business . . ."

That was the tip-off. Events moved fast thereafter. Handsome Henry Cabot Lodge, Jr., then Republican senator from Massachusetts, was chosen to head the Eisenhower preconvention campaign. In mid-November he went to Paris to discuss strategy with Ike, who agreed to enter the lists publicly in February. When Taft's

THE THREE PHOTOGENIC DAUGHTERS
of California's Governor and Mrs. Earl Warren are
(l. to r.) Dorothy, 21, Nina, 18, and Virginia, 23

campaign manager, Dave S. Ingalls, heard of this, he said: "The Eisenhower balloon will never get off the ground." Ingalls said Taft was rounding up pledges so fast that he would be nominated on the first ballot.

Scared, Ike's supporters decided he would have to get out in the open fast. On Sunday afternoon, Jan. 6, 1952, Senator Lodge called a press conference in Washington's plush Wardman Park Hotel. He said he had been authorized to enter Eisenhower's name in the nation's first Republican primary in New Hampshire on March 11, and concluded dramatically: "I invite you to check this in Paris."

The next day, at Rocquencourt, Ike told the press that his supporters were "exercising [their] right . . . to place before me next July a duty that would transcend my present responsibilities". But he added that "under no circumstances" would he come home to campaign for the nomination.

Now the battle was joined—a battle that was to prove more bitter than any other preconvention campaign in Republican history. The first skirmish was fought in New Hampshire.

New Hampshire has only 14 votes at the Republican National Convention, only 4 votes in the Electoral College. But the stakes in its primary were out of all proportion to the State's political strength. This primary was to test whether Ike had the pulling power his boosters claimed.

The primary was a double contest. First, the Republican voters would choose the 14 delegates—10 at large and 2 from each of the State's two Congressional districts—to the convention. Second, for the first time in the State's history they would also state their preference for the Presidential nomination.

Originally Taft had decided against entering the New Hampshire primary, since the State was considered "safe" Eisenhower territory. Governor Sherman Adams and many other prominent Republicans were on Ike's side.

But on Jan. 29—just a few hours before the filing deadline—Taft entered his name. He said the circumstances were "unfavorable" to him, but he thought the voters ought to have a chance to choose between him and Ike.

Actually, he didn't think the circumstances were too unfavorable. His agents had, in advance, reported that he had a good chance to win. Their reasoning: Primary day in New Hampshire is also annual Town Meeting Day, the day on which rural voters gather to vote local taxes. This means the turnout is usually heavier in the small towns than in the cities. Taft's agents had found—or thought they had found—strong Taft sentiment among small-town Republican regulars.

New Hampshire will not soon forget its 1952 primary. Never had so few been wooed by so many. For six weeks before election day, Taft and Eisenhower leaders beat up and down the snow-drifted valleys. In the last week, Taft came into the State for a whirlwind campaign. He was cock-a-hoop with confidence and bristling with challenge. "They said I was afraid to come into New Hampshire," he said sarcastically. "Now I'm in and they're afraid the 'will of the people' really will be shown." Newspapermen reported that Taft was riding high and might well win.

Against this background, the returns were a surprise. Eisenhower swept the preferential primary. He captured all 14 delegates. He lost only one city—Manchester. He took 140 of the 223 small towns.

Ike's forces were jubilant. Taft was "a little disappointed", but his campaign manager, Dave Ingalls, made no bones about the setback. He said that if Taft did not make a big showing in the Wisconsin primary on April 1, "the senator might as well get out".

But, while Taft was concentrating on Wisconsin, a storm was blowing up in Minnesota.

The Minnesota Republican primary was scheduled for March 18—a week after New Hampshire's. It had attracted no attention because no real contest was involved. Taft had not entered, out of deference to Harold Stassen, a former governor. Eisenhower's supporters in Minnesota had tried to enter his name, but Stassen followers had managed to keep it off the ballot on a technicality.

This maneuver had caused resentment in Minnesota, and after Ike's victory in New Hampshire it suddenly boiled over.

Some Eisenhower leaders in Minnesota got the idea of a write-in campaign for the general. They called Eisenhower headquarters in Washington. But Ike's campaign manager, Senator Lodge, was cool. He argued that the time was too short—only four days to go until primary day—and that, if Ike made a poor showing, the advantage he had gained in New Hampshire would be wiped out.

But Minnesota Citizens for Eisenhower now had the bit in their teeth. They organized telephone squads. They rang doorbells. A newspaper instructed the voters how to write in their preference on the ballot.

On election day, snow and sleet squalls lashed Minnesota. The morning turnout was light, but at noon the voters started pouring into the polls. In Minneapolis, the ballots ran out. In many polling places, officials initialed blank sheets of paper to make them valid ballots. The voters wrote in "Ihenhawer", "Eizenhuffer", "Ike".

When the count was completed, Eisenhower had almost 107,000 write-in votes—only 21,000 short of the vote for Stassen. Taft had only 24,000 write-ins. At Washington headquarters, Ike's lieutenants were overjoyed. Their man had shown his grass-roots appeal and now his aides were certain he would hold his own in the remaining primaries.

But it takes more than grass-roots appeal and primary victories to win the nomination. Only half the 1206 delegates to the Republican National Convention are chosen by the voters in State primaries. The other half are chosen by State conventions, and in State conventions the machine politicians usually call the turn. Taft was the favorite of most of the regular Republican State organizations. The regulars like a regular.

The big problem facing Ike's aides was to cut into the Taft strength among the professionals. The pros had been impressed by Ike's showing in New Hampshire and Minnesota, and by the pro-Eisenhower argument: "Ike can win in November; Taft probably can't." But Ike's warm personality was needed to capture wavering Taft supporters. His high command decided he must get home.

Fortunately, there was a top Eisenhower leader in Paris—Paul Hoffman, who had taken leave of the philanthropic Ford Foundation to help Ike. The transatlantic cables buzzed. Hoffman told Ike: "You are up against the facts of life . . . The people say they want you . . . You must face this and come home."

Ike thought it over. Two days after the Minnesota primary he told reporters: "The mounting number of my fellow citizens who are voting to make me the Republican nominee are forcing me to re-examine my personal position and past decisions." From that moment, it was taken for granted that Ike would be home before the convention.

As for Taft, Minnesota had put him on the spot. Somewhere, somehow, he had to demonstrate that he also had grass-roots

GENERAL DOUGLAS MacARTHUR waves from limousine following keynote address to convention. Famed soldier pulled no punches in attacking policies of Democratic administration

appeal. There was a made-to-order situation for him in Wisconsin.

For one thing, Eisenhower was not entered in the April 1 Wisconsin primary. For another, the State machine was controlled by able Tom Coleman, a Taft man, who had plenty of money and was using it to good advantage. Finally, the other two entries, Harold E. Stassen and Governor Earl Warren of California, tended to cancel one another out, because both represented the party's anti-Taft internationalist wing.

Stassen and Warren were making a play for the Eisenhower vote in Wisconsin. Warren and Eisenhower leaders had struck a bargain—any delegates Warren got would go to Ike at the convention if Warren could not get the nomination himself. Stassen, not to be outdone, promised to give Ike half of any delegates he won.

Taft made the most of this situation. He rode hell-for-rubber over the whole State, calling his opponents "hybrids". His supporters talked sarcastically of "Eisenstassen" and "Warrenhower".

When the votes were counted, Taft had won a smashing victory. He got 315,000 against 261,000 for Warren and 166,000 for Stassen. He collected 24 delegates against 6 for Warren and none for Stassen.

On the same day, Taft got a further boost in the Nebraska primary. In a straight write-in contest, he beat Eisenhower by 15,000 votes and captured 16 delegates against the general's 2.

Taft had put the brakes on Ike's hurtling band wagon. The day after the Wisconsin primary, Ike wrote to Secretary of Defense Robert A. Lovett, asking to be released from the supreme command of the North Atlantic forces on June 1. Ike would come home and make a fight for it.

The first four primaries—New Hampshire, Minnesota, Wisconsin, and Nebraska—seemed to indicate a pattern. Ike apparently was stronger along the eastern seaboard, where the internationalists were concentrated, and in those sections of the Midwest, like Minnesota, that had been voting Democratic in recent elections. Taft seemed stronger in the farm States which had been traditionally Republican and isolationist.

TRYING TO BE HEARD above din of convention, delegate holds his banner high and shouts his candidate's name. Many delegates had to be treated for painfully raw throats

The remaining primaries and conventions confirmed this pattern. Ike took New Jersey, Pennsylvania, and Massachusetts. But Taft sewed up Illinois, Ohio, Indiana, and West Virginia.

Taft was on the road constantly, meeting State leaders, corralling delegates. From October, 1951, through May, 1952, he was on the stump on all but two days. On one of those two days he had his tonsils out—and issued an attack on socialized medicine. On the other he filled out his income tax—and issued an attack on high taxes.

By mid-May it was even money whether Taft or Ike would win. Then suddenly it became apparent that the 1952 contest—like many in Republican history—would be settled south of the Mason-Dixon line.

Since the Civil War, the Republican Party in the South has existed chiefly for one purpose—to sell delegates at the convention in return for Federal jobs (as marshal, customs collector, revenue officer) after the election.

Republican "ins" in the South are always regular and conservative. The "outs" are always hoping for some dynamic candidate on whose coattails they can ride into power.

In 1952, the Southern regulars were for Taft nearly 100 percent. An insurgent group—mostly young people—was whoop-

"I SHALL WIN the nomination,' Taft tells nationwide audience on eve of convention

ing it up for Ike. But when reporters went South, they found that something new had been added.

This time the insurgents had found powerful allies—Democrats who had soured on the Truman administration and Democrats who desired a real two-party system in the South. Some of these Democrats were disgruntled politicians, but many—especially in Texas—were businessmen who had decided that their proper home was the Republican Party.

A battle royal was going on all over the South between Taft forces and the coalition of Republican insurgents and former Democrats. The biggest battle was in Texas, which had 38 votes at the Republican National Convention.

In Texas, precinct and county conventions elect delegates to the State convention, which chooses the delegates to the national convention. Early in the spring, Eisenhower forces had stormed into the precinct and county conventions in such numbers that they overpowered the Taft regulars and elected pro-Eisenhower delegates to the State convention.

When this happened, the Taft forces had walked across the street and held rump conventions. They charged that the Eisenhower forces were nothing but "Democrats in disguise", and proceeded to elect a rival slate of delegates to the State convention.

At the State convention, the Eisenhower delegates learned how politics are played in Texas. A Taft man was convention chairman. Taft forces controlled the crucial credentials committee, which decides on disputed seats. Of the 1060

PRETTY VOLUNTEER for Taft cries softly when nomination goes to Eisenhower. Taft forces fought well, but now the fight is over, and they are beaten

seats, the Taft forces were contesting 606. The credentials committee gave 10 to Eisenhower, 596 to Taft.

When the Eisenhower delegates tried to appeal the decision to the convention floor, the Taft chairman ruled that the disputed Taft delegates could vote on the contests, but the disputed Eisenhower delegates could not.

The Eisenhower forces went roaring out of the convention, waving banners reading: "Rob with Bob!" "Graft with Taft!" Now they, in turn, held rump conventions and elected their own slates to the national convention.

Thus arose the issue that came to be known as the "Texas Steal". The situation was duplicated in Louisiana, and there were also rival slates in Georgia and Mississippi.

On June 1, General Ike came home. He went to the White House, where President Truman pinned a medal on him for his services to N.A.T.O., and then showed him around the renovated Executive Mansion. Ike said: "Mr. President, if I get into this business, if I get the nomination, do I have to take my wife along on the campaign train?" President Truman is reported to have answered: "I'm afraid you do—that's the way it is."

Then Ike reported to the Pentagon, took off his uniform, and headed for his home town of Abilene, Kans., which was getting ready for the biggest show since Wild Bill Hickok drew both guns and brought down two bandits running in opposite directions.

Just seven years before—after V-E Day—Abilene had given its hero a home-coming. On that occasion Ike had said of Truman: "We've got a great leader in Washington." In 1952 he came not to praise Truman but to bury him.

The two-day celebration—June 4 and 5—was billed by Ike's managers as "non-political".

On the first day, Ike laid the cornerstone of the Eisenhower Museum in a lot next to his old home and made a moving speech on the simple life and virtues of his parents.

Between showers of rain, he watched a parade depicting his life from birth in Denison, Texas, to White House (Kansas was confident even then). In the evening, to a crowd standing in a pelting rain, he made a political speech on the dangers of class warfare, bureaucracy, high prices.

The next morning, at a press conference in the local movie theater, he got a baptism of fire from 300 correspondents. They threw the book at him—Korea, Fair Employment Practices Commission, McCarthy, China policy, farm prices, tariffs. When Ike didn't know the answer, he said so. The press was delighted with his candor, but puzzled by one statement.

Eisenhower said his philosophy "generally" was that expressed in the 1950 "Republican Statement of Principles". The chief author of that statement had been Robert A. Taft. Its theme was "Liberty vs. Socialism", and senators in the Dewey wing had attacked it as illiberal.

This was the first indication that on domestic affairs Taft and Eisenhower were kissing kin. Taft said he was glad to see that the general "apparently approves" the Taft policy.

Before leaving Abilene, Ike began the "meet the boys" routine. In the parlor of a white frame house across the street from his boyhood home, he received five Midwestern delegations. Reporters on the front porch heard roars of laughter as Ike and guests swapped stories. Then he flew to New York, met nine Eastern delegations, and held a picnic for Pennsylvania's key delegation on his farm outside Gettysburg.

Ike's smile and outgoing personality pleased the delegates. Many politicians believed he would be a natural on a campaign train. One reporter said: "The difference between Ike and Taft is the difference between a popular football coach and a high-school mathematics teacher."

Nevertheless, Ike's managers were worried. From Taft country came word that Taft supporters were "loyal to Bob and are going down the line for him".

The plain fact was that Ike didn't have the needed 604 votes for the nomination. It looked as if both he and Taft would go to the convention with roughly 500.

This meant that the nomination would hang on the outcome of the delegate contests in the South, about which Eisenhower leaders were scared stiff. And with good reason. In settling disputes over convention delegates, there are three steps, and Ike faced bleak prospects at each step.

First, a week before the convention opens, the National Committee meets and draws up a temporary roll call, thus making the first decision on disputed delegates. Taft controlled a majority on the National Committee. Thus, Taft's Southern delegates were almost certain to be put on the temporary roll.

Second, after the convention is organized, the decision of the National Committee can be appealed to the Credentials Committee, which is composed of one representative from each State and Territory. Taft controlled 29 of the 53 State and Territorial organizations which chose Credentials Committee members.

Third, the decision of the Credentials Committee can be appealed to the floor of the convention for a final-verdict vote of the delegates. Here Taft might have run into trouble except for one thing—a rule, adopted back in 1912, which says that disputed delegates on the temporary roll can vote in any dispute except their own.

This rule obviously favored Taft. When the convention voted on the Georgia contest, disputed Taft delegates from Texas who had been put on the temporary roll could vote to seat the Georgia delegates favoring Taft. When the convention voted on the Texas dispute, Taft's Georgia delegates would vote for Taft's Texas slate.

Senator Taft, feeling cocky, said he was prepared to compromise the delegate contests on a "fair basis". But he believed that, if former Democrats had gone into the county conventions in Texas, Ike's delegates from these counties should be thrown out of the Republican National Convention. Eisenhower leaders cried that Taft was making it impossible for the Republicans ever to set up a real party in the South.

When Ike's people were in control, Taft replied, they were "ruthless". He saw no reason why he shouldn't be "the same".

In mid-June, the mood at Ike's headquarters was grim. Then Herbert Brownell, the impassive Wall Street lawyer who had masterminded Dewey's campaigns for governor and President and who had become Ike's top strategist, came up with a brilliantly simple idea. It was to turn Taft's control of the convention into a boomerang by arousing the country with cries of "steal" and "steam roller".

Brownell also had a gimmick up his sleeve. It was an amendment to the rules that would prevent any disputed delegates on the temporary roll from voting on delegate contests. He decided the convention would support such an amendment because, with all the hue and cry about "steam roller", the Republicans would hesitate to go before the country with a candidate whose nomination was "tainted".

Time was short, but the Eisenhower organization went swiftly to work. Ike went to Texas armed with a hellfire-and-damnation speech. He said that Taft leaders in Texas had betrayed the people. "If

RUNNING MATES Richard Nixon and Dwight D. Eisenhower, joined by their wives, acknowledge delegates' cheers with victory salute. They can now look forward to four hectic months of campaigning

a businessman used the same tactics he would be indicted and sent to prison."

In the next two weeks, Eisenhower leaders cried "Robber!" up and down the land. Taft managers shouted that the whole thing was "propaganda". Eisenhower headquarters answered by publishing a letter to the National Committee from one of Taft's own supporters in Texas. The letter warned that, if Taft used his control of the convention to seat his Texas delegates, the Republican Party would suffer in November.

In this atmosphere, the National Committee met in Chicago the week before the convention to draw up the temporary roll. The hearings on the disputed Southern delegates began on Tuesday and lasted four days. The Taft forces on the

National Committee made an error at the outset. They voted down a motion by Eisenhower supporters to have the hearings broadcast. Ike's people screamed "Star chamber!"

The fight centered on 68 delegates in four States—all of Georgia's 17; 13 of Louisiana's 15; all of Mississippi's 5; 33 of Texas' 38. The contests were taken up alphabetically. In the first three days, the Taft committee members rode roughshod. They gave Taft all of Georgia and Mississippi, and all but 2 seats of Louisiana's contested 13.

At this point, the Eisenhower people pulled a master stroke. Republican governors were in convention in Texas. Governor Dan Thornton of Colorado, an Eisenhower leader, proposed sending a message to the National Convention urging that the rules be changed to prohibit contested delegates from voting on any issue until their contests were settled. The message said this was necessary so that the party could go into the campaign with "clean hands". All 25 Republican governors signed it.

The governors' resolution seemed to frighten Taft. When the National Committee met on Friday morning to consider the big Texas dispute, he made two conciliatory moves through National Chairman Guy Gabrielson.

In the first move, Gabrielson—at Taft's urging—laid before the committee a proposal by Herbert Hoover that Ike and Taft pick representatives to meet with Hoover and reach a compromise. Taft agreed to the Hoover plan.

In the second move, Taft made a direct offer through Gabrielson to split Texas—22 for Taft, 16 for Ike.

Taft's conciliatory moves proved too little and too late. By trying to arrange a deal, he convinced many people that the charges of "steal" were true. The Eisenhower people felt at this point that they had Taft on the hip. Senator Henry Cabot Lodge said curtly: "Eisenhower is a no-deal man."

The National Committee then went ahead and divided Texas according to the Taft offer—22 and 16.

Meanwhile, Ike had left Denver on Thursday on a slow, three-day roll into Chicago. At every whistle stop, he pulled down the cord and held it down in one long blast against the Taft "steam roller".

He was greeted in Chicago on Saturday

EISENHOWER, after winning, calls on defeated rival. Disappointed Senator Taft pledges Ike full support in campaign. Ohio's "Mr. Republican" said it was last time he would seek nomination

by roaring crowds carrying signs aimed at Taft—"Thou Shalt Not Steal". Forty years before, former President Roosevelt had come into Chicago under similar circumstances. From the balcony of a Chicago hotel, T. R. had roared: "This is a naked fight against theft and thieves."

The man who controlled the party machinery that year was William Howard Taft—the father of the senator—and Taft beat Roosevelt with 50 "stolen" delegates. But 1912 was not to be repeated in 1952.

On Sunday night before the convention opened in the Chicago Auditorium, Taft was desperate. At his urging, Chairman Gabrielson called a meeting to try to reach a compromise and prevent an open floor fight. The talks lasted until 2:30 A.M. Eisenhower's representatives would not budge, but they agreed to another meeting the next day at the big amphitheater just before the convention opened.

While the bands played and the delegates waited, the meeting was held in a room backstage. The Eisenhower leaders still said "nothing doing".

The air was charged as Chairman Gabrielson called the 1206 delegates to order. Ike's forces swung swiftly into the attack, offering their resolution barring any voting by disputed delegates. The argument was bitter, punctuated by boos and cheers. The vote was 658 to 548 for the Eisenhower proposal. This was a double blow for Taft; it was a psychological defeat and it cost him a net of 32 votes on the succeeding tests.

For the next two days—Tuesday and Wednesday—the scene shifted to the Gold Room of the Congress Hotel where the Credentials Committee—the second court of appeal—heard testimony on the Southern disputes. Mississippi was settled by agreement. Taft yielded on Louisiana. The Taft-controlled Credentials Committee supported Taft on both Georgia and Texas.

The convention was at fever excitement on Wednesday night as the Georgia and Texas disputes moved to the convention floor. There was a fist fight on the floor. In a final effort to head off the Eisenhower band wagon, the Taft forces launched an attack against Dewey, saying Eisenhower was his "stooge".

In the debate over Georgia, Senator Everett Dirksen of Illinois leveled his finger at the coolly smiling Dewey at the head of the New York delegation and said: "We followed you before and you took us down the road to defeat."

The vote on Georgia was 607 to 531. Taft threw in his hand and yielded on Texas without a roll call. It was all over but the shouting.

On Friday the balloting began just before noon. On the first roll call, Eisenhower had 595 votes—9 short of victory—against Taft's 500, the largest ever amassed by a candidate who failed to make the grade. Minnesota waved its standard, switched 19 votes from Stassen, and Ike was in.

When Eisenhower got the word in his Blackstone Hotel suite, he fought his way through crowds to the Hilton Hotel, went up to Taft's headquarters, put out his hand, called the senator "a very great American", and said his help was "absolutely necessary".

It was a bitter blow for Taft, but he played the political game. He managed a smile, said he would do "everything possible".

That night Eisenhower said to the convention: "You have summoned me . . . to lead a great crusade."

IT'S ALL OVER: Workmen use MacArthur and Taft placards to sweep up tons of debris after Republicans leave. Now huge Chicago Amphitheater must be readied for 1952 Democratic convention

The CAMPAIGN

BEFORE THE REPUBLICAN CONVENTION, General Eisenhower had said: "I will not indulge in personalities."

In his acceptance speech, Governor Stevenson had said: "Let's talk sense to the American people."

It was predicted that the 1952 campaign would be different—a campaign on issues, not personalities, a campaign looking to the future, not harping on the past. Said James Reston, political expert of The *New York Times:* "The campaign will be fought not from the gutter but on the higher ground in the middle of the road."

But other observers were cynical and the cynics were right. The 1952 campaign was one of the bitterest in U.S. history.

It was fought in four battles. The first lasted five weeks—from the end of the Democratic convention on July 26 until Labor Day week end, when the candidates took to train and plane.

VICE-PRESIDENT-ELECT and Mrs. Nixon with daughters Patricia (l.), 6, and Julie, 4. He achieved early prominence as able, dogged investigator of Communism

This was the period of headquarters planning and preliminary skirmishing. In temporary headquarters in Denver's Brown Palace Hotel, Ike's top-level strategists set to work on three big problems.

The first could be summed up in one word—Taft. Ike would need Taft's help to get out the Old Guard vote, especially in the Midwest. The Taftites, sullen over their hero's defeat, were sulking.

As for Taft himself, he was playing a waiting game. After the convention, he went off to his summer home in Murray Bay, Quebec. There he told a reporter that before he entered the campaign he wanted to learn from the general "what the Administration is going to be like".

Ike moved fast. He named several prominent Taft supporters to key positions on his planning staff. He held a series of harmony lunches for Taft leaders. Most important, he wrote to Taft, saying he would like to talk things over.

The second problem was what to do about two controversial Republican senators—Joseph R. McCarthy of Wisconsin and William E. Jenner of Indiana—both up for re-election. Both had violently attacked Eisenhower's old friend and patron, General George C. Marshall, wartime chief of staff and former secretary of state and secretary of defense. Jenner had called Marshall "a front man for traitors".

Taft supporters at Eisenhower headquarters put pressure on Ike to endorse Jenner and McCarthy. In late August, Ike said he would "not support unjust damaging of reputation". But he added that he wanted to "see the Republican organization elected" and therefore would endorse all the party's candidates. This O.K. for Jenner and McCarthy pleased the Taft wing, but it also gave the Democrats an opening.

The third problem was the line of attack Ike should take. About this, Eisenhower leaders held heated arguments. Those from the Taft wing wanted Ike to damn the New Deal root and branch, to condemn Truman for getting the nation into the Korean war, to promise reduction in aid to Europe, and to adopt the Taft-Hoover position that the U.S. should make itself a "Gibraltar" behind an impregnable U.S. Navy and Air Force.

The Dewey wing disagreed, arguing that the New Deal's basic reforms had become fixed in the American way of life, and warning that Ike would be defeated if he repudiated them. Furthermore, the Deweyites supported aid to Europe, although they criticized the Democrats for "losing China to the Communists". They held that Ike could not criticize aid to Europe when he himself had been the principal instrument of that policy as supreme commander of the N.A.T.O. forces.

While this debate was going on, Eisenhower went to Los Angeles for a trial-run speech before the Veterans of Foreign Wars. There was bad staff work. No crowds were at the airport, no crowds along the street to see the motorcade. Only 16,000 turned up in the Coliseum (capacity 102,000). The speech was tepid. Ike said he was for "honesty in government", "peace", "prosperity", "equality".

Back in Denver, his advisers decided this wouldn't do. Advance agents would have to whip up enthusiasm before Ike hit town. And he would have to hit harder. The next week in Denver he took a leaf from Taft's book. He accused the administration of "misleading us toward a third world war".

At the same time, he reassured Western farmers they would continue to enjoy benefits won under the New Deal. At Boise and Kansas City he promised high supports for farm prices, said: "All those things we call social gains are accepted overwhelmingly by the American people. We stand behind them." Then he

RELAXING with spaniel "Checkers", Sen. Nixon takes brief rest from campaigning after dramatic TV appearance to account for controversial political fund

waited to see what Stevenson would do.

In his headquarters in the Governor's Mansion in Springfield, Ill., Stevenson was having his own troubles.

His organization problem also could be put in one word—Truman. Stevenson needed the President's help in New Deal strongholds as badly as Ike needed Taft's in the Midwest. And the President was rarin' to go. But Stevenson knew he had to make it plain that he was his own man, not just Truman's heir.

Stevenson set out to establish his independence. By-passing the old party stalwarts, he appointed newcomers, most of them political amateurs, to key positions in the Democratic Party. He named, as his personal campaign manager, Wilson Wyatt, former mayor of Louisville and a leader in Americans for Democratic Action, an all-out New Deal organization. For new national chairman he picked Stephen A. Mitchell, Chicago lawyer, who had persuaded him to run for governor in 1948. He surrounded himself with aides and speech-writers little known in the party hierarchy.

At first, President Truman was hurt by Adlai's assertion of independence. Later he decided that Stevenson was doing what he himself would have done. In mid-August, he asked Stevenson to come to Washington, and in a cordial meeting the two leaders laid out their campaign roles.

The Democratic strategy was obvious. The country was prosperous. The nation was bothered by revelations of corruption, and the line would be that the wrongdoers must be exposed. The country also was unhappy over the seemingly endless Korean war, but Truman and Stevenson agreed that the people supported stopping the Communists in Korea. Therefore, the strategy would be: stand by the record.

Stevenson went back to Springfield—and immediately pulled a boner. In answer to a letter from an Oregon editor, he wrote: "As to whether I can clean up the mess in Washington, I would bespeak the

BRILLIANCE of Stevenson speeches won national admiration. Man who had not sought Democratic nomination proved hard-hitting campaigner. Here he works on draft of speech while sons John (l.), 16, and Borden, 19, nap aboard plane

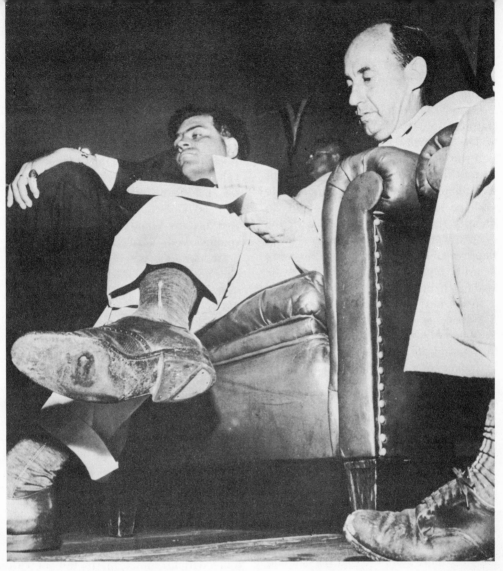

BARING HIS POLITICAL SOLE: Arduous campaign left Illinois governor little time for repairs. Homey shot was taken in Michigan whose Gov. Williams is at left

careful scrutiny of what I inherited in Illinois [from the Republicans] and what has been accomplished."

Somehow the quotation marks he had put around "mess in Washington", to show he was using the editor's own phrase, got left out in typing. Truman was furious. Stevenson moved quickly to assuage his feelings, but the damage was done. The Republicans welcomed the phrase from the enemy's own mouth and "mess

in Washington" became their battle cry.

The week before Labor Day, the country got its first real look at the two candidates in action when they came to New York City to address the American Legion convention in Madison Square Garden.

Ike spoke first. His speech was warmly but not enthusiastically applauded. But he got a big ovation when he marched up Fifth Avenue with the Legionnaires.

Two days later, Stevenson spoke to the

Legion on patriotism—a theme dear to Legionnaires' hearts. But no one else had ever talked to them about patriotism as he did.

He said the true patriot does not attack "faithful public servants"—a palpable hit at Joe McCarthy, a Legion favorite. He said the true patriot does not deny freedom of thought—a jab at the Legion for its attempted censorship of textbooks. He said too many organizations sought "to identify their special interests with the general welfare". The speech made a big impression. After it, Legionnaires were heard to say: "Well, I don't like what he said much, but he sure has got guts."

In the next two days, Stevenson gave five speeches to party workers in New York and New Jersey. It was a different Stevenson from the one who had solemnly spoken to the Legion. He said that standing on the G.O.P. platform was like standing in a "bushel of eels". The G.O.P. trying to get rid of its Old Guard reminded him of the Australian bushman who got a new boomerang and went crazy trying to throw the old one away. Democratic politicians were delighted. They feared he would be too high-brow to mix it.

As the first skirmish closed and the candidates prepared to go out into the country, the consensus was that Stevenson had got off to a fast start and that Ike had not. The pro-Ike New York *World Telegram* said: "Ike is running like a dry creek."

The second big battle of the campaign began on Labor Day and lasted to the end of September. In this period the two candidates perfected their strategy, got used to the grind of ten or twelve speeches a day, to ham-on-rye and coffee gulped from paper cups, to the endless handshaking on the campaign train.

Right after Labor Day, Ike opened with a two-day swing into Dixie. His strategists had decided he would have to hit hard. He did. He threw away his manuscripts and roared out at "the top-to-bottom mess" in Washington, which was full of men "too small for their jobs, too big for their breeches, and too long in power". It was time, he thundered, to clean out the "wasters, bunglers, and incompetents".

In Atlanta, Tampa, Birmingham, Little Rock, the crowds gave the "Yahoo!" rebel yell. When Ike returned to Philadelphia for his first formal speech, 300,000 jammed Chestnut and Broad streets so that his car could hardly pass. "We're rolling!" Ike's managers exulted.

Stevenson opened his campaign on Labor Day with speeches in and around Detroit. He had said, "I think we owe it to the people to talk sensibly . . . about actual issues," and he set out to do it. In Detroit, he dealt with labor relations, in Minnesota with farm policy, in the Northwest with conservation, in San Francisco with our Asian foreign policy.

In his set speeches in the big halls, before the TV cameras, Stevenson was at ease where Ike was nervous. He held his audiences with his eloquence. When he went over to the attack he used the rapier where Ike used the broadsword. Audiences laughed at his wit. Nevertheless, Stevenson's first whistle-stop tour through the Northwest was a failure. Said one labor leader: "Stevenson is definitely in touch with his subject matter but not with the men in the square."

Ike was making headway fast, but he still had the big problem—peace with Robert A. Taft. The senator did not return from Canada until Sept. 7. He seemed in no rush to see Eisenhower and he hinted that his help would have conditions attached to it.

In the second week of September, Ike headed into the Midwest, bent on bringing the Taftites into camp. In Cleveland he met with a group of Taft stalwarts. The air was frigid. But it began to thaw when Ike said they did "just right" to "give their

AMERICA DECIDES: A record-breaking 61 million Americans flocked to vote for nation's 34th President. Analysts had noted strong Republican trend among women

loyalty" to Bob Taft, and should keep him "at the top of the heap".

The next day Eisenhower went to Indianapolis, rode through the city with Senator Jenner—foe of General Marshall. Eisenhower winced when Jenner wrapped an arm around his shoulders and held his hand aloft as the flash bulbs went off.

Meanwhile, Eisenhower and Taft emissaries met in Washington. Then, suddenly, Taft took off for New York from Cincinnati. He carried with him the draft of a statement. The next morning at 7:30, Taft jumped out of a taxi in front of Eisenhower's residence on Morningside Heights. The two men had breakfast and retired to the study. Taft produced his statement. Ike read it, penciled in a few changes. As he left the house, Taft read the statement to the press.

The gist of it was that Taft and Eisenhower were in "100 percent" agreement on domestic issues, differed only "in degree" on foreign. Eisenhower agreed on a $20-billion budget cut at the end of two years and promised not to "discriminate" against Taft supporters in appointments. Taft promised to do everything possible to elect Eisenhower.

Democrats hooted. Stevenson said "the great crusade" had become "the great surrender". He described how Taft and Eisenhower had sat on a love seat "matching principles against pennies".

Some of Ike's earliest and closest supporters were unhappy about the Taft peace pact, fearing it would alienate independent voters. But Ike brushed their objections aside. He had made his reputation as a wartime leader through conciliation and he put high value on unity.

Now, with a united party behind him, Eisenhower again swept through the Midwest. Right and left, he endorsed bitter-

THE VERDICT IN, there are bets to be collected. The pie-in-face wager is an American favorite and here a gleeful Republican pastes rival with lemon meringue

end Republican isolationists—James P. Kem of Missouri, Zales N. Ecton of Montana, even Chapman Revercomb of West Virginia, whom Dewey had refused to endorse in '48.

His statements got increasingly tough. Taft said Ike "is advocating policies I've been preaching for fourteen years".

Ike's speeches were simple, full of homely platitudes. After one address, a reporter on his train gagged that "Ike had crossed the Thirty-eighth Platitude". But the crowds did not find his remarks banal. As the Eisenhower Victory Special pulled out of one small Minnesota town, a woman turned to her husband and said: "He's so sincere it gets me."

Then, while the Eisenhower train rolled through Iowa, all hell broke loose. It was Thursday, Sept. 18. Out in Cali-

fornia, the eleven-car special of Senator Richard M. Nixon, Eisenhower's running mate, was rolling up the Central Valley. At every stop, Nixon was scourging "this scandal-a-day administration".

Three thousand miles away in New York, the *New York Post* hit the streets with a story that Nixon during the past two years had received over $16,000 from a special fund collected by wealthy Californians. The story was soon chattering across the country. It caught up with Nixon at Merced.

He admitted the existence of the fund, but said it was used solely for "political expenses which I believed should not be charged to the Federal Government". He also said the whole thing was a "typical left-wing smear". (The *Post* was supporting Stevenson.)

The story reached the Eisenhower train at Des Moines. At first Eisenhower leaders, indifferent, failed to inform the general. But by Friday morning the Nixon affair was hot.

Ike called a meeting, but decided not to do anything until he had more facts. His aides had been unable to get through to Nixon. In the interim, Ike put out a statement saying he believed "Dick Nixon to be an honest man".

As the Eisenhower train rolled through Nebraska, there were frequent conferences. Should Nixon be asked to withdraw? Time was pressing. Ike was scheduled to speak on corruption that night in Kansas City. That speech might sound pretty funny if . . . In the late afternoon, the leaders reached Nixon. He promised a full accounting.

But by Saturday morning Eastern newspapers supporting Eisenhower were in a lather. *The New York Times* and the *Herald Tribune* suggested that Nixon offer to resign. On Saturday afternoon, the manager of the Nixon fund made public a list of seventy-five donors who had contributed a total of $18,235. Ike wasn't fully satisfied. He told reporters that Nixon had "to come clean as a hound's tooth—or else".

As the Eisenhower train headed back east toward Cincinnati, Taft's home town, the debate went on. Some Dewey Republicans urged that Nixon be dropped. But the Taft people were dead against it. Nixon himself was so angry, because Eisenhower wanted more facts, that on Sunday night in Oregon he scheduled a press conference. The rumor was that he was going to quit but that Republican Chairman Arthur E. Summerfield telephoned from Washington and persuaded him not to do so. All Monday, Summerfield

rounded up support for Nixon from national committeemen. That afternoon, Nixon left his campaign train and, with his wife, flew from Portland to Los Angeles. He buried himself in a hotel room and went to work on a speech. Summerfield had promised to get him a national TV and radio hookup to tell his story.

The show went on the air at 9:30 Tuesday night. Nixon was seated at a table. Nearby was his wife—rigid, pale, her lips frozen into a tense smile.

Two thousand miles away, in Cleveland, a crowd of 15,000 in the Civic Auditorium listened to the speech over loud-speakers. Backstage, Ike sat with Taft and his staff before a TV screen.

Nixon spoke slowly. He listed his possessions and obligations—a $41,000 house in Washington with a $20,000 mortgage,

JUBILANT sign appeared on house in Boston's sedate Beacon Hill after G.O.P. victory

a $13,000 house in California with a $10,-000 mortgage. The cameras panned to his wife. "Pat doesn't have a mink coat."

As for the fund, it had been used simply to "defray political expenses that I did not feel should be charged to the taxpayer". (A breakdown of the fund issued later showed that some $4000 had been used for Christmas cards to his constituents, other amounts for making platters in the Capitol Hill recording rooms for radio broadcasts back home.)

He rose from his chair, advanced into the cameras, his jaw tight, his fists clenched. "This is not the last of the smears," he said. He would continue his fight against Communists. He would not resign. The decision as to his own status was up to the National Committee. He asked the voters to send telegrams to help the Committee make up its mind.

In the Cleveland auditorium, women were weeping. Eisenhower threw away his prepared speech. He said, "Tonight I saw an example of courage." But he wanted more information. He had wired Nixon to meet him the next night at Wheeling, W.Va. He would talk to Nixon face to face, then make his decision.

But Nixon did not leave for Wheeling. He was furious with Eisenhower. He left for Missoula, Mont., to continue his campaign. He had a hunch that the reaction to his speech would be favorable. He was right. Telegrams poured into Washington headquarters at the rate of 4000 an hour.

At 10 P.M. Wednesday, Nixon's plane landed at the airport 10 miles outside Wheeling. Ike was there to meet him and went aboard. Nixon said: "You didn't need to come out here." Ike said: "Why, you're my boy." To a vast crowd in Wheeling, Ike said Nixon had been subjected to an "unfair and vicious attack", that he had completely "vindicated himself", that the National Committee had voted to keep him on the ticket.

Eisenhower did not ask for any further accounting from Nixon. This omission drew some criticism, since several political observers pointed out that all representatives and senators had to meet out of their own pockets the expenses for which Nixon had used his fund and that, therefore, Nixon had not in any way "saved the taxpayers' money". Furthermore, it was argued that the Nixon fund, even if not used for personal expenses, was wholly improper and that Eisenhower had lowered the tone of his "moral crusade" by accepting Nixon's explanation.

Many of those who condemned the Nixon fund as "unethical" were equally severe with Adlai Stevenson when it was disclosed that, while governor, he had used money left over from his 1948 campaign to supplement the salaries of some of his State officers.

The Nixon and Stevenson funds had got the campaign off the track. Now it got back on. Both sides had planned the first three weeks of October as a clean-up third phase. The candidates would take last swings through the Midwest, Northwest, Pacific Coast, and South to nail down votes on sectional interests, before they headed into the populous Northeast where the electoral harvest is richest.

Republican plans called for Ike to make a last quick visit to the farm belt, then to assure the Northwest that the Republicans would not halt conservation projects, finally to make an all-out effort to crack the Solid South.

But the first job at hand was one which he dreaded. That was to go into Wisconsin and endorse Joe McCarthy.

As Ike's train crossed the top of Illinois, Senator McCarthy—unannounced and not particularly welcome—swung aboard with Governor Walter J. Kohler. Ike talked with McCarthy for an hour at a hotel, had dinner with him.

A story, later denied, leaked out about

this meeting. It was said that Eisenhower showed McCarthy the speech he was to give the next night at Milwaukee. McCarthy urged him to delete two paragraphs praising General Marshall, and Eisenhower reluctantly agreed.

As the Eisenhower train rolled into Wisconsin, there were rumors first that McCarthy would, and then that he would not, introduce the general at the senator's home town of Appleton. In the end he did. At Milwaukee that night, Ike looked grim, but he called for the election of the entire State ticket "from the Governor right on to the Senate".

After telling people in the Northwest that he was all for big dams, public power, and watershed protection, but opposed the "whole hog" Federal approach of the Democrats, Ike went to New Orleans and cut loose on the offshore oil issue. President Truman had vetoed a bill to grant the States title to this oil. Ike called this a "shoddy deal".

Wherever he went, he bore down harder and harder on the Korean war. He accused Secretary of State Acheson of "inviting" it. In Champaign, Ill.—heart of the Taft country—he said: "If there must be a war [in Korea], let it be Asians against Asians." He spoke repeatedly of the mounting casualties. He said he knew it was a big job to end the Korean war, but maintained that in the past Americans had quickly finished the big jobs "when there was leadership".

During this period, Ike's relations with the press suffered a decline. Ike felt that many reporters had become antagonistic —possibly because a poll showed that most of those on his train were for Stevenson.

One night, Ike went into the press car and, after a beer with the boys, left with a parting shot: "I know you so-and-so's aren't for me, but the people are for me, and I'm going to win."

During this phase, the Democratic campaign was largely dominated by the figure of Harry Truman, who had entered the fray at the beginning of October. As he set out on a cross-continent whistle-stop tour, Truman was steaming mad. Deeply wounded by Eisenhower's attacks, he felt his place in history was being challenged.

The Democratic strategy at this phase called for Truman and Stevenson to work in tandem. Their objective was to "knock Ike's halo off" by claiming that he had sold out to the Old Guard and the isolationists. Meanwhile, they would blast the Republicans as the "same old depression party".

Truman was more relaxed than he had been in the campaign of '48—at least until he got warmed up. He would begin: "I like Ike—but I like him as a General." Then he would accuse Ike of "betraying" his former principles and endorsing senators who had "stabbed his chief [Marshall] in the back". Ike, he said, had become the tool of every lobby going—from electric power to China.

But at times the President was bantering. He said: "I don't think it's very nice of the Republicans to run on Bob Taft's program and leave him off the ticket."

Stevenson enlarged on the President's theme. He spoke of the Taft Republicans who "had to be dragged kicking and screaming into the 20th century". Taft, he said, now owned Ike "hoofs, hide and tallow".

But Stevenson also continued to talk on the issues, and he spoke his mind even when he knew his views were unpopular. In New Orleans he said he stood foursquare behind the Supreme Court decision that offshore oil deposits were vested "in all the people of the United States and not just those of Louisiana". In Texas, he said the same thing about Texas offshore oil.

Both Truman and Stevenson attacked Eisenhower's statements on Korea. The President said that the general, when he was army chief of staff, had joined in the decision to withdraw U.S. troops from Korea—the very decision that, according to Eisenhower now, had opened the way for Communist attack. He accused Eisenhower of playing politics with the casualty lists.

There was no easy answer to Korea, Stevenson said, and the people must not be led to expect one. "How long can we stay in Korea? . . . We can keep it up as long as we have to, and we will."

The final phase of the battle was fought in the Northeast. Stevenson and Truman were stressing the New Deal and prosperity issues. Truman said the G.O.P. was still wedded to the "trickle down" theory of distributing wealth. Stevenson said the Republicans had never relinquished their 1930 patent on "let boom and let bust". Replied Eisenhower: "We are not going to turn the clock back—ever."

Then the Republicans dropped their blockbuster. It had been devised early in the campaign by Emmet Hughes, a *Life* magazine staffer on the Eisenhower team of speech-writers. Eisenhower had decided it should not be used unless needed. Now it was wheeled out.

On Oct. 24, in Detroit, Eisenhower said that, if elected, he would "forego the diversions of politics and . . . concentrate on the job of ending the Korean war . . . That job requires a personal trip to Korea. I shall make that trip . . . I shall go to Korea."

The Stevenson forces did not recover for twenty-four hours. Then Stevenson said: "The root of the Korean problem does not lie in Korea—it lies in Moscow".

The Republicans probably would have won even without Eisenhower's dramatic pledge. But after that pledge the Democrats never got going again.

November 4 was ideal election weather throughout most of the country—crisp and clear. As soon as the polls opened at 6 A.M., the voters started pouring into the booths. All day long they kept coming. There had never been such a turnout. In district after district, 80, 85, or 90 percent of the registered voters marked their crosses or pulled the levers.

At 6:45 P.M., the first returns came in from Connecticut. From that moment, there was no doubt. It was a landslide.

When New York State went to Eisenhower, Stevenson knew it was hopeless. At 1:40 A.M., he stood before the TV cameras, amid a weeping, cheering crowd yelling "No! No!", and conceded. He said he had been asked how he felt. He borrowed from an Abraham Lincoln story. He was like the boy who had stubbed his toe. "He was too big to cry, but it hurt too much to laugh." This was the score:

	POPULAR	ELECTORAL
Eisenhower	33,927,547	442
Stevenson	27,311,316	89

Eisenhower had carried everything north of the Mason-Dixon line; had broken the Solid South by taking Texas, Virginia, Florida, and Tennessee; had carried eighteen States that had gone Democratic for twenty years. But the Republican Party—as distinct from its Presidential candidate—did not do so well. This was the Congressional box score:

	SENATE	HOUSE
Republicans	48	221
Democrats	47	213
Independent	1	1

It was Ike's victory.

A few weeks later, in a speech before the Gridiron Club in Washington, Stevenson began: "Let me tell you about something that happened to me the other day on my way to the White House."

"LET US UNITE . . .
the real job is still ahead"

EISENHOWER was born
in this plain frame house in
Denison, Texas, in 1890. Family
moved two years later

EISENHOWER

IKE EISENHOWER'S ELECTION TRIUMPH would not have surprised his mother. "Dwight," she once said, "always got what he went after."

Eisenhower's life had been one long climb, slow at first, amazingly fast later on. His career read like pages out of American and world history. Long before he set foot in the White House he had helped to shape the national destiny.

Dwight David Eisenhower was born on Oct. 14, 1890, in Denison, Texas— third of seven sons of David and Ida Eisenhower. He grew up on "the wrong side of the tracks". Father David failed as a railroad shopworker in Denison. Moving to Abilene, Kans.—which then was just emerging from its gun-totin' past as a frontier town—he got a low-paying job as night watchman in a creamery. Ike and the other boys had to work to help out.

Ike was a normal boy, though he did more than his share of schoolyard scrapping. His ambition was to be a shortstop like Hans Wagner, or a railroad conductor. In school he did best in English and history; he especially liked military history. Then, influenced by a friend who was trying to get into the Naval Academy at Annapolis, Eisenhower took examinations for appointment to both Annapolis and West Point. He placed first for Annapolis, but it turned out that, at 20, he was a few months overage. He placed second for West Point, but got the appointment when the winner withdrew.

At West Point, Eisenhower had an outstanding record in athletics (baseball and football). In studies he was average; he graduated sixty-first in his class. Commissioned a second lieutenant in 1915, he was assigned to the infantry at Fort Sam Houston, Texas. There he met, and soon married, pretty, vivacious Mamie Geneva Doud.

Dreary routine filled Eisenhower's early years as an officer. In World War I he did not get to France; he commanded a tank training center in Pennsylvania. After the war he was a major for sixteen straight years.

But he was making his mark. He graduated first in a class of 275 at the Army Command and General Staff School, where officers are groomed for high posts. In 1935, proud, brilliant General Douglas MacArthur went to the Philippines as military adviser; he chose modest, businesslike Eisenhower as his top aide.

Back in the U.S. in 1940, Ike became chief of staff of the Third Army—and won a reputation as the "brains" of the Third's "victory" in war-games maneuvers in Louisiana.

On Dec. 12, 1941, just after Pearl Harbor, came a summons to Washington. The stern-visaged army chief of staff, General George C. Marshall, asked Eisenhower how he would plan Pacific strategy. "Give me a few hours," Eisenhower said. Ike produced his plan and was on his way to renown.

What happened next is recent world history. In 1942–43 came the spectacular Allied invasion of North Africa, under Eisenhower's command. It drove the Axis forces back across the Mediterranean in-

TWELVE YEARS away from White House, Lt. Col. Eisenhower assumes new post at Ft. Lewis, Wash.

WEST POINT graduate courts a pretty, peppy Denver girl, Mamie Doud. He married her in 1916

D-DAY! Supreme commander sends paratroops into final campaign against Nazi Germany with tough simple order: "Full victory—nothing else."

to Europe. For Eisenhower the campaign meant endless labor to keep harmony among the American, British, and French Allies. The legend was: Ike doesn't mind if you call a man a "so-and-so". But look out if he hears you call anyone a "British so-and-so".

One day in Tunis, when the Allied assault on Italy was well under way, Eisenhower went to the airport to greet President Roosevelt. The President was homeward bound from talks with Stalin and Churchill at Teheran in the Near East.

When he was seated in his car, F.D.R. turned to Eisenhower and said: "Well, Ike, you are going to command Overlord." Overlord was the code name for the mighty Allied onslaught from England against Hitler's *Festung Europa* (Fortress Europe).

On June 5, 1944, at 3:30 A.M., Supreme Commander Eisenhower journeyed from his camp hideaway outside London to a naval headquarters a mile away. Gales howled in the darkness. The vast Allied armada was poised to move out across the English Channel next morning. Should Eisenhower brave the tempest

—and risk disaster? Or should he postpone D-Day—and give the enemy a chance to spot the array of Allied ships and men?

A last-minute report came in: weather would soon clear for thirty-six hours. Eisenhower, at 4:15, quietly ordered the go-ahead for June 6. It was the greatest and toughest decision of his career.

Eleven months later, the German generals surrendered in his headquarters at Reims, France. In the summer of 1945 he got a clue as to how much Americans esteemed him. President Truman, in Germany for the Potsdam conference with Churchill and Stalin, said one day while riding in a car with Eisenhower: "General, there is nothing that you may want that I won't try to help you get. That definitely and specifically includes the Presidency."

Ike laughed; he had no thought of entering politics.

But the Eisenhower-for-President talk persisted. Former heavyweight champion Gene Tunney, golfing with Eisenhower, told him he would be the next President. "Oh, my lord!" Ike exclaimed. Democrats and Republicans alike tried and failed to persuade Eisenhower to run on their tickets in 1948. He retired from the army, became president of Columbia University—"scared to death" of the faculty, he confided to friends.

Then came the final military assignment—supreme commander in Europe for the North Atlantic alliance. From his bright new headquarters at Rocquencourt, in the countryside near Paris, Eisenhower in the first days of 1952 finally gave the signal: he would run for President, as a Republican.

When the long, hard months of campaigning had ended in victory, Ike was aged 62 and in excellent health. His complexion was ruddy. He stood 5 feet 10 and weighed about 175 pounds. He liked to have two massages a day and exercised on a rowing machine and electric bicycle. He would eat practically anything, but in small portions. Once a chain-smoker, he had given up cigarettes while at Columbia because a doctor warned him they made his pulse beat too fast. Occasionally he drank a weak Scotch-and-water. He liked to get eight hours of sleep, but often had to settle for less.

Eisenhower was slightly farsighted; in the campaign he had got rid of his rimless glasses, which gave him a grandpa look, and adopted heavy horn rims. He was probably the baldest man elected President since John Quincy Adams.

Eisenhower's favorite pastimes were bridge (he was an expert) and golf (he scored in the pretty good high eighties). For reading, he liked Westerns. After leaving the army, he had taken up oil painting. He did mostly landscapes, and was good for a beginner. He liked to cook occasionally, specializing in Chinese dishes.

In manner, Eisenhower was like any American you might meet at a Rotary Club luncheon. He was warm, friendly, hearty. It was "Hiya, Joe," or "Golly, I'm glad to see you!" His wife Mamie matched his mood; she obviously liked her new life in the public eye.

In speechmaking, Ike was at his best talking off the cuff, from a few penciled notes. When reading a formal, written speech he was uncomfortable and looked it. He told reporters he knew he was not eloquent. But when he forgot about trying to be eloquent and spoke simply, he often touched his listeners' hearts.

So far as the problems of the Presidency were concerned, Eisenhower

NEW YORK CHEERS as Eisenhower, after victory over Nazis, rides in triumph up Broadway

PROUD FAMILY, Mrs. Eisenhower and son John, see Ike, in unfamiliar tasseled cap, march to his first presidency—that of New York's giant Columbia University

frankly had much to learn after forty years as a soldier. As one political writer said, "He had homework to do."

Ike went about his homework briskly. He used an approach that had served him well in the army. His technique was to organize an expert "team" that could do the spadework, analyze the problems, sum them up, and present them to the "boss" for a simple *Yes* or *No* decision.

Right after the election, Eisenhower moved fast. At Truman's invitation, he went to the White House to talk about the change-over from one administration to another. They smiled and shook hands for the photographer, but there was a chill in the air. The change-over problem was serious. Truman still had the powers of the Presidency, but Eisenhower was the real national leader. The country had no effective chief executive.

Eisenhower set up a "temporary White House" on the sixth floor of the Commodore Hotel, next door to Grand Central Station in New York City. He quickly

MATTHEW RIDGWAY JR. steals show as Eisenhower, flanked by Field Marshal Montgomery and Mrs. Ridgway, waits to greet successor in Paris

named his cabinet. For the most part, he chose conservative businessmen; he had an instinctive admiration for men who could get to the top in the hard give-and-take of business.

Not all the appointments pleased everyone. Senator Taft cried "Incredible!" when he heard the choice for secretary of labor—Martin Durkin, Chicago Democrat and plumbers'-union chief, little known nationally. Taft, who wrote much of the Taft-Hartley labor law, regarded labor as his own bailiwick. He was offended because Eisenhower had not consulted him about the Durkin appointment. Some predicted that the great Taft-Eisenhower battle in Chicago might prove to be only the first.

More urgent problems of the Presidency crowded in rapidly on Eisenhower. In the dark of early morning two days after Thanksgiving, he slipped out of a side door at his Columbia residence and stepped into a car at the curb. At a secret rendezvous at Mitchell Field on Long Island, he and a few trusted aides got into a big military plane.

Sixty-two hours later, the plane's landing wheels touched down at the airport in Seoul, South Korea's capital. Eisenhower had kept his campaign pledge to go to Korea. He toured the front in a "puddle-jumper" army car. He talked with G.I.'s and Allied soldiers. He lunched from a messkit on pork chops and sauerkraut. He met Allied commanders and South Korean political chieftains.

After three days, Ike took off for Guam, and there boarded the U.S. cruiser *Helena* for home. In mid-ocean, helicopters carrying men chosen for the Eisenhower cabinet landed on the *Helena's* deck. The President-elect and his "official family" started planning strategy for the Far East. The "new approach" to the Korean war was under way.

Despite the demands of the job he was soon to occupy, Eisenhower still found time to relax. Back at the Commodore, he liked to startle visitors with what his aides called an "Eisenhopper". It was a plastic grasshopper that you pressed unobtrusively on a desk top; after a few moments, it suddenly sprang high into the air.

One day a couple of visitors at Columbia found Ike in his shirt sleeves, painting. He said: "Take your jackets off. I don't think people can really relax unless they're in shirt sleeves."

In Washington, Harry Truman quietly passed the last days of 1952 tying up the loose ends of the twenty-year era of the Democrats. The spotlight already was focused on Eisenhower and the dawn of a new Republican era.

SEOUL GETS READY to greet Eisenhower as President-elect keeps dramatic campaign pledge

FIRES, BLIZZARDS, earthquakes, and human error took their toll of lives and property

DISASTER

FOR THE UNITED STATES, 1952 WAS A YEAR of exceptional decision in politics and diplomacy. Less portentous but often more important to most Americans were facets of their daily life: changes in the weather, accidents and crimes, the way people got along with their neighbors, the education of their children in school or college.

These things had local impact in the 48 States and in our territories overseas. Some local events also attracted national attention, had national meaning. Such events are recorded in this section.

WHETHER THEY WERE THE WORK OF MEN or nature, certain instances of loss, peril

and heroism in 1952 lingered in the mind.

The weather was its usual unpredictable self. In the year's first fortnight, blizzards swept the Midwest, 50-foot drifts piled up in the Rockies, and California was hit by the worst rain and snow since 1890.

In the Sierra Nevada, snow buried one town 9 feet deep, choked mountain highways, and marooned the Southern Pacific streamliner *City of San Francisco,* with 232 persons aboard, for three days. The locale was the infamous Donner Pass, and reporters drew obvious parallels with the plight of pioneers caught there a century earlier and, before the spring thaw,

MUDDY MISSOURI, on April rampage, swirls to the roofs of Kansas houses. Damage in eight States was nearly $300,000,000

forced into cannibalism. This time, snowplows freed the train's passengers.

In February, there were other mishaps: a blizzard in the Dakotas and Minnesota (21 killed), an Ohio River flood, a snowstorm in New England (31 killed, plus 14 drowned in gales off Cape Cod).

Then, on March 21–22, over Arkansas, a mass of warm, moist air from the Gulf of Mexico collided with a cold front from the north. The combination brought on a tornado which, before it blew itself out, ripped through five more States—Missouri, Kentucky, Tennessee, Mississippi, Alabama—and killed 239 persons (highest such toll since 1932), injured 1202, destroyed or damaged 2300 homes.

Now came the annual Midwestern water carnival: the spring floods which in other years had plagued the Ohio or

(before Tennessee Valley Authority) the Tennessee. In April, 1952, the upper Missouri-Mississippi basin had them.

They began high in Montana and the Dakotas, where warm winds melted the heavy snow and started the flow toward the Gulf. Thousands of freshets became a torrent and the rising Missouri, 10 miles wide in spots, rolled down into Iowa and Nebraska, Kansas and Missouri.

At the same time, to the east, the headwaters of the Mississippi were swelling, pouring south through Minnesota and Wisconsin, Iowa and Illinois.

In scores of big and little towns—Minneapolis, St. Paul, Pierre, Fargo, Sioux City, Omaha—the muddy water lapped up streets and into buildings, silting sidewalks, burying fences and autos.

Kansas City (Kans. and Mo.) and St.

Louis escaped the worst. But most of the nation's breadbasket was hard hit: 100,000 homeless, 2,442,000 acres of farmland inundated, and an all-time record of nearly $300 million in damage.

In ten ravaged States, Congress made available $25 million for emergency relief, and with the passing of the high water the land gradually dug itself free. Later, as President Truman pressed for flood insurance and active flood-control measures, Congress passed a $55 million appropriation to repair damage to flood-control projects.

Critics claimed Washington was still shirking its duty. The basic problem, far from originating in 1952, was born when man first plowed on the prairie and has grown steadily ever since. Many remedies have been offered; in 1952, none was adopted. Inescapable was the conclusion that Midwestern floods and their costly companions—erosion, dust storms, soil impoverishment—would go on indefinitely.

After spring's havoc, the land lay quiet through May and June. Then, on July 21, the little California town of Tehachapi, north of Los Angeles, awoke to terror.

Underground slippage along the State's great north-south fault line had set the surface trembling, shaking sun-baked Tehachapi as a terrier shakes a rat. The tremor, California's worst since the 1906 San Francisco holocaust, was felt well into Nevada and Arizona, an area of 100,-000 square miles, most of it, luckily, almost unpopulated. The quake killed 14, injured 150. Another shock on Aug. 22, in Bakersfield to the north, left 2 dead plus $20 million in damage.

The summer brought one double-barreled accident. On Labor Day, a thunderstorm hit Carswell Air Force Base at Fort Worth, Texas, and snapped the heavy cables tethering a fieldful of 139-ton B-36 intercontinental bombers. One craft was destroyed; 106 others were damaged. As taxpayers pondered the $48 million loss, commentators noted that this was the first admission that the air force possessed as many as 107 B-36's.

Another natural force was also at work, quietly, during the summer. Many Easterners noted that July was unusually dry; on Aug. 10, when rainstorms broke a month-long drought in New England and the South, it was reported that lack of rain had caused $1 billion in damage. The gov-

UMBRELLA OF DEATH: Trio of tragedies gets neighbors of Jersey airport fighting mad

THREE PLANES CRASHED into Elizabeth, N.J., within two months. Of the 119 killed, 11 had been "safe" at home. Furor closed Newark Airport for several months

ernment named all or part of ten States as disaster areas. By late September, the number of States eligible for drought-relief livestock feed stood at seventeen, and crop damage in Texas alone was estimated at $100 million. On Oct. 13, Oklahoma became disaster-area State No. 18.

As the rainless days and nights piled up, forests and grassland in twenty-eight States became tinderboxes. Fires broke out. In October alone, one State, Louisiana, lost more than 200,000 acres to more than 3000 separate conflagrations.

In Tennessee, the worst fires in the State's history swallowed 400,000 acres of timber. In Arkansas, a single blaze swept 10,000 acres. In Alabama, 100,000 acres burned; in Missouri, 450,000 acres. Oklahoma's drought was called its worst ever.

In Georgia, a government forester said: "It would take 100 years to replace the timber burned in the past week."

By Nov. 9, the drought loss to Texas farmers alone was estimated at more than $250 million. Cattle raisers there and in nine other States said they were facing ruin. In Dallas, the city council banned lawn sprinkling and car washing, and ordered a fine of up to $200 for a single leaky faucet.

Finally, in mid-November, rain fell over most of the country. Even prolonged downpours, however, could not repair the year's losses. They were cumulative. The 1952 drought actually had begun in 1950; it bore earmarks of a cyclical phenomenon, like that which brought on the Dust Bowl havoc of the 1930's.

Meanwhile, without nature's help, the country managed to get itself into a peck of trouble. The primary reason was the national preoccupation with fast transportation.

Never before had so many ordinary citizens taken so many airplanes so far, so often, so casually. Air travel is traditionally luxurious, but in 1952 travelers in the average air terminal looked much like those in the average bus depot: men in polo shirts, women in slacks, babies in arms.

The demand for wings was virtually unaffected by a spectacular series of crashes over Elizabeth, N.J., a stone's throw from the huge Newark Airport (one of three major fields serving Metropolitan New York).

Late in 1951, a nonscheduled C-46 had crashed in flames in Elizabeth, killing its 56 passengers and crew. Less than six weeks afterward, on Jan. 22, an American Airlines two-engine Convair, inbound from Buffalo, missed the airport in bad weather and, three quarters of a mile from the earlier crash site, plowed into two homes. All 23 persons aboard (including ex-Secretary of War Robert Patterson), plus 7 on the ground, were killed.

Then, on Feb. 11, a National Airlines four-engine DC-6, heading from Newark to Miami, developed engine trouble and crashed into an Elizabeth apartment house. Death toll: 33.

The tragedies raised an outcry for the closing of the Newark field. With 119 dead in two months, the Port of New York Authority finally complied. But there were dissenting voices. Eastern Air Lines President Eddie Rickenbacker pointed out that the field itself was safe. Field engineers stressed a new, 7000-foot, $9-million runway—already under construction—which would enable flights to avoid passing over Elizabeth. But for two months Newark's traffic (average number of daily flights: 220) was rerouted to La Guardia, Idlewild, and other fields.

Then, on April 16, Newark was reopened to the air force and the New Jersey National Guard; on June 15, to limited commercial use; on Nov. 15, to full commercial traffic. With the new runway and other safeguards in operation, Elizabeth seemed willing to wait and see.

The year's last two months were marked by a series of military-plane crashes in California, the Northwest, Alaska, and Japan. In three weeks, ten planes went down—mostly in bad weather—and 233 persons died. Then on Dec. 20 a giant C-124, flying 106 servicemen home for Christmas—plus 10 crew members—crashed on take-off at Larson Air Force Base, Wash., with 87 killed. This was the world's worst aerial disaster.

The commercial air lines, meanwhile, had their best year. The total death toll was 245 (down from 328 in 1951), of which only 5 occurred in accidents on scheduled carriers.

Two unusual marine sagas marked the year.

On Jan. 1, the 6711-ton Isbrandtsen freighter *Flying Enterprise,* bound from Hamburg to her home port of New York, was listing dangerously in a savage gale that had caught her northwest of the Bay of Biscay and nearly broken her in two. Three days before, with rescue ships from four nations pitching nearby, Danish-born Captain Henrik Kurt Carlsen had ordered his 10 passengers and 40 crewmen to abandon ship.

In New York, the freighter's owners radioed 37-year-old Carlsen against "further risking your life". His answer: "I am waiting till vessel saved or sunk." At home in Woodbridge, N.J., his wife began a lonely watch in which the whole Western World soon joined.

After six days, the *Enterprise* was still afloat; the British tug *Turmoil* reached her, first mate Kenneth Dancy got aboard, and he and Carlsen made fast a towline. For three days, tug and tow wallowed toward England through falling seas, but 50 miles from Falmouth the Atlantic stirred again.

As the waves rose, progress halted. The towline snapped. The *Enterprise* listed ever more steeply, forcing Carlsen and Dancy ever higher on her superstructure. On Jan. 10, both brave men jumped from the top of the funnel.

The *Turmoil* picked them up a few minutes before the *Enterprise* went down, 41 miles from land, and they came ashore to a hero's welcome. Carlsen, knighted by Denmark's King Frederick IX, finally arrived in New York City. There he was re-

OPERATION SANTA turns into world's worst air tragedy as crash of G.I.-laden plane kills 87

SEA SAGAS made absorbing news. In December, the French liner "Champollion", loaded with pilgrims en route to Holy Land, broke in two as it struck reef off Lebanon coast

warded with a ticker-tape parade up Broadway, a reunion with his wife, and command of the *Flying Enterprise II,* a new, 11,500-ton Isbrandtsen freighter.

Thereafter the deep-water records remained clear until April 26. On that night, the 27,100-ton airplane carrier *Wasp* was plowing east across the Atlantic. About her, in a choppy sea, were twenty-two other warships. One, the 1630-ton destroyer-minesweeper *Hobson,* drew near to stand by for possible rescue work when the *Wasp* set planes aloft for night maneuvers. When the *Wasp* turned into the wind to take back her airborne brood there came a grating crash: her bow had sliced full into the tiny *Hobson.*

Cut in two, the *Hobson* sank in four minutes. Most of her officers and crew were asleep or below decks; in twenty-four hours of searching, only 61 survivors were found. Lost with his ship were Lieutenant Commander William J. Tierney and 175 others. Damage to the *Wasp:* a 75-foot gash in her water line.

On Aug. 12, a navy court of inquiry reassessed the collision—worst, in number of lives lost, in modern American naval history—and fixed blame. The *Hobson's* skipper, it said, was at fault for a "grave error" of judgment committed when his ship made an "unexplained left turn".

Other disasters of 1952 excited less attention. The railroads got through the year without a fatality. The highways saw their accustomed slaughter, with every likelihood that traffic deaths would top 1951's 37,500, on Aug. 4, the nation's worst bus crash killed 29 near Waco, Texas. Mine disasters were far down from the year before, partly because of the Safety Board of Review appointed Aug. 21 by President Truman under the new Coal Mine Safety Law.

Even fire was sparing of human life. Deaths were recorded in various local blazes, but the year's biggest fire headlines emanated from Burbank, Calif., where the Warner Bros. motion-picture studios suffered $3 million damage.

On the lighter side was the standard quota of odd accidents. Among the oddest: a Baltimore man was shot by his pet rabbit (it tripped the trigger of a .22 rifle beside his bed); a Salt Lake City flier, forced down on a highway, made a perfect landing atop a moving car; when an Indiana motorist stalled on a railroad crossing, a train sheared off the front of his auto at the windshield, left him unscratched; in Atlantic City, N.J., a car suffered $300 damage when it ran into a 240-pound resident (who just laughed, helped the driver push the car to a garage).

One ominous note of the year was the progressive, long-continued rise in the level of the Great Lakes. The cause was obscure (geological, climatic, something else?), but water and wind kept nibbling at the shore lines of seven States. Beaches disappeared; houses, undermined, toppled over; property values were destroyed; in Michigan alone, the year's damage was estimated at $1 billion. No one did much about it, but something— Federal action probably in concert with Canada—certainly seemed needed.

LEBANESE FISHERMEN brave surf in fight to save 318 aboard the "Champollion". All were rescued except 26 who drowned trying to swim the short, turbulent way to shore

MURDERER Louis DiFraia continued struggling after capture by Pawtucket, R.I., police

BOOKIE BOSS Harry Gross goes behind bars. Off-again on-again witness implicated many N.Y.C. cops in pay-offs

CRIME

WRONGDOING DECREASED IN 1952—THANKS largely to the work of the Senate Crime Investigating (Kefauver) Committee in 1951. Echoes of that investigation continued to sound—not least around gambler Frank Costello.

Found guilty April 4 of contempt of the Senate investigators a year before, Italian-born Costello was sentenced to eighteen months in jail, in October, shortly after he began his term, the Justice Department filed a petition to revoke his citizenship.

Meanwhile, several cities—New York, Washington, San Francisco, and Kansas City—carried on "little Kefauver probes" of their own. Most headlined: New York's, which on Feb. 5 brought James J. Moran

a 15½- to 25-year sentence for heading a $500,000-a-year shakedown racket in his palmy days as first deputy fire commissioner. Three months later, Moran also was named as one of 120-odd city officials to whom big-time ex-bookmaker Harry Gross claimed to have paid $1 million a year as "protection".

Thereafter the New York State Crime Commission—also a Kefauver offshoot—took over the job of finding links between city politics and the underworld. A week of hearings in November revealed wide acquaintance between Tammany Hall and various shady figures. Chief among the latter was Thomas ("Three-Finger Brown") Luchese, who claimed friendship

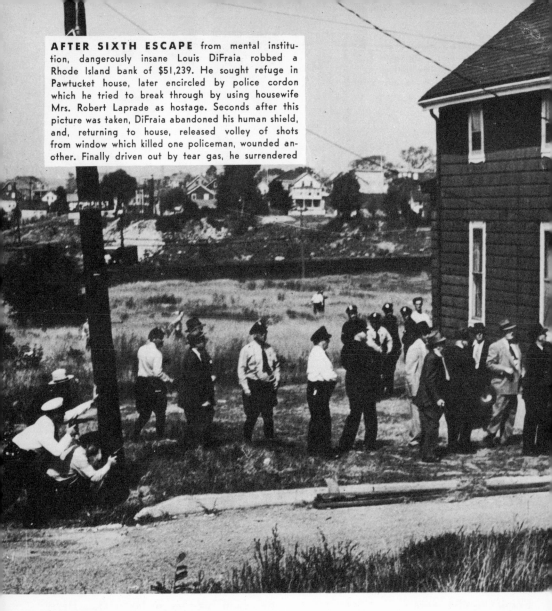

AFTER SIXTH ESCAPE from mental institution, dangerously insane Louis DiFraia robbed a Rhode Island bank of $51,239. He sought refuge in Pawtucket house, later encircled by police cordon which he tried to break through by using housewife Mrs. Robert Laprade as hostage. Seconds after this picture was taken, DiFraia abandoned his human shield, and, returning to house, released volley of shots from window which killed one policeman, wounded another. Finally driven out by tear gas, he surrendered

with judges, Congressmen, and district attorneys. At year's end Luchese, alleged heir to Frank Costello's empire, faced the threat of deportation.

In December the New York Commission and the New Jersey Law Enforcement Council turned a spotlight on the water front. What it revealed was shocking: a reign of lawlessness along 770 miles of docks in Brooklyn, Manhattan, and New Jersey that had cut the port's share of national tonnage handled from 22 percent to 15 percent in thirteen years.

In essence, the situation stemmed from labor bosses' control over the hiring of union longshoremen. A dishonest boss easily played both ends against the middle by squeezing kickbacks from the men (to hold their jobs), pay-offs from employers (to avert strikes). Known criminals got into the act; "pilferage" (in one case, 10 tons of steel vanished) was common.

Before the hearings recessed, not only businessmen, politicians, labor leaders, and police were implicated, but also some of the underworld's gaudier figures—such as Albert Anastasia of Brooklyn. Yet one observer commented: "The water front has stunk for years. Do you really think anything will come of all this?"

In New York City, also, occurred the year's most dramatic individual crime story. On Feb. 18, in a quiet, residential section of Brooklyn, 24-year-old clothing-store salesman Arnold Schuster told two patrolmen he had seen escaped bank robber Willie Sutton buying a battery for his car at a service station. At first incredulous, the patrolmen rallied to bring in one of the F.B.I.'s ten most-wanted criminals.

Thin, daring, hair-line-mustached William Francis ("The Actor") Sutton had made a specialty of banks and jewelry stores, got away with nearly a million dol-

HE PUT FINGER on Willie ("The Actor") Sutton. Arnold Schuster, young clothing salesman, spotted five-year fugitive getting car fixed and tipped off Brooklyn police

lars in two decades. Careful, adept at disguise, he had baffled New York and Philadelphia police with slick jailbreaks.

In 1947 he escaped from a Pennsylvania prison wearing a guard's uniform. In 1950 he appeared in New York just long enough to walk into a bank and out again—with $63,000. When he finally was caught, along with two henchmen, the law moved fast: on April 1, 51-year-old Willie was given thirty years to life.

Yet something of "The Actor's" legerdemain seemed to persist. On March 8, while Willie was awaiting trial, someone shot tipster Schuster dead. Rewards spurred a city-wide manhunt, but, at year's end, the murderer remained at large.

On Feb. 29, eleven days after Willie's capture, robbery made different headlines 2000 miles from Brooklyn. In Reno, Nev.,

realtor-recluse La Verne Redfield reported that someone had entered his mansion by the back door, bribed his watchdog with a ham hock, greased the bottom of his 400-pound safe, and dragged it away. In the safe: $1½ million in cash, jewelry, and securities.

Redfield, a casual type who kept an extra million in securities in a suitcase, was lucky: the thieves were caught and—despite the pretty ringleader's protest that Redfield had given her permission to take the loot—jailed.

Less fortunate were Leap Year victims of another type of crime: murder.

On the campus of Columbia University in New York, July 14, an 18-year-old secretary was shot by a total stranger, Bayard Peakes, insane self-styled "genius" whose scientific theories had been rejected by

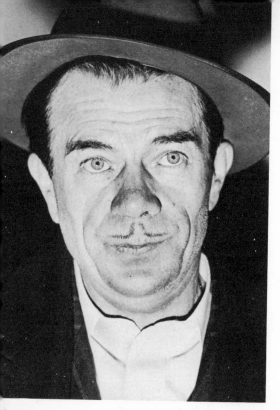

SLICK ROBBERIES and prison breaks made Willie Sutton famous. But he's jailed now for 30 years

the girl's employer, the American Physical Society.

In Chicago, Aug. 6, another 18-year-old was killed and her companion wounded by Bernard Richardson Jr., also a stranger to his victims, who then committed suicide. Both killers had previous records of emotional imbalance.

Near Baltimore, on Aug. 20, a car rolled downhill and turned over. In the wreckage was found the body of Mrs. Dorothy May Grammer, of New York. Suspicion fell on Mrs. Grammer's husband, George Edward. It was found that he had been pursuing another woman, whom he had wished to marry.

On Oct. 23, a Baltimore judge convicted Grammer of killing his wife, running her body downhill in their car to make her death look like an accident.

GANG REVENGE is good citizen Schuster's reward. A year· later, his killers are still free

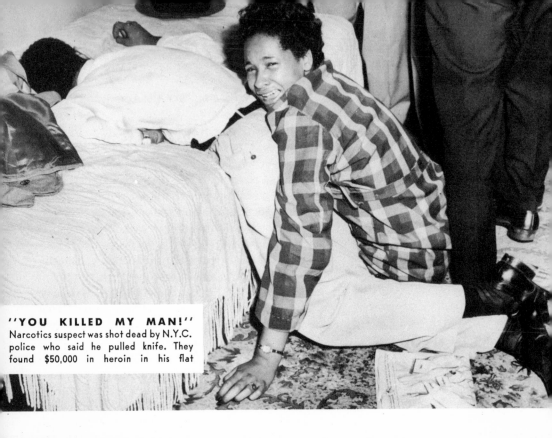

"YOU KILLED MY MAN!"
Narcotics suspect was shot dead by N.Y.C. police who said he pulled knife. They found $50,000 in heroin in his flat

Newspaper readers tsk-tsked over the year's "almost perfect crime".

"Almost perfect", too, was the peculation of prim, conscientious George Sponsler, who for fourteen years embezzled cash deposits at his teller's window in the First National Bank of North Baltimore, Ohio (pop., 2771). By juggling depositors' ledger cards, Sponsler hid his secret through 150-plus bank inspections. He might have remained undetected had not four cards turned up missing in the summer of 1952.

Pleading guilty before a Federal judge, Sponsler also bared a few background facts. When he became a teller in 1920, his annual pay was $1080; it was $1400 in 1927, the year he married and began embezzling to help support his family; it was only $1900 when he turned straight again in 1941. And the president of the bank, who haled him into court even though he confessed and repaid the $7541 he had taken, was Sponsler's own brother.

When the judge learned all this, he thundered: "The bank ought to be indicted here" for having "invited" Sponsler to steal by keeping him "a virtual pauper for at least 22 years." Sponsler walked out a free man, bewildered but grateful.

The year saw as varied, if not as many, crimes as most. Main remaining categories, listed alphabetically, are below:

Black Markets. In Chicago, discovery that horse meat was being sold as beef led to an investigation, indictment of Board of Health President Herman Bundesen (charges later dismissed), several fines.

Gambling. The Kefauver aftermath touched "numbers" operators, race-track betters, sports figures. A steady drop was reported in the number of slot machines in the U.S., but, despite the Federal tax on professional gamblers, the gradual return of bookmakers was marked in many areas.

Gold Smuggling. Sixty-five New Yorkers, mostly wholesale jewelers, were indicted on charges of shipping gold to overseas black markets.

Juvenile Crime. Wrongdoing by children aged 10 to 17, particularly serious offenses (robbery, sex crimes, even murder), was reported increasing in 48 of 61 major cities. Main cited causes were war tensions and "delinquent parents".

Narcotics. Teen-age addiction, scarehead story of recent years, was down in 1952. But the national war on dope continued—Brooklyn, for example, cracked "the largest ring yet uncovered"—and a familiar name turned up when, in the indictment of 23 alleged heroin peddlers in San Francisco, their source was identified as the deported Charles ("Lucky Luciano") Lucania.

Prostitution. The normal dreary parade of small-time offenders was colored by disclosure of a New York "café-society vice ring". Socialite oleomargarine heir Minot F. ("Mickey") Jelke, 22, and others —some of whom confessed—were charged with talking models and minor actresses into prostitution and with living off the proceeds.

The No. 1 crime story of the year, however, dealt not with transgression but with punishment. January began with the first drop in five years in the nation's prison population (164,896 adults, down 900 since 1950). Succeeding months made sociologists ask: "How are U.S. convicts being treated behind bars?"

The first warning sounded in New Jersey. On April 15, three outbreaks at the State prison in Trenton were climaxed when 69 inmates rioted, seized 4 hostages, and barricaded themselves in the prison print shop. Their complaint: bad food, brutal treatment. Three days later, 231 men in the State prison farm at Rahway, N.J., rioted "in sympathy" and held 9 guards as hostages. Both rebellions soon yelled themselves out, mainly for lack of food and water. But a spark had been ignited.

The spark landed in Jackson, Mich. On April 20–21, 2600 convicts rioted in Southern Michigan State Prison. Most were promptly cowed, but 171 kept control of one cell block and, using 7 guards as hostages, smashed everything smashable, set fires, finally forced Governor G. Mennen Williams to authorize a "peace". Officials agreed to the convicts' demands —a better parole system, dismissal of harsh guards—and Warden Julian Frisbie promised to take no disciplinary action.

As Deputy Warden Vernon Fox hailed the rioters for "the good faith with which they have bargained", damage was estimated at $2 million. Then public reaction set in: Fox resigned and Frisbie was fired.

The spark was still glowing. Louisiana, May 12: a four-day hunger strike of 120 convicts was broken with ammonia gas. Idaho, May 24: clubs and tear gas broke a five-hour, 250-man riot. Kentucky, June 26: a guard and 8 prisoners were hurt in a demonstration by 300 convicts. Massachusetts, July 2: 38 reformatory inmates held 4 guards hostage two hours before being subdued.

On Oct. 27 the spark touched off Illinois. In Chester, 362 inmates of Menard State Prison—which had had a smaller outbreak in September—rioted over alleged brutality of guards. A group of psychopathic convicts held 3 guards for four days; 7 more were seized by 300 men and released only when Governor Adlai Stevenson interrupted his Presidential campaign just before Election Day, flew to Menard, and, when peaceable overtures failed, ordered the locked cell doors cut with torches.

CONVICTS MUTINIED 22 times in 18 prisons. Riots raged until put down by tear gas, guns, hunger, or psychology. Here Michigan troopers dig out rebels

On Oct. 31, at the Ohio Penitentiary in Columbus, a series of riots involved 2500 prisoners and caused $1 million damage. When guards proved unable to cope with the situation, 240 armed National Guardsmen were called in. Before the rioters surrendered, one convict had been killed and several others were wounded.

All told, the year saw no less than 22 riots in 18 prisons. If the spark had died down by year's end, it was only temporarily. The underlying causes remained: bad treatment, bad food, unfair parole methods, "problem" inmates (psychopaths, four-time losers), overcrowding—e.g., Southern Michigan State Prison,

which was built for 5000 inmates, was jammed with nearly 6500. All of these conditions could be corrected with time, patience, and money. But in 1952, for an enlightened penal system, the U.S. too often substituted tear gas, clubs, and guns.

The year's crime record was rounded out by the brief press reappearance of names that had made tabloid scareheads in other days. Trunk murderess Winnie Ruth Judd escaped twice from the State Hospital for the Insane in Phoenix, Ariz., was twice recaptured.

Racketeer Irving Wexler—better known as Waxey Gordon—died, age 63, in California's Alcatraz Prison.

guts and everybody hates mine"), was executed in California.

Finally, the year that began in the afterglow of the Kefauver probe ended on a darker note. The American Bar Association, observing that current investigations had slowed underworld activity, predicted an early acceleration unless Federal and State authorities prevented it.

HOSTAGE GUARD is held at knife point as riot leader negotiates with officials

Puerto Rican chauvinist Oscar Collazo, doomed to death for his role in the attempt to assassinate President Truman in 1950, had his sentence commuted by the President to life imprisonment.

One-time bookmaking tycoon Frank Erickson, freed after sixteen months in a New York jail, entered New Jersey State Prison for twelve to fourteen months more.

Young Billy Cook of Missouri, who horrified the nation in 1951 with six brutal murders (arrested, he snarled, "I hate everybody's

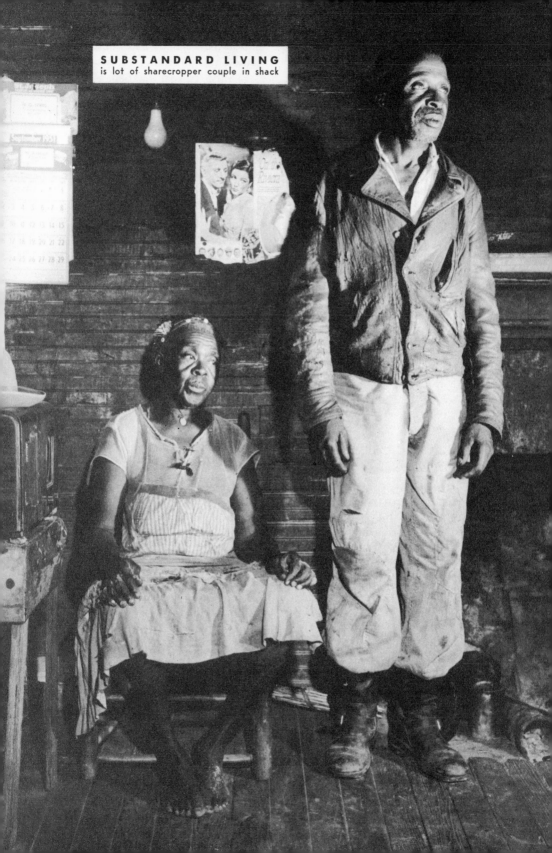

SUBSTANDARD LIVING
is lot of sharecropper couple in shack

SEN. McCARRAN'S immigration law beat President Truman's veto but drew wide criticism as racist

Race Relations

ON FEB. 16, IN THE ALL-WHITE SOUTH-wood district of South San Francisco, Calif., residents held an informal election. The proposition: Shall the Shengs stay?

Sing Sheng, 26, airline mechanic and former Chinese Nationalist intelligence officer, wanted to settle in Southwood with his Chinese-American wife and small son. But some of their potential neighbors objected. So Sheng suggested an election, on the theory that "everybody really believes in democracy".

The vote was 28 *Yes*, 174 *No*. Two days later, as outraged messages poured in from the country, the South San Francisco city council "deplored and disavowed" the election result. But the residents of

Southwood had spoken: the Shengs did not move in.

What those *No* votes meant to America, whose claims to fair dealing were on trial before the world's colored peoples, was debatable. The Sheng incident was the only one of its kind during the year, but the Communists could make use of it.

On June 27, Congress, over the President's veto, passed the McCarran-Walter Act, setting up annual quotas of 100 for each of eight smaller Asian countries—plus 100 for a much larger area including China and India—in a total annual immigration potential of 154,657. That did not sit well in Asia.

But the average American was far less

"MAY WE BE YOUR NEIGHBORS?" By 174-28, San Francisco suburb
said "No" to China war vet Sing Sheng. Too late, town council urged them to move in

concerned with the home-grown racial
problem: White vs. Negro.

Unlike many years that preceded it,
1952 saw little racial violence in the U.S.
There were no riots, no lynchings, no
bombing such as marred the last days of
1951 in the Miami, Fla., area. The nation's
progress in adjusting to its own racial
groups found expression largely in words.

As usual, some of the loudest words
were spoken on the topic of employment

opportunity. Agitation for and against a
national Fair Employment Practices Commission recurred throughout the Presidential campaign; General Eisenhower
was elected on a platform voicing hope
for legislation against "discriminatory
employment practices". But concrete action on F.E.P.C., even on the more likely
State level, was absent.

Less vociferously, the armed forces continued to integrate Negroes into white

units. Not all Whites, particularly Southerners, were made happy thereby; yet the
practice had become well established and
protests were not as influential in this as
in some other fields.

Chief of these fields was education. In
South Carolina, Governor James Byrnes
voiced indignation over possible U.S. Supreme Court action against the State's
right to segregate Negroes in schools. As
early as Jan. 8, Byrnes asked the legislature to submit a resolution at the November election to repeal the State's constitutional provisions for a public school
system. That would free the legislature to
set up separate school systems for Negroes
and Whites.

Thereafter, Byrnes kept busy in behalf
of his resolution, and in November it was
approved. Meanwhile South Carolina argued its case before the Supreme Court,
in hearings the outcome of which would
affect seventeen States with school-segre-
gation laws.

Important moves were made against
school segregation in 1952. The University of Tennessee enrolled its first Negro
student; so did the dental branch of the
University of Texas; so did a "white" public school in Baltimore.

Fisk and Howard universities became
the first Negro colleges in America to win
Phi Beta Kappa charters. The student
government of the University of California at Los Angeles withdrew recognition from three chapters of national music
sororities because of alleged bias against
Negroes.

On the other hand, a national fraternity
revoked the charter of its Dartmouth College chapter because the latter refused to
obey the fraternity's racial restrictions.
Special Federal courts upheld State laws
for public-school segregation in South
Carolina and Virginia. And the Florida
Supreme Court refused to admit five Negroes to the State university.

The Ku Klux Klan was heard from. In
July, in Florida, it announced formation
of an "American Confederate Army" to
fight, if necessary, against Federal attempts to ban racial segregation in that
State. That same month, in North Carolina, 63 Klansmen were brought to judgment in flogging cases and received jail
terms of ten months to six years.

Justice similarly was meted out in
Cicero, Ill., where a destructive riot ensued in 1951 after Mrs. Camille de Rose
(white) rented an apartment to bus
driver Harvey Clark Jr. (Negro). For having denied Clark's civil rights, the Cicero
police chief was fined $2000 and two pa-
trolmen $250 each.

In November, other police were involved in New Orleans in the roundup of
nine members of a "Nazi Storm Troopers
Club" which had been smashing street
lights, damaging railroad cars, and throwing bricks at Negroes.

The members carried swastika-deco-
rated cards in English and German and
pictures of Adolf Hitler, whom they professed to believe still alive in Argentina.
In their headquarters, an abandoned
store, were 2000 rounds of ammunition,
36 knives, a rifle. The members' ages: 13
to 15.

SKIN COLOR was less of a barrier to jobs,
education, and services in 1952. But the South
was still dotted by racial stop signs like this

Some Negro-White activities require close physical proximity, and in 1952 white Americans faced this fact in generally (but not always) constructive ways.

In the entertainment world, Georgia's Governor Herman Talmadge opened the year with a blast against Arthur Godfrey, Ken Murray, and other television figures. He said their programs violated the spirit of Southern segregation laws by offering Negro and white performers "on a purely social, equal basis".

But that same month, January, the first nonsegregated audience in Miami history heard Negro contralto Marian Anderson sing. A month later, Dorothy Maynor became the first Negro since 1939 to sing commercially in the D.A.R.'s (Daughters of the American Revolution) Constitution Hall in Washington, D.C.

FLOGGING VICTIM Ben Grainger said hooded mob took him across State line. F.B.I. invoked Federal kidnaping law, arrested 10 Ku Klux Klansmen

In sports, organized baseball opened its doors wider when the Texas League signed three Negro players—first in its 64-year history. Negroes also played with the Dallas Texans, a professional football team. The Professional Golfers' Association, spurred by protests from ex-boxer Joe Louis, modified its rule against Negroes in P.G.A.-sponsored tournaments.

But the U.S. Supreme Court ruled that a city-owned club in Miami Springs could bar Negroes from its golf courses; and in Kansas City, Mo., after a Federal court ordered the Swope Park swimming pool opened to Negroes, the park board voted not to operate the pool at all.

Among churches, the Methodists took the lead in Negro-White integration. First, 1½ million Methodist women adopted a forward-looking "charter of racial policies"; later, the General Conference gave Negro churches permission to join white jurisdictions and asked an end to discrimination.

In San Francisco, two Presbyterian congregations—one white, one Negro—merged under a Negro pastor. And Catholics named a New York mother of nine their first Negro "Mother of the Year".

For the record, it may be noted that in Louisiana a Negro entered the Democratic gubernatorial primary, for the first time ever (in a field of nine, he ran seventh). Probably the two most revealing human-interest stories of the year occurred in Colorado and North Carolina.

One morning in April, outside the mountain village of Fruita, Colo., a pickup truck carrying 12 persons braked suddenly to avoid a collision, skidded, turned over, and killed one of its passengers, a 14-year-old girl. She and the 11 others, all shaken up and some badly hurt, comprised the family of Melvin Minter, Negro lumber worker en route from Louisiana to a new job in Yakima, Wash.

When residents of Fruita heard of the

KLAN VENOM was not limited to Negroes. This North Carolina white woman was kidnaped and beaten. For series of terror raids, 63 alleged Klansmen stood trial

FIERY CROSS on a North Carolina hilltop dramatizes Ku Klux Klan's resurgence. Aftermath is shown (above right) as 10 sullen men are charged with kidnaping and flogging of white housewife

tragedy, they rushed to aid the Minters. Private cars took the injured to a hospital; one woman offered the whole family indefinite use of a house; other women furnished the house and stocked it with food; a construction company gave Melvin Minter a job; townspeople paid for repairing his truck, for the family's hospital expenses, for the daughter's funeral.

Only then did Fruita recall its Jim Crow ordinance forbidding Negroes to stay in town after sundown. In this all-White town, the law had been inactive. Now the city council held an emergency meeting and abolished it.

The scene of the second story was Yanceyville, N.C. There, seventeen months before, a 45-year-old Negro farmer, father of nine, had been arrested on the suspicion

of attacking a 17-year-old white tobacco grower's daughter. In his first trial, he had been given two years on the basis of a State law that says assault is possible without physical contact. Five months later, his lawyer appealed but a mixed jury was unable to reach a verdict.

This time, Willie Jean Boswell said Mack Ingram had approached her in a cornfield and "leered" at her. Ingram's defense was that he had mistaken her blue-jeaned figure for that of one of her brothers and had meant to ask if he could borrow the family trailer.

Willie Jean, married by now and a mother, admitted that Ingram had never come closer than "about 75 feet". She also confessed she had not known the meaning of "leer" till she looked it up. Nonethe-

less, an all-White jury swiftly returned a verdict of guilty. Ingram's sentence: six months (suspended), five years on probation.

Such cases as these brought forth a torrent of comment, generally heated. But the year's more meaningful statements were the result of long, thoughtful study.

Publishers brought out several good books on Negro-White dealings. Outstanding was Carl Rowan's *South of Freedom,* in which Rowan, a Tennessee-born Negro, now a reporter on a Minneapolis paper, returned to his native South and soberly totted up his race's gains and setbacks.

Another author, Swedish sociologist Gunnar Myrdal (*The American Dilemma*), told a U.N. group that, in the last ten years, there had been a "dramatic movement upward in the entire plane of living of the Negro people in America".

By contrast, the American Jewish Congress and the National Association for the Advancement of Colored People charged that government failure to eliminate discrimination against minorities was "hardly less inimical to our national security than actual subversion".

A Senate subcommittee report on Negro progress in the decade 1940–50 showed gains—both actual and relative to Whites'—in individual earnings, job levels, school enrollment, total schooling, death rate, and life expectancy.

But a similar report by the important interracial Southern Regional Council declared that failure to provide adequate public housing for Negroes had done "incalculable harm" to human relations in the South.

President-elect Eisenhower promised to create a commission to get all the facts on segregation in the U.S.

Yet probably no formal commission could achieve more impressive results than the Deep South community of Itta Bena, Miss., produced for itself at Christmas time.

There, when Negro students of the new Mississippi Vocational College set up an outdoor Nativity scene, four white youths wrecked it. But other white residents swamped the college with expressions of regret and offers of aid. So, in two days of joint Negro-White effort, the Nativity was restored. Said one resident quietly: "Christ rules again in Itta Bena."

CAMPUS SERENITY was disturbed in 1952 by the draft, budget troubles, and probes for subversives. In grade schools, postwar baby crop strained inadequate facilities

HARVARD President Conant started an academic uproar by his attack on private schools

EDUCATION

IN 1952, MORE THAN 32 MILLION BOYS, girls, men, and women were enrolled in U.S. schools and colleges. This colossal group seeking an education gave rise to all manner of problems.

Thanks to an unprecedented, unanticipated, ten-year population boom, the nation swarmed with youngsters for whom there were too few schools, classrooms, teachers. Thanks to inflation, there was too little money to remedy the lacks. Private colleges, perhaps hardest hit, began to form regional groups to make concerted fund appeals to business.

War complicated the situation. Draft uncertainty was reflected in June graduation figures, lowest in six years—315,000 collegians, 1,185,000 high-schoolers. Job-wise, these favored few were lucky. Starting salaries of up to $4500 a year were offered and sometimes went begging, for there were simply too few graduates to go around: 25,000 engineers for 30,000-plus openings, 50,000 teachers where 100-000 were needed.

In the fall, total college and university enrollment increased for the first time since 1949. But the reason was women: a 6 percent jump over 1951 (to 761,000), while the number of men dropped 1 percent (to 1,387,000).

The latter included thousands of Korea veterans—first to benefit from the new "G.I. Bill of Rights" passed in July—plus

WHEEEEEE! Eruption of "pantie raids" on campuses from coast to coast perturbed deans—but not coeds. Here embattled California damsels wait to defend their nylons

an all-time high of 300,000 youths enrolled in the draftproof Reserve Officers Training Corps (R.O.T.C.).

Good and bad news rounded out the 1952 statistics. In May, the nation heard that it had opened more college campuses in the past twenty-five years than in all its previous years put together. But at year's end the U.S. Office of Education estimated that the country needed 325,000 schoolrooms—$10.7 billion worth—and warned that, at the present building rate, the figure would be 600,000 needed by 1960.

In addition to budget troubles, educators had more than their share of ideological headaches. As part of the general concern over Communism, all kinds of people attacked school and college textbooks, teachers, and policies. Understandably, the educators rushed to defend academic freedom. The net results were confusion and acrimony.

In New York City, for example, ex-Communist, ex-teacher Bella Dodd told U.S. Senate investigators that in 1944 there had been some 1500 card-carrying Reds among the nation's teachers, with perhaps 1000 of them in New York. The Teachers Union, which Mrs. Dodd had helped found, promptly cried "Foul!" Meanwhile, some New York teachers lost their jobs for refusing to answer questions by school officials about leftist leanings.

Feeling ran high, coast to coast. Sarah Lawrence College (Bronxville, N.Y.) was such a frequent target that its president was forced to spend two thirds of his time answering attacks. Reed College (Portland, Ore.) installed a new president with the hope that he would be able to erase the school's pinkish reputation.

The American Legion turned on its onetime close collaborator, the National Education Association, calling it "one of the strongest forces today . . . for a socialistic America". The N.E.A., in its July convention of 7000 key educators, angrily "deplored" the accusation.

As one teacher put it, "A strong ground swell is running against us."

Another choppy sea was running over the relationship of education and religion.

The rarely militant Christian Science Church won a compromise with the New York legislature over the question of forcing Scientist children to attend public-school classes in subjects contrary to Science teachings. The legislature passed a bill requiring their attendance for certain courses (germ theory, public health) but not for others.

A broader controversy involved the Catholic Church. The first round came in April when Harvard University's President James Conant attacked the whole idea of private and denominational schools as a menace to "our democratic unity". Boston's Archbishop Richard Cushing and other Catholic leaders promptly counterattacked.

Among their arguments: Private schools are as American as public schools; the U.S. has been infected by a philosophy that says "everything is government's business".

November brought the second round. This time the nation's Catholic bishops decried the separation of religion and public education as a grave danger to the nation. Immediate criticism came from some Protestant sources. Baptist leaders, to cite one viewpoint, cried that the bishops wanted "a policy . . . rejected by the founders of the Republic".

As the controversy bubbled, a survey showed that more Catholics than ever before were being educated by the Church—some four million students in 11,500 schools and colleges. But the separation of church and state still seemed secure.

WHAT DOES IT MEAN? Sociologists, anthropologists, psychologists pondered. But zoologist Dr. Alfred Kinsey was calm, explained raids by saying, "All animals play around."

One charge leveled at U.S. education during the year carried high explosive. Its essence was that our basic approach to teaching is wrong.

The Carnegie Foundation's President Oliver Carmichael summarized it in a fourfold blast at college thinking.

He criticized: 1) arbitrary course credits which imply that "the educational value of typewriting, for example, is equivalent to that of calculus, literature or logic"; 2) overspecialization in limited fields of knowledge; 3) the idea that "education is primarily concerned with the communication of knowledge, whereas it is actually the communication of intellectual power"; 4) blind worship of facts for their own sake.

All this, he added, produces well-read spectators rather than intellectually alert participants.

No radical teaching innovations appeared in 1952, but the usual number of new courses popped up, indicative of adjustment to the changing times. Among them were a four-year course, leading to a degree, in television production and programming; a course in ghostwriting (for students at American U. in Washington, D.C.); courses on the Federal government's much-ramified departments and on civil-military relations.

In August, 35 Atchison, Topeka and Santa Fe railroad employees completed a six-week course at the University of Southern California on how to think about today's society, from child labor to Communism. In January, Columbia University turned its huge (10,000 students) adult-education program into a full-fledged liberal-arts college with its own faculty, degree, and Phi Beta Kappa elections.

During the year, educators were re-evaluating a onetime bogy, television. The most dramatic example occurred in Chicago, Ill., where Dr. Frances Horwich of Roosevelt College caused a minor sensation with her Ding Dong School.

This, Miss Frances' own idea, was a five-mornings-a-week telecast for pre-kindergartners. Presented with skill and understanding, it not only got the under-five set off Mother's hands but also taught thousands of tots clay modeling, group songs, arithmetic, good manners.

The end of the Federal three-year "freeze" on new video stations threw open 242 channels for educational use. A flood of applications ensued from colleges, cities, States, even private organizations.

Two incidents marked the year's lighter side. Foremost were the college-boy "panty raids". These began March 20 at the University of Michigan, where a mob of spring-fevered males suddenly invaded the women's dormitories to steal and brandish underwear. Within a few weeks, the same thing happened in Nebraska, Iowa, Minnesota, Connecticut, Miami—all over the land.

In a standard pattern, men moved en masse on dormitory or sorority house; women ran eagerly to windows or porches; general shouting broke out, punctuated by faculty protests and police whistles; the mob charged; the girls fled; the boys retired with their nylon loot.

Best analysis came from Dr. Alfred Kinsey (*Sexual Behavior in the Human Male*): "All animals," he stated, "play around."

In the spring everything went wrong for Alexander Stoddard, Los Angeles superintendent of schools. First he learned that some of a batch of 500,000 report cards spelled "language" as "langauge", while others bore "semeter" instead of "semester".

Reporting to the board of education, Stoddard wrote fervently: "There are two words, 'language' and 'semester', that we hope no one of our generation will ever mispell again." Then someone reminded him how to spell "misspell".

TERRITORIES

IN AN AVERAGE YEAR, AMERICA'S OVERSEAS possessions make little news. In this respect, 1952 was average, except in Puerto Rico.

Alaska and Hawaii put in twelve months of normal growth and equally normal frustration of their No. 1 political dream: to become States. Though Russian reconnaissance planes gave Alaska a scare, the year saw steady strengthening of the Territory's defenses. Hawaii recalled other planes at a historic moment —7:55 A.M., Sunday, Dec. 7—when ground was broken at Pearl Harbor, scene of the first Japanese attack on U.S. forces in World War II, for a memorial to an unknown sailor.

Otherwise, all was routine in Alaska, Hawaii, Guam, the Western Pacific, the Canal Zone, and the Virgin Islands. Not so in Puerto Rico.

July 25 was a real summer day in San Juan, the Island's capital. Sun lay on narrow Spanish streets and modern American-style homes like a blanket, lifted now and again by a breeze off the Atlantic. Outside the capitol, massed faces—white, brown, black—focused on the reviewing stand where Governor Luis Muñoz Marín was making a speech.

To Islanders, this moment was filled with almost unbearable emotion. Just fifty-four years before, the first U.S. troops had landed in the war that wrested Puerto

Rico from Spain. Since then, the under-endowed, overpopulated island had struggled to emerge from colonialism.

This day was dramatic proof that it had succeeded; Puerto Rico became the first U.S. overseas possession to win the status of commonwealth (or, in the Island's proud phrase, Free Associated State).

Governor Muñoz—heavy-set, bilingual, realistic, future-minded—symbolized the remarkable transition since his Popular Democratic Party came to power.

In twelve years, with some Washington help, the P.D.P. had led Puerto Rico from "tropical slum" to the most progressive land in the Caribbean, if not all Latin America. Sample statistics: life expectancy up from 46 years to 61; wages of sugar-cane cutters up from $1.40 a day to $3.20; public housing up from 4000 units to 40,000.

When Muñoz became, in 1948, the Island's first elected governor, he stepped the pace up further. Under him began "Operation Bootstrap", a long-range program to attract outside industry through tax and other benefits. In 1952 it brought dozens of new enterprises to Puerto Rico.

Muñoz also sparkplugged the new "model" constitution, a distillation of the best in the world's democratic thought, which Island voters and the U.S. Congress approved early in 1952 (although Congress insisted on the elimination of "human rights" guarantees it considered too advanced).

Now, in hot San Juan, Muñoz finished his speech and a morning of parades and eloquence reached its climax. For the first time, the single-starred Puerto Rican flag rose to flutter in the humid air beside the Stars and Stripes. And all over the Island cheers broke from choked throats.

OVERCROWDED PUERTO RICO could claim some of world's worst slum areas. The battle against poverty is gradually being won by the Islanders

Said a prominent banker: "Our mother, Spain, let us go. Our foster-mother has fed and taught us. Today we stand on our own feet. Next—forward!" In his words lay hope for all colonial people— and a sharp rebuttal to every critic of American colonial policies.

Puerto Rico made still other news in 1952, though none of similar importance. In April, a Pan American air liner crashed in the sea off San Juan and 52 were lost. The pilot, Captain John Burn, in a similar crash off Lisbon in 1943, had hit the headlines by rescuing singer Jane Froman, whom he later married. Her comment this time: "It can't happen to us again!" This time, Burn was one of 17 saved.

In July, in the heat and exhaustion of the Republican convention at Chicago, a long evening's polling of State delegations exploded hilariously when a short, balding Puerto Rican lawyer named Marcelino Romani demanded a roll call of his island's three delegates. By the time the chair had waded through the complicated Spanish names, including some of delegates temporarily absent, dead-pan Romani had reduced the convention (and countless televiewers) to helpless laughter.

In November, while the Fair Deal was taking a beating on the mainland, the Popular Democratic Party swept Puerto Rico. Not only was Governor Muñoz reelected; the P.D.P. elected every one of its candidates to both houses of the legislature and won control of all 76 municipal councils. The opposition got a look-in only because the constitution that Governor Muñoz inspired requires that other political parties be given a certain number of legislative seats.

The outlook was that Puerto Rican progress would continue and that Muñoz Marín would be heard from again.

MODERN APARTMENT HOUSE reflects Puerto Rico's growing prosperity, now based on industrial as well as agricultural economy. Island continues to be mecca for tourists

MARINES help load cargo of sugar bound for Mediterranean fleet

OLD WARRIOR John L. Lewis, boss of United Mine Workers. White House upheld his wage demands

BUSINESS

DROUGHT PARCHED THE LAND IN 1952. NOT since the postwar restlessness of 1946 were more work hours lost because of labor troubles. One crippling strike caused a loss of steel production equal to half the Soviet Union's yearly output and threw hundreds of thousands out of work. Our foreign trade slumped. So did farm prices. The cost of living climbed to a new peak. Any one of these events might have shoved us into hard times. And yet—

And yet the American economy—which means the business of making a living—had its greatest year in history. Our national income was highest. We bought and sold more. We made more things in our factories. On the land, we raised more things to eat. More people were at work. There were fewer business failures. Stocks reached their highest points in twenty-three years. And, even though we borrowed more, we also saved more.

How much of this 1952 prosperity was real? Contrasted with the 1939 dollar, the 1952 dollar's buying power was 53 cents. The U.S. Mint reported increased demand for quarters and half dollars and less for pennies, nickels, and dimes. To purchase what our 1939 national income would have bought in dollars of that year, our 1952 income would have had to total some $132 billion. Instead, after the tax collectors finished, it was $235 billion.

It is true, however, that millions of retired folk and others on long-fixed incomes were on the losing end. Inflation was not licked in 1952, but there were signs that it might be slowing down.

Among inflationary elements were defense spending, Federal debt, and governmental in-the-red budgets, all somewhat related. Ordinarily, their recital calls for out-of-this-world figures, hard to understand. But, for their informal discussions, officials of the Atomic Energy Commission, who must think and talk big, have dreamed up more compact units of measurement, the "megaton" and the "megabuck". One megaton is equivalent to one million tons of TNT. One megabuck equals $1 million.

Figured this way, defense spending is almost 50,000 megabucks a year, the annual cost of government is 80,000 megabucks, and the Federal debt is 267,000 megabucks. To keep the government in megabucks requires in taxes nearly a third of all the money we make. Many economists hold that, when government takes more than a quarter of income, there is bound to be inflation.

The year showed that our prosperity depends less upon defense spending than was imagined. Contrasted with output of civilian goods, defense production made a poor showing. Armament programs fell behind, either stalled by bottlenecks, or deliberately stretched out.

The real miracle was that, despite controls on materials for defense, a flood of consumer goods reached the market. And, for the first time since 1939, the market was ruled not by sellers but by buyers.

To attract the consumer's dollar, American business began the biggest-ever advertising and sales campaigns. Auto makers drastically restyled their new cars. Other big industrial corporations organized theatrical and road shows to publicize new products. Hopalong Cassidy, cowboy movie hero, enticed the young to start savings accounts. Glamour girl Faye Emerson's plunging neckline on TV helped to pull Pepsi-Cola out of the red.

New plastics and synthetic textiles reached the stores. So did novel household gadgets. Electric-appliance people stocked home freezers for their customers. Proctor and Gamble brought out "Zest", guaranteed to remove rings from bathtubs. Advertisers dreamed up new names for products. Sheaffer introduced the "snorkel" pen, mess- and leak-proof.

Employment and Labor Relations

Another year passed without fulfilling predictions of gloomy economists and Kremlin Communists that the U.S. is about to go into an economic tailspin.

Play-it-safe business forecasters frequently predict a high level of activity for the first half of a year and a decline in the second half. That was the prediction for 1952, but the decline did not occur.

Charts and columns of figures show *what* was done by American business in 1952, but not *how* it was done. That is the story of farmers who fed us, of people who punched time clocks and occasionally marched on picket lines, of men at big desks in front offices, of bankers who invested our money, of storekeepers who sold us goods, and of salesmen and advertising people who tried to persuade us to buy more. It is the story of the American people at work.

IN 1952, MORE PEOPLE WERE AT WORK IN this country than ever before. Newspaper classified advertisements were cluttered with "Help Wanted" and virtually bare of "Situations Wanted" notices. Applications for unemployment compensation were the fewest known.

All this was despite more work being done by machines which displaced men. In Texas City, for instance, three men at an instrument panel operated, without other human help, a giant chemical plant which produced one third of the nation's styrene used in paints, plastics, and synthetic rubber.

Nearly all of the 1952 wheat, three quarters of the corn, two thirds of the potatoes, and about one fifth of the cotton were machine-harvested. Two out of three retail groceries were self-service.

Some employers paid bounties for new hired help. One General Electric plant was in such need of toolmakers, testers, and janitors that it offered a $5 reward to any worker who lured a new employee to the G.E. payroll. The employee who got the most recruits in any given month won an additional prize of a TV set.

Theoretically, wages were frozen or under supervision of the Federal Wage Stabilization Board. Thus, many employers were balked in attempts to hold good workers by raising their wages. There were occasional ridiculous snafus, such as the one in Albuquerque, N.Mex., where a lawyer raised the pay of his efficient secretary from $170 to $225 a month.

"You can't do that," the local W.S.B. office told him. "The limit is $190." So the lawyer reduced the salary to that figure. Whereupon the girl quit and got a job with the W.S.B. at $225 a month.

Blocked from wage increases from employers, unions cast about for other benefits. Once, labor leaders rejected paid vacations and pensions as "gratuities". Later they included them in collective-bargaining demands. In 1952, the Chamber of Commerce of the United States estimated that these "fringe benefits" now cost American employers $25 billion annually.

At the year's beginning, a construction firm was convicted and fined for paying its bricklayers more than the rate approved by the Wage Stabilization Board. Toward year's end, the W.S.B.'s recommended reduction of wage demands by John L. Lewis' coal miners was overruled at the White House.

These two extremes show what happened to governmental attempts to "hold the line" by "stabilization" of both prices and wages. When the Truman administration yielded to pressure for wage increases, the end of price controls was in sight.

As long as price and wage controls remained in force, collective bargaining was not so much between unions and management as it was with government—i.e., with an administration which backed W.S.B.'s favoring of steel workers, and which reversed W.S.B.'s denial of some of the miners' demands. Up went wages and up went prices of steel and coal.

More workers (3,500,000) were on strike during 1952 than in any year since 1946. A month-long walkout of 90,000 oil workers closed down one third of the nation's refineries and sharply curtailed commercial and military aviation.

One of the year's longest strikes was by white-collar workers. When the Prudential (Rock of Gibraltar) Insurance Company did not agree that its agents were overworked and underpaid, 7500 of them went out on strike for 193 days. After a compromise settlement, the A.F.L. insurance agents' union vainly sought an insurance company willing to insure union members against future walkouts.

The year's biggest hot potato in labor relations was the steel wage dispute.

Eighteen million tons of production were lost. Workers lost several hundred millions in wages which would take months to make up at new wage rates. Lack of steel threw hundreds of thou-

"NEVER . . . have so few controlled so much." Brothers Irénée (l.) and Pierre du Pont discuss antitrust suit in which government named 117 Du Pont relatives as defendants

sands of people in other industries out of work. The probable nationwide loss in production and wages was $2 billion.

But instead of taking a year, as anticipated, the steel industry caught up with shortages caused by the strike in six months. The 1952 economy was strong enough to take in its stride all setbacks caused by the long steel strike.

Management

OUT WENT ONE CHARLIE WILSON; IN CAME another. Early in the year, C. E. Wilson, President of General Electric, resigned as director of defense mobilization because President Truman by-passed him in the steel strike. Late in the year, C. E. Wilson, President of General Motors, was designated secretary of defense by President-elect Eisenhower, who summoned top businessmen to top government posts.

Except for hosannas in board rooms, the unusual prospect of a Federal government administered largely by business executives had little impact upon the American economy in 1952. But there was evidence during the year of new attitudes not only toward businessmen but among businessmen themselves.

A former vice-president of the Hawaiian Pineapple Company is president of Cornell University. A former president of Trinity College, Hartford, is head of the New York Stock Exchange. A generation ago, only a handful of big businessmen got through high school. Today, only a handful did not attend college or professional school. And some are still going back to college to learn more.

Key executives of large corporations take part in the Advanced Management Program of the Harvard Graduate School of Business Administration. Last year's class at the Rutgers Graduate School of Banking included 5 bank presidents, 83 vice-presidents, and 212 cashiers.

Researchers examined businessmen in 1952 and reached conflicting verdicts. A California advertising man questioned more than five score executives in the $35,000-a-year bracket.

A third of the group turn up at the office around ten in the morning and quit about three in the afternoon. They are frequently out three hours for lunch and, if there's a chance for a golf game or a four- or five-day week-end, they're off. Most of these 30-hour-a-week slaves have their own companies.

The other two thirds are executives of big companies. Their work weeks range from 70 to 110 hours. They are driven more by ambition than by their families. They love their work more than they do their wives, and the divorce rate among them is high. The California adman found these hard-working top-management men happy in their jobs and swallowing less alcohol and sleeping pills.

Contrary findings came from an industrial psychologist. He pronounced them suffering from an emotional ailment he termed "executive neurosis", driven by inner feelings of insecurity to more and more overwork, excessive drinking, and nervous breakdowns.

Another diagnosis came from the head of a personnel firm. He divided management into the "stupid and industrious" and the "brilliant and lazy". The former, he said, comprise the greatest number. "Great damage can result from their actions. In backing ill-advised plans with zeal and energy, they may induce disaster." The brilliant and lazy executive is the best top-level business operator, said the personnel man, because his tendency to avoid time-consuming details enables him to maintain proper perspective and to plan simply, directly, and successfully.

Somebody must be right.

The take-home pay of the man of top management is less than it once was. An executive paid $75,000 thirty years ago had some $60,000 after income taxes. A generation later, when his salary was $175,000, he still had only $60,000 left after taxes

The result has been a custom, increasingly manifest in 1952, for a company executive in lieu of higher pay to get what union labor is already demanding and getting: fringe benefits.

Instead of a salary increase which would hike him to a higher tax bracket, the company pays his life-insurance premium and costs of his physical check-ups and health and accident insurance.

Another substitute for a salary raise is option on company stock at less than market price. The capital-gains tax involved would be less than surtaxes on increased salary. Another and newer substitute for higher salary is a long-term contract which stretches an executive's compensation into his retirement years.

Retailing

THE FAVORITE FRINGE BENEFIT CONTINUES to be the expense account. Because club membership may give executives better business contacts, the company pays the dues, and it pays also for theaters, night spots, and expensive dining places.

Retail storekeepers have a number of headaches and two nightmares. Among the headaches are half-trained sales personnel and new methods of competition. One nightmare is fear of having on hand more than customers can buy. The other is to have less on hand than customers want. In either case, the result is "No Sale" on the cash registers.

Those two nightmares were behind all the headlines in business sections of 1952 newspapers about "over-extended" and "under-extended" inventories. Yet, things moved on and off store shelves faster and in greater quantity during 1952 than the year before. Christmas sales were the biggest ever.

In 1952, Sears, Roebuck and Kroger's chain stores joined the "billion dollar" group, now numbering twenty-six corporations, whose annual sales reach $1 billion. On the other hand, the world's largest department store, R. H. Macy & Co., Inc., though not in trouble, had an uncomfortable year. Like many merchants, it guessed wrong when the Korean war began by stocking up big inventories in expectation of shortages which did not occur. Also, a screaming price war with a competitor, Gimbels, was costly.

Macy stockholders, whose dividends were cut from 50 to 40 cents a share, fumed at the 1952 annual meeting when they spotted Robert Montgomery on the board of directors. "Whatever my talents," explained the movie actor and TV m.c., "they are at Macy's service."

"What does he know about merchandising?" demanded a heckler.

When told that other Macy directors hadn't known much about retailing when chosen, the heckler heckled: "Maybe that's what's wrong with Macy's."

Other big-city department stores were uneasy. The trade of some fell off because competitors set up suburban branch stores to avoid traffic snarls.

Perhaps the year's most significant merchandising development was a general trend to night shopping. The eight-hour day gave more people time to shop after work hours. The five-day week moved payday shopping from Saturday to Friday night. With virtually the nation's entire work force now employed, retailers began to realize that the time to sell is when buyers aren't working.

Many stores are open two nights a week. Some are open until 9 o'clock five nights a week. About one fifth of last year's retail sales, food included, were made in the evening. These stores reported more man-and-wife shoppers, quicker sales, and fewer goods returned.

Night shopping increased retailers' personnel problems. Sales clerks want the five-day week which customers on the other side of the counter enjoy. Stores which observe a five-day week by closing on either Saturdays or Mondays found little or no decrease in sales, and some

reported their personnel troubles had "vanished overnight".

Elsewhere over the nation, personnel troubles kept retailers awake nights. Not only are they plagued by shortage of sales help; too many of their salespeople are lamentable specimens. One third of those engaged by a Chicago department store failed to show up for work. Nearly half of a Boston store's applicants went AWOL before their three-day training period ended. "Getting good sales personnel," a Houston chain-store manager said, "is just a matter of praying."

One answer to prayer is self-service.

Between 70 and 80 percent of all food stores are self-service or semi-self-service. Many retailers of everything from nuts and bolts to fur coats have adopted this supermarket technique.

With only four clerks, a hardware dealer in an Indiana small city serves two thousand customers in an afternoon. Two Sears, Roebuck stores have been trying "cash-and-wrap" centers to which customers take, for wrapping and payment, merchandise they pick out themselves. Store display cases are disappearing because, says one market expert, "they are the best way in the world to keep merchandise. We'd rather sell it."

When customers browse among the shelves, more buying and quicker sales result. Many food processors fight for favorable positions on cash-and-carry shelves. General Mills and Pillsbury give a quarter or a third of a dollar discount per case to retailers who display their pastry mixes prominently.

Self-service does away with sales clerks. Still another merchandising innovation does away with store cashiers. In 1952, automatic vending machines, once dealing almost wholly in chewing gum and

N.Y.C. SANITATION WORKERS, though not on strike, hold demonstration to bring attention to wage demands. Picketers said hoods were intended to hide identity, prevent reprisals

SUPERLINER "United States" won Blue Ribbon for west-to-east Atlantic crossing. Time: 3 days, 10 hours, 40 min. 1952's tourist exodus to Europe was biggest in history

salted peanuts, knocked down sales of nearly $1.2 billion, or more than the total business of Sears, Roebuck.

These silent salesmen offer nylon hosiery, cigarettes, magazines and paperbound books, lighter fluid, hot and cold drinks, and refrigerated fruits. The Lunch-o-Mat cooks and serves hamburgers, hot dogs, and coffee, as well as dispensing pies, milk, and fruit juices.

More than a thousand machines over the country shell out bags of crushed ice and ice cubes needed for emergency hospitality, and automatic fuel venders sell 5-gallon cans of kerosene and sacks of coal, charcoal, and briquettes.

Many odd and interesting novelties enlivened U.S. retailing in 1952. A supermarket outside Boston has a direct phone to a taxi company for the convenience of bundle-burdened customers. . . . A former Earl Carroll press agent in Los Angeles organized a "Master Charge" service, enabling carefully credit-screened clients to charge almost anything almost anywhere. . . . Another merchandising novelty: stores which merely display samples, then take customers' orders.

Hess Brothers, Allentown, Pa., department store, gives courses on infant care to expectant mothers and free art lessons to expectant artists. . . . The movie *Frogmen*, which glamorized the navy's World War II underwater daredevil swimmers, jumped 1952 sales of rubber fins and flippers and swimming goggles 400 percent. . . . After 17-year-old Maureen Connolly won the women's national tennis championship again, sales of junior-sized rackets leaped 50 percent over those of 1951.

. . . To stimulate sales of hunting rifles, Marshall Field, Chicago department store, equipped a target range for prospective hunters.

The year's most important new products in retail merchandising and in the chemical industry were synthetic clothing fabrics. Less than twenty years ago, the tree and the coal pile yielded rayon and nylon, which pretty nearly put the silkworm out of business. Less than five years ago came the mixing of natural gas with air to form a fiber which looks like wool and is bad news for Western and Australian sheepherders.

These acrylic fibers, as chemists call them, are blended in various proportions with wool, cotton, and rayon to be fashioned into blankets, suits, dresses, shirts, summer slacks, and knit yarns. Combined with wool, their chief advantage is washability and retention of shape without wrinkling and frequent ironing. Their disadvantage is low resistance to fire. Pipe and cigarette ashes and careless sparks melt holes which can't be rewoven.

One sweater manufacturer used so much acrylic fiber in his yarn that his garments went up in smoke when near a flame, with painful results to wearers.

It was the first big merchandising year for air-born fabrics. Hundreds of millions of dollars are being spent by the chemical industry in developing these new fibers under such trade names as Du Pont's Orlon, Union Carbide's Dynel, and Chemstrad's Acrilan.

American Cyanamid is working on X-51, Eastman Kodak is trying out M-24, and, when their makers are satisfied, these products will be marketed under more persuasive names. Enough acrylic fabric was produced last year to equal thirty million dresses or ten million suits. Facing a production this year three times that of 1952, some producers are wondering what they can do with it all.

The biggest splash made by the new synthetic, damp-proof, wrinkle-proof fabrics was in men's clothing. Tropical worsteds took a beating, and slacks "sweetened" with acrylics were popular.

Men found 1952 a good year in which to buy a new suit. Men's clothing prices came down; a further buying incentive was changed styles.

For at least a decade, American men favored double-breasted suits—even during World War II when controls and ration officials forbade waistcoats and trouser cuffs. But in 1952, more than two thirds of the suits sold were single-breasted. Tweeds, Shetlands, and unfinished worsteds were favorites.

More dinner coats and black ties were sold in 1952. White shirts recovered from an eighteen-month slump and two Troy, N.Y., shirt factories reopened.

Women's clothes cost more. Aside from usual year-to-year fashion changes, 1952's big development in women's clothing was a trend to higher-priced, quality goods.

This was good news for specialty shops with high price tags. In 1952, women didn't seem to mind paying more for a better-made, richer-looking dress or suit. Some stores found women customers happily paying twice as much as before.

The trend to more expensive clothing was widespread. In the Los Angeles area, aircraft workers' wives were no longer content with the cotton dresses they wore back home in Arkansas and Oklahoma, but sought *Vogue*-like numbers.

Store buyers attributed the popularity of better-quality clothes to the nation's continued high employment. Said one: "Folks are beginning to feel that it's going to last and want to live up to it."

There was one garment which early in the year some people, especially in Washington, seemed anxious to live down. That was the mink coat.

While Congressional committees investigated the subject early in 1952, the following appeared in the classified ads of the Gloucester (Mass.) *Daily Times:* "Owing to the controversy over mink coats, they will no longer be acceptable in rag bags. Clancy, Dealer in Junk."

One mink coat turned up in clothing sent to Korean refugees. By the year's end, $5000 coats were selling for $300 less. Nevertheless, two thirds of all dollars spent for furs are for mink. "If anything," said one of America's top mink ranchers, "the Washington mink scandals helped the market."

Other mink developments: "Jasmine", a new white mink, retails for $12,000 a coat. . . . A Chicago fur store rents out mink coats for $40 a night. . . . A California firm advertised silver-blue mink coats for dolls at $300.

Foreign Trade

AMERICAN ADVERTISED PRODUCTS HAVE INvaded foreign-language vocabularies. In Israel, "fresh" means canned salmon, that being the word in largest letters on U.S. labels of the product. To Haitians, whose politicians favor Buicks with Dynaflow transmission, "Dynaflow" means a Big Shot or something expensive—"Doesn't she dress Dynaflow?" And the Greeks have a word for a pretty girl. She's a "Nylon".

Nevertheless, both our exports (aside from government armament and economic aid) and imports fell off last year. Carrying on American foreign trade is like scrambling out of a bramble patch. Whatever move is made, we get scratched.

If we let tariff barriers down, a cry goes up that American industry and labor are suffering from cheap foreign competition. When duties on bicycles were lowered, British bikes sold here for less than American machines and in 1952 U.S. bicycle production slumped.

FINANCIER'S WIFE, Mona Williams, long listed among world's best-dressed women

If other nations raise tariff bars, a cry goes up that our export industries and those who labor in them are being hurt. When the U.S. restricted dried-fig imports, Turkey retaliated by slapping big duties on American typewriters, refrigerators, and washing machines.

Another disadvantage arose from our rearmament program. While Defense Department and N.A.T.O. requirements monopolized American jet-plane production, the British aircraft industry began turning out jet transport planes. The British inaugurated jet passenger-plane service between London and South Africa. American air lines have no jets and probably won't have for some years.

To enable dollar-short countries to get

on their feet and buy from us, some $14 billion in Marshall Plan economic aid was doled out to Europe in six years. The end of 1952 brought more pressure for ending this economic crutch. While he was secretary of state-designate, John Foster Dulles called for more private expenditure and investment abroad.

But just when the "trade not aid" slogan was making some headway in the country's thinking, the United Nations voted that it is all right for the government of a country to take over a private industry. After this encouragement of governmental piracy, many American investors wondered why they should risk money abroad.

Other trade developments in 1952 included the following.

Japanese Competition. The already unhappy American textile industry became unhappier over figures showing that Japan exports 25 percent more cotton goods than the U.S. The Ronson Lighter people got high blood pressure over the discovery that Ronson lighter replicas, consisting of cheap parts made in Japan, are assembled and sold in this country.

Italian Competition. Italian-made motor scooters, priced at $279.95, appeared on the American market.

Fashions and Films. Italy's renaissance in women's fashions vexed not only Paris couturiers, but New York City's garment district. Italy's movie industry, with franker—if possible—sex realism, invaded Hollywood markets. Hollywood also was pained by the continued popularity in this country of British-made films. In Britain, English film makers were sad because the year's best money-maker in their country was *The Greatest Show on Earth*, Cecil B. De Mille's Hollywood blockbuster.

U.S. Beverages Abroad. In France and Italy, vintners and Communists tried to arouse wine-drinker fury against the increasing popularity of Coca-Cola. . . . Some Arab kingdoms banned liquor imports even for American oil workers within their borders, and Pepsi-Cola and Coca-Cola ran neck-and-neck for the Middle East's soft-drink market.

In backward areas of the world, Borden Company's Klim (milk powdered and spelled backward) got a lot of free advertising. In East Asia and the Indies, Chinese Communist propaganda warned natives against Klim as an American imperialist plot against their babies. In the Belgian Congo, the popular song hit of the year was "Klim Abiski Mwana". In jungle rhythm and tribal dialect, it said: "Mama, oh Mama, the child cries! Give it Klim milk."

HARRISON WILLIAMS, wizard of American finance. New Deal ended billion-dollar dream

Hand-cranked phonographs were as popular among the natives of the Congo as TV sets are among natives of the U.S. As a result, 15,000 records of the Klim song were sold at $1.10 each, and Borden's powdered-milk sales went up 85 percent along the Congo.

Advertising

ALONG NEW YORK CITY'S MADISON AVENUE, advertising offices are thicker than market-research reports. Last summer, a sleekly decorated, new Madison Avenue restaurant was made ready. Its announced name, "The Huckster", was quickly changed.

Advertising men still wince when called "hucksters", the title of Frederic Wakeman's savage novel of six years ago. When *Tide,* one of advertising's trade papers, promised to banish the word from its columns, it suggested that a surer way of putting "h-ckst-r" out of circulation would be for advertising men to stop acting like hucksters.

To persuade its customers to buy more than in previous years, American business and industry during 1952 spent some $7 billion for advertising. Half of it went to newspapers, magazines, radio, and TV in that order of expenditure. The other half was for billboards, sales-promotion material, and solicitation by direct mail.

Auto, candy, washing-machine, and refrigerator makers told their salesmen and advertising people to get set for hard selling days which may rival those of the 1930's. Banks, railroads, steel companies, tire manufacturers upped their advertising appropriations, sometimes by 50 percent.

Gasoline refiners, producers of antidishpan soaps, and tooth-paste purveyors have come forward with pet names supposedly descriptive of special, exclusive ingredients. "Medicated" is a favorite radio-plug word for cold remedies and soothing pills for aches and pains.

One brewer of lager beer thought "lagered" might boost his product, but advertising psychologists reported that nearly 40 percent of persons approached believed the word meant "lazy", "tired", or "drunk".

Despite the fact that recognition tests showed that Elsie, a dreamy-eyed cow, is more familiar than pictures of Senator Taft and Van Johnson, Borden's withdrew her from advertising circulation, except as a trade-mark.

The charge for four hours of spelling out words in the sky is $6000. Last year, Sky-Writing Corporation of America stopped using a single plane to form letters in wispy white smoke. It now sends up a fleet of seven planes in tight formation. Pilots were chiefly Air Force Reservists willing to pick up extra money, and all they had to do was keep on flying. The rest was handled in a control plane by an electronic mechanism which releases puffs of brightly colored chemical smoke from each of the planes. In a few seconds, these puffs form letters, and within ninety seconds a five-word advertising message is written out.

Television

DURING THE LAST FORTY YEARS, MANY A new device, appearing as a luxury, has finally become a mass-purchased near-necessity. Examples: the automobile, electric icebox, oil burner, washing machine, radio. After World War II came air-conditioning units, deep freezers, and Television with a capital T.

Around Christmas, 1951, TV makers and dealers were biting their nails. The market was flooded; well-known makes appeared at cut rates. Still, prospective buyers hesitated, afraid that early color television might render current sets obsolete. But color still seemed far off as 1952 progressed. The Federal Communications Commission (F.C.C.) failed to make up its mind; the Great Decision was left dangling into '53.

F.C.C. did take the freeze off licenses for new TV station outlets and issued some 2053 authorizations for localities not previously served by television. Extension of reception area whetted appetites for new sets. Other spurs were the political conventions and the Presidential campaign. Still another was owners' dissatisfaction with 10- and 12-inch sets and desire for 21-inch screens. But the wider TV area boosted advertising rates, already painfully high for most sponsors.

About five million TV sets were made and sold during 1952. By year's end, television was in about one third of all American households. Installment-buying TV owners still owed $750 million, and will have to pay out hundreds of millions yearly for repair and maintenance. But they loved it.

With production and sales running nearly 50 percent ahead of 1951, manufacturers had another cause for worry when 1952 ended. How big a bite would the excess-profits tax take out of their earnings, up 350 percent from the year before? TV manufacturers showed a greater percentage of increased net earnings than any other American industry.

Law Business

FEDERAL ANTITRUST LAWS AND THEIR court interpretations through the years are such a jungle that many businessmen do not know in particular cases whether they are acting within or without the law. Sometimes one government department urges firms to activities which other governmental agencies, such as the Federal Trade Commission and Department of Justice, later declare illegal.

Into last year's political campaign was tossed an 860-page F.T.C. report which assailed five American and two foreign oil companies for uniting their operations in a world-wide cartel.

There was a time when the F.T.C. and Department of Justice indicated whether certain proposed corporation mergers might be antitrust-law violations. By 1952, they were tying things in knots by declaring that some projects would "create conditions which might tend to violation of antitrust laws"—like forbidding a car to be taken out of a garage lest someone drive it through a red traffic light.

By the end of 1952, some 140 antitrust suits were pending in the courts. Many of them had taken years to prepare and would take months and millions of dollars to prosecute and defend. By December, 1952, a trust-busting case involving seventeen leading investment-banking houses had been argued in New York for twenty-five months. The defendants were charged with conspiracy in bidding for and in floating new security issues.

The case was heard by Judge Harold R. Medina, nimble-witted survivor of another judicial endurance contest, the turbulent nine-month trial and conviction in 1949 of eleven Communist Party leaders.

Opening arguments in the securities trial consumed four months. Government attorneys presented their case for a year, then rested. When weary Judge Medina called for a respite before hearing the defense, he exclaimed, "Holy cats! This is the damnedest case I've ever seen."

The U.S. government threw the book at two corporations of which it is the biggest customer. Without International Business Machines (I.B.M.) mechanical calculators, tabulators, and other office equipment, government business would be thrust back into quill-pen days. Yet I.B.M. was hauled into court on monopoly charges because it usually leased

HOT DOGS ARE BIG BUSINESS: Americans eat 42 apiece every year, total of 6½ billion! Butcher in Frankfurt, Germany, invented them just 100 years ago

rather than sold its ingenious contraptions. I.B.M.'s answer was that, if the machines were sold, only 5 percent of civilian renters could afford to buy.

Granddaddy of all antitrust suits was the one against Du Pont which began in December, 1952. In war and peace, the government has turned to Du Pont. For a fee of $1, Du Pont is building a gigantic hydrogen-bomb plant for the Atomic Energy Commission (A.E.C.) on the banks of the Savannah River. The Defense Department and Du Pont are co-operating to expand production of titanium, a "wonder metal" twice as strong as steel and half as heavy.

While the A.E.C. and Defense Department were. working with Du Pont because it was big enough to give them what they needed, the Department of Justice sought to cut Du Pont's size.

Beginning in 1949, antitrust attorney Willis L. Hotchkiss and an assistant leafed through 100,000 documents, narrowed them down to eight volumes of 1200 exhibits. At the same time, a slim young government lawyer named Dorothy M. Hunt, an ex-Wave with a pageboy bob, climbed through the many-branched Du Pont family tree. She came down with a list of 117 defendants and alleged "conspirators" raked out of 2000 Du Pont relatives.

The government charged that Du Pont companies, controlled by the defendants, had created a monopoly by owning 23 percent of General Motors stock and 18 percent of U.S. Rubber.

Of the 117 Du Ponts and relatives named as monopolist conspirators, 59 were minors. Of these, Alletta du Pont Bredin was born in July, 1951, two years after the first suit was filed.

The trial opened in Chicago before U.S. District Judge Walter La Buy, who heard the case without a jury. Opposing the 3 government lawyers was a platoon of 33 defense attorneys who were billeted on a whole floor of the Palmer House. Du Pont legal forces so crowded the courtroom that Pierre du Pont, 82-year-old head of the family, and Irénée, his 75-year-old brother, were crammed with younger relatives into the idle jury box.

"Never in the history of antitrust legislation have so few people controlled so much," said U.S. Attorney Hotchkiss. Although "much merriment" had been aroused by the tender years of some Du Pont defendants, the purpose of including them in the suit was so that "family control can be destroyed".

After seven days, Hotchkiss collapsed and was taken to a hospital with nervous exhaustion. The decision to continue the suit was left to the Eisenhower administration's Department of Justice.

Meanwhile, there were important trials of business cases between nongovernmental litigants, some big, some strange.

Strangest suit. When Columbia Records reissued some early recordings of trumpeter Louis ("Satchmo") Armstrong, it found dealers selling disks re-pressed from Columbia originals. What galled Columbia particularly was that these piratings bore the trade-mark "Jolly Roger". Accordingly, it brought an injunction suit against Paradox Industries, owner of the trade-mark.

The court decided that Columbia had no case because Paradox had not pirated its trade-mark. The court held that copyrights apply only to things seen, like words, pictures, and sheet music, and that they could not protect sounds, even the hot licks from Satchmo's trumpet.

Biggest. Harrison Williams, 80, ran a tricycle factory in Ohio when he was 19. Moving to New York, he acquired control of one group of utilities after another. By the late 1920's, he ruled one sixth of all U.S. public utilities and had taken for his second wife decorative Mona Strader Bush of Lexington, Ky. His fortune soared to $680 million.

"Why not quit?" he was asked.

"Not until I make it an even billion," he replied.

He lived magnificently in a sumptuous place on Fifth Avenue, on magnificent estates in the South, in a stately house in London, an elegant home in Paris, a place in Italy, and on the world's biggest yacht. Mrs. Harrison Williams became known as one of the world's ten best-dressed women.

Then came the depression and the Roosevelt administration. The New Deal's death sentence on public-utility holding companies destroyed Williams' hope of parlaying his fortune to a billion dollars. Next came legal troubles. Trustees of Central State Utilities brought suit, charging that Williams had appropriated its assets.

After seven years of court skirmishes, a Federal district judge directed Williams to return to the utility company $11.4 million, plus interest since 1929. This decision was the biggest judgment against an individual in American legal history and might ultimately have cost Williams between $17 and $20 million. A U.S. court of appeals, however, reversed the judgment and late in 1952 the Supreme Court upheld the reversal.

Taxes

IN 1952, A HOUSTON, TEXAS, MAN BROUGHT out a "Junior Tax Return". Income space had such items as allowances, paper routes, mowing lawns, and other chores. Deductibilities included Sunday-school contributions, gifts from family, and repairs to toys. The purpose of this playful inquisition is to teach children the meaning of income taxes.

Their elders needed no such lesson. At least 30 percent of last year's national income was siphoned off in taxes, and the cost of all government—Federal, State, and local—was three quarters of the total wages and salaries of the nation's nongovernmental employees. So high are Federal and State gasoline taxes that oil men proposed renaming motor fuel "taxoline".

Companies showing losses instead of profits became attractive buys. They were sought by profitable firms anxious for consolidation to absorb losses and thus

come within the regular 52 percent corporation tax rather than the 68 percent excess-profits tax. Typical of many such offerings advertised in *The Wall Street Journal* during the year was a 75 percent interest in a concern whose losses for the last three years were $200,000 and "available for carryovers" on 1952 tax returns.

1952 Federal levies hiked the tax on distilled spirits from $9 to $10.50 a gallon, putting legal whisky beyond many American pocketbooks. Federal liquor-tax collections dropped more than $125 million, 900 million gallons of bonded whisky piled up in warehouses, and the bootlegger returned to his furtive yet profitable calling of the 1920's. Outraged legitimate distillers estimated that illegal stills had cut their business in half.

In the Bronx, operators of 500-gallon-a-day stills, which deprive the Federal gov-

WORLD'S ONLY floating sulfur plant was built to extract sulfur from Louisiana marsh. Feat was another triumph for American engineers

ernment of $5250 a day in taxes, vainly tried to disguise odors of the illicit distillations by using chlorophyll.

Finance

FOR LONG YEARS, THE PERSON WHO BANKED his savings was a forgotten man. He got next to nothing in interest, then 2 percent, and then 2½ percent. Last year's savings-bank interest was quite often 3 percent. And along with interest rates, deposits in and borrowings from banks went up.

The typical banker of seventy-five years ago, solemn in mutton-chop whiskers and Prince Albert, sat behind a roll-top desk so big one could sleep in it. He might well turn in his grave at some recent innovations. For banks are after new business as determinedly as any Fuller Brush man. They have increased by 25 percent appropriations for advertising, which is often of a chatty, neighborly style. In 1952, the millions they spent to give a new look to their banking houses brought a 15 to 50 percent increase in deposits.

The banks of the 1920's resembled glorified mausoleums or big-city railroad stations and scared away humble people. Now that banks seek the patronage of small-income groups, the trend is to more friendly interiors. In place of zoo-like tellers' cages are low, glass-fenced counters. Cold marble interiors have yielded to soft pastel shades and thick carpeting. Last year's biggest bank-carpeting job was nearly an acre of floor covering for the lobby of Washington's Union Trust Company.

Some banks now have special accommodations for motorists. An Ohio bank is building five glassed-in teller units in its

parking lot. A Texas bank has ramps to an upper-floor parking space for three hundred cars. For motorists who won't use even this convenience, there are ten car ports on the ground floor, where a bank official roams, ready to negotiate small loans to auto users.

One bank has a baby-carriage garage, with nurse service, for check-cashing mothers. A Long Island, N.Y., bank issues credit cards to depositors, who may go to stores and say "charge it", while the bank picks up the check. At the end of a month, the bank sends a statement to card holders, who then pay four weeks' bills with one check. Eight hundred local merchants say the scheme has increased their sales 15 to 20 percent among twenty-seven hundred credit-card holders. A bank in the Midwest issues left-handed checkbooks to southpaws: stubs at the right instead of the left of the book.

Bowing to custom of the times, the New York Stock Exchange adopted the five-day week. This left plenty of time for trading, for the number of men and women who are shareholders in American business and industry was less than expected, some 6.4 million. Also, the stock-exchange people were bothered by the tendency of corporate management to borrow money on bonds and mortgages rather than dilute ownership by new stock issues.

For nearly a century, brokers gathered in the streets of the financial district and dealt in securities not on the lists of orthodox stock exchanges. Thirty years ago, the New York Curb Exchange gave up competition with the weather, moved indoors, and became the second-largest securities market place in the country. In 1952, it voted to assume the name "The American Stock Exchange" on Jan. 2, 1953. Meanwhile, it stretched trading from 10 A.M. to 3:30 P.M., thirty minutes longer than conventional hours. Late in 1952, it proposed to open at 11 and close at 5 to accommodate Western security dealers in a time zone three hours later than New York's.

Farm and Food

THE AVERAGE FARMER'S NET CASH INCOME for 1952 was $2200, about $20 less than in 1951—roughly a 3 percent return on his land and building investment. But he needs less money for living expenses than the city man. His home is usually part of his business investment and he often raises much of his own food. So he didn't do so badly last year. In fact, in only four of the last twenty-five years did he ever have it so good.

But when retail food prices reached their highest peak in August, 1952, farmers' prices began to fall. They were still falling at year's end when farm-belt Congressmen were about to return to Washington. And although causes of depressions vary, hard times are generally heralded by a drop in farm prices.

The situation of the farmer at the end of 1952 caused concern, but was not necessarily dangerous. Mortgage-loan totals were magnified by inflationary dollars. Mortgage foreclosures on old and new farm homesteads were less than two for each thousand loans. Basically, farm prosperity remained high. Anxiety over the economic condition of the American farmer was over what *could* happen rather than what *was* happening.

Hardest hit during 1952 were dairy farmers. Those in some drought areas had to import two thirds of their hay for winter feed. The American dairy farmer's cow gives a quarter more milk than the animal of twenty-five years ago. Yet, despite drink-more-milk campaigns, the 1952 consumption of milk per person was the lowest on record. The chief reason is that the palm tree, the soybean, and the peanut gave the cow stiffer competition.

Over the opposition of legislators from dairy States, Congress repealed the punitive Federal tax on oleomargarine, and most States relaxed their bans against selling oleo colored like butter. Housewives paid 35 cents for margarine, as contrasted with 80 or 90 cents for butter. By the end of the year, oleo had caught up with butter consumption. Many big dairy-products distributors began selling oleo as well as butter.

Dairy-products people also took another swipe at the cow. Just before hot weather came, a synthetic "ice cream" composed of vegetable oils instead of butterfat appeared in the Midwest and Southwest.

The new frozen dessert comes in chocolate, strawberry, and vanilla flavors, and sells for less than half the price of genuine ice cream. The vegetable-oil base can be coconut, cottonseed, peanut, or soybean oil—whichever is cheapest at the time. It is hard to distinguish between the real stuff and the substitute. The vegetable-oil product lacks certain vitamins found in milk, but they can be added.

Lower butter consumption and ersatz ice cream could strike heavy blows at dairy farming. The cow's peak milk yield comes in summer. Ice cream is most popular then and siphons off most of the farmer's surplus milk. But there is little prospect that the cow will go the way of the dodo, for other outlets for surplus milk developed during 1952.

Although dried milk had been on the market for a half century, there were few takers. Last year saw a spurt of converting whole and skimmed milk into powder. Production was nine times that of 1951.

Another innovation is a method of keeping whole milk fresh in cans for a year or more without refrigeration. The new canned milk has virtually the same taste as fresh. By year's end, three plants in Western dairy country were equipped for production. A New Yorker expected to sell the product in vending machines at 10 cents for a 6-ounce can.

DAIRY CATTLE have begun to slip in importance. Margarine is outselling butter; vegetable oils are replacing butterfat in ice cream; milk consumption dropped in 1952. One cow just scratched her head and wondered what world was coming to

The WORLD

The WAR
of WORDS

WHO'S WHO OF THE KREMLIN is seen at first Communist Party Congress in 13 years, held in Moscow. Stalin is in first row at far left, Deputy Premier Molotov third from left. Making address, which lasted four hours, is Georgi Malenkov

THE FRANTIC ARMAMENTS RACE CONTINUED in 1952, and, in the main, it was conducted during a lull in the actual shooting. For most of the year, there was only small-scale fighting in Korea, Indochina, and Malaya, the three scenes of armed conflict.

But all was far from quiet on the propaganda front.

In February, a smallpox epidemic broke out in North Korea. It was probably imported by Chinese "volunteer" troops. But the Communists blamed in on the United Nations. On Feb. 22, a broadcast from Pyongyang, capital of North Korea, told the world that Allied airmen had rained down "fleas, lice, bugs, ants, grasshoppers, and spiders".

Spread by the Party lie machine, this whopper got international circulation.

On March 14, 1952, U.S.S.R. Deputy Foreign Minister Jacob A. Malik charged in the U.N. that the U.S. was using germ warfare for "mass killing of civilian populations". He disdained a U.S. suggestion that the Red Cross be asked to investigate.

BIGGEST BLUNDER OF THE COLD WAR was made by Major General Robert W. Grow (left). Red propagandists had a field day when his diary, which they stole, provided ammunition for their "warmongering" charges against United States

The Red Cross, he said, was "a Swiss national organization", neither international nor impartial.

On March 28, Malik told the United Nations Disarmament Commission, meeting in New York, that the U.S. had dropped bacteriological bombs. These contained germ-infested "crackers, crows, pork, spiders, ants, yellow leaves, crickets, canned food, fleas, and goose feathers".

At this point, the Disarmament Commission decided it had heard enough from Malik. By a vote of 11-1, it ruled him out of order.

Meantime, Chinese Red newspapers published photos of bombs, insects, and germs which "Americans had dropped" on North Korea, Manchuria, and China's Shantung Province.

The Chinese radio said Red prisoners on Koje Island, off the southeast coast of Korea, had served as guinea pigs for U.N. germ-weapon experiments. A United Na-

tions LST (Landing Ship, Tank), they said, was used as a floating laboratory.

On April 28, General Ridgway, supreme commander of U.N. forces in Korea, was transferred from the Far East to replace General Eisenhower as Supreme Commander, Allied Powers, Europe. Ridgway arrived in France at the end of May. The Far Eastern flea circus traveled with him.

French Reds labeled him General Plague, held anti-microbe demonstrations in Paris, and, with sticks, bricks, and iron bars, fought the police.

Among the 700 arrested was Jacques Duclos, acting head of the French Communist Party, caught masterminding the riot from a nearby limousine. In the seat beside him were a short-wave radio, a pistol, a blackjack, and two dead pigeons. They turned out to be not homing pigeons, as the French government suspected, but month-old eating squabs.

On June 16 and 17, Rome and Naples

also staged anti-Ridgway riots. Later, Togliatti, Italian Communist chief, delivered a vicious anti-Ridgway talk in Parliament. De Gasperi, Prime Minister, turned on him fiercely.

"Remember this," he shouted. "If present laws are not sufficient to curb you, we shall make new ones."

Britain's Very Reverend Hewlett Johnson, Dean of Canterbury, got into the bug act. Johnson, 77, who looks and talks like a medieval saint, was once described by former F.B.I. agent Herbert A. Philbrick as an underground member of the Communist International. The dean told the press that he had seen "conclusive and irrefutable evidence" of U.S. germ warfare. With his own eyes, he had seen Chinese children pick up infected bugs with chopsticks and place them in bottles.

"No truth whatsoever in the disgraceful and fraudulent accusations," said the British Foreign Office. But on July 15, British Prime Minister Winston Churchill and Dr. Geoffrey Fisher, Archbishop of Canterbury, rejected demands in Parliament that Johnson be expelled from the Church of England and tried for treason.

"Free speech," Churchill declared, "carries with it all the evil of the foolish, venomous, and unpleasant things that are said." The archbishop told the House of Lords that the dean was "a public nuisance", but "not yet a danger to public safety".

He had "misused and compromised his office", but was "no atheist" nor "an official member of the Communist Party". Hence, no proper grounds existed for ousting him.

SIDEWALK SCRIBBLING, part of all-out Communist campaign to incite anti-American demonstrations, greeted General Ridgway's arrival in Paris to command N.A.T.O. troops

The dean "sincerely believes that the Christian principles of peace-making and social justice are better applied in Communist countries . . . That is not in itself heresy. We all have a right to be wrong."

On July 20, from the pulpit of Canterbury Cathedral, the Red dean repeated his germ-warfare charges. Americans at the services hurried to the exits.

And the Kremlin, as well as the Red dean, continued to twist truth into pretzels. A tragicomedy involving war prisoners on Koje Island was exactly their cup of tea.

Koje is about twice the size of Manhattan. Until May, 1952, it held 80,000 Red prisoners of the U.N. within seventeen barbed-wire enclosures. Few U.N. troops could be spared for guard duty, and fanatical Communists among the prisoners kept hostility at boiling point.

In February and March, riots resulted in the death of 90 prisoners. By mid-April, tension was high.

U.N. guards, fearing for their lives, moved out of Compound 76—Koje's Alcatraz. By May, the situation was largely out of control. The unguarded prisoners conducted military drills, held courts to punish nonconformists, and established a system of communications among prisoner compounds and between Koje and Communist North Korea.

It was this last that made the fantastic General Dodd incident possible.

At Panmunjom, truce talks between North Korean and U.N. representatives had been deadlocked for months. The stumbling block was prisoner repatriation. The Communists wanted an all-for-

ANTI-RIDGWAY demonstration gets under way as Paris Reds parade against N.A.T.O. commander. Stories of alleged U.N. atrocities in Korea were circulated throughout the world

ALL PARIS WAS CONCERNED with Ridgway's arrival. General and Mrs. Ridgway (above) exchange social pleasantries with British Foreign Secretary and Mrs. Anthony Eden at N.A.T.O. reception

PARIS POLICEMAN ignores two Communists with head injuries during anti-Ridgway demonstration

PESTE, TIFO COLERA: NUOVE ARMI U.S.A.

all exchange. The U.N., having polled the prisoners of war, had found that 100,000 out of 170,000 were not Communists, did not desire to be repatriated, and wished to be segregated from their Communist fellow prisoners. The U.N., therefore, suggested repatriation on a voluntary basis.

On May 8, Communist delegates at Panmunjom took turns delivering tirades against the "dishonesty" of the U.N. statistics regarding prisoners' desires, and accused the U.N. of screening prisoners forcibly.

Meantime, leaders of Koje Compound 76 requested a conference with Brigadier General Francis Dodd, bespectacled West Point graduate.

Dodd had often conferred with the compound leaders, and so, virtually unguarded, he went to the compound gate. While prisoner representatives engaged him in talk, a group darted through the gate, overwhelmed the general, and dragged him into the compound.

For the next three days, negotiations took place between the U.S. Army's prisoners and the U.S. Army.

Dodd was reported "still well". Periodically, he telephoned from the enclosure to a sentry at the compound gate. What he said was passed on to General James Van Fleet, Eighth Army Commander, or, after the first day, to Brigadier General Charles F. Colson, who replaced Dodd as commandant.

Dodd asked that no force be used: "Conferences are being held on a peaceful plane."

On May 10, Van Fleet disclosed that, to gain Dodd's release, the Allied Command already had granted some concessions to the Communist prisoners. However, he said he would never yield to "unreasonable" demands and force would be used if Dodd were not released.

Next day, Dodd was released, but the release had been bought at a steep price.

Dodd related his experiences. He had been given "a blanketed room with rice mats on the floor, a built-in bunk, a table with flowers".

As he negotiated with the prisoners, "the best parliamentary procedure" was followed. If force were used, the Communist commissar of the compound told him, he would be killed, and "there would be a simultaneous break from all compounds on the island".

He had spent his last day writing and rewriting letters for Colson's approval. These described Communist-dictated concessions to be made in exchange for his release. The concessions in the letter which Colson finally signed—under pressure—Dodd laughed off as "minor and of no importance".

But, used as propaganda at Panmunjom, that letter was a diplomatic triumph for the Communists.

"In the future," the letter stated, "prisoners of war can expect humane treatment." And, "there will be no more forcible screening of prisoners."

At Panmunjom, North Korea's chief delegate, dapperly uniformed General Nam Il, read the passage on forcible screening triumphantly. "Your absurd principle of voluntary repatriation," he crowed, "has collapsed."

The Communists accused the U.S. of "tearing up the Geneva Convention" in its treatment of war prisoners, and the charge echoed around the Red world. The National Committee of the United States Communist Party announced it had sent President Truman a telegram denouncing the "bestial massacre of war prisoners on Koje Island".

The U.S. had lost face in the Far East, not so much because of the extorted letter as because a U.S. general had fallen into so crude a trap. General Mark Clark, hero of North Africa in World War II, who had assumed the Korea command in place of General Ridgway, quickly removed General Colson, who, Clark said, had acted on his own initiative in the Dodd matter.

General Haydon Boatner was named commandant on Koje. Known as "the bull", he was expected to crack down. He did. Compound 76 was broken up, and its fanatic ringleaders were scattered in small groups all over Koje. Communist banners were ripped down and burned. But, in Asia, the Koje Island in-

PRO-COMMUNIST RELIGIOUS LEADER, Church of England's Dean of Canterbury, the Very Rev. Hewlett Johnson, repeated Red charges of germ warfare. He is shown with royal couple

HOMEMADE SPEAR pierces heart of North Korean prisoner. He was murdered by his own officers when he attempted to surrender to U.N. forces during Koje Island prison riots

ESCAPE from Koje Island prison compound is chanced by anti-Communist POW.
Plan is dangerous but preferable to certain death at hands of fanatical Red fellow prisoners

HOPES FOR KOREAN PEACE centered on Military Armistice Conference site, Panmunjom. Truce negotiations have been going on there since July, 1951

cident had proved a godsend to Communist propagandists.

And, in Europe, the diary of U.S. General Grow was to prove another.

Major General Robert W. Grow, 56, was U.S. military attaché in Moscow from July, 1950, to January, 1952. In the summer of 1951, while he was visiting Frankfurt, Germany, General Grow's diary was stolen from his hotel room, photographed, and returned.

Later that year, a book entitled *The Road to War* appeared. Its author, English Communist Richard Squires, sought to pin a warmonger label on the U.S. and prove that Grow was a spy. Featured were photostats from the general's diary, containing such passages as:

"War as soon as possible! Now!"

"We must start by hitting below the belt."

"Anything, truth or falsehood, to poison the thoughts of the population."

Early in January, 1952, East German newspapers carried excerpts from the diary as they appeared in Squires' book. As a result, the general was recalled from his post. Only in March did the Russian press take it up.

On March 11, while the Iron Curtain press headlined germ war and American brutality to Koje prisoners, the Moscow *Literary Gazette* called Grow a typical American militarist, saying his diary revealed "the real plans of the American warmongers". Later that month, the Cominform journal *For a Lasting Peace, For a Peoples' Democracy* spoke of an American "imperialist, militarist, bloody butcher", whose "monstrous crimes" make pale "the cannibalism of savages and the horrors of the Inquisition".

Early in July, the State Department suspended publication of the magazine *Amerika,* written in Russian to tell the truth about America. It was the only U.S. publication still permitted in the U.S.S.R.

Late in July, George F. Kennan, U.S. Ambassador to Russia, declined an invitation to attend the annual Russian air show when Soviet posters advertised it by depicting Soviet planes shooting down American aircraft.

Then, in September, the Russian youth magazine *Smena* described "beizbol", the American national sport, to its readers in this pipe dream: Baseball was nothing but the ancient and peaceful Russian game of lapta. In America, said *Smena,* it had taken on a bloody and militaristic flavor. Players frequently kill or maim their opponents.

Traded around like slaves for six or seven seasons, cast out when they are "ruined in health", players spend their remaining days begging in the streets. Teams go by horror-inspiring titles. *Tigrov!* (Tigers). *Piratov!* (Pirates). (*Smena* did not say that, in 1952, both of these terrors finished in the cellar.)

That same month, in Berlin en route to England, Ambassador Kennan told the press of the "icy cold" atmosphere in which he lived in Moscow. He said it had become impossible for an American to engage a Russian even "in simple conversation". He deplored the Communist "hate campaign" against America, and said that until Soviet leaders put a stop to anti-American propaganda no faith could be placed in their professed desire to improve relations with the West.

Pravda called Kennan a "slanderer under the mask of a diplomat" and the Soviet government demanded his recall.

From the start, Kennan had two strikes against him. He had formulated the West's "containment" policy, designed to prevent further Soviet expansion into any foreign country. Also, he understood the Russian language and the Kremlin mentality.

OFFICIAL RECORDS of truce talks at Panmunjom tower over official navy stenographer

PARTIALLY OPENED GRAVE reveals bodies of some of ten thousand Polish officers slain in Katyn Forest Massacre in 1939. Mass murder was originally blamed on Nazis, but more recent evidence traces it to the U.S.S.R.

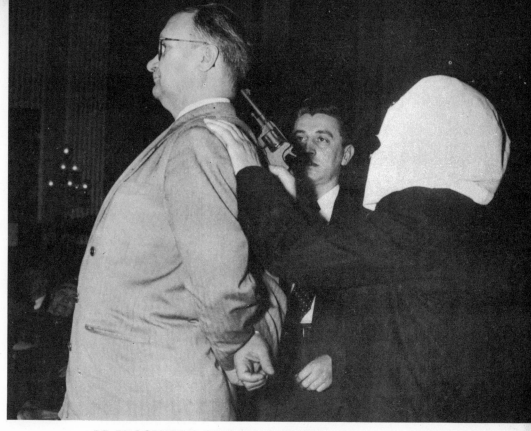

RE-ENACTMENT OF GRISLY CRIME: With a newspaperman posing as victim, witness shows U.S. Congressional committee how Russian soldiers shot Polish officers in Katyn Massacre. Ghoulish disguise is to protect family of witness from Soviet revenge

However, he had gone to Moscow hoping somehow to ease existing tensions, and he was unhappy about the ending of his mission.

The "hate America" campaign reached a climax when the 19th Congress of the Russian Communist Party opened in Moscow on Oct. 5.

Deputy Premier Vyacheslav M. Molotov, speaking in the Great Hall of the Kremlin, declared that U.S. "reactionary circles" were "blowing up war hysteria", preparing to unleash a new war.

Malenkov, Stalin's probable successor, likened U.S. aims to Hitler's. "The leaders of the United States," he told the assemblage, "knew it was impossible even to dream of world supremacy without the use of force, without launching a new war. They decided to break the peace, to prepare a new war."

Then Beria, head of the Soviet Gestapo, amid thunderous applause, predicted that the launching of World War III by the U.S. would bring about "its downfall and ruin".

America's hands were bloody, Moscow implied, but its own were full of olive branches. While preparing for war, Moscow paid lip service to peace. In the U.N., early in the year, Soviet delegates double-talked of atomic disarmament.

On April Fool's Day, Stalin issued a reply to questions submitted to him by fifty U.S. newspaper and radio editors.

Question: Is world war nearer now than two or three years ago?

Stalin: It is not.

Question: Is peaceful coexistence of Capitalism and Communism possible?

Stalin: Fully possible, given the mutual desire to co-operate . . . and non-interference in the internal affairs of other states.

"In the answer of Comrade Stalin," *Izvestia* declared, "there is expressed the readiness of the Soviet Union to solve all international questions by peaceful means."

That same day, at the World Economic Conference meeting in Moscow, Mihail Nesterov, Soviet Chamber of Commerce head, expressed the Soviet desire to buy $7 to $10 billion worth of goods from the West in the next two or three years.

Stalin, interviewed by India's ambassador in Moscow, spoke hopefully of peace, and gave the Indian the erroneous impression that he was thinking in terms of a Big Three conference, with Premier Nehru of India as mediator.

In June, Communist parties in Western Europe and the U.S. were instructed to soft-pedal revolution and join with non-Communist groups on issues of "bourgeois democratic freedoms".

Thus the Popular Front tactic of 1934–38 was revived. At that time, fearing Hitler, the Soviet Union sought friends among the anti-Fascists and antimilitarists of the West. The revival of this tactic in 1952 meant that the U.S. had taken Hitler's place in the Soviet scheme of things.

The objective of the Soviet war of words was to stamp the U.S. as an aggressor and make temporary friends with the masses in countries allied to America, on the alleged basis of a common struggle for peace.

Like other abrupt switches in the Party line, this one caught some Red chiefs flat-footed—for example, the French Red André Marty, commander of the pro-

Communist International Brigade in the Spanish Civil War of 1936–39. Brought up on charges of deviationism, he refused to conform.

"I am an old man," he said. "I am tired. Leave me alone." He was ousted from the Party.

All in all, the U.S. did not fare well in the 1952 war of words. It refused to use the Big Lie against the Big Lie. However, the U.S. had something that seemed like a Big Truth up its sleeve, and made good use of it.

On a witness stand in Washington, on Feb. 6, sat a weird-looking figure. Grim-faced members of the Congressional committee investigating the Katyn Massacre in Poland surrounded him. A ghoulish white hood was over his head, so that his family in Poland would not suffer from his revelations.

In halting words, the witness, a Polish ex-soldier, told how, from a hiding place in a tree, he had seen the Russians murder 200 Polish army officers in October, 1939.

In April, 1943, Joseph Goebbels, Nazi propaganda specialist, had broadcast a ghastly discovery. The German army in Poland's Katyn Forest had come across a mass grave containing the remains of 10,000 Polish officers. He blamed the slaughter on the Russians, who had held the Katyn area from September, 1939, when the Red Army invaded Poland, to June, 1941, when Germany invaded the U.S.S.R.

In 1943, as they have done ever since, the Russians angrily denied the charge. Anxious at the time not to offend Stalin, the U.S. and British governments brushed aside Polish demands for an international Red Cross investigation. However, the Polish Red Cross conducted an investigation independently. Probably for diplomatic reasons, it made no report of its findings.

In the fall of 1951, urged by Arthur Bliss Lane, former ambassador to Poland, and various congressmen, a Congressional committee was appointed to examine the Katyn evidence. The committee set up shop in Washington and in Frankfurt, Germany, heard dozens of witnesses, mostly displaced persons, and compiled mountains of testimony.

The main point to be determined was the date of the murders. This would establish the identity of the killers, since it would indicate whether Russians or Germans were then in possession of Katyn.

As witness after witness testified, the evidence grew damningly anti-Soviet. In 1943, captured American officers had been forced by the Nazis to view the gruesome burial site. They reported their conviction that the Russians had perpetrated the crime. The uniforms on the bodies were in good condition; they did not look as if they had been worn in prison camps for two years.

The former Polish Red Cross spoke up. In examining the corpses, it had found no letters or papers dated later than May, 1940—just before the German advance. The last entry in one diary described the Polish officers entering Katyn Forest under Russian guard.

Whatever the truth of Katyn, as anti-Russian propaganda in Poland the effect of the committee investigation was electric. Every newspaper in Communist-controlled Poland had to carry an eight-year-old Soviet communiqué blaming the crime on the Nazis.

VOICE OF AMERICA broadcasts are most effective means of penetrating Iron Curtain despite Russian "jamming" to prevent reception on Soviet radio sets

"I ACCEPT the full responsibilities . . ." In May, General Ridgway succeeded Eisenhower as supreme Allied commander in Europe

The ARMAMENTS RACE

IN 1952, WHILE THE HOT AND COLD WARS raged, the Western world at last acquired a military shield against the danger of a smashing Soviet assault.

No longer did it tremble lest the Kremlin, at a twitch of Joseph Stalin's finger, send Soviet hordes crashing from the Elbe River to the English Channel. For the North Atlantic Treaty Organization filled the military vacuum in Western Europe so as to make a Red blitzkrieg unlikely.

Moreover, the U.S. and Britain unveiled a secret arsenal of wonder weapons, atomic and otherwise, which probably could devastate any aggressor.

But the new shield made the N.A.T.O. nations relax. The Allies, on both sides of the Atlantic, stretched out or slowed down defensive efforts. The Western Europeans lost their sense of urgency as they lost the leadership of General Dwight D. Eisenhower from N.A.T.O.'s key command. Soon they worried as much over economic emergencies as they once did over the Red threat. Perhaps they put too much trust in atomic weapons.

Thus there arose a new crisis—a crisis of complacency.

Zero hour was 7:15 A.M., Nov. 1, 1952, for the most sensational atomic event since July 16, 1945, when the first A-bomb was detonated in New Mexico. At that hour, near Eniwetok Atoll in the western Pacific, the U.S. exploded the first test-tube model of the hydrogen bomb.

This H-bomb, or "Hell bomb", was nicknamed "Lulu" by the servicemen of Joint Task Force 132, the composite group of soldiers, sailors, and airmen who staged the epoch-making experiment. From their uncensored letters home, the bomb seemed indeed a Lulu. One eyewitness, wearing black glasses 35 miles away, said it exploded with the glare of "at least ten suns".

The *Lima News* in Lima, Ohio, printed this letter: "About 15 minutes after shot time, the island on which the bomb had been set off started to burn, and it turned a brilliant red. . . . Within six hours, an island that once had palm trees and coconuts was now nothing. A mile-wide island had actually disappeared."

The most colorful description was contained in a letter published in the *Los Angeles Examiner:* "Early this morning, we stood on the deck facing the islands we couldn't see. Everyone waited tensely as the loudspeaker announced the minutes, then seconds—four, three, two, one.

"Then, right on the nose, through glasses so dark absolutely nothing could be seen, appeared a huge orange ball, materializing out of nothing, which grew larger and brighter until it appeared as if no dark glasses were there at all.

"An intense heat struck us almost immediately and the ball of fire started to rise and slowly lose its intensity. We took off our glasses and saw water vapor suddenly form around the column.

"Then it rushed into the base of the column and up, clearing the air so that you could see countless tons of water rushing skyward—drawn up the column by that tremendous unseen force. The column went up and up and finally mushroomed.

"About three minutes later, the report, like a nearby cannon shot, hit us and was followed by several seconds of dull rumbling. Then the mushroom expanded into a free halo, growing with tornado-like speed and reaching nearly over our ship before it appeared to cease growing. Then it appeared to connect itself to the main column by a web of filmy vapor.

"Typical comment from the oldtimers: 'Holy cow! That sure makes the A-bomb a runt!' "

Not until Nov. 16 did the U.S. Atomic Energy Commission confirm what the letters had divulged. Then it simply announced the conclusion of "experiments contributing to thermonuclear weapons research".

The H-bomb was so powerful that an A-bomb was used as a mere percussion cap to provide heat and pressure to set it off. Some scientists claim that it could be made 1000 times more deadly than the A-bomb. A single H-bomb could destroy Moscow—or New York.

The Eniwetok test of the H-bomb took place within three years after President Truman, on Jan. 31, 1950, had ordered the A.E.C. "to continue its work on all forms of atomic weapons, including the so-called hydrogen or superbomb".

This test was the U.S. reply to the Soviet Union's explosion of its first A-bomb. President Truman announced the Russian explosion on Sept. 23, 1949.

The A-bomb, thus relegated to the horse-and-buggy age, derived its power from the *fission* into lighter elements of heavy atoms of either uranium or plutonium. The H-bomb, in contrast, got its power from the *fusion* of isotopes of hydrogen, the lightest element, into helium, the second-lightest. This is the same process which lights and heats the sun and the other stars. Thus the H-

GIANT HOWITZER is dropped to ground forces from C-119 "Packet" plane. The 5000-lb. cannon is lowered by three 100-foot parachutes

TOUGH, COMPETENT Lord Ismay is N.A.T.O. secretary-general. Close friend of Churchill, "Pug" Ismay has fine reputation for getting things done

bomb caught the secret of solar energy.

Presumably, as the mightiest weapon in all history, the H-bomb would serve as the gravest warning against Red aggression. Yet the American people, surfeited by stories of wonder weapons, took its test casually.

For the atomic-weapon age of plenty dawned in 1952. The U.S. stockpile of A-bombs now was numbered in four figures. A whole family of atomic weapons grew up for a variety of strategic situations. A-weapons were reduced in bulk and in weight but not necessarily in explosive power.

Atomic explosives were made small enough to be carried by guided missiles. Baby A-bombs were hung onto special shackles on the F-84G Thunderjet, the fleet Republic fighter which, being refuelable in mid-air, was limitless in range. Atomic shells were made to fit the new 280-millimeter atomic gun.

This atomic gun weighed 85 tons and was hauled at 35 miles an hour by twin transporters at front and rear. Having a 20-mile range, it was more accurate at night and in bad weather than were atomic bombers.

With a plenitude of raw material for atomic energy available, the U.S. buckled down to using it to propel American warships and warplanes. On June 14, at Groton, Conn., President Truman laid the keel of the *Nautilus,* the first atom-powered submarine, scheduled for launching in 1954. Only "a few pounds of uranium", Truman said, would drive her at "a top speed of more than 20 knots"

FRENCH MARSHAL Alphonse-Pierre Juin relaxes at veterans' ball. A strategy expert, he heads S.H.A.P.E. ground forces in central Europe

and would make it possible for her "to stay under water indefinitely".

The *Nautilus*, the President added, heralded an era of "atomic-powered merchant ships and airplanes, of atomic power plants producing electricity for factories, farms, and homes".

The U.S., in sum, was believed to be outstripping the Soviet Union in the atomic race—although to be the probable target of the relatively few Russian A-bombs was hardly a pleasant prospect.

In addition, the British, in Operation Havoc, exploded their first A-bomb on Oct. 3, when an orange-red flash flared like the setting sun over the desolate Monte Bello Islands off Australia and then gave way to a soaring, Z-shaped, gray cloud instead of the usual mushroom.

Winston Churchill disclosed that the British had set off their bomb inside the frigate *Plym* so as "to investigate the effect of an atomic explosion in a harbor".

Churchill described the result: "Thousands of tons of mud and rock from the sea bottom were thrown many thousands of feet into the air, and a high tidal wave was caused. . . .

"H.M.S. *Plym* was vaporized except for some red-hot fragments which were scattered over one of the islands and started fires in the dry vegetation. . . . When the flash first burst through the hull of *Plym*, the temperature was nearly 1,000,000 degrees."

The prime minister added the reminder that the British had built their own A-bomb, because the wartime pooling of atomic secrets among the U.S., Britain, and Canada had been banned in 1946 by act of Congress. Now he needled Washington for "a much closer American interchange" of atomic information.

Joining Churchill in urging that atomic

"BRASS HATS" make impressive array at Paris' Hotel Iena. 69 top-ranking officers of 14 nations gathered for S.H.A.P.E. staff exercises, called "Paper Maneuvers"

secrets be shared with America's allies was General Omar N. Bradley, chairman of the Joint Chiefs of Staff. Bradley was worried that the N.A.T.O. allies were slowing their rearmament effort because of an unjustified faith that atomic artillery and baby A-bombs were all that were needed to repel a Soviet assault.

He argued that Western Europe's military leaders should be taught what atomic weapons could do, if they were to use the atom effectively, and also what such weapons could not do, if they were not to rely on the atom unduly. The trouble with atomic wonder weapons was that they gave rise to a false sense of safety.

So also was it with other wonder weapons throughout 1952. Each event was so sensational that it created no special sensation.

Only a ripple was made by the navy's midsummer boast that its D558-II Skyrocket had flown at 1238 miles an hour, as fast as a rifle bullet and twice as fast as the speed of sound. So that its metal would not melt from the friction of the air, the Skyrocket carried enough apparatus to refrigerate a 3000-seat theater.

So fast and so intricate did new aircraft become that their human pilots were obsolescent. The air force unveiled semiautomatic interceptors such as the Lockheed F-94C Starfire and the D model of the North American F-86 Sabre. Each fired 2.75-inch rockets rather than conventional but less lethal guns, and was laden with 1000-odd pounds of electronic gear.

This electronic brain, faster and surer than the human brain, picked up the enemy bomber, charted its course, guided the interceptor toward the target, and selected the instant to fire the rockets.

Even these interceptors were to be replaced, in time, by supersonic fighters. And the army's first antiaircraft battalions to be armed with guided missiles were being organized.

These battalions were one concrete result of the $1,000,000,000-a-year guided-missile program. They were to use the so-called Nike missiles, with electronic brains, to destroy enemy bombers.

But futuristic weapons did not provide an air defense or offense that would be available should the Soviet Union strike. Never was this more plainly proved than just before 6 P.M. on Sept. 1.

At that instant an unpredicted tornado, as lethal as any Red assault, swept across the Carswell Air Force Base at Fort Worth, Texas. It was recorded at 91 miles an hour before it blew away the anemometer. It destroyed one $3,500,000 B-36 bomber, damaged 106 more, and caused a total loss of $23,000,000.

Thus it temporarily knocked out more of the giant bombers, whose wings stretch 230 feet and whose tail fins reach five stories high, than the air force ever had admitted having. And, for many weeks, it drastically reduced America's capability to deliver the A-bomb.

America's leading allies helped to mold the shape of things to come. The French developed the Mystère, a swept-wing jet interceptor. They boasted that it was speedier and more deadly than the American F-86 Sabre. But they admitted the Mystère was still in the testing stage.

The British, putting various aircraft designs into what they called "superpriority" production, pinned their greatest hopes on the delta wing.

This triangular shape, resembling the Greek letter delta, enclosed jet engines, gas tanks, radar, guns, and bombs within a single streamlined case. Two delta designs—the Gloster Javelin, an all-weather fighter of supersonic speed, and the Avro Vulcan, a four-jet bomber of sonic speed—were ordered into quantity production.

Even though such wonder weapons

were no insurance of present security, still the picture was not all black. American arsenals really got rolling during 1952 and spewed out military material in increasing quantities.

For example, they were so speedy in turning out the new M-47 and M-48 Patton tanks, with high-velocity 90-millimeter guns and automatic turret controls, that three out of the five tank factories were ordered to shut down their production lines. They delivered 666 planes to the air force in November to reach the loftiest production level since World War II. They did so in the face of repeated "stretch-outs".

President Truman's administration pushed back, from 1954 to 1955, the timetable for the proposed 143-wing air force, comprising 7500 combat aircraft, despite a warning from the Joint Chiefs of Staff that 1954 would be "the period of maximum peril".

It took this "calculated risk" even though General Bradley cautioned: "The stretch-out program will seriously reduce the anticipated military capabilities of the United States and the North Atlantic Treaty Organization to withstand successfully any all-out attack on the part of Russia prior to 1956."

Prime Minister Churchill took a similar calculated risk by disclosing that Britain's rearmament program, laid down in 1951, "is much more likely to be carried out in four years than in three". Despite such stretch-outs, N.A.T.O.'s military leaders made real progress during 1952 in getting ready to withstand successfully any all-out attack on the vital front between East and West—the Iron Curtain frontier of Western Europe.

"The specific purposes for which I was recalled to duty have been largely accomplished," General Eisenhower wrote to Defense Secretary Robert A. Lovett on April 2, 1952. It was the first anniversary of his activation of his N.A.T.O. headquarters as Supreme Allied Commander, Europe (SACEUR). "The command has been formed, its procedures established, and basic questions settled."

He felt that "we have made considerable progress" but he did not pretend that Western Europe had yet been provided with "the required shield".

Eisenhower was hard to replace, in view of his immense prestige as the Allied commander in Europe during World War II. But he had to be replaced. He recommended General Alfred M. Gruenther, his brilliant chief of staff and bridge-playing crony. But Gruenther was deemed lacking in command experience.

Instead of Gruenther, President Truman appointed General Matthew B. Ridgway, General Douglas MacArthur's successor in the Far East. General Gruenther was retained as chief of staff. Thus the President turned over to a fighting commander, who had stopped the Communists in the hot war in Asia, the task of stopping them from precipitating a hot war in Europe. Truman did so at the urging of the Joint Chiefs of Staff.

Now 57, with a springy stride, General Ridgway had parachuted into Normandy before dawn on D day in 1944. This time he landed, more sedately, at Orly airfield outside Paris with "Penny" Ridgway, his 31-year-old third wife, and their 3-year-old son Matty. He even put away the live grenade, strapped to his paratrooper's harness, which he had worn as a personal insigne in the Korean fighting.

On May 30, on a green lawn outside the new S.H.A.P.E. headquarters at Rocquencourt, Ridgway shook Eisenhower's hand. He said simply: "I accept, sir, the full responsibilities from you with a deep sense of pride and privilege. . . . We wish all people to know that we are determined to resist aggression."

GIGANTIC Globemaster transport can carry 200 troops or 30 tons of cargo. Here it takes aboard record-breaking navy Skyrocket which flies at twice speed of sound

Sharing Ridgway's duty of letting "all people" know was Lord Ismay, formerly Britain's secretary for commonwealth relations.

Lord Ismay, a 64-year-old, India-born, polo-playing general known as "Pug" for his bulldog jaw, took over there in April as secretary-general of the North Atlantic Treaty Organization.

Of him Churchill had written in *The Gathering Storm*: "We became hand-in-glove, and much more." American leaders had known him in wartime as "the man with the oil can. When he's around, the wheels turn." More recently, Ismay had referred to the cumbersome N.A.T.O. complex as "rather a lot of harness and not much horse". There was "a hiatus at

the summit", he had said. Now he had to fill that hiatus.

Admiral Lynde D. McCormick rounded out the top N.A.T.O. hierarchy as it was revised in 1952. Already commanding the U.S. Atlantic Fleet, in April he broke out a blue-and-gold flag in front of his two-story brick headquarters at Norfolk, Va. Thus he signified that he had taken over as Supreme Allied Commander, Atlantic (SACLANT), the naval counterpart of SACEUR.

However able Ridgway, Ismay, and McCormick might prove, the loss of General Eisenhower deprived N.A.T.O. of its most forceful leader. This contributed to a gradual slowdown of N.A.T.O.'s dynamic drive during the rest of 1952.

"Dawn is breaking," U.S. Secretary of State Dean Acheson exulted, "and a new day is dawning for all of us." It is "the beginning of a new era", British Foreign Secretary Anthony Eden rejoiced. "One rarely attends a conference which accomplished as much as this one did," Robert Schuman, Foreign Minister of France, summed up.

The foreign ministers of the Western Big Three were talking about the February meeting of the N.A.T.O. Council. This was held in the flower-bedecked Portuguese Parliament in Lisbon. To silence any possible sour note, the strongman premier, António Salazar, jailed 400 Lisbon beggars for the duration.

The Lisbon conference blueprinted the N.A.T.O. goals for 1952. "The N.A.T.O. nations," the Council revealed, "agreed to provide approximately 50 divisions in appropriate conditions of combat readiness" by year's end, so that they would have enough strength to deter the Kremlin from attacking with its 175 divisions.

Of these 50 divisions, 25 were to be ready for instant combat, and 25 were to be held in reserve. They were to be backed up by 4000 tactical aircraft. In addition, 30 more divisions were brought into N.A.T.O. by Greece and Turkey, the newest of the fourteen allies.

The N.A.T.O. Council at Lisbon also made the historic decision to rearm West Germany within an international European Army. Furthermore, it decided to set down permanent roots in Paris.

General Eisenhower was satisfied. "Visible and within grasp," he said, "we have the capability . . . of such strength as the Communist world would never dare challenge."

During 1952, the Lisbon blueprint led to a remarkable build-up of N.A.T.O.'s power. In the springtime the saying went: "Two years ago, nothing stood between the Russians and the Channel.

Now they would have to struggle past committee after committee." N.A.T.O.'s first command-post exercise, involving 199 generals and admirals, was nicknamed "Venus de Milo—no arms but plenty of S.H.A.P.E.". But in the fall, a whole series of mammoth maneuvers flexed N.A.T.O.'s new muscles.

Exercise Holdfast tested how the British and Benelux divisions in northern Germany could stop the Russians, before they got to the Rhine, by means of a "hedgehog" defense—based on heavily armored pockets rather than an old-fashioned unbroken line.

Exercise Rosebush demonstrated how the Americans and French in south Germany could hold the thorny Rhine line.

Exercise Ancient Wall showed off how the Italians, with their crack Alpine troops, hoped to shore up their age-old Alpine wall.

Exercise Mainbrace brought together the carrier-studded naval power of both SACEUR and SACLANT, boasting 200 ships and 1000 aircraft, to show what could be done to aid the isolated Scandinavian allies, Norway and Denmark.

All these war games employed a multinational command, multinational tactics, and even multinational spelling. The British went so far as to surrender the "u" in "harbour".

Yet N.A.T.O.'s new power contributed to a mood of complacency that produced a "slowdown in action", as General Ridgway called it, at the N.A.T.O. Council session in Paris in December, 1952. In advance Lord Ismay had cautioned that there would be "no spectacular decisions". There were none.

First, the N.A.T.O. Council set aside the ambitious goals, tentatively agreed upon in Lisbon in February, to build up from 50 to 70 divisions in 1953 and to 98 in 1954. Anthony Eden explained that "quality rather than quantity" would be the future aim. But General Ridgway huffed: "Unjustifiably dangerous."

Second, the Council bowed to economic necessity by agreeing to a new budget of only $229,600,000 for "infrastructure" (logistical installations). Yet Ridgway said S.H.A.P.E.'s plea for twice that much was the "irreducible minimum".

Third, the Council stretched the moral commitments of the Atlantic alliance all the way to Southeast Asia by promising "continuing support" to France's "valiant and long-continuing struggle" in Indochina. But it did not specify what this support would be.

Fourth, it salved British pride by naming Britain's Vice-Admiral Earl Mountbatten, the dashing uncle of the Duke of Edinburgh, as Commander in Chief, Mediterranean, in charge of sea communications there. But it kept the atom-carrying U.S. Sixth Fleet, the most powerful Mediterranean force, under U.S. Admiral Robert B. (Mick) Carney's separate authority.

Both Mountbatten and Carney were to be coequal under S.H.A.P.E. and were to "co-ordinate" with each other. Lord Is-

may defined what this word meant: "Co-ordinate is fixing it with the other chap."

Finally, the N.A.T.O. Council urged that "paramount importance" be placed on the "rapid" ratification of the European Army treaty for adding German divisions to its ground forces. But it thus reflected what grievous delays were stalling off the only real reinforcements which could be foreseen for Western Europe.

"We have to do what we can do, not what we'd like to do," Dean Acheson observed as he was leaving his last N.A.T.O. Council session. The Western alliance was "not going as fast as we would like", but "we are going forward; we are not standing still".

Admittedly, by the end of 1952, N.A.T.O. had fulfilled its Lisbon goal of having 25 divisions combat-ready, including 5 American, 5 French, and 4 British in West Germany. It also had on hand 3500 combat aircraft, which fell only slightly short of its Lisbon quota of 4000. N.A.T.O.'s most serious "shortfall" was in the pledged 25 reserve divisions; most of these troops were available on

ROCKET CLUSTER heads for target after leaving Starfire jet. Electronic gear on plane picks moment to fire rockets, each one of which could bring down biggest bomber ever built

WORLD'S RECORD was equaled when this rocket soared 135 miles into space. 7½-ton, 42-foot missile reached speed of 3900 miles per hour

paper but were nowhere near ready to fight.

Still, N.A.T.O.'s "covering forces" were approaching the level which the potential Red aggressor was maintaining in East Germany. If the Soviets were to launch an all-out assault, they would first have to strengthen their spearhead and, in doing so, presumably telegraph their punch.

But that was not enough to satisfy General Ridgway as he looked into the future. He rejected "the view that potential aggressors do not want war, are not ready for war, and will not precipitate war; that we are in for a long cold war and, therefore, should adjust our plans. . . . There can be no excuse for . . . lessened effort. . . .

"My responsibility for the military defense of the N.A.T.O. nations of Europe is not qualified. I am not told to defend just parts of them and their peoples. Nor am I told that my responsibility is to become effective at some future date. I have it today."

STALIN STATUE in Erivan, Armenia, is 164 feet high, won Stalin Prize for Soviet sculptor Merkurov

Behind the
IRON CURTAIN

DURING THE 13TH CENTURY THE GREAT Mongol Khan, Kublai, ruled over an empire which extended from Korea to Poland. His power was absolute; his word was law; he was looked upon as divine.

Soon after Kublai died, in 1294, the empire began to crumble. Rivalries broke out among candidates to the throne; then conquered areas broke away from Mongol sway. Lastly, the Mongol provinces themselves were split into tiny khanates.

The history of Russia, since 1380, has been a long process of picking up these pieces and putting them together again.

Stalin and Company had rewritten much Russian history to make it more palatable to themselves. But Russia's rulers knew the truth. They knew what could happen when the Great Khan died.

Stalin was 73 in December, 1952. For

CHIEF CONTENDERS to succeed 73-year-old Stalin were (l. to r.) Vyacheslav Molotov, Lavrenti Beria, Georgi Malenkov. None had record of friendship for West

years he had not left the side of his physician except to appear in public once or twice a year—often enough to let the world know he still lived. He and those close to him knew that the end might be near. That could not be permitted to occur without careful preparation.

The first problem to be solved was the designation of a successor; otherwise, the throne might be left to internecine struggle. During 1952 there was doubt who would inherit the mantle. Many were betting on Malenkov.

Georgi Maximilianovich Malenkov was born 51 years ago in southern Russia, of nonproletarian parentage. Soviet panegyrists, always seeking the factory worker in their hero's family tree, rarely mention Malenkov's family background. Malenkov himself has attacked Soviet executives who "pick subordinates by their proletarian ancestry rather than by capacity".

At 17, Georgi joined the Red army, then fighting against the Russian Whites. At 20, he was head of the Political Department of the Turkestan army. Sometime between 1925 and 1930, he became Stalin's private secretary. From that time on, his rise was meteoric.

By the time the Germans invaded Rus-

sia, in 1941, he was one of four secretaries of the Communist Party's Central Committee. During the war, he supervised the production of aircraft. In 1946, he was made a full member of the Politburo. After that, in official photographs of that Soviet ruling body, Malenkov's chubby, sharp-nosed face usually showed up next to Stalin's.

In December, 1949, half the world "celebrated" Stalin's 70th birthday. Malenkov's personal tribute to the exalted one appeared, at the head of all other congratulatory messages, in every newspaper printed in the Soviet Union.

But there was still room for conjecture. What about Vyacheslav Molotov — a friend of Stalin from way back? Would not memories of the underground, bank-robbery, and Siberia days bind these old coconspirators?

And what of Lavrenti Beria, the secret-police chief, a Georgian like the boss?

Even dashing Vasili, Stalin's aviator son, was not considered out of the running. The Soviet press had given him a good deal of space. Of course, this build-up may have been sentiment, like the name *Svetlana's Breath,* given to Russia's best-smelling perfume in honor of Stalin's daughter.

The year 1952 just about wiped out doubt.

On Jan. 8, Malenkov reached the half-century mark. Page One of every Soviet newspaper ran a large photograph of him. With it went the official Party greeting to this "true pupil of Lenin and co-adviser of Comrade Stalin", for "fulfilling the most responsible assignments, in all posts of Party and State activity, with energy and heroism".

In Stalin's time only two men had received this kind of write-up. One was Stalin himself. The other, Lenin, had long been safely dead. To paint the lily, Malenkov was awarded the Order of Lenin and, in the 1952 edition of the *Soviet Encyclopedia,* his biography was overhauled. Most noticeably altered was the description of Malenkov's role at the 18th Party Congress of 1939. It was rewritten to fit his heroic stature of 1952.

The clincher came in October, 1952, at the 19th Party Congress. Molotov was the first speaker, but the star of the occasion was Malenkov, who gave the traditional secretary's report—a meaty speech several hours long. Stalin spoke only ten minutes.

Malenkov's report dealt with international, cultural, and inter-Party affairs. However, economic matters took up the bulk of his speech, which hymned the superiority of Soviet over capitalist production. The figures cited, while impressive, revealed that Soviet heavy industry produced only about one third as much as heavy industry in the U.S. Soviet light industry was far behind, but Malenkov declared that the Soviet pace of production increase was greater.

Lesser Party lights arose to comment upon the brilliance of Comrade Malenkov's analysis. Subsequently, the Soviet press praised Malenkov's solution of problems hitherto regarded as beyond solving. Malenkov's speech was reprinted in an edition of three million copies.

One aim of the Congress was to avert chaos in the event of Stalin's death. The Politburo, long the policy-making center

SECOND IN COMMAND at Kremlin, Malenkov, here seen addressing Czech Communist Party Congress, began rapid rise to fame as Stalin's secretary. Circle indicates Czech Rudolf Slansky, Red hatchetman, himself purged at end of 1952

of the Party, was abolished. The Party's Central Committee was increased in size, with representatives from each of the Soviet republics. At its head appeared a Presidium of twenty-five members, including most of the former Politburo and some newly risen lights besides.

Actual supreme power was relocated in a newly created Secretariat. In this body of ten members, Stalin and Malenkov probably would pull the strings.

Foreshadowing new purges, Party rules were made stricter. A definite, if wishful, warning was given that the day of the protected and often corrupt Party bureaucrat was over. Not *whom* but *what* the Party official knew, would count.

One basic purpose of the 19th Congress was preparation for war, which Party leaders apparently believed imminent.

In 1945, Soviet author Feodor Pankerov wrote an article for which his knuckles were rapped. "It is true," he noted, "that in World War II millions of Soviet people answered Stalin's call, girded their loins for battle, and stopped the Germans at Stalingrad. But the question is: How could the Germans reach Stalingrad at all?"

A good question. It hit the heart of Soviet weakness—popular discontent with the brutality and corruption of the regime and the low standard of living.

During World War II, millions of Soviet citizens had flocked to Hitler as a savior until they learned that they had jumped from the frying pan into the fire. Stalin was determined this would not happen again. He had cause for worry.

During 1952, the little fellow in the Soviet Union showed scant respect for the "official in charge". Popular discontent revealed itself through critical letters to editors. In *Krokodil*, the Soviet humor magazine, the following unfunny letter appeared. "Dear *Krokodil*: I write you

and my hand trembles. Comrade Elizarov, chief of the management of the Rospishchestra building materials trust No. 14 dislikes it very much when one complains about him.

"Recently the paychecks of the workers of the Pskov region were withheld. The chief of the region, Comrade Menshikov, after several unsuccessful attempts to straighten out the matter of giving pay to the workers, complained to the Food Ministry of the Russian Soviet Republic. The workers . . . quickly recovered all that was coming to them.

"Only Comrade Elizarov remained displeased and proceeded to issue decree No. 24:

It is categorically forbidden to all regional chiefs, without previous approval by the managing chief, to send letters and telegrams to the Ministry and other higher ranking organizations.

"I am sending you this letter, dear *Krokodil*, without 'previous O.K. by the chief' of the building materials administration. What will happen?—I. Ivanov

Representative of the general committee of trade unions of local industry"

A strikingly similar letter appeared in the Moscow *Literary Gazette*. It was written by a Mrs. Chui, wife of the chief engineer of a Donets Basin mine. She complained that for months her husband had slept only two or three hours out of twenty-four and had had no holidays.

The boss of the mine was in constantly recurring, often imaginary, critical situations. The mine, for a number of years, had not fulfilled its production quota and four or five times weekly the trust ordered "days of increased mining".

On Sept. 11, the lady phoned her husband at 9 P.M.

"My husband answered in a sleepy voice: 'I can't talk. We will disturb people.'

"I was surprised—what people? He

answers that mechanics and workers of the mine are sleeping in his office waiting for the third shift to start."

Mrs. Chui wrote the letter without a word to her husband. "The manager doesn't like criticism . . . But I am in such desperation for the health of my husband that I will stop at nothing."

Judging from the fact that such revealing letters were printed, the government disliked bureaucrats who made the regime unpopular. Seeming to side with the masses against such officials, it nevertheless knew that its own impossible production demands forced them to their brutal impositions upon the workers—an inevitable part of a planned economy geared to fantastic acceleration.

Letters to editors do not tell the whole story. Incidents of what the Party termed corruption and sabotage, on the part of regular Soviet officials, cropped up.

In Baku, the oil center, there was Shaburov's now famous wedding party. In the words of Azerbaidzhan Party Secretary M. D. Bagirov:

"A certain Shaburov, up to most recently, was head of the department for trade among cotton pickers in the organization Azzerttifak. His salary was 950 rubles a month. Recently he gave a wedding party for his son in which more than 200 persons, among them his subordinates and his chiefs, including Communists, participated.

"The character of the wedding is indicated by the fact that one of the guests stole the watch of his neighbor . . . found later in the pocket of the thieving guest. The participants held a drumhead court over him, beat him up, and threw him out.

"Nobody among the participants, including the Communists, thought about questioning from what funds and what sources a person who receives 950 rubles in monthly salary can allow himself to give such a luxurious wedding party."

In Central Asiatic Kazakhstan, top Party functionaries were ousted for failing to cope with collective-farm violations. The Kazakh minister of justice, Nurbaev, was expelled from the Party on a charge of moral disintegration after an inquiry by a special committee sent from Moscow to "correct abuses".

In Kiev, capital of the Ukraine, three men were sentenced to death by a special military court. Their crime—heading a gang of "counterrevolutionary wreckers". This sounds like industrial sabotage, but the actual crimes, according to the Soviet press, were speculation, embezzlement, and trade racketeering which cost the state "hundreds of thousands of rubles".

The "criminals" ran their racket from, of all places, the Chief Office of Light Industries, which supplied the Kiev area with retail goods. The gang's profits were said to have been converted into illegally purchased gold, which was buried in secret hiding places. Members of the gang were recruited from persons "of dark pasts and anti-Soviet attitudes". All this, the press stated, explained why the workers of the area had not gotten their share of consumer goods.

Something was rotten in the state of Stalin. At any rate, from October, 1952, on, the Party was slated to undergo an almost military type of reorganization. First and foremost, however, everything possible was being done to improve living conditions. The new, fifth, Five-Year Plan, announced at the 19th Congress, while more than ever geared to war production, also promised a 60 percent increase in consumer goods. Actually, the process of raising the general standard of life, culturally as well as materially, had been under way for the past few years. The results were becoming noticeable.

How well did Ivan Ivanovich live in 1952? Nowhere near as well as the aver-

age American, but certainly better than American opinion assumed.

Frank W. Rounds, Jr., U.S. Embassy aide, left Russia in 1952 after an eighteen-month stay. While in Moscow, he noted that people passing him in the street would gaze in fascination at his well-shod feet. Russian shoes are of inferior quality and are crudely fashioned.

The "squeak, squeak, squeak of Russian shoes," he reported, was everywhere to be heard, "even on the stages of the theaters. The most renowned actresses, who wore the best and fanciest clothes available, had some difficulty in making their own voices heard above the various voices of footwear."

As yet there were no big department stores in Russia. Shop windows contained little that was eye-catching. Consumer goods, by U.S. standards, were still painfully skimpy.

However, nylon stockings, evening gowns, refrigerators, and washing machines were appearing. In Moscow alone, according to Cyril Ray, British journalist, there were 10,000 TV sets. Perfumes and lipsticks were cheap and beauty parlors, run by the state, were available.

Housing was insufficient, but there were no serious food shortages.

Cyril Ray also revealed the existence of stores bulging with "beefsteaks and pork chops, sausages (in wide variety), butter and cheese and bacon, and delectable mountains of caviar that would make a Western millionaire's eyes pop".

Though still lacking in many rudimentary comforts, the Soviet citizen knew that conditions were slowly improving. A clear sign of progress came on April 1 —large-scale price reductions, the fifth since the end of the war.

FOOD STORE IN MOSCOW. Imports from satellite nations helped Russians eat better than people of most European countries during 1952

Frank Rounds told of Moscow subway riders deeply engrossed in books. Throughout the country, he had gone to theaters, movies, concert halls, and museums. All were jammed. Much of the "culture" was propaganda—one reason the people got so much of it. But a good deal of it was classical literature, drama, and music. The government put out tons of scientific and technical literature and this was avidly read.

If the Soviet way of life was improving, how was this being accomplished? Russia had had to repair war damages, produce arms at a rate higher than ever before, draw labor from farms to factories to meet higher industrial production norms. And she had had to send millions of tons of grain abroad to help embattled Communist China and to get rubber and machines from Britain.

One answer to the question of "how" lay in the dismal conditions in the Soviet satellites. Caught in the Kremlin wringer, the so-called Peoples' Republics, normally self-sufficient, bitterly watched freight cars of produce rumble eastward loaded and come back empty.

In the satellites, eggs and butter were obtainable only on the black market. In Czechoslovakia, even the black market could not supply butter.

Hungary's famous salami had vanished from the shops—gone east in a cloud of garlic. By December, as Vice-Premier Ernö Gerö stated, the food situation was so desperate that "in the old days famine would have resulted".

Romania's Premier Gheorghe Gheorghiu-Dej blamed it all on "subversive elements". In December, the East German government fired Supply Minister Karl Hamann and his deputy for allowing "criminal elements to operate within the ministry". State-owned grocery stores were shut down to prevent "enemy agents" from buying up the food.

RUSSIAN GIRL ATHLETES perform at Moscow Stadium under sign proclaiming "Long Live the All-Union Communist Party of Bolsheviks, the Party of Lenin and Stalin"

In Poland, after Feb. 15, the government used force to compel deliveries of beef cattle. The Ministry of Agriculture admitted that more than a million farmers had been holding out against "voluntary contracting" with the government.

On April 1, the day food prices dropped in Moscow, food rationing was tightened in Poland. Food riots punctuated the rest of the year, growing more intense by November, when the potato supply dropped to 40 percent of the country's needs.

But in 1952 at least one Pole got out from under Soviet oppression. Mycyslav, a blond and handsome 13-year-old lad, knew that his dad, Ludwig Tomkiewicz, was somewhere in England. There the fates of World War II had landed him. Being anti-Communist, he had not been able to return to Poland.

The boy's first attempt to join his father had led to his arrest in Breslau, Germany.

Returned to his home village, he lived with his mother and the man she had married when she had learned that her husband would never return.

In August, young Mycyslav gave it another try. A short train ride took him to the Polish-German boundary. From there on, his exodus became a contest of youthful determination against a system designed to keep millions of would-be fugitives behind the Iron Curtain.

The youngster displayed courage and resourcefulness. Coming upon a pair of wire shears dropped by a frontier guard, he cut his way through two successive barbed-wire fences. As he was approaching the third and last, he stepped on a signal wire and a bell clanged. Quickly he snipped the wire, then crawled under the fence into East Germany. There he ran as long as he could.

"I ran until dark," he later related,

"then I dried myself, climbed into a tree, strapped myself to the tree, and slept."

Now he had to walk through East Germany to Berlin—without asking for directions or food—a distance of 150 miles. Somehow he made it, digging for potatoes on the way. In East Berlin, he had his first brush with authority. He was stopped by a policeman who wanted to know where he was headed.

"Do not stop me," the boy snapped. "I am the son of a Russian officer." The policeman apologized and stepped aside. A few minutes thereafter, the youth was in West Berlin, in a free world.

Days later, Mycyslav was in the arms of his father, a textile worker in Blackburn, England.

Short of food, the Soviet satellites found themselves yoked to a large-scale industrial speed-up. In Hungary, the Supreme Court, on Jan. 3, ruled that a man who quit his job without permission was liable to two years in jail. In November, the vice-premier reported a "tremendous upsurge of our industry" but deplored an "anti-machine attitude" on the part of the workers. This had caused the coal mines to fall "112,000 tons short of their target".

In November, a Polish housewife wrote to Radio Warsaw: "We have so many coal mines; yet coal is rationed. Where is it all going?" The answer: "For the great construction of Socialism." Next question.

In Bulgaria, the Ministry of Electrification rationed light bulbs—one to every household. In Romania, the government advised the peasants to "remedy the shortage of fuel" by making use of agricultural waste, sedge, and other materials.

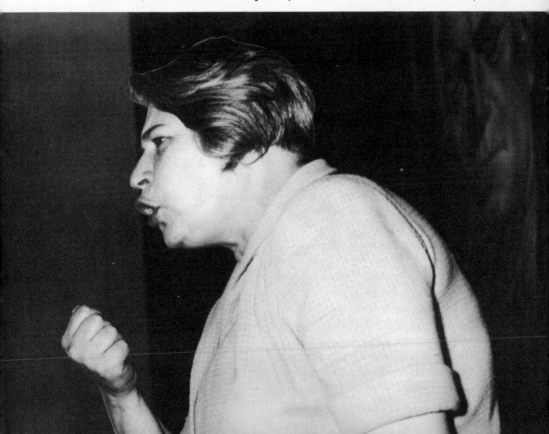

REPRIMANDED for "rightest deviations", Ana Pauker, Romanian foreign minister since 1945, fell from favor during the year and was relieved of all official positions

Through 1952, the Russians mercilessly bled the Czechs of their wealth. On March 3, the Prague *Rude Pravo* announced that 10,000 youths would be recruited to work in mines. They would be given "special care" to discourage them from quitting. By May, there were said to be 300,000 at forced labor, mainly in the uranium mines under the direction of Soviet police.

In July, the Prague radio announced a "purge" in the trade-union movement. Prime Minister Antonin Zapotocky told of unions infiltrated with "spies and traitors". Corruption, he said, was rampant both in trade unions and in industrial management. Trade-union leaders were to blame for the "calamitous" situation in the power industry—the many breakdowns and power cuts.

By August, workers were forbidden to change jobs without official permission.

Thus the U.S.S.R. was embarked upon one of the most highly systematized exploitations known to history. This was the Molotov Plan or KOMEKON (Council for Mutual Economic Assistance), as the Russians call it. While the U.S. was dumping wealth into Western Europe, the U.S.S.R. was looting Eastern Europe.

But somebody besides the Kremlin would have to take the blame for it. It would not do to leave the satellite populations with an everlasting grudge against Russia. What if war came?

A crude answer to this problem was revealed to a shocked world in the fantastic Prague trials held late in the year.

In 1948, bushy-browed, red-haired Rudolf Slansky, born Saltzman, then general secretary of the Czech Communist Party, headed the *coup d'état* which brought Czechoslovakia behind the Curtain. Probably taking orders from him at the time were moderate Communists Klement Gottwald and his friend Vladimir Clementis. These gentlemen later became

president and foreign minister, respectively, of the new Red Czech republic—front men, as it were, for behind-the-throne Slansky, who himself, allegedly, was under the thumb of Bedřich Geminder, chief Cominform agent in Czechoslovakia.

Slansky, with zealot Josef Frank, at once proceeded to purge the Czech Party. In 1949, they jailed Evzen Loebl, Deputy Minister of Foreign Trade. In 1950, Arthur London, Deputy Minister of Foreign Affairs, was imprisoned.

That same year, while representing Czechoslovakia at the United Nations in New York, Clementis received a summons to return home. Fearing hatchet-man Slansky, Clementis began to make inquiries about remaining in the U.S. as a refugee. But his friend Gottwald sent Clementis' wife to New York and she convinced him there was nothing to fear.

In January, 1951, Clementis, having returned, was arrested. Boasted Slansky's aide, Frank: "We have, in the last six months, purged 169,544 members of the Party." By the end of 1951, the figure was 300,000 members. All of this met with the hearty approval of the Kremlin.

On Nov. 20, 1952, the great Prague trials began. Heading the list of defendants was Slansky. Sitting alongside him on the bench of the accused were Clementis, Frank, and Geminder, as well as his chief victims of the past few years; in all, fourteen persons. The charges—Titoism, conspiring with U.S. agents, and, especially, Zionism. (Eleven of the fourteen on trial were Jews.)

The trial, like those in Moscow in the 1930's, spared no theatricality to discredit the culprits. Confession after confession went from the marionette-like performers onto the Czech radio network.

Said Slansky: "I am a two-faced Jew. . . . I was never a true Communist." He went on to describe his murder in 1944 of

Slovak Communist hero Sverma. He told of recruiting Sverma's widow to his scheme to get rid of President Gottwald and betray Czechoslovakia to U.S., French, British, and Yugoslav agents, all with the help of a Zionist conspiracy.

Sverma's widow appeared, tearfully described herself as defendant Otto Sling's mistress.

Lisa London, wife of defendant Arthur London, told the court that, after long doubt, she was finally convinced of her husband's treason. She had told her two children what their father had done. They were indignant and had promised her that they would remain good Communists. All she asked was a "just verdict" against her husband.

Ludvik Frejka, the man responsible for Czechoslovakia's Two-Year and Five-Year plans, admitted that he had "sabotaged in such a way that there is still rationing of electricity and food in Czechoslovakia".

The heights of tragicomedy were reached by André Simon, who described himself, absurdly, as a contact man for Overseas News Agency, which he said was a Jewish spying organization, with headquarters in a Times Square sea-food restaurant. Only hanging, said Simon, was fitting desert for his crimes. "I can be happy," he said, "with no other penalty."

Clementis, once almost clear of the noose, also admitted plotting to murder Gottwald. He further admitted contacts

Butterworth in The Manchester Daily Dispatch

BRITISH VIEW OF KOREAN PRISONER ISSUE. Mao: "I can't understand those prisoners for not wanting to come home—we have everything ready for them."

with "spies" such as John Foster Dulles, Sir Gladwyn Jebb of Britain, and the Americans Noel and Hermann Field. The Fields mysteriously vanished behind the Curtain in 1949. At the trials, it was revealed that they had been in the custody of the Czech police.

On Nov. 26, the state prosecutor demanded the death penalty. "It is no accident," he declared, "that, of the fourteen accused, eleven are the product of Zionist organizations. The danger of Zionism has increased with the foundation of the State of Israel by the Americans. Zionism and Jewish bourgeois nationalism are two sides of the same coin, which was minted in Wall Street."

As he was speaking, the 30,000 Jews still in Czechoslovakia received chilling reminders of Nazi horror. On the doors of houses in Bratislava appeared in chalk the phrases, "Down with the capitalist Jews", "Jews live here", or, simply, "Jew".

On Nov. 27, sentence was pronounced. It was death by hanging for eleven, including Slansky and Clementis. Three minor figures, among them Arthur London, got off with life imprisonment.

Prague's *Rude Pravo* had only contempt for the convicted persons. "The accused," it said, "are creatures who long ago lost the right to be called men."

The trial raised many questions.

Why were such loyal Stalin men as Slansky, Frank, and Geminder given the ax rather than less reliable men like Gottwald? Why were enemies Slansky and Clementis tried as partners? Why were anti-Zionists Slansky and Clementis accused of Zionism? Why was Zionism featured in the state's accusations?

Under Soviet instructions, the Czech government, during the Israel-Arab war of 1948–49, had supplied arms to Israel. With Britain out of Palestine, it became Soviet policy to get a toehold in the Suez region. Now it was necessary to placate the Arabs for injuries done in sending arms to Israel.

Thus, as demonstrated by the trials, it was not Communists who did the dirty work, but Zionist traitors to Communism —agents of Western imperialism.

Also, anti-Zionism—translated to mean anti-Semitism—could be used to woo former Nazis of East Germany. The Kremlin wanted them for an East German army. And, no doubt, Nazi-indoctrinated West Germany also figured in Russian calculations.

The Kremlin also seemed ready to use anti-Semitism in other trouble spots behind the Iron Curtain. In Romania, Ana Pauker, a Jew, was deposed. She had ruled the Red roost in Romania since 1945. On June 3, it was announced from Bucharest that the lady vice-premier had been reprimanded for rightist deviations and dropped from her Party posts.

Shortly thereafter, she lost all of her official positions. Foreign experts wondered how much of 1953 she would live to see—and, of more importance, what would be the fate of the three million Jews trapped behind the Iron Curtain.

Of course, there was always the chance that the people of the satellites might refuse to swallow the kind of swindle foisted upon them in the Prague trials.

The Czechs, apparently, were not diverted from hating Communism. On Dec. 16, only twelve days after the execution of the "Zionists" had been announced, Premier Zapotocky delivered an address before some miners at Kladno.

"People," he said, "complain, among other things, that they cannot buy coal for the winter and that their food rations are insufficient . . . Among the people, there is discontent and rebellion. . . ."

PIPE-SMOKING Czech Foreign Minister Clementis and U.S.S.R.'s Vishinsky at U.N. headquarters. Clementis was hanged after Prague trials

WEST GERMAN POLICE race after refugees from Red zone who have slipped across border under cover of darkness. Hundreds try it nightly

WESTERN EUROPE

WESTERN EUROPE, IN 1952, MOVED TO make the dream of European unity come true. Its central aim: to end the 1000-year feud between the French and the Germans, the two strongest peoples of continental Europe outside the Iron Curtain.

Said British Prime Minister Churchill: "The first step in the re-creation of the European family must be a partnership between France and Germany."

The impetus to such a partnership came from fear of the Soviet Union and from prodding by the United States.

In May, twin treaties were signed to give West Germany virtually full freedom in return for its entry into the Western coalition against Communism. The Germans would be rearmed to join the Allies in the defense of the free world.

By the end of 1952, however, the dream of unity seemed to be fading. For, as the Soviet Union pulled its punches and as the U.S. concentrated on its Presidential election, the West Europeans relaxed. New domestic crises and old international rivalries in France and Germany stalled the ratification of the twin treaties.

These pacts to unite France and Germany within the framework of a united Europe were signed in Bonn and Paris.

In Bonn, on May 26, the severely simple Bundesratsaal, overlooking the Rhine, was bedecked with flowers. This home

PEACE AGREEMENT between Germans and Western Allies is signed at Bonn. Konrad Adenauer signs for West Germany; looking on are Britain's Eden, France's Schuman, and America's Acheson

of the upper house of parliament was packed with spectators. Others huddled in the rain outside the chamber's picture window, watching what went on inside at a small table draped with gray velvet.

There Foreign Secretary Anthony Eden of Britain, Foreign Minister Robert Schuman of France, Secretary of State Dean Acheson of the United States, and Chancellor Konrad Adenauer, acting as foreign minister of West Germany, signed a peace agreement between the Germans and the Western Big Three. The negotia-

tions had lasted eight months. But the signing of the English, French, and German texts was over in two minutes.

The pact was entitled "The Convention on the Relations Between the Three Powers and the Federal Republic". For short it was called the "contractual agreement". It could not be a true peace treaty without including the U.S.S.R.

The keynote of the 120,000-word agreement was "to integrate the Federal Republic on a basis of equality within the European Community, itself included in a developing Atlantic Community".

West Germany was granted "full authority over its internal and external affairs". However, the Western allies retained their rights to station armed forces in the country.

"The mission of the armed forces . . . will be the defense of the free world," the pact stated. "The Federal Republic [West Germany] will participate in the European Defense Community."

The signing of this pact, said Eden, "opens a new window in Europe". It gives the Western allies "a new partner", said Acheson. Adenauer called attention to "the aim that is before all our eyes—to create a new, unified Europe".

In Paris, on May 27, the baroque Salon de l'Horloge (Clock Room) of the Quai d'Orsay, along the Seine, was as garish as ever with its cute cupids. It was set up with an E-shaped table, covered with green baize, for the signing of seventeen separate documents creating the European Defense Community.

Since *Allemagne* (Germany) came first alphabetically, Chancellor Adenauer was the first to sign. He was followed by Robert Schuman for France, Alcide de Gasperi for Italy, and their opposite numbers for the so-called Benelux nations, Belgium, the Netherlands, and Luxembourg. Dean Acheson and Anthony Eden, whose nations sponsored the E.D.C., looked on happily. The ceremony was over within an hour. It had taken fifteen months to negotiate the treaty.

Blueprinted on the white parchment of the E.D.C. treaty, with its 131 articles and 15 annexes, was a European Army composed of units from the six member nations. Its target: forty standing divisions—fourteen from France, twelve from Germany, eleven from Italy, and three from Belgium, the Netherlands, and Luxembourg combined. The goal also included fifteen reserve divisions.

These divisions were to wear a common uniform, fight with common weapons, and obey a common commander. Their chief was to be Marshal Alphonse-Pierre Juin of France. In turn, he was to be subordinate to the Supreme Allied Commander, Europe, representing the North Atlantic Treaty Organization. A tactical air force was to include 1100 German aircraft in its total of 4500.

West Germany was not admitted to N.A.T.O., which includes Britain and the U.S. But all N.A.T.O. nations, as well as all E.D.C. members, promised to treat a threat to any E.D.C. member as a threat to themselves.

The whole E.D.C. setup was given: (1) a policy-making Council of Defense Ministers; (2) a nine-member supranational executive body known as the Defense Commission; (3) the same legislative Assembly and judicial High Court that were envisaged for the Schuman Plan (see below).

As the ink was drying, Acheson spoke of "the realization of an ancient dream—the unity of the free peoples of Western Europe".

But during the ensuing seven months of 1952, not one of the six signatories ratified the E.D.C. treaty. Also, although the U.S. Senate and the British House of Commons approved the agreement, neither France nor Germany did so.

Nevertheless, a beginning was being made toward a united Europe. Only a few days after the E.D.C. treaty was signed, the Schuman Plan, uniting the coal and steel industries of the same six E.D.C. nations, moved out of the realm of ideas into the world of fact. This happened when Italy, despite Red ragings and by a 265-to-98 vote in its Chamber of Deputies, became the sixth and last nation to ratify it.

The crucial test had come in Bonn

TOTTERING ON BRINK of political and financial disaster, France had unusually rapid turnover of premiers. René Pleven (left) was replaced by Edgar Faure (center). Faure was followed by Antoine Pinay (right), France's 11th premier since the war

in mid-January. Konrad Adenauer had pleaded: "The beginning must be made. The decision . . . is truly for or against Europe." In opposition, Socialist Kurt Schumacher protested that the Schuman Plan was a conspiracy of "capitalism, clericalism, conservatism, and cartelism".

Then a wooden box was passed around the Bundestag (lower house of parliament). Into it the deputies dropped 232 blue cards signifying *Ja* votes, 143 pink for *Nein,* and 3 yellow for abstentions.

Thus West Germany voted to join with France, Italy, and the Benelux trio of nations to create a tariff-free market for the 230 million tons of coal and 40 million tons of steel produced each year by the 155 million people of the six nations.

This idealistic plan bore the name of Robert Schuman. A German-speaking Lorrainer, Schuman spent his first thirty-three years under the German flag, was educated at German universities, and served in German arsenals during World War I. But the plan was the brain child —as was the E.D.C.—of Jean Monnet, the European-minded idea man for the French government.

Fittingly, Jean Monnet became the first president of the Schuman Plan's High Authority when it set up shop in August. His friends dubbed him "Mr. Europe".

As his temporary headquarters, Monnet chose a five-story building at the end of a long stone bridge spanning a deep ravine which traverses the center of Luxembourg, the steelmaking capital of the grand duchy of the same name.

The steel-and-coal community's job was to move toward European unity through a functional approach involving the two basic materials of heavy industry. It had to wipe out tariff barriers and cartels, modernize production methods, foster competition, expand output, and let all Schuman Plan members buy coal and steel on "equal terms". Thus it aimed at a single market in place of the tight little islands which had been the preserves of prewar cartels.

The city of Luxembourg, the closest thing to a European capital since Charlemagne, was jestingly called "Monnet Carlo". And the Schuman Plan's dedicated leaders were indeed gambling, on behalf of a high ideal. On Sept. 10, its policy-making Council of Ministers entrusted its 78-member Assembly with the job of drafting a constitution for a Western European federation by March 10, 1953.

Inevitably the European Defense Community had a tough time getting under way, for many French politicians wanted to stall off German rearmament lest a rearmed Germany again menace the peace of Europe. The E.D.C.'s long road ahead was foreshadowed as early as Jan. 7, 1952. Then its original sponsor, France's Premier René Pleven, quit after only five months in office. The cause was a domestic political feud over how to balance France's record 1952 rearmament budget of $9.6 billion. Pleven's replacement was Edgar Faure, at 43 France's youngest premier in the 20th century.

A former justice minister, Faure had served as a prosecutor of German war crimes at Nuremberg, wrote mystery stories under the pseudonym Edgar Sanday, and spoke Russian. He dangled a cigarette from his lower lip and sported bow ties and horn-rimmed glasses. He lasted only forty days, during which he lost 12 pounds and rested only five hours a night. On Feb. 29, Faure quit when the National Assembly rejected a tax boost of 15 percent to pay for the increased defense budget.

Just when the whole future of European rearmament seemed as shaky as the French government, France found a leader, Antoine Pinay, to be its eleventh premier since the war.

Mild mannered, with a small mustache

DEFENSE-OF-THE-FRANC CAMPAIGN was launched by conservative Antoine Pinay, who tried to bring price reductions to inflation-ridden France

FUNERAL PROCESSION of General Jean de Lattre de Tassigny, leader of French forces in Indochina, advances along Paris boulevard. Fellow soldiers following caisson include Field Marshal Montgomery (l.) and General Eisenhower (r.)

and a gray felt hat popped on top of his head, Pinay did not look like a leader, but he was as able a politician as postwar France had seen. He was a 60-year-old leather manufacturer and co-owner of Scandale, a firm which makes girdles and brassières. His right arm had been crippled during World War I.

His policy was right-of-center.

He constructed his cabinet out of his own conservative Independents, the middle-roading Radical Socialists, and the liberal Catholics of the Popular Republican Movement. He was confirmed in office on March 11.

Thereupon, Pinay launched a "save-the-franc" drive. He succeeded so spectacularly as to win applause in newsreel theaters. Yet he refused to move into the Hôtel Matignon, official home of French premiers, "because my job is so temporary". He was so thrifty that he wouldn't leave his office until he had darkened every light.

"When the franc has regained its position," Pinay preached, "France will soon recover its rank." He argued simply: France should not spend more money than it had; it should not waste money; it should pay its debts. Accordingly, he pledged not to devalue the franc again. He insisted on balancing the budget without raising taxes. He bludgeoned fellow businessmen into cutting prices. He promised an "amnesty" to past tax evaders if they would pay up in the future.

He carried his thrift campaign to French housewives by reporting what happened when two halves of a Camembert cheese were priced differently: "Always—you hear me, always—the women asked for the more expensive piece."

The Pinay cabinet sent the Communists into a tailspin. It forbade a Red rally which had been called for Paris on May 28 to protest the arrival of "Le Général Microbe", General Matthew B. Ridgway. The Reds rallied anyway, but

were repulsed by a small army of 8000 policemen and Mobile Guards in the bloodiest Paris riot in almost two decades.

A Red call for a nationwide sit-down strike for June 4 pulled only one of every fifty French workers from his bench. French police, in steel helmets, raided Red headquarters. They grabbed riot arsenals, stolen seals for forging documents, and, in the naval base of Toulon, Red espionage reports on Indochina convoys, guided missiles, and radar research.

In late June, Étienne Fajon, French member of the Cominform, laid down a new line for French Reds. It ordered them

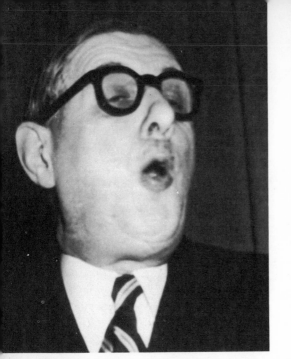

GENERAL CHARLES de GAULLE, leader of right-wing faction, has support of many Frenchmen

to avoid "sectarian faults such as riots and sabotage by hard-core militants".

Preoccupied with crusades to save the franc and crush the Communists, the Pinay cabinet felt no urgency about ratifying the European Defense Community and the contractual agreement. Premier Pinay himself was busy trying to prod Washington into boosting its offer of American aid from $525 million to $650 million. Thus France's ratification was put off until 1953—or later.

At least, Pinay was officially in favor of French-German unity. President Édouard Herriot of the National Assembly, at 80 France's grand old man, came out against the E.D.C. document.

Herriot quoted the only Assembly speech ever given by Georges Heuillard, who was crippled by captivity at Buchenwald and died on Oct. 11:

'I am dying as a result of the treatment given me by the German Army. I do not want my sons or my grandsons to be enrolled in an army alongside the executioners of their father."

Then, on Dec. 22, Premier Pinay suddenly resigned. Faced with political bickering over his balanced budget for 1953, he challenged the National Assembly: "What are the real problems in this world? The war in Asia, the intrigues in North Africa, and the uncertainty in Europe. In this situation let us not forget what we owe France."

Without waiting to be beaten on a vote of confidence, he announced that he could not go on "without a solid majority". Refusing even to join in a new cabinet, Pinay exclaimed: "If any one thinks I'm going back into that bear cage, he's crazy."

Thus France was tossed into a year-end crisis. At the least, this put a new roadblock in the way of a European Army. At the most, it endangered the whole European idea, personified by Pinay's foreign minister, Robert Schuman, and by his defense minister, René Pleven.

"The signing of the contractual agreement," Otto Grotewohl, Prime Minister of Soviet-run East Germany, had threatened, "will produce in Germany the same conditions that existed in Korea. . . . It will bring Germany to the brink of a civil war and of a new third world war."

Grotewohl's gruntings epitomized the Red campaign to bluster West Germany out of either signing or ratifying the contractual agreement and the E.D.C.

Meanwhile the Reds chopped Germany in two even more sharply. They sliced an 11-yard-wide gash all along the 850-mile boundary. Within this strip, they felled trees, plowed land, and barricaded roads, so that their *Volkspolizei* (People's Police) could stop any West German from entering or any East German from fleeing. Behind this 11-yard strip, they created a

"No Man's Land", as much as 5 miles wide.

They went so far as to build a barbed-wire fence out into the Baltic Sea where West and East Germany meet. "The Communists are not content with splitting our country," a Western eyewitness gibed. "They are even splitting the sea."

A pinprick policy was imposed all along this boundary and also between West Berlin and the Soviet sector of the city. Western patrols were repeatedly stopped on the autobahn, West Berlin's motor-road life line to West Germany. Rail and road traffic were often blockaded at border crossings. Dial telephone service between East and West Berlin was severed. No fewer than 137 roads leading out of West Berlin were closed.

All West Germans and West Berliners were forced to get special visas even to enter the Soviet areas. Most spectacularly, two Soviet MIG-15 jets riddled a Berlin-bound Air France DC-4 on April 29, wounding five persons aboard, though the French transport was flying inside its assigned air corridor.

Daily and nightly, Red thugs invaded West Berlin to riot, to shoot, to kidnap. During 1952, a pitiful tide of 118,000 East Germans flowed into West Berlin for sanctuary.

Ernst Reuter, West Berlin's spunky mayor, pledged: "Berlin will stand, just as it has before." He had faith in his two million people, in his six-month stockpile

COMMUNIST LEADER Jacques Duclos presides at the bar of justice in Communist artist's painting on exhibit in Paris gallery. Duclos swings considerable weight in turbulent France and is personally responsible for much of its turbulence

HITLER'S GHOST continued to hover over Germany with rebirth of Nazi movement. War criminal Gen. Hermann Ramcke (right) is given hero's welcome upon his release from French War Crimes Prison

of necessities, in a new *Luftbrücke* (air bridge) should the Communists turn their "creeping blockade" into a full-fledged siege. And his city stood.

Meanwhile, the Kremlin sang a siren song. On March 10, in identical notes to Washington, London, and Paris, Moscow suggested a four-power conference, to draft a German peace treaty.

Desperate to prevent the rearming of West Germany in alliance with the West in general, the Russians proposed that a united but neutral Germany should have "national land, air, and sea forces essential for the defense of the country". With transparent cynicism, they also said: "The German people . . . should enjoy . . . freedom of speech, press, religion, political convictions, and assembly."

Said Secretary of State Dean Acheson: "A united Germany cut off from defense with and by the West could not be a free Germany." Thus debunked, the Red initiative produced only a futile diplomatic correspondence to and from Moscow.

The task of achieving French-German harmony was not made easier by reviving fears of a rebirth of German military spirit along either Prussian or Nazi lines.

In September, West German police discovered that the "German Youth Association", set up with mysterious American aid to fight a guerrilla war in case of a Russian conquest, had marked 80 anti-Red Socialist leaders for liquidation.

In October, Hermann Bernhard Ramcke, a former paratrooping major general, aroused the first reunion of Nazi *Schutzstaffel* (S.S.) troops by shouting: "Who are the war criminals? They are those who destroyed German towns like Dresden . . . who dropped the atom bomb on Nagasaki and Hiroshima. . . . Eisenhower is a *schweinehund!*"

Lest the European Army be blocked by worries over German militarism, Theodor Blank, the stocky ex-lieutenant who was Adenauer's chief military adviser, took to the radio in November.

He promised that West Germany would have a "citizens' army in uniform". The goose step would be *verboten*. The German general staff would not be reborn. The common soldiers would be encouraged to vote. They would not even be "German soldiers", but rather "European soldiers of the German nation".

Not so, said the West German Social Democrats (Socialists), the most powerful opposition to Chancellor Adenauer's Christian Democrats. They fought the E.D.C., the Schuman plan, and every other proposal for European unity that might delay all-German unity.

Not even the death on Aug. 20 of Kurt Schumacher, the one-armed, one-legged Socialist chief, eased the Socialist opposition. The fanatically nationalistic Schumacher, who was equally anti-Nazi, anti-Communist, and anti-Western, was succeeded by the less fanatic but equally stubborn Erich Ollenhauer.

Not until December did the showdown

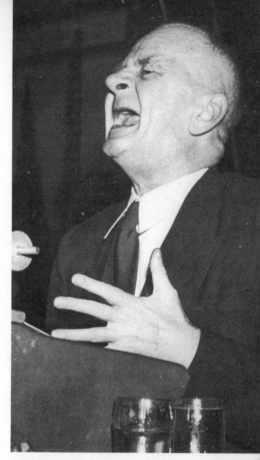

SOCIALIST CHIEF Kurt Schumacher (above) opposed all proposals for European unity that might delay Germany's unification. Chancellor Konrad Adenauer (below) favored treaties with Western allies

BISECTED by barbed-wire barricade, French-German border town of Kehl am Rhein shows evidence of life only on German side of street

come in the modernistic Bundestag with its glaring white neon lights.

"It is the fateful hour", said Adenauer. "A vote of *No* on these treaties means *Yes* to Stalin. . . . Germany is divided and torn, disarmed and defenseless. She is overshadowed by a colossus [Russia] that is trying to enslave and swallow her."

In reply, Ollenhauer besought Adenauer to give up his "teen-age enthusiasm for European unity".

Withstanding gibes at his "one-man democracy", the chancellor pushed the twin treaties, by a 50-vote majority, through a preliminary test. But, as a tactical trick, he delayed the decisive vote until 1953.

By this newest delay, he gave the Federal Constitutional Court the chance to decide on legalisms, raised by the Socialists, to the effect that the whole ratification technique was unconstitutional.

However, the biggest barrier on the road to German-French unity was the 900 square miles of the coal-rich Saar Basin. The French wanted to keep it politically autonomous but economically united with France, because otherwise they would be far outmatched by the Germans in coal and steel production. The Germans argued that the 950,000 Saarlanders speak German, think German, even eat and dress German, and should be allowed to rejoin the *Vaterland.*

"French shoes just don't fit German feet," they said.

For seven weeks, Schuman and Adenauer tried to compromise the Saar issue. The Frenchman proposed that Saarbrücken, the Saar's capital, be made the permanent headquarters of the Schuman Plan and that the whole Saar be "Europeanized". The German agreed on a temporary "European" solution under the Schuman Plan. But he specified that the Saar's permanent fate must be decided by a future peace treaty.

Schuman and Adenauer failed to budge each other. Their deadlock was proclaimed in late October. Then the Saar issue broke out in full fury.

The Saarlanders' local election on Nov. 30, to choose their *Landtag* (legislature), was converted into a plebiscite like the 1935 ballot on which they had voted to rejoin Nazi Germany. The issue this time was between their pocketbooks, in terms

KITES marked "F" for "Freiheit" (Freedom) are launched in West Germany, fly over Communist-held cities. Such propaganda devices have proved important weapons in cold war

of their prosperous present ties with France, and their hearts, in terms of a closer future link with Germany. They chose their pocketbooks.

Two thirds of them voted for the pro-French parties. Thus they kept Saar Premier Johannes ("Joho") Hoffmann and his Christian centrist *Volkspartei* (People's Party) in power. One third showed their sympathies with the outlawed pro-German parties. Only 7 percent stayed away from the polls that rainy Sunday, but 25 percent cast blank or mutilated ballots in accordance with the pro-German slogan, *Wahle weiss* (Vote blank).

The Saar result was a rebuke to German nationalism. It agreeably surprised the French. As such, it was a vote in favor of the European ideal. Still, virulent voices in both France and Germany were threatening to go no further toward European unity until the Saar issue was settled to their own satisfaction.

Yet the basic story of 1952 in continental Europe was that all the free nations, as well as France and Germany, were moving, though fitfully, toward the high ideal and hard-headed necessity of a unified Western world.

In Italy, Premier Alcide de Gasperi, Rome's European-minded counterpart of Schuman and Adenauer, rolled on to a new record for political longevity in postwar Western Europe. For fourteen years a filing clerk in the Vatican Library, the 71-year-old De Gasperi finished his seventh straight year as premier on Dec. 10. But his middle-of-the-road Christian Democratic Union was increasingly threatened from both left and right.

The Communists provoked pitched battles in the Chamber of Deputies. They

HUNGRY AND RAGGED, a child of Rome begs handout from tourist. Italy's widespread poverty causes many to believe Communism is sole solution

MIDDLE-OF-THE-ROAD Alcide de Gasperi has been Italy's premier for seven strife-torn years. He is under constant attack from both left and right

stained its carpets with both ink and blood, and forced the frock-coated ushers to remove inkwells and nail down desks.

The neo-Fascist *Movimento Sociale Italiano,* together with the right-wing Monarchists, became a threat by amassing 21.3 percent of the popular vote, against the Christian Democrats' 29.7 percent, in the May 24-25 municipal elections. They even captured control of Naples, Foggia, Salerno, Bari, and other southern Italian cities.

Promptly, a curious coalition of Christian Democrats and Communists enacted a new law making Fascism illegal and punishing even a Fascist salute with three months in jail.

ITALIAN COMMUNIST LEADER Palmiro Togliatti speaks before portrait of Joseph Stalin. Similarity of their gestures makes Stalin appear a puppeteer

With regard to Austria, Washington, London, and Paris proposed to Moscow a short peace treaty of only eight articles. The proposed treaty would relieve Chancellor Leopold Figl's regime of the four-power occupation. It took the Kremlin from March until August to say *Nyet*. Then the Russians had the gall to propose that the four powers begin again, from scratch, the peace-treaty negotiations. These already had stretched over 258 meetings and six years before they broke down in January, 1952.

The Russians also ignored the U.N. General Assembly's resolution, passed by 48 to 0 on Dec. 20, calling for a peace treaty to restore Austria's sovereignty.

In Yugoslavia, in September, the invitations to a formal reception for the visiting Anthony Eden read: "Marshal Josip Broz Tito and Mme. Jovanka Broz invite . . ." Thus the 60-year-old marshal revealed his 3-month-old third marriage to a tall, dark, handsome Yugoslav army major of 28. A partisan fighter from the age of 17, Tito's wife turned out to be a

YUGOSLAVIA'S strong man and anti-Kremlin Communist, Marshal Tito enjoys bottle of beer at vacation retreat. Note pipelike cigarette holder

MARRIAGE OF MARSHAL TITO to a handsome, poised Yugoslav army major was revealed at formal reception for Britain's Anthony Eden (left) in Belgrade. It was the Balkan dictator's third marriage. He's 60; she's 28

poised and charming hostess in a burgundy gown—capitalistically low cut.

Marshal Tito, in 1952, won an American promise to deliver jet aircraft, artillery, and tanks, and engaged in a merry-go-round of military talks with the Greeks and Turks. Thus Yugoslavia, although not a N.A.T.O. member, was inseparably tied into N.A.T.O. strategy.

But Marshal Tito, the anti-Kremlin Communist, was no docile ally of the West. Feuding with Italy over the Free Territory of Trieste, he challenged Premier de Gasperi: "Do you wish to be friends or enemies?" He broke off diplomatic relations with the Vatican in December. He argued that the elevation to cardinal of the "convicted war criminal" Archbishop Aloysius Stepinac betrayed Vatican meddling in Yugoslav business.

At the Yugoslav Communist Congress at Zagreb in November, Marshal Tito had to referee a marital dispute. Without preliminaries, Ljubodrag Djuric, the secretary-general of Tito's government, shouted: "I hereby accuse Comrade Petar Stambolic of stealing my wife."

As Stambolic, Premier of Serbia and a Tito crony, sat poker-faced nearby, Djuric's microphone was cut off, his words were outshouted, and he was thrown out bodily. Then Tito himself stepped in and predicted that Djuric would be proved to be a Cominform agent.

In Greece, on Nov. 16, Field Marshal Alexander Papagos, the aging hero of World War II and the Greek civil war, proved himself a hero to the Greek voters also. His Greek Rally Party, a right-wing counterpart of General Charles de Gaulle's Rally of the French People, won 49 percent of the popular vote and a land-

A ROW OF SEVEN WINE GLASSES before him, Spain's Generalissimo Francisco Franco appears contented at state banquet. Though his country does not belong to N.A.T.O., Franco entered into negotiations for providing sites for U.S. military bases in Spain

slide of 241 of the 300 seats in Parliament.

While King Paul had refused to offer the premiership to Papagos after the 1951 election, he had to do so now. The American Embassy was undiplomatically delighted at the Papagos victory. For the old centrist coalitions had proved too weak and too graft-ridden to check Greece's galloping inflation or to make the most out of $2 billion in postwar American aid. Premier Papagos would try to reform most Communist sympathizers into loyal Greeks. "But . . . the most dangerous must be interned," he said, on prison islands in the Ægean Sea.

In Spain, in January, 1952, Generalissimo Francisco Franco's regime went all out to welcome thirty warships of the U.S. Sixth Fleet on its first visit. American sailors were given free movie tickets, free streetcar rides, and free wine in flamenco (gypsy) dives. The Falangists' black uniforms were kept in their closets. Their saluting hands were kept in their pockets.

But the Franco regime was not as hospitable in its diplomatic dickerings with the U.S. throughout the rest of the year. The U.S. wanted to set up a permanent home for the Sixth Fleet in Spanish ports. Previously, this naval armada had roamed the Mediterranean without any real base. The U.S. also wished to fly its strategic bombers from Spanish airfields. Admittedly the Spanish harbors and airdromes were ill-developed. But they were protected by the Pyrenees, and they were far enough from Russian bases to be relatively secure from a sudden air assault.

The U.S. was so anxious for the Spanish bases that it was willing to welcome Fascist Spain, a strange bedfellow, into a Western coalition. Yet Franco set his price so high in military and economic aid that no deal was made during 1952.

In Sweden, Premier Tage Erlander's coalition of the Social Democratic and Peasant parties learned that its policy of armed neutrality was no shield against Soviet missiles.

At 4:09 A.M. on June 16, an unarmed Catalina of the Swedish air force, searching for a missing Swedish DC-3 over the Baltic Sea, radioed: "Two MIG-15's make a feigned attack toward us." Two minutes later, it said: "We are being shot at with 20-millimeter ammunition." At 4:15 A.M. came its last message: "Hit several times."

Luckily, the Catalina's seven-man crew was rescued. The DC-3's rubber life raft also was picked up, riddled with bullet holes. Stockholm protested these "outrages" in sharp notes to Moscow.

Simultaneously, it staged a sensational trial of seven Swedes for Communist espionage and sabotage. In this trial a pale, 33-year-old Red named Johan Fritiof Enbom, who passed himself off as a salesman of pornography, confessed plotting with Soviet Embassy officials to blow up the Boden fortress, keystone to Sweden's northern defenses against Russian assault. Enraged, the Swedish people spat on the Soviet Embassy's grounds and shouted: "Hang Stalin!" But still the Swedes stayed away from any N.A.T.O. link.

As one Swede defined the effect of the Soviet provocation: "Last week 95 Swedes out of 100 were for neutrality. This week the number has dwindled to 92."

SENORA FRANCO,
wife of Spanish dictator, holds her granddaughters after baptism of youngest

England and Canada

"THE KING IS DEAD, LONG LIVE THE QUEEN!"

On Feb. 6, George VI, beloved British monarch, died in his sleep at Sandringham House. The throne "Bertie" had ascended after the abdication of Edward VIII (now Duke of Windsor) was to become the property of a buxom young beauty of 26. The heart attack that had killed her cancer-ridden father found Elizabeth, with her husband the Duke of Edinburgh, at an East African hunting lodge, en route to Australia. They boarded the next plane back to England.

On Feb. 8, Elizabeth took her oath of succession. All over Britain, artillery blasted welcome to the new ruler. Heralds in medieval garb rode in procession from St. James's Palace to bear the tidings of a new reign to the lord mayor of London and his sheriffs and aldermen.

At St. James's, as Big Ben—London's famed tower clock—struck eleven, four trumpeters strode forward on the balcony to introduce the proclamation of Elizabeth II. Afterward the throng sang "God Save the Queen".

George VI lay in state in lofty Westminster Hall as crowds of Britons moved slowly through cold, sleety weather to pay their last respects. Black-bordered newspapers carried endless histories of the throne and empire.

For the first few days of the mourning

THREE QUEENS WEEP for George VI after sudden death of Britain's beloved king in February

period, the British Broadcasting Company (B.B.C.) closed down almost entirely. People in outlying areas, not having heard the news, called repairmen to fix their radios. Sometimes repairmen who had not heard of the king's death spent hours puttering with undamaged sets.

On Friday, Feb. 15, to the music of Chopin's funeral march, the casket was borne from Westminster to Paddington Station. A million people lined the route.

Many had reserved their spots by sleeping in the streets and eating breakfast—thermos-flask tea and sandwiches—sitting in the gutter. At Windsor Castle, the new queen sprinkled dust onto the coffin as it was lowered into the vault.

Since 1936, times had been hard in England. There had been, first, the threat of war, then war itself and the "blood, sweat and tears" of the Battle of Britain. By war's end, most of Britain's Asiatic empire had fallen away. Then the Labor government introduced austerity, trying to get Britain's economy back to normal on a diet of low calories and Socialism.

To the average citizen, the fresh young queen symbolized a happier future.

"Famous," Prime Minister Winston Churchill said, "have been the reigns of our Queens. Some of the greatest periods in our history have unfolded under their sceptres."

The British could not be blamed if they hoped for better things. Economically, the country had hit bottom by the beginning of 1952. On Jan. 27, the weekly meat ration was reduced from 20- to 16-cents worth per person. War clouds still darkened British skies, potential battle arenas for U.S. and Russian aircraft. The country was divided into two political camps with widely differing views on England's best path to the future.

On Jan. 29, Chancellor of the Exchequer Richard A. ("Rab") Butler told the

AFTER CORONATION CEREMONY in May, 1937, George VI and family appear on Buckingham Palace balcony to acknowledge London's cheers

BRITAIN WORRIED over George VI's haggard appearance when he said good-by to Elizabeth, off on Empire tour. His sudden death came at Sandringham seven days later

House of Commons that Britain's retrenchment on imports for 1952—made so that it could "pay its own way"—would reach $1.4 billion.

Production of radio and TV sets, washing machines, and bicycles would be cut one third. U.S. tobacco imports would be slashed by $61 million. Individual allowances for foreign travel would be reduced to $70 a year—about enough for a few days in Paris.

Other ways would be adopted to make ends meet. Ten thousand civil servants would be fired, saving $14 million. National Health Service prescriptions, before then gratis, would cost 14 cents apiece. Dental treatment would cease to be free. The new cost: £1 maximum, children and expectant and nursing mothers exempted.

This new budget the National Union of Mineworkers termed "an affront to the people". The Labor *Daily Herald* described it as "bad and unjust". A poll questionnaire made the rounds shortly afterward. One question: "Given a reduction of one-tenth in your income, where would you make your cut?"

"Across my throat," read one anonymous scrawl.

In other quarters, Butler's budget was popular. It provided new incentives. Extra earnings made by extra work were subject to an easier tax rate. But labor critics argued that this would benefit only the better-off. The lowest wage earners would not qualify for tax relief.

From Jan. 5 to 8, Winston Churchill and President Truman conferred in Washington.

1. Truman agreed that U.S. air bases in England would be used "in an emergency" only, after "joint decisions" by both governments.

2. Churchill gave his blessing to the European Army plan and the Schuman coal-steel pool.

3. Churchill, defending the fact that Britain had recognized Red China, at the same time admitted the need for joint U.S.-British containment of Red aggression. He also supported U.S. protection of the island of Formosa, off the south coast of China, held by China's Nationalists. He approved a plan to bomb Manchuria if a Korean truce were broken by the Reds, or if they used Manchurian bases for bombing raids on Korea.

Back in England, Churchill was greeted with mixed emotions. Many thought he had committed Britain too far to U.S. policies. And national pride was stung by his failure to get a Briton named to head the naval forces of the North Atlantic Treaty Organization.

Labor Party leaders Clement Attlee and Herbert Morrison decided the time had come to call for a vote of censure on the Conservative Party's "war policy". On Feb. 26, on the floor of Parliament, Morrison accused Churchill of failing, in Washington, to give adequate expression to England's policy on Korea.

"Peace," he thundered, "was safer with the last [Labor] prime minister."

Churchill's reply started innocently enough. In May, 1951, and again in September, he told the House, his honorable predecessor had made certain wise moves. The old fox paused for effect, then exploded the dynamite.

On these occasions, he revealed, Prime Minister Clement Attlee had signed secret agreements with the U.S. promising that, under certain conditions, Britain would help bomb Red bases in Manchuria. These agreements, he said, he had merely affirmed.

In the uproar that followed this statement, Attlee sat and doodled.

Question: Why had the Labor Party leaders walked into their own trap?

Answer: They had been forced into it by left-wing party leader Aneurin Bevan

THE QUEEN COMES HOME. On her return from Africa, Elizabeth II is greeted by her country's top government officials. Prime Minister Churchill is at the right

who had charged his party's right wing with being "tails to the American kite". At the poorly calculated risk that Churchill would not expose the secret agreements, they had tried to acquire antiwar coloration—at Churchill's expense.

That same day, Churchill gave the Laborites another left-handed pat on the back. His predecessors had developed an A-bomb. Good job, said Churchill, but why had they "concealed this vast operation from the House, not even obtaining a

FROM A ROYAL SCRAPBOOK. (Above) 8-year-old Princess Elizabeth visits Westminster Abbey with grandparents George V and Queen Mary. (Below) Queen Mary was important influence in upbringing of Elizabeth and younger sister Margaret (right)

TRUE TO TRADITION of British love for the sea, Elizabeth, 18, poses in Sea Ranger uniform

vote on the principle involved . . . while at the same time accusing their opponents of being warmongers?"

Thus Churchill revealed a second war-like skeleton in the closet of the "peace loving" Labor Party. As Attlee squirmed in embarrassment, Churchill taunted him for being one who "did good by stealth and blushed to find it fame".

"Nye" Bevan is a husky, round-faced, bellicose man. In 1952, he lived with his in-laws in a charming home in Chelsea, the artistic section of London. His radicalism dated from his youth in depression-ridden Welsh coal fields. Bevan could never forgive capitalism for the years he half-lived on the dole.

A onetime journalist, Bevan once worked for George Orwell, author of

BRITAIN REJOICED when Elizabeth married Philip, Duke of Edinburgh, in November, 1947. Wedding in Westminster Abbey was gala event for country long accustomed to drabness of postwar austerity. Here Philip wears uniform of British naval lieutenant

Nineteen Eighty-four, a satirical novel of totalitarianism triumphant. He is not a Stalinist, though American opinion loosely labels him as something of that nature.

"It would interest the American people," Bevan has said, "to know that it is the existence of people like myself in the Labor Party which enables millions of British workers to maintain their faith in Social Democracy, and therefore keep the membership of the Communist Party to the proportions of a small and comparatively powerless sect."

About his supposed anti-Americanism, he says: "I have far more friends among Americans than I have among British Tories. To be against a particular American policy is not to be anti-American."

On April 4, Bevan's book, *In Place of Fear,* was published and got front-page notice in most English papers. Bevan's main argument: Soviet Russia was not a menace to Britain but only to the panicked minds of U.S. capitalists.

"The weapons of the Soviet Union," he wrote, "are, in the first instance, economic, social and ideological, only secondarily military." Some U.S. leaders, he charged, hoped to convert the Korean situation into a war against Communism in Asia. Bevan maintained that the $13-billion British rearmament program would wreck British economy.

Through the year, Bevan went all out for Socialism (fought bitterly in Parliament for free wigs, though he has a good shock of hair), arms reduction, and tax cuts. On several occasions, he mutinied against moderation and, at party conferences, tried to unseat Clement Attlee.

Converts came to him from the rank and file of the unions. In July, the Gallup poll estimated that half of England's organized workers stood behind the Welshman. Many thought he was most likely to succeed Churchill as prime minister.

Bevan's biggest triumph came at the big Morecambe Labor Party Conference, held Sept. 29 to Oct. 3. In the smoke-filled Winter Garden Theatre, to the cheers of the twelve hundred delegates, he harangued his party on to Socialism.

"Let's don't be mealy-mouthed about it," he cried. Then he lashed out at American capitalism "hagridden by fears: fear of war and unemployment, and fear of peace".

When the votes were counted, Bevan's faction had won six of seven seats on the party's Executive Committee which were allotted to local groups. Herbert Morrison, thirty-year occupant of an executive seat, had been displaced by a Bevanite.

Morecambe was not necessarily fatal to Attlee and moderation in Labor. The trade-union leadership remained fiercely anti-Bevan. At Morecambe, the defeated Morrison, still deputy leader of the party, made the final speech. He pleaded for realism regarding America, without whose aid world problems could not be solved. "Do not let us think," he said, "that America is Senator McCarran."

But Bevan rode a leftward wind before which even the Conservatives bowed. If it was guns or butter, the Conservatives chose butter. It was that, or defeat in the next election. Though pressing for denationalization of steel, trucking, and railways, they slowed down rearmament and sought trade with the world's Reds.

By September, Britain had exchanged $76 million in rubber for $120 million in Russian grain. On Oct. 17, said the London Export Board, eleven hundred British firms were seeking business with Red China. On Nov. 5, 500,000 yards of cotton cloth were sent to China and contracts were signed for office machines, textile machinery, and refrigerators.

Despite hard times, the British people carried on. Spring came early; so did summer. Large crowds took advantage of the weather and opportunities for

FUN-LOVING Princess Margaret enjoys the theater but must spend long hours performing duties as queen's sister. Favorite question among British: Whom will she marry?

cheap enjoyment. In March, throngs visited the Royal Academy to see the Leonardo da Vinci Quincentenary exhibition; two hundred of Leonardo's drawings, the world's finest collection, were loaned by Windsor Castle.

Football matches were sellouts. On week ends, the big cities disgorged multitudes bound for country or seashore despite raised transportation costs.

Sitting by the seashore one fine day in June, Major John Evans, to thrill his children, made out a check for £1 million, stuck it in a bottle, flung the bottle into the ocean. Four months later, F. W. van Houten of Noordwijk, Holland, fished the bottle out of the water. On Oct. 22, Major Evans received a letter from him.

"What," it read, "do I have to do now?"

The passing scene was changing in London. Despite protests, the famous helmets of the bobbies were changed to peaked caps. The double-decker trams were changed to busses.

In the factories, work was enlivened by the B.B.C.'s "Music While You Work". However, the hit song, "Sugarbush", was banned. According to the B.B.C.: " 'Sugarbush' features intricate handclapping as a part of its rhythm, and some machine-shop workers have been hitting machinery with their tools in time with the handclaps."

In June, Queen Elizabeth announced that the date of her coronation would be June 2, 1953. This announcement caused great excitement; many persons hoped to be assigned to certain duties in the ceremonies in Westminster Abbey.

Mrs. Elizabeth Earle said she had the right to carry a towel in the procession of the queen, because she owned Heydon Hall in Norfolk and the towel tradition went with the ownership. (The Special Court of Claims turned her down.) A number of peers, no longer well off, asked the queen for permission to be excused from wearing expensive velvet and ermine robes, or even dyed rabbit.

Tradesmen, cashing in on the precoronation enthusiasm, were using questionable business-getters. Conservative Major Sydney Markham complained in Commons that one firm advertised "ladies undies, decorated with the British flag at the rear".

Road hazards came in for attention. On Oct. 15, in the House of Lords, Lord Hampton, surprisingly, said he had knocked down a pedestrian in Trafalgar Square. The victim arose and apologized, and they parted "on the best of terms".

Lord Hampton noted that the pedestrian had not been looking where he was going and had been saved only by his, Lord Hampton's, alertness. Lord Lucas took the floor to say that the pedestrian was the greatest menace on the roads. "I hope," he exclaimed, "the time will come when it will be an offense for pedestrians to cross the road . . ."

Other peers, at this point, interrupted ironically: "Get them off the face of the earth!"

Lord Lucas looked hurt, but completed his sentence: ". . . except at recognized crossings."

In Manchester, organized gangs twice attacked American G.I.'s. Consequently, on Oct. 25 the city was placed off-limits to U.S. airmen at the air base of Burtonwood, 21 miles away. However, the whole matter was subsequently smoothed over. It was all blamed on English girls trying to hook up with more money than English boys could manage.

The Presidential election in the U.S. created great interest. In October, the odds were three to one in favor of Stevenson.

Canada

AN AMERICAN TRIPPER TO CANADA IN 1952 was likely to get a shock. Say he was on his way by rail from New York City to the Canadian capital, Ottawa, a miniature Washington without Washington's bustle. Say he changed trains at Montreal and finished a leisurely breakfast on the diner. The check came to $1.58 and he had the right change.

"Sorry, sir," the waiter would explain apologetically, "that will be $1.62, on account of American money."

The great American dollar, the only "real" money in the world to the average citizen of the U.S., was worth only 98 cents (or a little more or less, depending on exchange fluctuations) in Canadian money. Canadians could boast that their dollar was one of the soundest in the world—sounder even than the American.

The big news from Canada in 1952 was that this northern neighbor—still pictured by many Americans as a snow-blanketed stamping ground of Eskimos and scarlet-coated Mounties—was rapidly becoming one of the industrial bulwarks of the Western World.

There was, for example, the Pacific coast province of British Columbia, Canadian equivalent in climate and countryside of the States of Oregon and Washington. It is bigger than Oregon, Washington, and California combined but has only 1,165,000 inhabitants.

Thriving on their lumber, salmon, apples, lead, zinc, newsprint, and farm products, the people of British Columbia

RADIANT ELIZABETH on her way to open first session of Parliament held during her reign. This is Winston Churchill's favorite picture of the queen

WASHINGTON RECEPTION in his honor brought together Winston Churchill, his actress daughter Sarah (left), and another famous daughter — Margaret Truman

have always said that they live in God's pocket. In 1952, that pocket was beginning to bulge.

The most sensational example of B.C.'s increasing wealth was springing up around the sleepy little Indian village of Kitimat, 400 miles up the mountainous coast from Vancouver.

The Aluminum Company of Canada (Alcan) was spending $1 million a week on the Kitimat project. Its engineers were reversing the flow of the Nechako River and dumping it over a waterfall sixteen times as high as Niagara into an atombomb-proof powerhouse carved out of mountain granite. This would generate power for the largest aluminum smelter in the world, being built at Kitimat.

Alcan expected the town (former population, 580 Indians) to grow into a city of 50,000. The whole area probably would become a thriving industrial center. So, on a smaller scale, would other empty spaces in the province.

Eastward across the Rockies, new oil wells were gushing all through the wheat fields of Alberta, Canada's Texas. Less than fifty years ago Alberta was mostly farms and ranch land. It had no industries, few towns of any size, no fences, no roads, and only a lonesome railroad line or two. But in 1952 it produced 163,000 barrels of oil a day.

Capital was pouring into the province by the millions; local industries were expanding; new ones were moving in. A visitor could stand on any street corner and watch the capital, Edmonton, grow. Alberta was getting rich.

Saskatchewan, the province next door, was off on a more newfangled boom than Alberta's. In the northern wilderness of deep bush and jack pine above Lake Athabaska, the first uranium rush in history started on Aug. 4. As modern-style sourdoughs, equipped with Geiger counters instead of picks and shovels, staked out their claims, Canada looked forward

SOCIALIST Aneurin Bevan has background of poverty in depression-ridden Welsh coal fields, won't wear formal dress even on state occasions

to the day when it would excel the Belgian Congo as a source of nuclear fuel.

Far to the east, in the wilderness along the Quebec-Newfoundland border, another treasure had been found: proven reserves of 418,000,000 tons of iron ore. A railroad was inching its way 360 miles north from Seven Islands on the St. Lawrence River. When it reached Burnt Creek, the steel mills of the U.S. and southern Canada would have more than enough ore to replace the fabulous but rapidly dwindling store of the Mesabi Range in Minnesota.

These were only the high spots. Here, there, and all over Canada new sources of wealth were being discovered and developed. "And this is only the beginning for Canada," eager-eyed Canadians insisted. "Nothing but war can stop her growth," Finance Minister Douglas Abbott asserted, more soberly.

There were natural limitations, of course. Much of northern Canada is uninhabitable wasteland. And the country is sadly underpopulated. It is a third again as large as the U.S., but has fewer inhabitants than New York State. Nevertheless, economically, Canada was clearly on its way.

It was moving toward political ma-

NINETY-FOOT PROTEST against Bevan appeared on embankment near Houses of Parliament. But poll estimated half of British workers supported the Welshman

BOOT OUT BEVAN

turity, too. Once a British colony, it has advanced gradually to self-governing nationhood; allegiance to the same queen and membership in the Commonwealth of Nations are now its principal political bonds with Britain.

In 1952, formal recognition was given to that fact. Early in the year, Prime Minister Louis S. St Laurent admitted that in official documents he had quietly but deliberately removed "Dominion", with its suggestion of subservience to Britain, from the old title, "Dominion of Canada". And in December he agreed with other Commonwealth prime ministers that the phrase, "British Dominions Beyond the Seas", should be dropped from the new Queen Elizabeth's title.

In Canada she would be "Elizabeth the Second, by the Grace of God, of the United Kingdom, Canada and her other Realms and Territories Queen, Head of the Commonwealth, Defender of the Faith". So it would be as queen of Canada that Elizabeth would rule in that country. Some enthusiasts suggested that she be crowned in Ottawa after the coronation in London.

As a self-governing country, Canada had its political problems. In some ways, they were like those of the U.S. before the November elections. The Liberal Party, Canadian equivalent of the U.S. Democratic Party, had been in power uninterruptedly for eighteen years. Canadians had seemed satisfied with scholarly, slow-spoken "Uncle Louee", Liberal Prime Minister Louis S. St. Laurent, and they kept re-electing his party.

In 1952, however, Canadians appeared ready for a change. The Progressive Conservatives, counterparts of U.S. Republicans, were picking up one seat in Parliament after another in by-elections. They were cautiously optimistic about their chances in the general election scheduled for 1953. All they needed was an issue.

In December, one dropped into their laps.

It was packaged in an official report on goings-on at Camp Petawawa, a large army base near Ottawa. There had been, the report charged, a "general breakdown in the system of administration, supervision and accounting". One specific charge was that $3000 or $4000 had been spent at the camp to build an artificial lake. The army called it a fire reservoir. Critics said it had been stocked with trout for the benefit of officer-anglers.

Another item. A large quantity of rails belonging to the Canadian Pacific Railway had been torn up and sold by what the report called "a handful of crooks". When the C.P.R: asked embarrassing questions, "a spur line of the Canadian National [Railway] running into the ordnance depot was taken up and the rails used to replace the missing C.P.R. track".

The most sensational charge was that "horses were hired by army personnel and placed on the payroll under the names of non-existent laborers". This turned out to be untrue, but it gave opposition humorists a field day. One Conservative member of Parliament wanted to know if the horses had paid income tax. Another produced a telegram, signed "Pinto", saying: "Understand that horses now eligible for regular army pay. . . . On behalf local nags, all category E and not fit for service, I appeal to the government for old-age pensions. . . . As alternative, appointment to Senate will be considered."

As it turned out, the whole report was exaggerated, and the public did not take it too seriously. But it did create a certain amount of confusion which weakened the prestige of the Liberal government. In the closing weeks of 1952, Canadians were wondering under which party's auspices their glowing economic future would develop.

WORST FOG OF CENTURY blanketed southern England in December, 1952. London's red double-decker busses crawled while passengers led the way with torches. Effects of fog brought death to many

The MIDDLE EAST

IN 1952, FOR THE WESTERN WORLD, THE story of the Middle East became an Arabian nightmare.

It was a story of riot-torn cities and oil-rich lands, of weakling kings and ambitious soldiers, of ultranationalistic politicians and bloodthirsty fanatics, of torches and bombs.

The nationalism that burned in the Middle East was aimed, more often than not, at Western imperialism. Its main target was the British, who had long shouldered the colonial burden. But the U.S., which was taking on world-wide burdens, also was assuming its share of blame.

The Communists generally were not the cause of these troubles. But they were always delighted with the effects. They labored to widen the gap between the great colonial powers and the emerging nations.

It suited the Kremlin's devious purposes that the Arab nations were steering a neutral course in the cold war between West and East, and that the Arab bloc was balking at joining the West in some sort of Middle East defense organization.

The nationalistic fires in the Middle East did not always die down into desolation and despair. Out of the embers

مشانق دنشـواى
انتظار اعناف الانجليز

EFFIGY of British soldier hangs as mobs attack British and American centers in Cairo. Final toll of extremist-led riots: 62 persons killed, $300 million in property destruction

there sometimes arose new hope. Nowhere was more promise shown than in Egypt, keystone of the entire area.

Flames licked at the Long Bar of Shepheard's Hotel in Cairo, raced through the garish lobby, swept the 350 antique bedrooms. A grenade arced through the smoky air and exploded. Fiery brands stoked the bonfire. Soon the old hostelry, symbol of British supremacy in the Moslem world, was a ruin. It was Black Saturday—Jan. 26, 1952.

That day, everything Western was the target for the Egyptian mobs. The British Barclay's Bank was burned out. The Turf Club was wrecked, its liquor bottles smashed, its wicker chairs piled high and burned.

The Parisiana Restaurant, the Ritz Café, the American-owned Metro theater,

the offices of British Overseas Airways and Trans-World Airlines, the Cicurel department store, the Bahri office building —all were turned into ashes. Burned-out skeletons of Western automobiles littered Fuad I Street and other avenues.

The sacking of Cairo was the sequel to the bitterest battle between the British and the Egyptians since Queen Victoria's forces moved in seventy years earlier.

It was touched off when Lieutenant General Sir George ("Bobby") Erskine, British commander in the Suez Canal Zone, ordered the Egyptian police there, who had been waging guerrilla war against the British, to hand over their weapons and get out. Otherwise, he warned, they would be "destroyed by force".

Fuad Serag el-Din Pasha, Egypt's fleshy interior minister, ordered his police

to "resist to the last bullet". They did. Only after their four-story barracks had been pounded for six hours did 800 of the "Gyppos" surrender. They left 40 of their number dead.

Egyptian mobs got revenge in Cairo. But theirs was not a spontaneous reaction. They were carefully and coldly organized by leaders, who sped through Cairo by jeep to co-ordinate 220 separate attacks within half an hour. Egged on not only by Moslem Brotherhood fanatics but by known Communists, they shouted not only "War with Britain!" but "Long live Russia!"

Not until 62 persons lay dead and $300 million in destruction had been wrought did King Faruk use his trigger-happy soldiers to restore some semblance of order. He did so at the urging of American Ambassador Jefferson Caffery. The am-

bassador warned that otherwise the British might have to occupy Cairo.

While Cairo burned, the pudgy playboy monarch had been staging a luncheon party at Abdin Palace to honor the birth of his first son and heir. The 7-pound, 7-ounce boy was delivered on Jan. 16 to the 18-year-old commoner queen, the former Narriman Sadek, whom Faruk had married the previous May.

In triumph, the royal physicians exclaimed: "Walad! Walad!" ("It's a boy!"). In gratitude, the king promoted the obstetrician, Ibrahim Magdi Bey, to the rank of pasha. He also declared a two-day holiday, gave $28.70 to every other boy born that same day, and presented $86,100 to the families of the so-called "martyrs" killed in the undeclared conflict with the British.

He named the boy Prince Ahmed Fuad,

NATIVE POLICEMEN patrolling Anglo-Egyptian Sudan on 2½-miles-per-hour camels stare at British jet-engined "Comet", which does 600 m.p.h.

in keeping with his dynasty's tradition that all personal names begin with the lucky letter "F". Ex-Queen Farida, whom Faruk had divorced in 1948 for bearing him three daughters but no son, sent him congratulations: "Am very happy that your dearest wish is now realized."

At long last, King Faruk displayed courage. He tossed out Premier Mustafa el-Nahas Pasha, Serag el-Din, and the rest of the cabinet. He thus broke with the Wafd, Egypt's most powerful, most corrupt, and most xenophobic (foreign-hating) party.

Still, his ability to ward off revolution depended on his chances for reaching some working agreement with the British. London was prepared, if necessary, to withdraw its garrison from the Suez Canal Zone on condition that the Egyptians join in a common effort for Middle Eastern defense. But it was insistent on guaranteeing self-government and self-determination to its colonial showcase in the Sudan, to Egypt's south.

It thus balked at Faruk's claim to be "King of Egypt and the Sudan".

Now the Egyptian premiership spun like a revolving door. First, Premier Aly Maher Pasha tried a modest cleanup, even cutting his cabinet members down to one Ford each. But he was sacked by the king because he failed to move quickly enough against the Wafd.

Second, Premier Ahmed Naguib al Hilaly Pasha sought to prove Serag el-Din to blame for letting the Cairo riots get out of hand, and pointed to him and to ex-Premier el-Nahas as sharing in big-time graft. But he failed to get a dramatic deal from the British such as was required to overshadow the Wafd's popularity. His anticorruption crusade also came too close for comfort to Faruk's own palace guard. He resigned in despair.

Third, Premier Hussein Sirry Pasha,

while friendlier to the Wafd, sought to insure the army's support by appointing, as war and marine minister, a soldier's soldier named Major General Mohammed Naguib.

He resigned when the king insisted on giving the job to his 30-year-old brother-in-law, Colonel Ismail Sherin Bey. Colonel Sherin was married to Faruk's favorite sister, Princess Fawzia, whom the shah of Iran had divorced.

Faruk had declared: "In a few years' time, there will be only five kings in the world—the king of England and the four kings in a pack of cards."

At 2:00 A.M., July 23, General Naguib (*nah-geeb*), rather than wait for Faruk to exile him to some far-off oasis, grabbed control of Cairo in a bloodless *coup d'état*. While the city of Cairo slept, steel-helmeted soldiers, backed by tanks and armored cars, took over the telegraph and radio offices and government buildings. They even surrounded Abdin Palace —while the king was summering at Alexandria.

The corrupt gang of palace-picked generals and colonels was hustled behind bars. Into their places went a younger, more honest, better-educated clique who called themselves the Free Officers Club.

At 7:15 A.M., Radio Cairo aired a Naguib communiqué: "Egypt has been subjected to bribery, corruption, and instability in government. All this has had a grave effect on the army. For this reason we are cleansing ourselves."

At Naguib's urgent "request", King Faruk named the reputedly incorruptible Aly Maher Pasha as "Emergency Premier". He also promoted General Naguib to farik (marshal).

So far, there was no indication that Naguib intended to rid Egypt of Faruk. But the king made a fatal error. Although the British Foreign Office suggested that he make up with Naguib, the king called

EGYPTIAN EXTREMIST, captured in Moslem cemetery where 20 tons of ammunition were discovered, is guarded by British soldier

EX-QUEEN FARIDA was divorced by Faruk in 1948 because she bore him 3 daughters but no son

upon the British to seize both Cairo and Alexandria. The British refused.

When Naguib heard of Faruk's appeal, some of his supporters urged that the king be shot. Premier Aly Maher urged a softer fate. He went to Ras el Tin (Promontory of Figs) Palace in Alexandria and ordered the king to give up the throne and get out in six hours.

As a last desperate effort, Faruk summoned Ambassador Caffery and appealed for assistance. The American ambassador, instead, advised the king to leave.

With only a handful of bodyguards still loyal to him, Faruk bowed. He announced he was "submitting to the will of the people", and abdicated. His 6-month-old son was proclaimed "King Ahmed Fuad II of Egypt and the Sudan".

Before nightfall on July 26, Faruk, in a white admiral's uniform, strode to the quayside in Alexandria, offered his fat hand for General Naguib to shake, and accepted the general's salute.

Tears streaked his pudgy cheeks as the Egyptian anthem was played and a 21-gun salute sounded. Then he boarded his royal yacht *Mahroussa* ("Protected") along with his wife, the infant king, his three daughters Ferial, Fawzia, and Fadia, and 204 trunks.

He sailed off at 32, as H.R.H. Prince Faruk Fuad, to exile, first in a 20-room suite at the Eden Paradiso Hotel on Capri, then in a rented hotel, with 31 rooms and 31 baths, in the Italian resort village of Santa Marinella.

Now *lèse majesté* ran rampant in Egypt. Freed from royal censorship, the newspaper *El Akhbar* of Cairo noted:

FARUK'S SECOND WIFE is 18-year-old commoner Narriman Sadek, who joined him in exile. She bore Faruk first son shortly before abdication

"Today, history records the name of an oppressive and unjust king . . . who used the influence of the monarchy to flog the backs of the liberals, who imposed misery and slavery on the country and forced the country to call his tyranny justice, his corruption reform, and his immorality piety."

The army opened up Faruk's four palaces, two villas, and one country estate. His favorite yellow-stucco Koubbeh Palace, outside Cairo, was stuffed with 100 suits, 50 canes, 1500 ties, 2000 silk shirts, diamond-studded dice, 400 decks of playing cards bedecked with pin-up girls, huge safes full of gold coins and stamps, pornographic paintings, two autographed photos and one bust of Adolf Hitler, four drawers full of solid-gold fountain pens, a "Magic Tricks" box including something to "Measure Nuclear Energy Yourself", a lush set of Kodachrome nudes, several stacks of American comic and cowboy magazines in the royal bedroom, and 20 exercise machines for the futile task of keeping Faruk lithe.

THEN AND NOW: (Above) Slim, dapper King Faruk at 18. At 32, in exile (right), he strolls beside pool of singer Gracie Fields at Capri

All Egypt rejoiced now that Faruk was gone. But Naguib sternly brought his people down to earth. "We've had enough of carnivals and demonstrations," he cautioned. "Today we work."

Quickly the word "boukhrah", which means "tomorrow" in Egyptian slang, vanished from the vocabulary in government offices. Egypt's new strong man himself, at 51, set the example by working eighteen hours a day.

More often than not, he slept on a shabby army cot on a glassed-in balcony at his Abbasiya Barracks headquarters. There he pointedly turned Faruk's photo toward the wall. He sustained himself on yoghurt and brown-bread sandwiches and read a chapter of the Koran before breakfast every day. He did not hesitate to break off the most vital conference to turn toward Mecca and offer his prayers to Allah.

In scathing contrast to his predecessors as Egypt's bosses, he asked nothing for himself or his relatives. He turned down the promotion to marshal which Faruk had bestowed. In rounding up the old-guard generals, he included his own brother Aly, the Cairo garrison's commander. When Aly was freed from jail eight days later, he shook hands with the strong man and said: "Remarkable man, my brother. Always has been."

"Our aim is reform," General Naguib vowed. "We will leave politics to the politicians." But he wanted to reform in a hurry. Premier Aly Maher was too slow-moving, especially on land reform. On Sept. 7, he bowed to Naguib's demand: "Authority should be concentrated in the

MUSTAFA EL-NAHAS heads powerful, corrupt Wafd, Egypt's largest political party. He opposed Naguib's reforms but was helpless to stop them

EGYPTIAN STRONG MAN Naguib vowed to clean up corruption, improve relations with Britain. Reforms may include making Egypt a republic

hands of the armed forces." By nightfall, the general was sworn in as premier.

Thus was climaxed the sensational rise to authority of the nonpolitical fighting man who had been so obscure that a British Foreign Office cable as recently as July 24 referred to him as General "whatever his first name is" Naguib.

One reform quickly followed another. All noble titles such as pasha and bey were abolished. To attract foreign capital, non-Egyptians were given the right to own 51 percent of Egyptian companies.

A land-reform decree limited all holdings to 200 acres, promised to distribute the excess to landless peasants and called

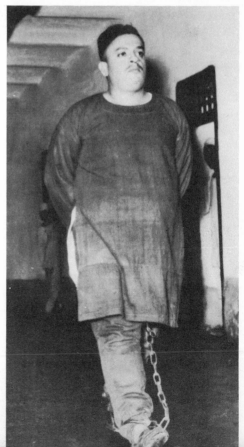

WEALTHY EGYPTIAN LANDOWNER Adly Lamloam begins life prison term. He led armed attack on police station to protest land reforms which limit property ownership to 200 acres per person

for compensation to the expropriated owners—including Faruk, whose 200,000 acres made him Egypt's biggest land-owner.

Premier Naguib also carried out his vow, made when he was the thrice-wounded hero of the recent war in Palestine, to "clean up this mess" involving arms-profiteering scandals reaching into the highest places, even the royal palace. He clapped suspiciously wealthy politicians into jail.

He even dared to order the mighty Wafd and other political parties to "purge themselves of corrupt elements". The Wafd expelled a few smaller fry. But Naguib was relentless: "I am not satisfied . . . We have had enough of corruption."

Still the Wafd's chief, ex-Premier el-Nahas, who had kissed Naguib in public and hailed him as "the savior of our nation", balked. Naguib now had the people on his side. He made a triumphal tour of Wafd strongholds in the overpopulated Nile delta. In Tanta, his guards had to bludgeon frenzied admirers to keep the strong man from being suffocated. In Sammannoud, El-Nahas' birthplace, he was welcomed with a shower of flowers. At last, El-Nahas bowed. At 73, the five-time premier retired to the Wafd's new figurehead position of "honorary president". Thereupon Naguib united all the political cliques into a national front.

He climaxed his Egyptian revolution on Dec. 10 by abolishing the "feudal" constitution granted in 1923 by Faruk's father, King Fuad I. In a nationwide broadcast, Naguib stated that the old constitution had put Egypt under the thumb of an "irresponsible king". He revealed that a new constitution would be drafted "making the people the source of all power". He implied that it might abolish the monarchy in favor of a republic.

Naguib, so far, was a benevolent dic-tator. While his predecessors had made a profession out of twisting the British lion's tail, he frankly admitted: "We want to be on friendly terms with Britain." He gave short shrift to the propaganda that the Egyptian monarch was "King of Egypt and the Sudan".

Half-Sudanese himself, Naguib got together with Sayed Sir Abdel Rahman el Mahdi, the pro-British apostle of Sudanese independence. Under their tentative agreement, the Sudan was guaranteed full home rule at once under its British governor-general, and a plebiscite by 1955 on whether it wanted to be an independent nation or to be united with Egypt.

The Arab League

THE STORY OF EGYPT IN 1952 WAS, IN ESsence, the story of its partners in the Arab League, the organization of independent Arab states. The abdication of the monarch was duplicated in Jordan. The rise of the military strong man was duplicated in Syria. The rioting in Cairo was duplicated in Iraq.

King Talal's trouble in Jordan was a mental disease, schizophrenia. Although pronounced cured when he succeeded his assassinated father, King Abdullah, in September, 1951, he went from bad to worse. He was flown to Europe in mid-May for treatment. But he attacked his royal physician with a stick, tried to strangle his Arab driver and to toss his 5-year-old son Prince Hassan out of a window.

He beat his wife Queen Zaine until she fled for her life to the protection of the Swiss police. He drank cocktails and champagne incessantly and squandered his fortune on miscellaneous women.

Thrice he tried to kill himself. Though his martyred father had been Britain's good friend, Talal screamed: "To hell with Britain and America! Long live Stalin!"

By early August, with Talal back home in Amman uncured, Jordan's parliament had had enough. It decreed: "It is with greatest pain that both houses decide to end the reign of King Talal and proclaim his son king."

The new king was the 17-year-old Hussein. He was then an introspective student at Harrow, Winston Churchill's old school, and soon after ascending the throne he entered Sandhurst. He liked automobiles, horses, and spaghetti. The removal of his rabidly anti-British father left power in the hands of pro-British Premier Abdul Huda Pasha.

Syria's version of General Naguib was Colonel Adib Shishekly. He was frugal, sad-eyed, publicity-shy, afraid of assassination.

After serving as the power behind the premiers since 1949, he took over the reins in Damascus in August, 1952, with the title of deputy premier. His avowed intention was to combat Communism and corruption. Within two months in 1952, he ground out 200 decrees.

He abolished such titles as pasha and effendi, banned alcohol, dissolved all political parties, loosened the big landowners' grasp on large estates, barred foreigners from owning "immovable property", bestowed the honor of "Grade Excellent" on all mothers of sixteen children. He made such a showing that neighboring Lebanon also moved in the direction of more benevolent authoritarianism.

Colonel Shishekly's most promising move was to sign up with the United Nations Relief and Works Agency for a $30 million irrigation project on which to resettle all of Syria's 80,000 Arab refugees from Palestine. Aware that Communist agitators were infecting the squalid refugee camps, he said: "We hope the democratic countries—first of which is the U.S.

—will help us. With money, we can raise the standards of our people and fight bad ideas."

In Iraq, the counterpart of the Cairo riots swept Baghdad on Nov. 23. Nationalistic mobs ran amuck and looted stores in protest against a caretaker government's failure to reform the electoral system.

But the fanatic nationalists also capitalized on domestic discontent to attack Anglo-American interests. They stoned the British Embassy. They wrecked the $125,000 United States Information Service building. After 15 or 20 persons were killed and hundreds wounded, General Nur el-Din Mahmoud, the tough army chief of staff, was appointed premier. Reputedly pro-British, he clamped down martial law in the old-time Garden of Eden.

Iraq was no Eden for Western interests. The Baghdad rioters flaunted slogans reading: "Down with foreign imperialism!" This was a direct assault on the Iraq Petroleum Co., owned jointly by the British, Americans, French, and Dutch. Only a few days earlier, Iraq's boy king, the 17-year-old Feisal II, who had been a Harrow classmate of King Hussein of Jordan, had opened a new $115 million pipe line to the Mediterranean which would triple the output of Iraq's oil and thus boost Iraq's whole economy.

Iraq had signed up with the oil companies on the same 50-50 profit-sharing basis which was bringing new hope to its oil-rich neighbors of Kuwait and Saudi Arabia. But now the Iraqi fanatics threatened to cut off their oil to spite their faces. They also raged against "Anglo-American plans" to create a mutual-security setup, aimed at the Soviet Union, to protect the Middle East.

Significantly, it was not only nationalist fanatics but out-and-out Communists, masquerading under the "Partisans of

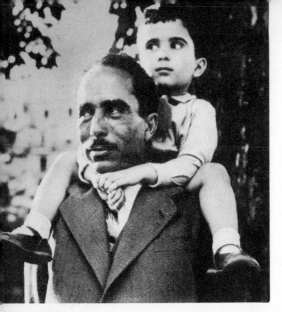

DANGEROUSLY INSANE, Jordan's King Talal was deposed from his ancient throne by Parliament

Peace" front, who led the Baghdad riots. And they were ominously reinforced by Red leaders from across the Iranian frontier.

But the changing Arab world remained unchanging in its refusal to accept the existence of the Israeli island in the Arab sea. It made no move to write a formal peace treaty, even though the shooting war—except for isolated border incidents —long since had been ended by a U.N.-mediated truce. It kept up its boycott, which helped undermine Israel's rickety economy.

The Arab League, in a protest to West Germany, even tried to block its ratification of a bilateral agreement to give Israel $715 million worth of iron ore, steel, electrical equipment, machinery, and other goods during the next fourteen years.

This pact was signed in September at Luxembourg's City Hall because the Jews balked at setting foot on German soil. It was intended, said Chancellor Konrad

THE GRAND MUFTI, supporter of Hitler during World War II, wields power in Near East politics

Adenauer, to "make moral and material amends" for "unspeakable crimes committed in the name of the German people".

Amid all its pressing problems, Israel lost the father of the country, President Chaim Weizmann, who died at 77 on Nov. 9 after a long illness. It tried to persuade Albert Einstein, as "the greatest Jew alive", to succeed President Weizmann. But Einstein was a naturalized American citizen and had never been an all-out Zionist. Now professor emeritus at the Institute of Advanced Study in Princeton, N.J., the mathematics genius explained: "I have neither the natural ability nor the experience to deal with human beings."

Instead, the Israeli Knesset (parliament) elected to the five-year-term, as president, Yitzhak Ben-Zvi (ben-tsvee).

Ben-Zvi was a weather-beaten archeologist of 68, noted for his threadbare suits and untied high-top shoes. He was a fast

ARABIAN ROYALTY recently studying at England's famed Harrow: King Hussein of Jordan (left), who succeeded his deposed father King Talal, and his cousin, King Feisal of Iraq

ISRAEL'S Premier David Ben-Gurion (top) continued efforts to lead nation out of economic wilderness. Yitzhak Ben-Zvi (center) became Israel's president after Albert Einstein declined position

friend of Premier David Ben-Gurion and a leader of the Mapai (Labor) Party.

"Death to the traitor Qavam!"
"Give us Mossadegh or we die!"
"Down with the traitor Shah!"

The screams of the Moslem fanatics swept through the streets of the Teheran bazaar for three steaming July days. Some 2000 rioters marched on the Majlis (lower house of parliament), only to be blocked off by troops.

"Pierce our breasts with your bayonets," the fanatics dared The army fired warning shots and used tear gas. When the rioters kept coming, the soldiers drove them off with bayonets, rifle fire, and the guns of their Sherman tanks. Soon 20 persons were dead, 100 wounded. The fanatics dipped white cloths in the blood and used them as battle banners.

Premier Ahmed Qavam es-Sultaneh saw the handwriting in blood. On July 21, the multimillionaire landlord, an ambitious pro-British politician who had been jailed, exiled, and thrice previously premier during his 77 years, quit. He scurried off into hiding to save his skin.

His fatal mistake had been to promise that his "prime objective" would be to solve the oil dispute with Britain, even though he stuck to the policy of nationalization of the Anglo-Iranian Oil Co.

And so he lasted only a few revolutionary days.

Now ex-Premier Mohammed Mossadegh came back more powerful than ever. Stepping on the balcony outside his yellow brick house, Mossadegh told the

CHAIM WEIZMANN, distinguished scientist and first president of Republic of Israel, died in 1952

PATRIARCH: In the ancient homeland of his forebears, where at last he is safe from the terrors of anti-Semitism, an orthodox Jew contentedly spends his remaining days studying Biblical lore

mob: "Your sacrifice today saved the country. I wish I had been killed instead of so many innocents." Then, as usual, he fainted away.

What had caused "Old Mossy" to give way temporarily to Qavam was his failure to break the oil deadlock. Iran had gone from poor to poorer without the $100 million a year which Anglo-Iranian had pumped into its economy. The Abadan refinery, the world's largest, had remained idle. The International Bank's plan to compromise the dispute had been rejected by Premier Mossadegh.

The army, the police, the civil service had gone unpaid. The Majlis elections, after being delayed over six months, had been called off because sentiment was running heavily against Mossadegh.

In desperation, Mossadegh had demanded that the Majlis grant him the dictatorial right to rule by decree. He also demanded that Shah Mohammed Riza Pahlavi give him control of the army by appointing him minister of war. When he failed to win his wishes, he quit.

Now the weak-willed shah of 32, fearing for the future of his throne, brought Mossadegh back as not only premier but war minister. Thus the shah surrendered control of the army, traditional bulwark of the monarchy.

However, Premier Mossadegh himself was to some extent a prisoner of the fanatics. They could get rid of him whenever they wanted. They were led by an uneasy and unholy alliance among Mossadegh's own National Front, the theoretically outlawed Tudeh (Communist) Party, and the extremist Moslem Combatants of Seyed Ayatollah Kashani, a top-ranking Moslem mullah (literally, interpreter of Islamic doctrine).

Kashani now emerged as a powerful prop to Premier Mossadegh. He was elected president of the Majlis. A tiny, turbaned man of 68, he looked mild and cheerful enough, with his blue eyes and gray beard. But he had been sentenced to death in Iraq for battling the British, exiled from Iran for fighting the present shah's father, and repeatedly jailed.

He hated the "British dogs". He often boasted: "I hold the fate of Iran in my hands. I can summon 1,000,000 martyrs for any cause."

His causes were an unusual assortment. He was allied with the wily conspirator who calls himself the "Grand Mufti of Jerusalem". He had plotted with the Nazis to "open the gates of Iran" in 1941. More recently he had welcomed Communist money. Indeed, he made a public alliance with the Communists during the anti-Qavam riots, although he privately promised to crush his Red allies.

Under dictatorial powers voted by the Majlis on Aug. 3, Mossadegh decreed a social revolution for Iran. Himself a wealthy landowner, he wiped out the centuries-old feudal fees and servitude. He also ordered the landlords to surrender one fifth of their share of the crops to their poverty-stricken peasants.

By so doing, he moved to take the hot air out of the Communists' sails. But he also alienated Kashani, who wanted to return to that old-time Islamic religion with its feudal ways of life.

Whether Iran could be saved from Communism seemed, to both London and Washington, to be a 50-50 wager. The U.S. and Britain agreed that to support Mossadegh now was their best bet.

To keep Iran from bankrupting itself into the Kremlin's grip, President Truman and Prime Minister Churchill, on Aug. 30, joined in a supreme effort to break the oil deadlock, then eighteen months old.

They sent Mossadegh the most gener-

AILING Premier Mossadegh of Iran tried to make oil-thirsty U.S. and Britain dance to his tune

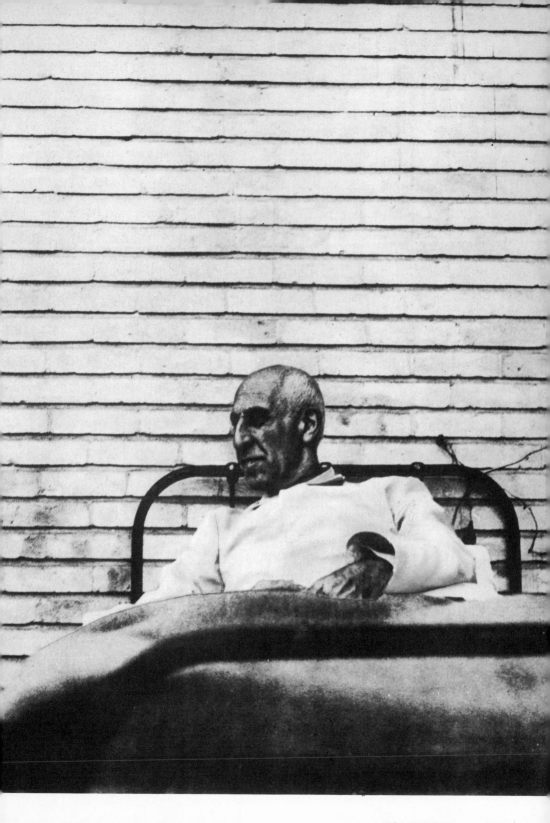

ous Western offer yet. In it they proposed the following. (1) The World Court should set the compensation for the Anglo-Iranian Oil Co.; thus the British, for the first time, accepted the Iranian nationalization law as valid. (2) Iran should negotiate with Anglo-Iranian the proper "arrangements for the flow of oil from Iran to world markets"; thus the British no longer insisted that Anglo-Iranian or any other British technicians must operate the oil wells and refinery. (3) The U.S. would grant Iran $10 million, the British would remove their restrictions on Iran's sterling balances and foreign trade, and Anglo-Iranian would sell for Iran some $25 million worth of oil now stored in Iranian tanks.

At that "Old Mossy" proclaimed over the Teheran radio: "This government can never agree to this message."

He insisted that it was a "trap" to get Anglo-Iranian back into Iran. He said the U.S. offer of $10 million was really a bribe. In reply, Mossadegh served on Britain an ultimatum that it pay Iran $137.2 million in royalties. This is the sum that would have been owed if Iran had not nationalized its oil. Mossadegh further insisted that Britain give up its claim for compensation for future profits under its long-term oil concession.

The British called these terms "unreasonable and unacceptable". Thereupon Mossadegh announced: "They have thus forced Iran to cut relations with them." He knew something about the technique of cutting relations. His foreign ministry had borrowed a book on the proper protocol some weeks earlier—from the British Embassy. On Oct. 22, for the first time in ninety-three years, the British hauled down the Union Jack and removed the Lion and the Unicorn from the entrance to their parklike embassy in Teheran.

Such was the temper of the moment in Iran that a bearded fanatic, who had assassinated pro-British Premier Ali Razmara in 1951 and thus paved the way for the Mossadegh regime, was pardoned for murder.

In November he emerged a free man from the Teheran jail. Named Khalil Tahmassebi, the assassin promptly called on Kashani for a cup of tea. The Moslem mullah, the spiritual leader of the Fadayan Islam (Crusaders of Islam) which had plotted the murder, stroked Tah-

FREED ASSASSIN Khalil Tahmassebi, confessed slayer of pro-British Iranian premier in 1951, receives pat on head from Moslem extremist Ayatollah Kashani, head of the Majlis (Chamber of Deputies)

massebi's beard to show his approval. He gushed: "You are a brave son of Islam."

Premier Mossadegh, who welcomed all callers while wearing a camel's-hair bathrobe and lying on his iron cot, also asked the murderer to drop around. It was the safe thing to do. Then Tahmassebi declared: "Politics is not my business. I will go back to my job as a carpenter."

The U.S. State Department, meanwhile, stuck to its job of resolving the dispute between London and Teheran. Seeking at any cost to keep Iran from going Red, it announced on Dec. 6 that it no longer objected to American companies buying oil from Anglo-Iranian's national-ized properties. It also called in top officials of American companies familiar with Middle East oil and asked them to unite to market the oil of Iran.

The British disagreed with these moves, but a State Department emissary assured them a few days later that any agreements made would be contingent on prior settlement of the Anglo-Iranian dispute.

At year's end the Americans and British were agreed that to yield to Iran's nationalists and their fair-weather Red allies might prompt the entire Middle East to throw out the Western-owned oil companies.

VIOLENCE swept South Africa on occasion as natives rioted against segregation laws of Premier Malan's Nationalist government

MAU MAU death symbol: Strangled cat warns natives against working for Whites

AFRICA

THE EPIDEMIC OF VIOLENT NATIONALISM swept out of the Middle East to the far corners of Africa. It infected the French territories along the Mediterranean, the British colony of Kenya along the equator, and the Union of South Africa. But its spread was fitful. It left some bright spots in the Dark Continent.

The Gold Coast became a stable rock in a restless stream under Dr. Kwame Nkrumah (*nah-croom-ah*), the first Negro to become prime minister of any British colony.

Reared in the jungle and educated at the all-Negro Lincoln University in Pennsylvania, he was a Marxist Socialist who had served a term in prison for his radi-

cal activities. His self-governing regime made such progress toward eventual Commonwealth status that the British planned to develop the Gold Coast with the biggest single colonial development project in history.

In November, they announced a $560 million plan to dam the Volta River to produce 560,000 kilowatts, half as much as Hoover Dam, and to use the electric output to smelt 235,000 long tons of aluminum each year. Thus the Gold Coast, sandwiched between the old Ivory Coast and the Slave Coast, would become an Aluminum Coast.

In Ethiopia, His Imperial Majesty Haile Selassie I, King of Kings, Conquering

GOLD SCISSORS are used by Haile Selassie in ceremony uniting his country and ex-Italian colony of Eritrea. Ethiopia now has outlet to Red Sea

Lion of the Tribe of Judah, painlessly won an outlet to the Red Sea for his land-locked tableland.

He merely used golden scissors in October to cut a ribbon at the border of the ex-Italian colony of Eritrea. He thus united that part-Moslem, part-Coptic Christian land to Ethiopia in a U.N.-sponsored federation. This solution to Eritrea's future was worked out by the U.N. commissioner, Eduardo Matienzo of Bolivia. The Eritrean constitution included in its preamble these unique words: "Grateful to the United Nations." It was "a Bolivian concept of a Swiss federation adapted to an African absolute monarchy".

Nowhere did a darker shadow hang over the Dark Continent than in the twin French protectorates of Tunisia and Morocco. Yet the nationalistic leaders of the Moslem Arabs there were relatively reasonable. They were seeking home rule rather than full independence.

"It is not a question of throwing the French into the sea," said Habib Ben Ali Bourguiba, the gray-eyed president of the Neodestour (New Constitution) Party and the most powerful and popular person in Tunisia. "But we must let them know that their presence here wounds our pride."

Convinced that the French were offering too little and too late, the Tunisian cabinet dispatched a delegation to the United Nations in January to plead for self-government. Simultaneously, week-long riots against French rule left 54 persons killed and 500 wounded.

The French cracked down. Their new resident general, Jean Marie François de Hauteclocque, had Bourguiba and a dozen other leaders, both Neodestour and Communist, arrested in their beds. He turned Tunisia into an armed camp.

At 3 A.M., March 26, the resident general had Premier Mohammed Chenik arrested and whisked away with some of his colleagues to a desert oasis. According to Chenik's son, the premier was picked up "like a common murderer".

To succeed him, the nominal chief of state, Sidi Mohammed al-Amin Pasha, Bey of Tunis, appointed Salah Eddine Ben Mohammed Baccouche to be a puppet premier for the French. The bey did so under Hauteclocque's threat to force his abdication. But the French finally offered to bow to the bulk of the nationalists' demands.

Tunisian terrorists spoke for themselves with a "bomb-a-day" program beginning on May 12. The French ringed the bey's palace with troops. They banned his eldest son, the 47-year-old Prince

DESPOTIC REGIME of South Africa's Premier Malan, shown with his wife, is anti-native, anti-British, has brought country to explosive state

POWERFUL Habib Bourguiba, leader of fight for home rule in Tunisia, carried self-government demands to U.N. before being jailed by French

Chadli, who was a Bourguiba henchman, from the bey's presence.

They also kept away Princess Zakia, another of the bey's twelve children, whom they blamed for financing the bomb-throwing Comité Secret de Résistance. They "persuaded" the bey to rubber-stamp a plea for peace.

Lest the U.S. side with the Arab bloc, the French directed warnings toward Washington, saying in effect: If we have to choose between the U.N. and the integrity of the French Union, we will have to give up the U.N. They had not been investing $750 million a year since the war in their North African territories merely to preside over the dissolution of the French Union. They were genuinely afraid that they would cease to be a great power if they lost these storehouses of strategic minerals.

Just before the U.N., willy-nilly, took up the Tunisian question in December, the staccato burst of a machine gun shattered an uneasy calm. An unknown gang of assassins murdered Farhat Hached, 39, the No. 1 Tunisian nationalist then at liberty, on a lonely road outside Tunis.

The nationalists placed the blame on "The Red Hand", a sort of Ku Klux

Klan composed of French colonials. The French suspected the Communists or an anti-Hached clique of Neodestour nationalists. Hached was hated by the Reds for taking the General Union of Tunisian Workers out of the Red-led World Federation of Trade Unions.

Whoever the murderers were, a new wave of nationalist gunplay broke out. A three-day general strike was called. A number of nationalist and labor leaders were hustled off to "controlled residence" in the southern desert. The French executed three Tunisian terrorists, gave death sentences to three more, and condemned four others to life imprisonment. Again the French served an ultimatum on the bey. They forced him to okay two decrees creating what they called a "democratic system of representation".

The Hached murder echoed even more ominously in Casablanca, the gleaming white metropolis of Morocco. There a Moroccan sympathy strike flamed into open rebellion. Five Frenchmen were murdered. Three of them were caught in a stone quarry by a raging mob. Their skulls were crushed with rocks, their hands were chopped off, their throats were cut, and their bodies were burned beyond recognition.

In Morocco's bloodiest outbreak since the Riff War a generation earlier, some 300 natives were killed. General Augustin Guillaume, the French resident general, ordered French, Senegalese, Berber, and Foreign Legion troops to pacify the city. They did. Twelve European Communists were flown off to France. Perhaps 300 Istiqlal (Independence) Party leaders were sent to desert isolation. About 2000 Moroccans were arrested. No fewer than 167 were given jail terms on a single day of mass-production justice.

The French government felt that the Tunisian and Moroccan violence was deliberately plotted to call attention to pending Arab and Asian protests against its rule in the U.N. The French themselves boycotted the U.N.'s debate on the ground that their domestic affairs were no outsider's business.

The U.N. General Assembly went on to shelve stiff Tunisian and Moroccan resolutions which the Arabs and Asians were pressing with the best wishes of the Communist bloc. Instead, it adopted compromises devised by the Latin-Americans. These merely requested that steps be taken in Tunisia and Morocco in the direction of self-government. Supporting these compromises, the U.S. avoided making an out-and-out choice between the French and the Afro-Asian bloc.

Yet only if the French and Arabs could bury the hatchet would the U.S. be able to rely on the strategic bomber bases it was rushing to completion in Morocco.

The French were faced by only sporadic bloodshed from relatively civilized Arabs in North Africa. But the British were plagued by an unceasing eruption from barbaric natives in Central Africa. Their crown colony of Kenya was ravaged by a black-magic society known as the Mau Mau (The Hidden Ones).

Its 300,000 members among the 1,000,-000 Kikuyu tribesmen took pagan oaths involving the circling of their heads with a cup of goat's blood and the sipping of the blood or the biting of the goat's meat —all seven times.

They swore: "If I am asked to bring the head of a European and I refuse, this oath will kill me. If I reveal any secrets of Africans who are Mau Mau members, this oath will kill me."

The Mau Mau promised: "Africa for the Africans." It swore to drive out of Kenya the 29,500 Whites who ruled the 5,600,000 natives. It especially aimed at the fertile "White Highlands", with their lush green pastures, their coffee and tea plantations, their polo and pink gin.

Its methods were as barbaric as its oaths. During 1952, its fanatics stabbed two white women to death, tore native policemen to bits, shot the Kikuyu's senior chief Waruhiu in cold blood as he drove up to a church mission, chopped a British settler into pieces in his bathtub with broad-bladed *pangas*, slashed a British colonel and his wife in their bed, drowned Kikuyu "traitors" or burned them alive, disemboweled cattle and sliced off the noses of sheep.

The Mau Mau ringleader was a London-trained anthropologist of 50 named Jomo ("Burning Spear") Kenyatta. Kenyatta sported a black beard and an ebony cane. He was married to a white schoolmistress from Sussex. He was believed to be a Communist; he spent the 1930's studying in Moscow.

The Communist organ *Pravda* thundered its approval of the "national liberation struggle of the people of Kenya", which was going on under his leadership. Besides his Mau Mau activities, Kenyatta was president of the Kenya African Union, the only political party for natives.

So menacing had the Mau Maus become by October that the British proclaimed a state of emergency. To meet

FRENCH POLICE search residents of the Medina, native quarter of Tunis, following uprising by party seeking home rule

terror with force, they flew a battalion of Lancashire Fusiliers from the Suez Canal and sent the cruiser *Kenya* steaming over from Ceylon. They arrested Kenyatta himself, along with some 5000 Mau Mau suspects. Some were given 24 lashes with bamboo canes; some were sentenced to jail; and others received death sentences.

Whole Kikuyu villages were punished by having their cattle and crops seized. To remove causes of the unrest, Governor Sir Evelyn Baring framed an $18.9 million program to improve the health, welfare, housing, and farm production of the land-shy natives. The British even used witch doctors to cleanse the Kikuyus of their Mau Mau memberships.

"We will free Kenya from fear," British Colonial Secretary Oliver Lyttelton vowed. But Lyttelton's predecessor in the Labor government, James Griffiths, was gloomy: "We are in danger of converting what began as a struggle of all the decent, moderate, loyal people—Africans, Asians, and Europeans—against the Mau Mau into a Black-White struggle."

What racked the Union of South Africa during 1952 was not only a Black-White struggle but a White-White struggle.

On one side fought the Nationalist Party of Prime Minister Daniel F. Malan (*m'lawn*), whose followers spoke mostly Afrikaans and wanted a republic. On the other side stood the United Party of the late Jan Christiaan Smuts, whose heirs spoke mostly English and wanted to retain their British monarch. This White-White struggle boiled up, ironically, over Malan's policy of *apartheid* (*apart-hate*, meaning "apartness"), with its twin

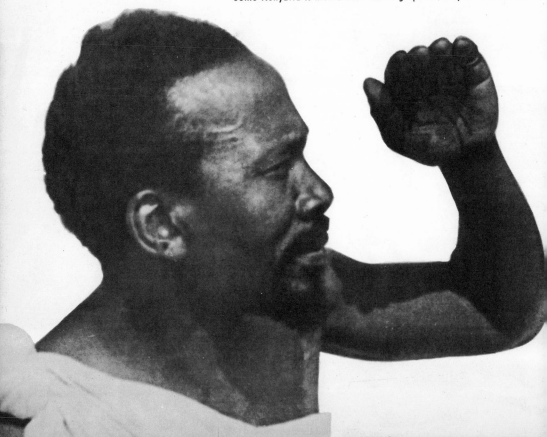

TERRORIST leader of Kenya's Mau Maus, anthropologist Jomo Kenyatta is nicknamed "Burning Spear", may be Communist

themes of racial segregation and white supremacy.

The Appellate Division of South Africa's Supreme Court in March, 1952, struck down, as unconstitutional, Malan's Separate Representation of Voters Act which would have removed the 50,000 Colored (half-caste) voters from the common rolls. Thereupon Malan promised to straitjacket the court with a new law to insure "the sovereignty of parliament".

Accused of refusing to bow to the Supreme Court's ruling, the former *predikant* (pastor) in the Dutch Reformed Church nodded his big bald dome and retorted: "I do refuse."

In June he shoved through the legislature the High Court of Parliament Act. This would supersede the Supreme Court, on constitutional questions, with a new High Court consisting of the two branches of the legislature sitting jointly. Thus the legislators, in effect, would decide for themselves whether their own laws were in accordance with the constitution.

The new High Court ruled in August that to deprive the Coloreds of their voting rights was indeed constitutional. But the Appellate Division ruled in November that the High Court itself was unconstitutional.

Malan promised to wage his 1953 campaign for re-election on this issue and, if victorious, to "place the sovereignty of Parliament beyond all doubt". If he should succeed in abolishing the "entrenched right" of the Coloreds under the constitution, the opposition United Party feared he would next outlaw the English

WIRE BARRICADES surround natives rounded up in drive against Mau Maus. British troops flown from Egypt help quell outbreaks against white settlers

WHITE WOMEN cower as violence erupts around them in an Africa seething with racial tension. Generally, protests against rigid segregation laws were nonviolent

language and then, perhaps, secede from the British Commonwealth. A gaping gulf thus split South Africa's 1,500.000 Boers from its 1,100,000 British just when its white minorities were being challenged as never before by its 8,400,000 Negroes, 1,100,000 Coloreds, and 360,000 Asians.

On June 26, the non-Whites fed Malan's fears of the "black peril" by launching a "Campaign for the Defiance of Unjust Laws". Thereafter, they courted arrest, with the deliberate intention of "filling the jails", by such tactics as entering a "Europeans Only" coach on a railroad train or a "Europeans Only" doorway to a station. By November, some 26,000 of them had been jailed for their fight against Jim Crow statutes.

In October, the arrest of 2 Negroes for swiping one can of paint touched off eight hours of rioting in Port Elizabeth. Eleven persons were killed and 27 injured. As the South African press put it, this was "the first major riot of natives based on no more than a murderous impulse to kill the white man". In November, police killed 13 Negroes who ran wild in the diamond center of Kimberley. It was reported that many more were killed in the port city of East London.

There Sister Aidan, an Irish Dominican nun and practicing physician, drove into the segregated Negro shanty town to take food baskets to her patients. But the raging Negroes dragged even their benefactor from her car, stoned her to death, and burned her body.

The Malan regime replied by ordering its police to "shoot first" and by deciding to clamp troublemakers into concentration camps without bothering to put them on trial. But such stiff measures obviously were no cure-all.

For, as Jacobus Strauss, Smuts' successor as United Party leader, charged, Malan's *apartheid* had put South Africa "on a boiling cauldron".

BEJEWELED AND GLAMOROUS Eva Perón rose from humble beginnings to become First Lady of Argentina and most important woman South America has ever known

PUBLICITY SHOT
of actress Eva before her
marriage to Col. Juan Perón

LATIN AMERICA

ON A JULY DAY IN 1952, PRESIDENT JUAN D. Perón of Argentina presented his suffering, bedridden wife Evita with the Collar of the Order of San Martín. It is Argentina's highest decoration; never before had it been given to anyone less than a chief of state.

The gold-and-platinum collar held more than 750 diamonds, emeralds, and rubies. It was one of Evita's most glittering treasures. It was also the last gift she ever received.

On July 26, crying, "I am too small for so much pain," Evita died at the age of 33. It was rumored she died of cancer.

Not many women have traveled so far so fast. She was born María Eva Duarte, on May 7, 1919, but she preferred to be called Evita (Little Eva). Evita and four older brothers and sisters lived with their unmarried mother in the squalid, dusty little pueblo of Los Toldos on the silent pampas some 200 miles west of Buenos Aires.

Her father, who had a legitimate wife and family in a nearby town, was only a

SHARING POWER AND GLORY, Perón and Eva acknowledge ovation after his inauguration for second term. Death was near for woman called nation's "spiritual chief"

part-time parent, and he died when Evita was 2.

The thin, white-faced little girl grew up in a noisy, disorderly household where there was never actual want but seldom enough of anything. She was quiet and in no outward way remarkable. But she was hotly ambitious for a richer life.

Before Evita was 16, she eloped to glamorous Buenos Aires, "Paris of South America", with a wandering guitar player who promised to open stage doors. The little sparrow of a girl had no talent and no particular looks. She never got beyond the roles of a bit player in the theater, a soap-opera queen in radio.

Then she discovered that, if she had no gift for acting, she did have a way with men. She began to use them to fight her way up in the world. But she was bitter against the stuffy, male-dominated society that made this the only way a lone Argentine girl could get ahead. She grew

steadily tougher and more unscrupulous.

Her big chance came in January, 1944, when, at a charity rally, she met a tall, genial colonel named Juan Domingo Perón. Perón was then a comparatively minor figure in the group of army officers who had taken over the government the year before. But he was smart and ambitious and on his way up.

He liked Evita and she played up to him. In 1945 they were married and in 1946 Perón was elected president. The ugly duckling from the pampas by now had grown into a strikingly beautiful woman with an imperious temper. She was First Lady of the Land.

For almost six years Perón and Evita ruled Argentina side by side. Evita never forgot the slights, real and imaginary, she had suffered at the hands of the "oligarchs", wealthy aristocrats who were the traditional rulers of Argentina.

She gloried in helping her husband

beat them down and raise up in their place, as the real rulers of the country, the *descamisados,* the long-neglected "shirtless" workers on farms and in factories. They were grateful for her lavish charity; her Cinderella-like career captured their imaginations.

At the height of Evita's power, the cancer struck. She died, a shrunken, pain-wracked shadow of the glamorous young queen who had been the second—some said the first—most powerful figure in Argentina.

Buenos Aires had never seen anything like the mourning for Evita. It was raining the night she died, but great crowds of *descamisados* kept vigil in the streets. Women wept. Some knelt in prayer on the rain-soaked pavements.

The next day, her body was taken to the Ministry of Labor, to lie in state in a white mahogany casket with a glass cover. The casket stood on a bier blanketed with white orchids. The funeral had to be postponed as endless lines of mourners from all over the country filed, day and night, through wind, rain, and cold, to pay their respects.

Old women and children broke into sobs as they passed by. Some flung themselves on the casket to leave a parting kiss for the woman who was described as a "martyr of labor, protector of the forsaken, defender of the workers, and a guiding light to the children".

Several persons were trampled to death, thousands injured in wild demonstrations of grief. The army had to be called out to help the police maintain order. Flowers covered the street, piled up against the

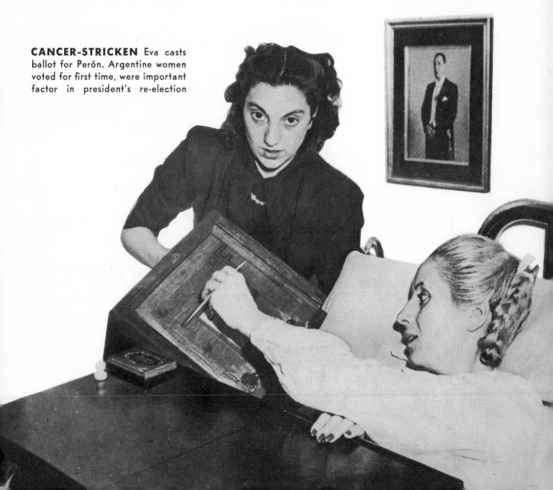

CANCER-STRICKEN Eva casts ballot for Perón. Argentine women voted for first time, were important factor in president's re-election

walls of the building, and carpeted the improvised chapel. Every florist shop in Buenos Aires was stripped. Flowers had to be flown in from as far away as Chile.

Funeral services finally were held on Aug. 10. Then the body was to be hidden from view for a year while embalmers prepared it for permanent display in a monument yet to be built.

Some of Evita's followers hailed her as a saint. One newspaper told of a little girl who said: "Eva was a saint. I know, because she cured my mother." It added: "Many sick are now well, many sorrowful are happy because of her."

At last, after this orgy of grief, the country went back to work—and to politics. One question the politicians asked was what effect, if any, Evita's death would have on the strained relations between Argentina and the United States. The answer: It was hardly likely to improve them. The teachings of Evita, the martyr, would now have more authority than ever. And those teachings were generally anti-U.S.

Like her husband, and in fact like most Argentines, she was jealous of the U.S. Argentines consider their country the richest and strongest in South America and think they, rather than the United States, should guide and influence their neighbors.

Perón would like to form a bloc of South American countries, led by himself, that he could play off against Washington. He made some headway in 1952, for in three South American countries men with Argentine connections became president.

One of these countries was Bolivia, the landlocked republic to the north. Bolivia is bigger than Texas and California combined. But for all practical purposes it is one big tin mine. It has rich valleys and plains where grains and fruits could be grown in abundance and cattle could

ARMED MINER guards leader of "Bolivia for Bolivians" party which ousted army government

graze fatly. But this farm land is neglected. Three fourths of Bolivia's three million people live on the altiplano, a desolate plain more than 2 miles above sea level, flattened out between jagged mountains whose peaks stab another mile into the cold sky.

Mostly these people are rock-faced Indians, illiterate, often drunken, numbed by the cocaine-bearing coca leaves they chew to dull their pain and hunger. Since the days of the Incas, they have been digging the tin on which Bolivia lives. The food they eat and practically everything they use is bought abroad with the money the tin brings in Britain and the U.S.

Until 1952, the Indians worked for the three big tin companies which owned most of the mines, the Patiño, Hochschild, and Aramayo interests—the Rosca, or ring, Bolivians call them. The Rosca paid better wages than most Bolivian employers and gave the workers free housing, free schools, and some free medical service. The listless Indians were more or less content.

But in La Paz, the 12,000-foot-high capital, a few educated, independent-minded Bolivians felt that Bolivia would be better off if it raised its own food and developed other kinds of wealth besides tin. They accused the Big Three tin companies, all foreign-owned, of draining the nation's wealth into other countries.

"These three companies are bigger than the government, and that cannot be," they declared. Under the slogan, "Bolivia for the Bolivians", they formed a political party called the Nationalist Revolutionary Movement (M.N.R.).

The tin companies practically controlled the government and the army as well as the mines, and the M.N.R. did not get far. It was in power briefly during World War II, but was thrown out by a revolution.

But it plugged along, concentrating on pushing the tin miners into unions and lining them up behind the M.N.R. In the spring of 1951, to everyone's surprise, the M.N.R. leader, Victor Paz Estenssoro, led all other candidates in a presidential election. But before he could take office, the army seized the government.

At dawn on April 9, 1952, machine-gun

CUBAN STRONG MAN Fulgencio Batista is sworn in as provisional president after almost bloodless coup. He promptly suspended Congress, dissolved all political parties

and rifle fire broke out in the thin, chill air of La Paz, as the M.N.R. and its armed miners moved in.

For three days rebels and soldiers fought through the deserted streets of the 2½-mile-high city, while residents cowered behind shuttered windows and doors. Finally El Alto airport, last stronghold of the government forces, fell, the army was destroyed, and the M.N.R. was in control.

Paz Estenssoro, 45-year-old professor of economics, a neat, alert man with a pleasant personality and convincing speech, became president. On Oct. 31, while thirty thousand cheering miners looked on, he signed a decree ousting the Rosca and taking over the tin mines for the government.

The M.N.R. used to be anti-Semitic, anti-United States, and pro-Argentina. Paz Estenssoro says it isn't any more. But he has many connections in Argentina, and an Argentine company already has been set up to help the Bolivians with the tough job of handling their own tin.

In two other countries, old friends of Perón were elected president: colorful Ecuador, the country astride the equator; and the string-bean republic of Chile (2600 miles long, 100 miles wide).

Ecuador is small—about the size of New Mexico—and picturesque, with steaming jungles checkered with barren plateaus and snow-topped mountains. Ninety percent of its people have Indian blood; about 60 percent are pure Indian. It is a land of poverty and political disorder; it has had twenty-one presidents in the past twenty-five years.

In 1948, things began to look up for Ecuadorians. They elected as their president Galo Plaza Lasso, 46-year-old, 6-foot son of a former president. Plaza was born in New York City and educated in the States. He admired the North American way of doing things, and he tackled his country's staggering problems with most un-Latin energy. He would work three hours at home, be in his office by 11, and stay there until 8 at night. He installed dictation machines and electric typewriters in the staid Government Palace.

But he couldn't make the country over in four years, and he couldn't legally run again. Nor would he pick his own successor, because that wasn't the democratic way. As a result, his followers quarreled among themselves. In an election held on June 1, 1952, José María Velasco Ibarra became president.

The bony, professorial Velasco Ibarra, known as *El Loco,* the crazy man, looks something like Don Quixote. For years he has been the idol of the Ecuadorian masses, and a headache to any government he was not running himself.

An orator whose speeches have been called "cascades of words", he is erratic, impatient, and highhanded. Twice before he has been president and twice has been thrown out of office because he acts like a dictator when "politicos with mouse minds . . . put banana peels in my way".

His ties are with Argentina rather than the United States. This fact may have helped him win the presidency, for many suspicious Ecuadorians think Galo Plaza was too friendly to the *Yanquis.* Velasco has an Argentine wife. Also, he lived in Argentina for five years before his election and the Argentines openly helped his campaign.

Chile is one of the most civilized, democratic countries in Latin America, and there was no monkey business about the Sept. 4 election. But here again the winner was an old friend of Perón's, and a stormy figure out of Chile's past.

Swarthy, square-jawed General Carlos Ibáñez del Campo has been in and out of the presidency, in and out of plots and revolutions, in and out of the country for thirty-five years. Now 74 years old—but not looking it—he had spent the last three years quietly in the Senate.

Chileans laughed when this apparent has-been announced that he was going to try for the presidency again. They stopped laughing as the campaign rolled on, and it became obvious that Ibáñez was making an impression on the voters. His technique was simple. The high cost of living was pinching Chileans badly. So Ibáñista speakers played on the theme that they never had it so good as when Ibáñez was president before.

"How much did you pay for bread when Ibáñez was president and how much do you pay now?" campaign orators would ask. This appealed to the women, who for the first time were voting in a presidential election. When the votes were counted, Ibáñez had won. Perón had helped him with money and propaganda.

Like Perón, all three of these new presidents are strongly nationalistic. This statement means, in practice, that they are suspicious of the U.S. "Chile, yes, Yanquis, no!" was a slogan in the Chilean election. And there are noisy nationalists in other countries, too. Even in normally friendly Brazil, street crowds shouted "The oil is ours!" while the Brazilian Congress debated whether to let foreign oil companies into the country.

The nationalists are encouraged by Latin America's Communists, who are ready to help anybody against the United States. In most of Latin America, the Communists are a nuisance rather than a danger. But in one country they really have been throwing their weight around.

This country is Guatemala, land of coffee and bananas, of steaming coastal regions and blue, volcano-shadowed

TROUBLE MOUNTS, MOUNT TROUBLED: Panama policeman helps horse after animal slips on corn kernels thrown by rioting students who demanded extension of school year!

MURDERERS (above) face firing squad and 15,000 spectators at public execution in Guatemala. Robbery was their motive for killing five with large knives called machetes. Officer administers traditional coup de grâce (opposite)

mountain lakes, of Indian communities so primitive that they still worship old Mayan gods.

The Communists moved into Guatemala during the presidency of Juan José Arévalo Bermejo, whose term expired in 1951. No Red himself, Arévalo was a liberal social reformer and he let the Communists take over the labor unions. He got so dependent on their support that he became virtually their prisoner. Jacobo Arbenz Guzmán, now president, is in the same fix. He and his government are not Communist, but they need Communist votes and backing, and so they let the Reds have things their own way.

Most Guatemalans are not Communists. They do not like to see their country falling into Red hands. In March, the anti-Communists revealed their feelings in a public demonstration. Warned in advance, the Reds breathed fire, scattered inflammatory leaflets over Guatemala City, and threatened to stage a counter-demonstration. But on the appointed day the graver anti-Reds began gathering in the Central Plaza. When nothing happened to them, more and more men and women joined the throng, until there were perhaps thirty thousand.

The crowd was well behaved and good natured, but determined. "We have come to this place," a spokesman said, "to remind the government . . . that the people do not believe in Communism, and to state that the government should wipe out Communism." Then the gathering broke up.

But the Reds evidently were stronger than public opinion. At the end of the year, they seemed to be as firmly in the saddle as ever.

The threat of Communism in this area is to the Panama Canal, important U.S. life line. Except in Guatemala, the Communists did not make much headway in the Caribbean area around the Canal.

They tried to move into El Salvador. But in September the young, anti-Communist president, Oscar Osorio, learned of their plans. He immediately declared a thirty-day state of siege. Then National Guard troops in fleets of police cars and trucks raided homes and hideouts of suspected Communists. Their families, servants, and boarders were carted away for investigation. Caches of guns, bombs, and other weapons were raided. Thus, apparently, the Communist threat in El Salvador was eliminated.

In the republic of Panama itself, around whose waistline the Canal is wrapped, the Reds had little chance against a new president, Colonel José A. ("Chichi") Remón.

In his off hours, before he became president, Remón, plump and fortyish, could usually be found at some Panama City sports event or drinking with friends—sometimes Yankee businessmen—at El Rancho café. Generally he wore a short-sleeved, white sport shirt and slacks, with a handkerchief-covered gun butt sticking out of his right hip pocket.

But in business hours he was chief of the National Police. Panama has no army, and so Remón's 2500 smart, well-equipped, heavily armed police could call the country's tune. Remón didn't like to be called a president-maker, but no enemy of his was likely to run for the job. He and his attractive young wife Cecilia ("Ceci") put on a whirlwind campaign.

Chichi stayed comfortably at home. Ceci took to the road. By oxcart, jeep, plane, launch, canoe, and on foot, sometimes with a caravan of doctors and dentists who gave free treatment to all comers, she hunted votes all over the republic. She gave away pots, pans, and packages of seeds, all stamped "Remón serves the people." She also passed out soda pop. When the election was held on May 11, her husband was an easy winner.

Remón always has been friendly to the United States. He got part of his military training at Fort Riley, Kans., and during the past war Eleanor Roosevelt personally

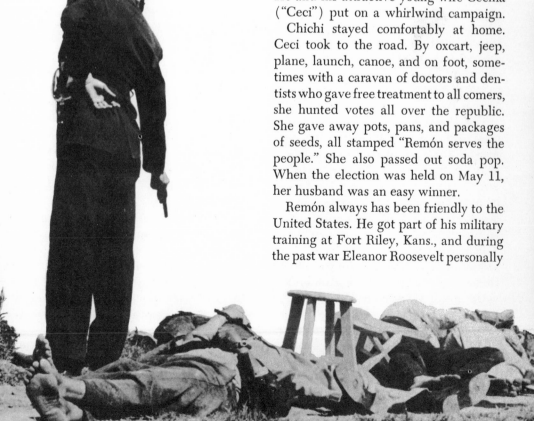

presented him with the U.S. Legion of Merit. And there are not many Communists in Panama, anyway.

Another important Caribbean country changed hands in 1952—but without benefit of election. For four years, Colonel Fulgencio Batista y Zaldivar, stenographer by trade and onetime sergeant in the Cuban army, then maker and unmaker of presidents, and finally president himself, had been living in the United States.

"I just felt safer there," he said after his candidate had lost the 1944 election. He commuted luxuriously between a New York City hotel and his home in Daytona Beach, Fla. But he kept his finger in Cuban politics, got himself elected to the Senate *in absentia* in 1948, and returned to the island.

In March, he decided that the Cuban people were fed up with their government. In a 77-minute, almost bloodless coup he and a group of young army officers turned out President Carlos Prío Socarrás.

At 51, Batista was a little plumper than he had been, solid in build, muscular and fit. He plunged at once into a fifteen- to eighteen-hour working day. But by the end of the year there were signs that he was accomplishing less than he had promised, and that the Cubans might be getting a little tired of him. Meanwhile, he was helping out in the Caribbean by cutting the Cuban Communists down to size.

In two other Latin American countries, there was confusion and unrest in 1952, although in neither were nationalists or Communists especially involved.

In Colombia, things went from bad to worse. For four years, a Conservative government had been trying ruthlessly to break up the opposition Liberal Party. The Liberals had fought back. In the llanos, the backland plains region east of the Andes, there had been bloody battles, with hundreds of casualties, between police and soldiers on the one side and "bandits" on the other. Some of the "bandits" were Liberals, forced off their farms or afraid to stay on them.

In 1952, for the first time, fighting erupted in the capital, Bogotá. Funeral services for five police, killed in a battle with guerrillas, touched off a mob which ran riot, shouting "Down with the Liberals. Down with the assassins!" Liberal headquarters and the offices of two important Liberal newspapers were burned, and prominent Liberal leaders fled the country.

In Venezuela, the three-man military dictatorship, in power since 1948, decided to take a chance. Sure it would win, it called an election for Nov. 30. But when the count of votes began, the opposition Republican Democratic Union quickly took the lead. With almost a quarter of the votes tallied, it was leading the government party by nearly two to one.

Then in mid-morning on Dec. 1, wire-service correspondents in Caracas reported to New York: "Unable to file." Telephone circuits were closed. For more than twenty-four hours, censorship was airtight.

On Dec. 2, the announcement of returns was resumed. The tide had turned, the government declared. It had won the election. Lieutenant Colonel Marcos Pérez Jiménez, one of the ruling triumvirate, had himself declared provisional president.

Two weeks later, seven opposition leaders arrived in Panama insisting that the whole thing was a frame-up, that their party actually had won but had been counted out. They themselves had been seized by the government and dumped on an outgoing plane without money, extra clothes, or even toothbrushes.

So the political pot boiled in Latin America. Anything could happen in 1953.

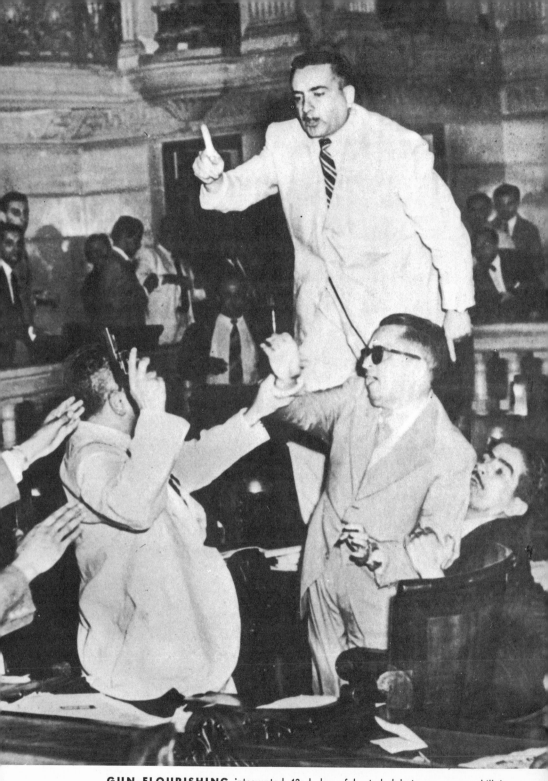

GUN-FLOURISHING interrupted 42nd day of heated debate on revenue bill in Rio de Janeiro city council. Shot was fired and microphone hurled but no one was hurt

WAR in ASIA

RED CHINA

TEN DEJECTED MEN STOOD UNDER A TRAFfic light in the heart of Red Shanghai's "Times Square". From their elegant appearance, they were obviously gentlemen of means. But alert constables standing by indicated they were under arrest.

Presently, two coolies began to beat drums and clash cymbals until a crowd had collected. Then one of the officers spoke. The men had been caught gambling at cards—a crime against the people of New China. These criminals were to be given a chance to plead publicly for the forgiveness of their sin.

One by one the gamblers stepped forward. Tearfully, they confessed their guilt. They were sorry for their misconduct and grateful to Communist authorities for the chance to purge themselves.

The crowd laughed and applauded, the men were released.

But they had lost face—a punishment more devastating than imprisonment to a self-respecting Asian.

Something of the same sort has happened to the Westerner in Korea. The Communists have made him lose face. For the first time in a full century, Asians have been able to push him around—and get away with it. In terms of human life, it has been a costly adventure. But it has enhanced Chinese prestige immeasurably.

There is, however, much more significance to the Chinese invasion of Korea.

It is part of a sinister psychological war being waged against millions of their fellow Asians in Thailand (Siam), Burma, Malaya, Indochina, and Indonesia—in the whole crowded vastness to the south of Red China which is the source of 90 percent of the world's rubber, 75 percent of the world's tin, and a high percentage of the world's oil, tungsten, and other vital materials.

By marching into Korea, the Chinese Communists proclaimed in effect:

"We don't hesitate to cross our borders to take what we want by force, if need

MAO TSE-TUNG, Dictator of Red China. Army is estimated at 4 million troops. Women, too, are drafted; many have seen combat

be. Moreover, to prove that we are strong enough to do it, we shall take on the whole United Nations, including the mighty United States."

As 1952 drew to a close, millions of non-Chinese Asians had begun to look fearfully to a localized peace in Korea— a peace which would free the Chinese Reds to step up their aggression to the south, and thus further their dream of dominating all Asia.

The invasion of Korea enabled the Chinese Communists to solve many of their most pressing domestic problems. The "Resist-America-Aid-Korea" campaign, as they call it, gave the Communists a handy pretext for crushing dissidents against the Red regime. By their own admission, thousands of "enemies of the people" were put to death without formal hearing.

Shih Liang (*shir lee-ang'*), China's bloodthirsty female minister of justice, declared that her Russian-styled People's Courts had been too soft on those suspected of opposing the government. "Now," she said, "let the heads roll."

In February, the Peking authorities initiated another terror campaign which virtually liquidated private enterprise in the name of a "people's drive against dishonesty and corruption".

The inquisition, popularly called a "tiger hunt", lasted for three terrifying months, and affected every businessman from the lowliest noodle seller to the topmost industrialist. Throughout China, these businessmen were brought before "denunciation meetings" to be judged by employees and neighbors. Varying degrees of guilt were established. The *wu fan* or "five cardinal sins" were bribery, tax evasion, fraud, stealing state property, and theft of state economic secrets.

Threatened with imprisonment or conscription for non-co-operation, employees were urged to report graft, hoarding, ex-

cessive profits, and abuse of authority. Whether these accusations were real or falsified, the victim was given little opportunity to defend himself. Before mobs whipped to anger by local commissars, the accused "tigers" were ordered to "confess" their sins and beg for mercy. Punishment varied with the whim of the mob, from a simple fine to summary execution.

The executions were staged as public spectacles, often broadcast on a nationwide radio hookup. Hysterical mobs yelled "*Sa! Sa!*" ("Kill! Kill!") as the victims were marched before a People's Court. A presiding officer asked a few

CHINESE WORKERS celebrate anniversary of founding of People's Republic of China. Placards are of Mao, but high tribute was also paid Red China's good friend, Joseph Stalin

formal questions—name, age, residence—and then waved the condemned man to a seat where he wrote his will or final statement. Then the prisoner's hands were tied behind him and a rigid, 3-foot pennant listing his crime was fastened like a huge feather to the back of his head. An attendant stepped forward with a tray of steaming noodles and pork chops and fed the trussed man with chopsticks while a circle of guards watched with guns drawn.

When the prisoners had been fed, they were loaded into trucks. With sirens screaming, the convoy raced through the crowded streets to the selected execution ground, often a busy downtown intersection. The condemned were quickly lined up, pushed to their knees, and shot twice in the back of the head.

As the victims fell forward, a roar rose from the crowd. Then, suddenly, silence. As if ashamed of their blood lust, the onlookers quickly melted away.

As a result of this campaign of terror, the government was able to raise vast sums of extra revenue for the national treasury by means of heavy fines, punitive taxes, and outright confiscation of property. Accumulated cash ran into the billions of Chinese dollars.

In addition, about 200 million American dollars and other "hard" currencies—the hoarding of which had been declared "traitorous to the interests of the people"—was uncovered and confiscated. This foreign exchange made it possible for the Peking government to offer high prices, in cash, for much-needed machinery, transport, and supplies purchased in the Hong Kong and East European markets.

Although the purge ended almost as suddenly as it began, nevertheless it had broken both the will and the economic back of the middle-class businessman. It dealt a death blow to what remained of capitalism in Red China.

Most major economic and industrial enterprises long since had come under government control. The small businessman, however, had expected comparative freedom to operate. For this he had the word of Communist leader Mao Tse-tung (*mah'-oh dzuh'-doong'*), who some years ago had declared in his book, *New De-mocracy*, "big banks, big industries, and big business shall be owned by the state, so that unscrupulous individuals can not manipulate the life of the people". But, said Mao, for the time being small business would not be restricted.

Mao Tse-tung's rise from leadership of a political minority to mastery of all China, with life-and-death authority over five hundred million people, has been meteoric. He is tall for a Chinese, broad-shouldered and loose-boned. Although 59, he looks much younger. His sensitive face, its unusually high forehead topped by a shock of bushy black hair, is enlivened by expressive eyes. He smiles easily, speaks softly, and is often almost boyish in his enthusiasms.

The Communism of Karl Marx, which he studied in Chinese translations, is, and always has been, Mao's ultimate objective. He has devoted a lifetime to its fulfillment. But the old order dies hard in

SIGNING OF SOVIET-CHINESE TREATY: From left, A. S. Panyushkin, A. Y. Vishinsky, N. P. Fedorenko, V. M. Molotov, Su Yui, Chang Wen-tien, G. I. Tunkin, Li Fu-chun, J. V. Stalin, Chou En-lai, G. M. Malenkov, L. P. Beria, A. I. Mikoyan, L. M. Kaganovich, N. A. Bulganin

China, and social changes must necessarily be slow and evolutionary. As a Chinese, no one knows this better than Mao.

He has, accordingly, introduced what he calls "New Democracy" as a compromise form of government to fit the practical needs of the "liberated" millions in China today. In his own words, the government allows of a "limited capitalism". This outlaws big business, but includes small-scale private enterprise such as restaurants, workshops, retail merchandising, and similar small businesses.

Indeed, the place of this special "capitalism" is fixed in the new Communist Chinese national flag. It is comprised of a large yellow star and an arc of four smaller stars on a red background. The large star symbolizes the leadership of the Chinese Communist Party; the smaller stars represent the four most important classes in the "New China"—farmers, wage earners, merchants, and "national" (as distinguished from "foreign") capitalists.

One reason for the government's decision to call a sudden halt to the "tiger hunt" was the fact that there had been little rain or snow in the first three months of 1952. The drought had delayed spring plowing, and with a million nonproductive "volunteers" in Korea, and twelve million government workers to be fed, drastic measures had to be taken lest the nation suffer the worst famine since the terrible Honan famine of 1943, in which more than five million people perished in the "Ohio" of China, and thirty million more were affected to some degree.

To meet the threat of another such disaster, the Communist authorities in early 1952 mobilized millions of peasants into "volunteer" work battalions. It was slave labor on a vast scale. In the colder northern provinces these labor battalions cracked the ice on frozen lakes and rivers,

and sluiced the water into adjoining fields. In the semitropical south they dug wells and irrigation ditches. Canals and rivers were dredged and dammed, to back up water to levels sufficient to provide a flow into irrigation systems.

A contributing factor to this threatening calamity was the government's order to complete land distribution by the end of the year. Like other government-sponsored campaigns, this one was conducted with violence. Stirred to frenzy by party leaders, farmers neglected their fields in their *tou cheng* (struggle dispute) against the local landlords. As a result, the nation's agriculture was seriously dislocated.

By the end of 1952, the Communists were already able to control virtually every aspect of China's social, economic, and political life. They had a firm hold

REFUGEE gnaws bark of tree as famine brings death, suffering to eastern China. Child (below) weeps beside body of mother who died of starvation

upon schools, wages and prices, the press, the police, the courts—even the council of elders in the tiniest crossroads village.

This totalitarianism had been building up since the Reds came to power in 1949. By 1952, full control was made possible through a system of universal registration whereby one could not spend a night away from one's home without permission from the local Communist Party representative.

It was not enough, however, to submit one's daily routine to surveillance. The mind as well as the body had to be regimented, and throughout China everyone was expected to join a "study group", closely supervised by a Party worker. Having joined, the individual found it difficult to remain passive. He was expected to participate in endless discussions, usually centered upon self-criticism and criticism of others. Silence was suspect, even dangerous, and required *hsueh hsi* (brain-washing) to bring about "ideological reform".

The time wasted attending these endless "study groups" was bound to affect a man's production efficiency as well as his peace of mind. The *Shanghai Liberation Daily*, official newspaper of the Communist Party there, reported that the heavy strain placed upon "Model Workers" was causing grave concern to officials and insisted that "steps be taken to end it".

"Model Workers" were not only hard pressed to maintain the high production levels which earned them the title, but were burdened almost beyond endurance with social and political demands on their time after working hours.

The paper told the story of Yuan Kai-li, a "Model Worker" of the Second Steel

HUMAN BEINGS, cheaper to maintain and more plentiful than farm animals, are used to till Chinese soil. China has population of 475 million on area about one-third larger than United States

Mill in Shanghai. Yuan not only worked at top speed to set a shining example for his co-workers, but was called upon to contribute his free time to the following duties. He was a member of the executive committee of the factory's trade union, a member of the production committee, propaganda officer of the Communist Party, vice-director of a committee for the elimination of counterrevolutionaries, workers' representative at the People's Representative Conference of All Circles of Shanghai, people's representative of the New Municipal Center, district vice-chairman of the Consultative Council of the New Municipal Center, and district people's representative in the Yangtzepoo residential area.

Yuan, the paper concluded, had to have "at least five injections of glucose each month to keep him going", but even so he complained of dizziness and inability to work because he had to "think all the time what to say at the meetings".

A special attack was directed against the family system which has motivated the Chinese way of life for over four thousand years. In a society rooted in the principle of respect for one's elders, the cruelest blow came when Communist-indoctrinated school children were deliberately encouraged to denounce their "reactionary" parents.

Mothers-in-law, traditional matriarchs in the home, were hauled before housewives' unions for real or fancied abuses. Sons and daughters were urged to break away from the family hearth and devote themselves to political activities.

By the end of the year, scores of once-prominent industrialists, bankers, professors, engineers—often graduates of American and European universities—publicly disavowed appreciation for the West. Their written "confessions" filled the press.

Meanwhile, Western-endowed colleges and medical schools were taken over by the government and turned into political centers. And in the summer, an orgy of book-burning began.

The year was also high-lighted by an assault upon Western religions, especially their missionary work in China. The Communist authorities seemed reluctantly willing to tolerate religious belief and worship, provided the Western churches would submit to the will of the state, but the compromise was obviously unworkable.

When the foreign missions refused to knuckle under, the Communists hit back with wholesale arrests and humiliating trials. Scores of missionaries were jailed and tortured. Many died in prison or were shattered in health before being permitted to cross into the British crown colony of Hong Kong.

Unlike the Nationalists, who had ruled through loose working agreements with semi-independent provincial war lords, the Communists made no deals with regional strong men.

There was still some anti-Communist guerrilla activity, but it appeared to be on the wane. And as the Communists tightened their hold, opposition seemed destined to diminish.

Apparently Red China and Red Russia see eye to eye on most political considerations concerning Asia. But what is the relationship between Mao Tse-tung and the Kremlin? Is he a willing colleague, a reluctant partner, or a puppet? Opinions differ, but the facts are these.

The deference accorded Mao during his 1950 visit to Moscow was not in keeping with the Kremlin's normal treatment of a puppet. The reception was perhaps the most elaborate ever given a foreign visitor. Its very sumptuousness betrayed something of the Soviet's apprehensions. For Mao was the conqueror of a nation larger than the United States, containing more than one fifth of the earth's people. He could be neither pushed around nor patronized.

As do most Chinese, Mao Tse-tung regards all Westerners, including probably the Soviet Russians, as "long-nosed" barbarians who are his social and intellectual inferiors. This attitude perhaps explains why Mao and his aides look upon the Soviet dictator and his comrades as, at best, colleagues, not masters.

It may also explain why the Kremlin does not entirely trust Mao. A "colleague" of Mao's stature can mean only a rival. Undoubtedly, it must have irked Stalin to know Mao controlled almost twice as many people as he.

With victory in China already assured, Mao felt strong enough to talk up to the Russians. He demanded the return of vast areas in North China which the Soviet had virtually detached from China. These included Manchuria, Inner and Outer Mongolia, and Sinkiang, which collectively form sovereign China's northern half.

Mao was especially adamant in his insistence that the Russians get out of Manchuria, the "New England" of China. Manchuria is China's principal source of iron and coal, prime essentials for industrialization.

Shockingly backward industrially, China manufactures only an insignificant part of her vast requirements. Mao himself has repeatedly stated that without Manchuria and its industrial potential China can never achieve economic independence.

It is little wonder, then, that Mao Tse-tung took an uncompromising stand. He insisted that the Russians withdraw from Manchuria, which they had occupied since their armies entered it to engage the Japanese six days before Japan's capitulation in August, 1945, to end World War II.

Normally a man of even temper, Mao

LANDOWNER confesses "crimes" after being denounced at mass rally. Whether she will be released, imprisoned, or shot depends on whim of mob

PEOPLE'S COURT hears case of farmer Huang Chin-chi. A few minutes later, sentence is carried out (right). Huang's "crime" was exploiting peasants who worked his two thirds of an acre

can be a terror when he gets angry. His long black hair bristles like a lion's mane. A master of invective, much of which he invents, his language gets earthier by the moment.

The Soviets were flabbergasted by his increasing arrogance but they knew better than to antagonize the Chinese leader at a time when the cold war with the West hung in the balance. An open break between Red China and Red Russia would be disastrous to the cause of world Communism.

At that 1950 meeting, the Soviets agreed to withdraw their troops from Manchuria, return the railways and the principal ports to China by 1952, and advance credits of $300 million to be used for the purchase of capital equipment and raw materials from the Soviet Union.

Beyond promising to return what they had grabbed from China since 1945, the Russians didn't give Mao much. But it was significant that he was able to *get* something from Moscow, instead of *giving* something. This success gained him much face throughout Asia as well as in China.

To be sure, it was a postdated check Moscow gave Mao. But he had no inten-

tion of waiting until the end of 1952 to collect. When the Russian-backed adventure in Korea collapsed in the winter of 1950, Mao saw his chance to kill two birds with one stone. By sending a million Chinese "volunteers" to the rescue of the North Koreans, he regained immediate control of Manchuria, through which these "volunteers" had to pass en route to the Korean border.

Whatever the outcome in Korea, therefore, one thing is sure—Manchuria, the densely populated, industrialized south of it at least, is again firmly in Chinese hands.

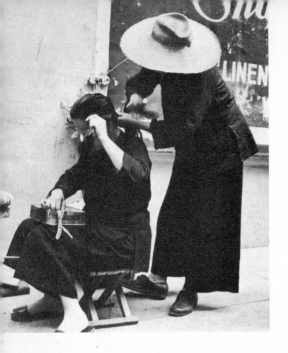

HONG KONG

A LITTLE BRIDGE ACROSS THE SHUMCHUN River on the border between Hong Kong and Red China today forms the only direct contact between the Western democracies and the vast stretches behind the Communists' "Bamboo Curtain".

The Communists had long ago thrown a barrier across their end of the bridge. Freight-bearing trains bound for Canton passed through without much difficulty, since Red China needed imports from the outside world, especially scrap iron, medicines, and rubber tires.

Passengers for British Hong Kong, however, were herded into barbed-wire pens, where they stood in broiling sun or pelting rain to await processing and Customs examination before being permitted to leave Red China. A half day or more might be spent in this processing before the refugee was permitted to cross into British-controlled territory. Here he was processed by British Customs and funneled to a medical tent to be vaccinated for smallpox and inoculated for cholera.

Finally, he was permitted to move on to a tiny station where he might buy a ticket for the train to take him the remaining 20-odd miles to Hong Kong proper.

On their side of the bridge-border, the Communists had set up a loud-speaker over which all refugees were sternly warned not to try to smuggle hoarded money or treasure out of Red China. The man on the microphone often padded these warnings with tirades against "foreign imperialists", particularly Americans.

In the center of the bridge was a barbed-wire enclosure which might be described as something of a limbo. In there were placed those luckless ones who had been passed by the Reds but were refused entry by the British. They could go neither forward nor backward. Usually, they stayed there until the 7 o'clock curfew, when a compromise was worked out between the British and the Communists, who agreed to divide them up.

The guns of both sides watched day and night to prevent illegal crossings. The

Communist border guards were especially trigger-happy and fired without warning at anyone who approached the river bank, except at the check point on the bridge.

The British had thrown up a high barbed-wire fence which extended for miles along their side of the Shumchun River. Even so, scores of refugees braved the dangers nightly in a desperate swim to freedom. Once on the British side, they climbed over or burrowed under the fence. Many of them were picked up by British patrols. The few who were able to prove close family connections in Hong Kong were usually permitted to remain. The others were returned to the Communists, who imposed severe penalties on them—in many cases, execution.

In 1952, Hong Kong became known as a political no-man's-land. Its importance as a listening post for what went on behind Red China's Bamboo Curtain was attested by the United States Consulate-General, which had expanded its personnel from a mere handful to several hundreds.

In the furious local propaganda war, the Americans spent the most and got the least for their money. The Communists spent the least and got the most. The Nationalists spent a lot of money and got almost nothing.

Almost every Chinese-language bookshop in Hong Kong was Communist-controlled. Stocked with propaganda books published in Red China, they offered such curious volumes as the *Cartoon Propaganda Reference Book*. This textbook for artists, cartoonists, and stage designers showed the right way to present such groups as "foreign imperialists" and "Nationalist runnings dogs" (traitors). One sketch brazenly depicted a Red underground terrorist crushing a Hong Kong Englishman's skull with a stone.

From the standpoint of getting reliable news about Red China there was, of course, no substitute for being able to

OVER A MILLION REFUGEES from Red China have poured into Hong Kong. Feeding and housing are acute problems for British authorities

MINE DETECTOR is used by Hong Kong police to check for concealed weapons. Next step for new arrivals is compulsory vaccination for smallpox and cholera

travel freely in the country and to talk freely with the Chinese people and their leaders. This, however, was impossible. Hong Kong, therefore, served as a communications center for news filtering in from all parts of China. Actually, Hong Kong was a better place than Peking or Shanghai to collect information about Red China, for political controls inside China itself had reached the point where a Chinese courted danger merely by talking publicly with a Westerner.

Similarly, the Communists found Hong Kong useful as a clearinghouse for their agents, who traveled freely between Red China and the countries in Southeast Asia. They came and went without check or control, inasmuch as Britain had formally recognized the regime of Mao Tse-tung as China's legal government.

Meanwhile, espionage and counterespionage went on behind the scenes in a charged atmosphere which threatened to explode whenever the time was deemed right by any of a dozen different underground factions. The British were fully aware of this danger. Yet they knew there was almost nothing they could do about it. In spite of an impressive array of warships riding at anchor, sweating Tommies swarming over the countryside, and jet warplanes streaking overhead, the fact remained that almost every pound of food for Hong Kong's three million people came from Communist-controlled farm lands beyond the city's limits. Even the precious water reservoirs were located within range of Red Chinese gunners just across the Shumchun River.

In normal times, Hong Kong lives almost entirely on commissions it makes as a transfer point for southern China's foreign trade.

When the Western Powers, at the insistence of the U.S., imposed restrictions upon strategic materials destined for Communist China via Hong Kong, the Chinese turned toward the Soviet Union and its Eastern European satellites. By the end of 1952, 70 percent of Red China's foreign trade was reoriented overland to and from Communist-dominated countries in Europe. Hundreds of firms in Hong Kong were caught with warehouses filled with goods, valued at $100 million, intended for sale on the mainland. Alternate markets in Asia could not be found.

Hard times came not only to Hong Kong; the vast British interests in China itself were virtually killed by restrictions and taxation. Indeed, it was their $2 billion investment in China which had prompted the British to step forward with recognition for the Communist regime, a recognition rudely snubbed by the Red Chinese government.

In mid-May the British decided they had had enough. After a century of profitable trade relations with China, London sent a note to Peking announcing that British firms remaining in China would close their doors. An effort would be made to salvage tangible assets, but the Britishers were resigned to leaving virtually everything behind.

In July, further evidence of a more realistic attitude toward Red China came when the Privy Council in London dramatically reversed the Hong Kong court's decision to award 40 former Nationalist planes to the Red government.

The planes had been flown to presumed safety in Hong Kong when the Nationalist armies collapsed on the mainland in November, 1949. The Communists demanded the return of the aircraft to the "people of China". Hong Kong authorities announced that British recognition, then expected momentarily, would give the Communists ownership of the planes "by right of inheritance".

The Nationalists reacted swiftly. Before Britain formally recognized the Red regime in January, 1950, the planes were sold to Civil Air Transport, Inc., a corporation chartered in the U.S. by Major General Claire Chennault, wartime commander of the famed Flying Tigers.

Following the Privy Council's decision, the planes were turned over to General Chennault's agents, who removed them from Hong Kong to Formosa. Inasmuch as the planes, with thousands of spare parts, were worth an estimated $30 million, it was a conspicuous loss to the Chinese Communists. At year's end, the British were nervously awaiting reprisals against Hong Kong.

CARGO FROM HONG KONG to Red China is carefully screened by British authorities on lookout for forbidden war materials or other contraband

HE'S HOME! HE'S SAFE!

HIS BUDDY DEAD,
a G.I. weeps without
shame somewhere in Korea

KOREA

A UNITED NATIONS' SUMMARY OF THE WAR in Korea noted that 1952 had been a year of "relative inactivity", although at least 150,000 casualties had been inflicted upon the enemy. In two and a half weary years of fighting, Red forces had suffered a total of 1,299,961 casualties. U.N. casualties totaled 366,055, of which 128,530 were American.

Our losses in the air were twice as many as the enemy's. The figures, however, were deceptive. According to the U.S. Air Force, F-86 Sabre jets had maintained a 9-to-1 combat ratio over the Russian-built MIG-15's—shooting down nine MIG's for every F-86.

The high American air losses were explained by the fact that Allied air units concentrated upon bombing enemy strongholds heavily defended by antiaircraft guns. Communist aircraft, on the other hand, rarely attacked United Nations ground stations.

On the ground, a virtual stalemate ex-

RUSSIAN-TRAINED General Nam II, head of North Korean peace-negotiation team, dons coat to leave Panmunjom after futile armistice conference

isted, so far as high-level military strategists were concerned. For the men in the front lines, this could never be so.

On Nov. 27, 1951, armistice negotiators established a line of demarcation based on points where opposing forces were then locked in battle, roughly along the 38th parallel. This line was to serve as the temporary boundary for a cease-fire zone should an agreement be reached within thirty days. The cease-fire was not reached within the time limit, and although neither side was thereafter obligated to respect the line, it nevertheless influenced the 1952 pattern of fighting.

In February, the Communists launched a "creeping offensive". Firmly dug in on the demarcation line, they began inching forward, adding a bunker here, strengthening another there, while moving vast quantities of ammunition up to the front.

To contain this offensive, U.N. patrols were sent out nightly to destroy the new fortifications as they appeared. Action stemmed largely from these patrol clashes.

The toughest fighting flared on the night of Oct. 6, when the Chinese attacked more than thirty Allied hill posi-

tions along the western two thirds of the front. In twenty-four hours, they poured more than 93,000 rounds of artillery and mortar fire into U.S. 8th Army positions. It became apparent, however, that the enemy's main objectives were White Horse Mountain, which guards the western edge of the Chorwon Valley, and nearby Arrowhead Ridge, protecting the gateway to the capital, Seoul.

In a determined defense of Arrowhead Ridge, a French battalion of 800 men shattered a full regiment of Communists.

White Horse Mountain was defended by the Republic of Korea's 9th Division. The Chinese sent five regiments of their "elite guard" against the ROK's. In the hand-to-hand fighting which followed, the ROK's were repeatedly driven from the crest, but each time fought their way back before the Chinese could dig in.

This resurgence in ROK morale was perhaps the most notable achievement in 1952. In the early days of the war, American commanders had little confidence in the ill-equipped, ill-trained ROK's, who often broke ranks and ran at critical moments. Following an intensive training program directed by American officers, the new ROK army was expanded to twelve divisions and armed with the latest U.S. weapons, including artillery.

On April 15, 1000 Chinese struck at an outpost held by 150 ROK's who stood their ground until virtually all their officers and noncommissioned officers were casualties. When the survivors fixed bayonets in a charge which sent the Chinese reeling down into the valley, it was apparent that a new Republic of Korea Army had been born.

President-elect Dwight D. Eisenhower expressed the hope that the South Koreans would eventually relieve American and other U.N. troops in the actual front lines. By the end of the year, 60 percent of the U.N. front lines in Korea was already held by South Korean troops. Even so, General Douglas MacArthur declared before a Senate committee that:

GEN. MARK CLARK (r.) became U.N. supreme commander in Korea, succeeding Gen. Matthew Ridgway (l.), who was assigned to N.A.T.O. headquarters in Paris as commander

"There is a large potential of manpower in South Korea; but to train it and to supply it is a matter of gravest difficulty. . . . To build up an army it takes years, tradition, standards, and there is no way to substitute for that."

First at Kaesong, in July, 1951, and later in a roadside tent at Panmunjom, Vice-Admiral C. Turner Joy met to discuss armistice terms with North Korean Lieutenant General Nam Il and his Red Chinese associates. Hopes that a truce could be achieved in a few weeks were soon dashed. By 1952, the Communists had turned the meetings into sounding boards for wild propaganda and vicious abuse directed against the United States and her U.N. allies. They haggled interminably, and whenever an agreement appeared about to be reached they suddenly injected more impossible demands.

Day after day Admiral Joy entered the truce tent and faced ramrod-stiff General Nam Il across the green-covered conference table. The 38-year-old Russian-trained Nam Il, immaculate in well-tailored Russian-style uniform and glistening boots, chain-smoked nervously as he spoke and waited for interpreters to translate. Once he attempted to light one of his Russian cigarettes with Chinese matches. He struck a dozen or more; none fired. He reached into his pocket and brought out an American cigarette lighter, which clicked and flamed instantly. Then, apparently feeling he had somehow been disloyal to Communism, he threw the lighter disdainfully out the window behind him.

The talkathon dragged on from month to month. On May 22, 1952, Admiral Joy faced Nam Il for the last time before

BETTY HUTTON drops in for chow. Film comedienne toured Korea with U.S.O.

leaving for his new post as superintendent of the Naval Academy at Annapolis.

"There is nothing left to negotiate," he said. "The decision is in your hands."

His place as senior U.N. delegate was taken by Major General William K. Harrison Jr., a deeply religious World War II hero who neither drinks nor smokes. There was little left for General Harrison to do, however, for a stalemate had obviously been reached. The deadlock hung on Item Four on the agenda—the exchange of war prisoners.

The United Nations had captured 173,-000 Communists; the Communists, 12,000 Allied soldiers—all but 4400 of them South Koreans. The U.N. insisted that prisoners on both sides be given the right to refuse repatriation. The position was based upon post-World War II experiences. Many Polish and Russian prisoners captured by the Germans had committed suicide rather than return to their homelands, and possible execution.

The U.N. declared that about 55,000 of its prisoners of war had said they would resist repatriation to the death.

The Communists rejected voluntary repatriation, aware that they would lose face in Asia if it were revealed that many of their soldiers refused to return to the Communist Utopia.

The West believed that forcible repatriation would betray a promise made to POW's. United Nations planes had regularly "bombed" the enemy with handbills which guaranteed humane treatment and ultimate freedom to any trooper who brought one of the leaflets to Allied lines. Thousands of Chinese and North Koreans had done so. It would be sentencing them to death to send them back.

SOUTH KOREA'S first popular presidential election won Syngman Rhee, 77, another 4-year term. Opponents charged he sought dictatorship

The repatriation issue was inflamed by bloody outbreaks among Communist firebrands in U.N. prisoner-of-war camps and by the stern countermeasures taken by Allied authorities.

When the U.N. General Assembly convened in New York City in the fall, the Allies sought endorsement of their POW stand. India offered a compromise proposal. The plan called for an immediate cease-fire, after which all POW's would be turned over to a neutral five-member repatriation commission which would return prisoners from both sides to their homes, on a voluntary basis. After debate, and negative votes by the Soviet Union and its satellites, the resolution was adopted by an overwhelming majority and cabled to Peking on Dec. 5. It was rejected by Foreign Minister and Premier Chou En-lai (*jo en'-lie'*).

This rejection reinforced a growing Western suspicion that the Reds were not anxious to resolve the war on any but their own terms. Indeed, they seemed more interested in keeping Korea a festering sore in the side of the West. At year's end, a re-examination of the Korean situation seemed warranted.

Anticipating this need, General Eisenhower voiced as a campaign pledge his determination, following his election to the Presidency, to visit Korea for a first-hand look-see. Shortly before Christmas, he flew to Korea for a whirlwind tour of the fronts, and conferences with the military command. On his return, he said little to reveal what he thought of the situation and of possible remedies. It was assumed he would wait until after his inauguration before he took formal action.

He did, however, say that he saw no "panaceas" for settlement of the war. With ominous emphasis, he added: "We must go ahead and do things that will induce [the Communists] to want peace."

Early in 1952, there were reports of an alarming spread of disease in both China and North Korea, due perhaps to a shortage of medicines and medical practitioners. As of October, 1950, according to the Communists, China had only one doctor or medical assistant for every 10,000 persons. Inspired to give emphasis to an "anti-epidemic mobilization" on the home front, word was spread that Americans were engaging in bacteriological warfare and that germs were being passed on to China by returning soldiers.

In a radio broadcast from Peking on Feb. 25, Foreign Minister Chou En-lai gave the charge official standing.

At first the U.S. ridiculed the Chinese "evidence" to "prove" the charge. When, however, the Soviet Union repeated the

FUTURE KOREAN VOTER learns election procedure by watching mother cast first ballot

charge in the United Nations Assembly, the U.S. offered to submit the matter to impartial investigation by the World Health Organization or the International Red Cross. The offer was rejected by both the Soviets and the Chinese.

One outstanding event took place on the nonmilitary scene in Korea. This was the first presidential election by secret ballot since the Republic of Korea was born on May 10, 1948. Without speeches, without campaigning, and without even acknowledging the party that nominated him, the white-haired, iron-fisted "father of his country" Syngman Rhee (*sing-man ree'*) achieved an overwhelming victory in the August elections with more than 70 percent of the seven million votes cast at the polls.

Uncompromising President Rhee has been something of a problem child for the United Nations. More than once he has embarrassed his Western democratic allies with his high-handed rule in South Korea. He has repeatedly ignored the law of the land when it suited him, and once actually jailed some legislators when they objected. Even so, while many Koreans dislike his methods, he is popular with them and they back him as the only national figure who has the stature, toughness, and political skill required to deal with the U.N. and the U.S.

Throughout 1952 he was outspoken in his determination to reject any negotiated peace for Korea. While conceding that the ROK's alone were not yet strong enough to drive the Chinese Reds out of Korea, he declared on Dec. 2 that if any peace plan that divided North and South Korea were accepted by the United Nations, South Korea would have to stand alone against the Chinese invader.

"The Korean people want to live united, or die," he said, and scoffed at what he considered overrated reports of the Chinese "volunteers'" battle efficiency. He was confident the enemy would collapse like a house of cards if only the U.N. forces would take the offensive by establishing beachheads in North Korea behind the present battle fronts.

His aggressive views were both applauded and denounced abroad.

G.I.'S CONTRIBUTED thousands of dollars for Korean war orphans. Two half-starved children (left) wander around Seoul streets; (above) youngster seeks warmth from paper banner

Akihito, 18, is Crown Prince heir to throne

Emperor Hirohito

JAPAN

THERE WAS LITTLE TO MARK THE HISTORIC occasion on April 28, 1952, when the treaty of peace with Japan took effect and the Japanese people regained their political independence. Emperor Hirohito penned a poem, Premier Shigeru Yoshida and his cabinet toasted the future, and the Japanese flag was raised on all public buildings—including the Dai Ichi skyscraper which, for seven years, had been the headquarters of the Supreme Command Allied Powers (S.C.A.P.).

With the peace treaty, the Japanese signed a security treaty with the U.S. which provided for the retention of American troops and military bases in Japan.

These peace and security treaties were denounced by the Soviet Union as "illegal". So far as Russia and Red China

were concerned, they were still technically at war with Japan.

A Communist-led May Day celebration in Tokyo exploded into an anti-American demonstration which left two Japanese dead and scores of persons, including several Americans, injured. U.S. troops looked on helplessly. Rioters stoned American military establishments, set fire to American-owned automobiles, and shouted "Go home, damn Yankees!"

In the months that followed, a growing antiforeign feeling seemed apparent. Not only was every little incident involving American military personnel magnified— even such "crimes" as jostling and barbrawling—but the press began to play up what it termed an "American crime wave" in Japan.

But most Japanese and Americans continued to live together on terms of easy friendship arrived at under the Occupation. To foster better relations with the Japanese, now that Allied troops were "guests" in the country, the U.S. Army abandoned its Dai Ichi headquarters for more modest accommodations in the suburbs. Army sedans were painted black instead of olive drab and military personnel were encouraged to wear civilian clothes when off duty.

The year was marked also by the coming of age of 18-year-old Crown Prince Akihito and his formal investiture as heir apparent to the throne—the oldest continuously occupied throne on earth. In November, he closed a week of celebrations with a speech before 75,000 cheering Japanese. The reception accorded him dramatized, as nothing else since the end of World War II, the deep-rooted place occupied by the imperial family in the hearts of the Japanese.

As he stepped from his black sedan, with the gold chrysanthemum insignia of Imperial Japan embossed on its door, he was greeted with a roar of applause. Wearing a morning coat and striped gray trousers, Akihito walked to the podium erected on the upper level of the bridge leading into the palace grounds.

Almost the entire front section was reserved for schoolgirls wearing the familiar navy-blue middy-blouse uniforms. The prince is the idol of Japanese bobby-soxers and at one point police reserves were called to hold back the squealing teenagers straining at the rope barriers.

Without an army to defend itself against possible Communist invasion, Japan remained dependent upon U.S. gar-

YANKEE, GO HOME! Disciplined Tokyo Reds turn May Day rally into a raging anti-American riot which left two dead, hundreds hurt, millions dismayed

G.I.'S STAY although Occupation ends. Here a lonely group whiles away time in one of the few night clubs not "off limits". Language differences are prime social barrier

THE ORIENTAL MIND runs into trouble when it tries to master the English language

risons for protection. The situation irritated ultranationalistic Japanese and afforded the Communists a fertile field for propaganda.

A more serious problem facing the new Japan was the necessity to achieve economic independence. A nation that had staked its all on a war intended to guarantee sources of food and raw materials, together with monopolistic control of markets for its overpopulated islands, it now found itself even more dependent upon the world outside.

Historically, Japan's principal potential for self-sufficiency has been trade with her Asian neighbors, of which China was most important. But as long as the U.N. was at war with Red Chinese forces, the Japanese were forced to seek elsewhere. Although Japan did find new avenues for commercial development, it ended 1952 with a trade deficit of over $8 billion.

Indirectly, the Korean war served to ease what might have been even more serious economic problems. In addition

NOT ALL ARE LONELY: The geisha girl is
trained to charm, as this corporal discovers

private Western capital helped Japan
develop a healthier foreign trade.

Japan's race for economic self-sufficiency was desperate. The pressure of a
steadily increasing population demanded
increasing food imports which could be
paid for only with exported manufactured goods. If the one could not keep
pace with the other, an economic conflict seemed inevitable.

The alternative was a reduction in the
standard of living which might weaken
resistance to Communism. The Western
world had too much at stake in Asia to
permit this. That realization, perhaps, explained its unusual confidence in Japan
as a financial investment.

to the $2 billion poured into Japan since
the beginning of the Occupation, the U.S.
spent millions for "special procurement
orders" for the Korean war.

In 1952, the mainstay in Japan's shaky
economy was the production of goods
for the U.N. forces in Korea. Meanwhile,

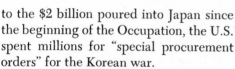

DOMESTICITY CLAIMS MANY. Some of
them marry; some do not. With men at war, heart-
break awaits many Japanese-American families

FREE CHINA SYMBOL: Controversial Chiang Kai-shek rules the island of Formosa, lays plans to regain mainland lost to Reds

CHIANG'S SON, Gen. Wei-kuo, sends tanks into practice action

FORMOSA

THERE SEEMED LITTLE DOUBT, AT THE END of 1952—if the Korean war should end without settlement of problems involving Formosa—that the Chinese Communists would launch an invasion across Formosa Strait. The Reds had built strings of air bases along the mainland coast opposite Formosa. These were backed up by a vast network of airfields—constructed by the U. S. Air Force during World War II—which could be speedily activated.

The U. S. Seventh Fleet, patrolling Formosa Strait, could do little to stop the Reds' new jet-propelled air force. Nationalist pilots, with obsolete World War II planes, could do even less against the Soviet-built MIG's.

A Red airborne invasion would be met by Nationalist forces numbering about 650,000 men, of whom only 370,000 men could be classed as operational ground forces. Of these, less than 120,000 were combat-worthy troops equipped with weapons matching those of the Chinese Communists. This army was commanded by 1600 generals, 2 of whom were the sons of Generalissimo Chiang Kai-shek (*jeh-ahng' ki'-shek'*) himself.

Forty-two-year-old Lieutenant General Chiang Ching-kuo (*jing-gwoh'*) commands the army's corps of political officers. The generalissimo's elder son by his first wife, he has spent a third of his life in the Soviet Union. He was 14 when he quarreled with his anti-Communist father and fled to Moscow. For the next thirteen years he lost no opportunity to criticize the generalissimo's pre-World War II campaigns against the Chinese Reds. Meanwhile, young Chiang worked his way up to manager of a Moscow factory, married a Russian girl, and took an

MORE GUNS, more planes, more tanks, China's Nationalists beg of the U.S. While Washington debates, this gunner guards skies against raids by Red Chinese

active interest in Soviet political affairs.

The Russians liked young Chiang and were grooming him for big things when Japan attacked China in 1937. With his homeland at war, blood proved thicker than politics and Chiang Ching-kuo returned to China with his Russian wife and infant son.

The generalissimo's second son, Major General Chiang Wei-kuo (*way-gwoh'*), is presently in command of the armored corps on Formosa.

The armored corps had approximately 1000 old tanks with few spare parts and less gasoline to run them. The air corps had about 500 propeller-driven planes, less than one third of them able to get off the ground at any one time. The navy had a 1400-ton-destroyer, 6 tiny destroyer escorts, a converted Japanese merchant ship, and some minesweepers and landing craft—a total of 80 vessels— with 125 admirals to command them. But by the end of 1952, a flow of more modern equipment had already begun from the U.S.

A U.S. Military Assistance Advisory Group (M.A.A.G.) had been functioning on the island officially since May 1, 1951. M.A.A.G. was not concerned with possible use of Nationalist troops outside Formosa. Its sole duty was to reorganize and rehabilitate the Nationalist military establishment for the defense of Formosa. Its personnel operated as advisers; they screened Chinese requests for military equipment and demonstrated its use and maintenance when received.

While Nationalist leaders expressed their gratitude for this aid, they believed the U.S. sent the weapons only because it was in America's interest to aid Formosa's anti-Communists.

Formosa was not high on the U.S. priority list for military build-ups abroad. In Asia, Korea came first. Indochina and Malaya followed because of the "hot wars" being fought against Communism there. Formosa was envisioned principally as a defensive base, not as a base for aggressive operations, except perhaps for sporadic commando raids.

While observers were divided as to whether Chiang Kai-shek could muster enough popular as well as military support to lead a crusade for the reconquest of Red-held China, most were willing to concede that at the very least he served as a symbol of militant anti-Communism in Asia.

The most notable achievement on Formosa in 1952 was the increase in rice production. In an area not much larger than Maryland, the semitropical island grew enough rice to feed its own seven million Formosans, as well as two million Nationalist refugees from the mainland, with enough surplus to export to Japan.

Bumper harvests were attributed largely to an enlightened Nationalist policy of land reform divided into three stages. First, all rents were reduced from 50 percent to 37.5 percent of the tenant farmer's cash crop. This reform immediately brought a measure of prosperity to Formosans. The second stage called for the sale of vast public lands once owned by the Japanese who had occupied Formosa since their war with China in 1895. The third stage, slated to begin on Jan. 1, 1953, was designed to cut up large landholdings into 5-acre plots, with only one such plot permitted to a single family.

The entire program was intended as an answer to the Communists' land-reform program on the mainland. The difference was that the big landowner's estate was not confiscated outright; the government would pay for what was taken. Although belated, it was now the national government's avowed purpose to fulfill the admonition of Sun Yat-sen, the "George Washington" of China, that the "land must belong to the tiller".

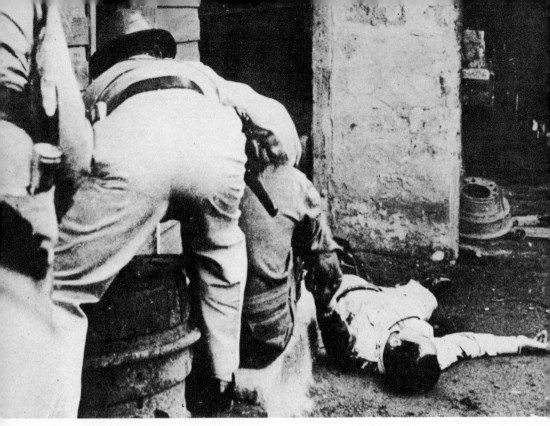

FIGHTING HUKS was costly business, as these Filipino policemen learned. But the problem of the Red-incited, land-hungry guerrillas dwindled in 1952

PHILIPPINES

ABSENTEE LANDLORDISM HAD LONG BEEN the curse of Asia. According to 1952 official reports, 35 percent of all Filipino farms were operated by tenants. While the percentage was not as high as it had been in China, it was still sufficient for the Communist-directed Hukbalahaps to base and maintain a bloody revolt against the Philippine government. In Pampanga Province, headquarters of the

Huks, 98 percent of the land was owned (on the record, that is) by barely 2 percent of the people—absentee landlords with palatial residences in big provincial towns, few of whom had ever seen their estates. In addition, thousands of smaller estates were likewise owned by absentee landlords who received up to 30 percent of the harvest from sharecroppers.

One of the first steps taken by Ramon

Magsaysay (*mag-sigh'-sigh*), when President Quirino (*kee-ree'-no*) appointed him secretary of national defense in 1950, was to order a court-martial for any soldier or constable who accepted a bribe from a landlord to deny a tenant farmer his legal rights. It was a dramatic gesture calculated to prove to an oppressed peasantry, highly susceptible to Communist propaganda, that it could expect justice.

In an unprecedented move, Magsaysay ordered the judge advocate's department of the army to defend any tenant against an eviction order demanded by a greedy landlord. When army lawyers lost their cases in the local courts, they were directed to take them to the nation's supreme court.

Those, and other progressive measures for land reforms, initiated by hard-hitting Magsaysay, a dedicated anti-Communist, had done much to undermine the once-powerful Huks. In 1950, the Huks numbered at least 20,000 well-armed and disciplined partisans openly supported by more than 2,000,000 Filipinos. By late 1952, defections from their ranks had reduced them to a hard core of 5000 Communist diehards based deep in the hills.

Early in 1952, Magsaysay persuaded the government to give increased attention to Huks who surrendered and forswore allegiance to the Communists. Some were given vocational training; others were encouraged to become small merchants and businessmen. Those with farm skills were given grants of land in large resettlement projects in northern Mindanao. These were ambitious undertakings, planned on a long-range basis.

By late 1952, however, only a bare fraction of the 1,500,000 impoverished Filipino families had been resettled. Moreover, the projects themselves were clouded with corruption and abuse by greedy administrators, as well as by speculators and loan sharks who preyed upon the settlers. As the muddle grew to a scandal, the government moved in, and Magsaysay promised a thorough cleanup.

DEFENSE MINISTER Magsaysay tells captured American Huk, William Pomeroy, of reforms

REBELLION CHARGE awaits Huk propagandist Pomeroy, bidding wife good-by. Both got life

HER MAN IS AWAY fighting the French in what his Red leaders call a war against hunger. She is left to fend alone and face the questions of Vietnam troops

Indochina and Malaya

HANOI, THE CAPITAL CITY, SYMBOLIZED beleaguered Indochina in 1952.

The battle front was less than 20 miles north of the city; yet Hanoi was doing business as usual. There were no barricades, no pillboxes, no barbed wire—as if retreat from the fighting lines were unthinkable.

Shoppers thronged the streets in the morning, but at noon all doors closed while the city took its customary siesta. Late in the afternoon, the sidewalk cafés filled with Frenchmen and their ladies while string trios played soft music as a backdrop to the latest gossip. The war was a million miles away.

At least it seemed so. But when the sun set, scattered rifle shots punctuated the night. Periodically, the distant thunder of artillery rumbled in on a tropical breeze. There was no curfew, but it was safer to stay indoors, except in the brightly lighted downtown section where there was music and laughter. Cabarets bulged with Foreign Legionnaires whooping it up on an overnight pass from the front lines. Taxi-dancers—doll-sized Annamites, Chinese, Thais—giggled as they tried to keep up with their partners.

Out from Hanoi, blockhouses and fortresses segmented the highway. They looked exactly like sets in a Beau Geste movie, except that instead of standing in the midst of a vast desert landscape, they were surrounded by rice paddies, orchards, bamboo groves, and sometimes the jungle itself—surroundings which came alive with guerrillas after dark.

Constructed largely of mud and bricks, they had proved reasonably adequate for defense against small-arms fire. The Communist-led Vietminh (*vee-ut-min'*) rebels, however, had begun to attack them with homemade bazookas. A well-fired projectile cut through the mud and brick like a hot poker through butter. The French were becoming worried.

Most of the blockhouses were encircled with head-high fences made of sharpened bamboo staves. Tin cans were strung along the inside to warn the defenders if the fences were disturbed during the night. They looked fearsome and formidable. But the bamboo was sun-dried and a flaming arrow from the darkness was enough to make a torch of the whole structure.

"We have no alternative," shrugged a lieutenant. "Those bamboo fences are indeed primitive, but they must do until we receive barbed wire along with the artillery, tanks, and planes we have been promised by the Americans."

The first shipments of this military aid arrived in 1951. In 1952 it began assuming sizable proportions. By the end of the year, the United States was shouldering almost one half of the cost of military operations in Indochina.

The year's most significant development affecting Indochina was the North Atlantic Council's mid-December ruling that the French defense effort in the Far East deserved "continuing support" from France's Western allies.

It was the first successful attempt to establish a direct relationship between the European nations in the North Atlantic Treaty Organization and Communist aggression in Asia.

Specifically, it recognized that France's contribution of arms and men to Europe's defense was determined largely by her military commitments in Asia. For as long as France had to spend a billion dollars a year on her Far Eastern campaign, while losing about one half of each year's officer graduates from St. Cyr (the French "West Point") in the fighting, the war in Indochina would be a matter of concern to France's Western allies.

The N.A.T.O. Council recognized, too, that should Communist aggression not be stopped in Indochina, it would not only immensely damage French prestige but would spread to Thailand and Burma. These three nations constituted Asia's greatest sources of rice export. Their control by the totalitarian world would give the Communists possession of one of the most powerful of all weapons—hunger. And, if the Communist tide continued southward to engulf Malaya and Indonesia, Southeast Asia's fabulous sources of rubber, tin, oil, and other vital raw materials would fall to the Soviet bloc.

Militarily, 1952 was high-lighted by two major actions. In February, Hoabinh (*hoh-bin'*), a strategic communications center 40 air miles from the northern

make the Nasan siege so costly for the Vietminhs that it would fail and the garrison could then take the offensive.

A dusty airstrip within Nasan's defense perimeter was the only contact with the outside world. A steady stream of aircraft began pouring men and supplies into Nasan. The Vietminhs attacked repeatedly and each time were thrown back with losses. Newly arrived light bombers surprised the enemy with rocket fire and jellied gasoline.

On Christmas Eve, the French broke out a force of 5000 men from Nasan to link up with Vietnamese paratroopers dropped behind the Vietminhs. The enemy, however, decided it had had enough and withdrew before the battle was joined.

The battle for Nasan uncovered a sinister development in international Communism's plans for conquest of all Asia. Among weapons and supplies left behind by the retreating Vietminhs were 25 tons of Russian-made mortar shells and four Russian Molotova trucks. The presence of those heavy trucks meant that Vietminh forces in Indochina had a direct rail link with Red China and the U.S.S.R.

In October, 1951, the Chinese completed the final section of the railway from Yungning in southern China to Chennankuan on the border of Indochina. Here the railway linked with the French-built rail system in Indochina, the northern sections of which were controlled by the Vietminhs. The Russian-made trucks captured at Nasan proved that the 7000-mile rail link from Indochina to Moscow was now operating—a grave danger for all Southeast Asia.

Malaya

IN LATE 1952, FOR THE FIRST TIME IN MORE than four years of grim war in Malaya, the initiative seemed to have passed from the Communists to the British. Monthly

MALAY ABORIGINE meets High Commissioner Templer, who's lots tougher than parasol indicates

capital, Hanoi, was evacuated by 22,000 French and Vietnamese (*vee-ut'-nahm-eez'*) troops in the face of heavy Vietminh pressure. Officially, it was described as a "tactical maneuver" to strengthen the defense of rich farm lands in the Red River valley, "bread-basket" for the northern half of Indochina. Actually, it was a resounding defeat for the French and Vietnamese.

In November, the Communist-led Vietminhs struck again in force at Nasan, an isolated mountain bastion 110 air miles northwest of Hanoi.

Completely surrounded by enemy troops in enemy territory, full evacuation in face of overwhelming odds was impossible. The French command decided to

MOSCOW-TRAINED Ho Chi Minh runs campaign to oust French and open Southeast Asia to Reds

FRENCH HOPES center on ex-emperor Bao Dai, who heads Vietnam. Rebels call him U.S. puppet

casualties among the Reds rose to an average of 150, more and more Communist leaders were coming out of the jungles to surrender, and a "whispering" campaign was proving eminently successful.

The authorities attached much importance to these "whispers". The posting of high rewards for secret information leading to the arrest or death of Communist guerrillas was paying off. A considerable number of key Communists had been ambushed and killed as a result of intelligence supplied by unnamed informers.

From the time General Sir Gerald Templer arrived in February to assume the post of high commissioner, British forces gained ground against Communist terrorists.

Where the promise of generous rewards did not bring desired results, General Templer resorted to a harsh policy of collective punishment. When the people of Tanjong Malim, a haven for underground Communists, refused to

divulge the identity of terrorists in their midst, the high commissioner ordered the entire population of 20,000 people confined to their homes with only two hours allowed them daily to buy a reduced ration of rice.

Four days later, the names of twenty-eight Communists, among them several prosperous shopkeepers, were turned over to the British.

When a town was suspected of supplying food to the jungle-based Communists nearby, troops were ordered to throw a cordon around it. Such a blockade was imposed on the city of Seremban in August. Seremban is the capital of the Malay State of Negri Sembilan, and is an important commercial center with a population of over 36,000. For several weeks, every person and vehicle moving in and out of the city was carefully screened, while a barbed-wire fence was built around the area to facilitate the quarantine.

To further deny the Communists

sources of food, the government undertook a vast program for resettling small farmers living in or near the jungles. Willingly or not, these had provided sources of food for Red guerrillas. By the end of 1952, about a half million of these farmers were resettled in five hundred wire-enclosed villages, closely supervised by government officials.

Meanwhile, General Templer asked London for helicopters to wage a form of chemical warfare against the Communists. The helicopters sprayed plant-killing chemicals on inaccessible jungle garden plots where harassed Communists had begun to grow their own food. More chemicals were sprayed on strips of jungle flanking the roadways to destroy natural cover favoring Communist ambuscades. "Operation Starvation" appeared to have won a major victory over the Reds by the end of the year.

Officially, there are no Communists in Malaya. Contemptuous reference is made only to "bandits" or "terrorists"—despite the fact that Red regulars distribute unmistakable Communist propaganda decorated with the sickle-and-hammer insignia, and call themselves the "Malayan People's Liberation Army".

To suppress this "banditry", the British government has been forced to commit thousands of troops, squadrons of bombers, and a fleet of warcraft to maintain a tight coastal patrol. And yet, after more than four years of full-scale military operations, frustrated authorities admitted at the close of 1952 that "banditry" in Malaya was still far from being liquidated.

The Chinese comprise about 38 percent of Malaya's 5,400,000 population. Communist strength in Malaya is composed of about 5000 well-armed, well-disciplined regulars, about 95 percent of them Chinese. They are backed by an estimated half million civilian sympathizers, and the *min yuen*, or "people's militia", also largely Chinese.

Their campaign is directed by the Central Executive Committee of the Malayan Communist Party, headed by a slim, British-educated Chinese named Chin Peng. Chin Peng won a high British decoration for his leadership of a guerrilla movement against the Japanese who occupied Malaya during World War II. He was further honored with a prominent place in London's Victory Parade.

When the British reoccupied Malaya after the Japanese surrender, Chin Peng co-operated with them for a time, but rough treatment at the hands of shortsighted officials culminated in his flight to the jungles in June, 1948. From there, he proclaimed his determination to drive the British out of Malaya.

FAR FROM PARIS, a lonely soldier, alert for guerillas, cools his heels in a rice-paddy ditch

The over-all strategy of the Reds is clear. It is to force the British to fight on the Communists' terms. In essence, it is a deadly game of hide-and-seek in the jungles, where snakes, leeches, and poisonous insects add to the dangers from Communist mines, bullets, and grenades.

Except for the regulars who rarely leave their jungle bases, the Reds operate in small units. Often they are composed of no more than a dozen men who emerge for a swift strike and dash back to the jungle for cover.

The British, then, are obliged to split their forces into thousands of small patrols who trek more or less haphazardly through the jungle underbrush. Their only hope of contacting the elusive Communists is to come upon a fresh trail or to be fired upon from ambush.

The troopers call it "Operation Decoy".

Sept. 15, 1952, ushered in a new era for Malaya. A law, effective on that date, provided full Malayan citizenship to approximately 1,100,000 Chinese and 180,000 Indians, who previously had enjoyed no political status in the Malayan Federation. Indeed, before then there had been no such thing as citizenship for any resident of Malaya.

The new law confirmed, for the first time, the existence of a common nationality for all Malayans, and marked a long step toward the creation of a national unity for the multiracial peoples in the Federation. It could be expected to have far-reaching effects on the struggle against Communism in Southeast Asia.

As 1952 ended, two ominous situations confronted the West. The first was the stalemate in Korea, where truce negotiations were stranded high and dry. Neither side was willing to give an inch, and the United Nations were about convinced that the Communists did not really want a truce in Korea, and never had.

The second was the growing crisis in Southeast Asia, and the fear that the Chinese Communists were getting ready to divert their hot war from Korea to Indochina. According to reliable reports, the Reds were already massing vast numbers of troops in southern China, which borders on Indochina.

The problem of dealing with these dilemmas was complicated by considerable difference of opinion among the Allies. Britain was convinced that should the U.N. expand its military operations and begin bombing Manchuria and key centers in China, the Chinese Reds would retaliate with an attack on British Hong Kong. The French, on the other hand, feared that a settlement in Korea would free the Reds to launch a full-scale invasion of French-held Indochina.

There was, however, general agreement on an over-all policy which aimed at the following objectives:

1. To make a continuation of military aggression in Korea and elsewhere in Asia so unprofitable for the Reds that they would sooner or later be forced to make peace.

2. To create conditions whereby the mainland Chinese could be weaned away from Soviet Russia's influence. If wishing could make it so, this situation might be realized through a sharp Tito-like break between Mao Tse-tung and the Kremlin. The hard way would be to increase military, economic, and political pressure to the point where a breakdown of the Red regime in Peking might open the way to a non-Communist Chinese government.

Whatever course of action might be decided upon for 1953, it was clear that a general peace in Asia was not in the immediate offing.

THE DIRTY WAR, French soldiers call it bitterly. They, with their native allies, flush Red snipers from the jungle, lie on guard in paddy fields, or dig the foe from well-hidden foxholes

Arts, Sciences, and Entertainment

OPERATING ROOM in new Paris Hospital has domed ceiling ablaze with spotlights

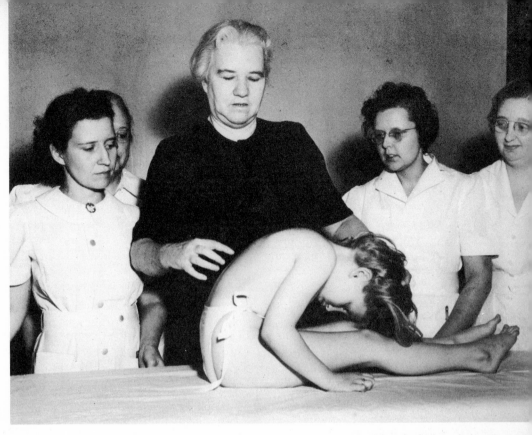

SISTER ELIZABETH KENNY, Australian nurse whose heat and physical therapy treatment for polio victims proved controversial issue among doctors, died in 1952

SCIENCE

THE AVERAGE TAXPAYER CONTRIBUTED ALmost $100 to the Federal government's $6 billion science budget in 1952.

As in previous years, the biggest share of this immense hoard went to the Atomic Energy Commission. Bigger and better weapons were still main goals of the A.E.C. During the year something akin to the first hydrogen bomb was set off at Eniwetok atoll in the Pacific. Tactical-size atom bombs, smaller than any previous atomic explosives, blasted the desert flats in Nevada. And military men smiled grimly when they talked of an atomic cannon shell in the final stages of development.

At Groton, Conn., the keel of the first atomic submarine took shape on the ways of the Electric Boat Company. Power for this craft would come from an engine being designed at Schenectady, N.Y., by the General Electric Company. Another nuclear naval engine was being readied by the Westinghouse Electric Corporation at A.E.C.'s Arco, Idaho, laboratory. And atomic scientists were confident they could build an atomic airplane engine within a few years.

Although most A.E.C. dollars were earmarked for defense, 1952 was the first year the average man could see tangible evidence of atomic power that might light his streets and warm his home.

At Arco, physicists and engineers achieved the first "breeder" atomic pile. While "burning" its uranium fuel, this furnace creates an even greater amount of another fissionable element, plutonium. This fantastic economy is like that of an imaginary coal furnace which would burn a pound of coal and simultaneously manufacture two additional pounds from thin air. On a large scale, the breeder pile would mean cheap electricity for everyone.

Success at Arco was not merely theoretical. The engineers harnessed 100 kilowatts of their power to operate pumps and light their laboratory building.

For the first time, private enterprise began to shoulder into the atomic-power field. A new firm, Walter Kidde Nuclear Laboratories, Inc., went into business for the express purpose of designing atomic-generator plants for anyone who wants one.

The slender, scholarly vice-president of the new firm was Dr. Karl Paley Cohen, a 39-year-old veteran of wartime atomic-physics research. There was nothing new, he admitted, in the idea that the atom would furnish light, heat, and power in the future. "The new element is that this future is now so close that it is time to prepare for it."

Whoppers The atom had no monopoly on scientific bigness. At Brookhaven National Laboratory, on Long Island, an atom smasher called the cosmotron generated 2,200,000,000 volts for a few hectic moments. Physicists at Brookhaven were not yet satisfied. They had a scheme for raising an atom smasher's output to 100,-000,000,000 volts. But first they planned to build a smaller, 30,000,000,000-volt model. Theoretical reasoning told them that this machine would be amply powerful to create matter from energy.

Easily the biggest scientific word of the year was the name of a new synthetic chemical called, to the despair of typesetters, 2-methylcarboxymercaptobenzothiazole. Researchers at the Connecticut Agricultural Experiment Station had hope that it would quell the Dutch elm disease fungus which has withered fine elm trees all over America.

At least one scientist came into big money. The British government rewarded its roly-poly radar genius Sir Robert Watson-Watt with $140,000 for his wartime inventions. Since the grant was tax-free, it was equivalent to an award of more than 5,000,000 taxable dollars.

Robot Brains Electronic brains were getting faster, more compact, more numerous. One of the newest and most remarkable was a black box no larger than a portable typewriter. It was conceived to solve the dilemma of the jet fighter pilot, who resembles a trapshooter asked to bang away at clay pigeons from the hip and on the dead run. As one Korea veteran put it: when two planes close head-on, "there is no time for anything but split-second jockeying to avoid collision".

With the little black box stowed in his cockpit, all a fighter pilot has to do is maneuver so as to center the enemy plane on his radar screen. Thereupon, his rockets fire automatically.

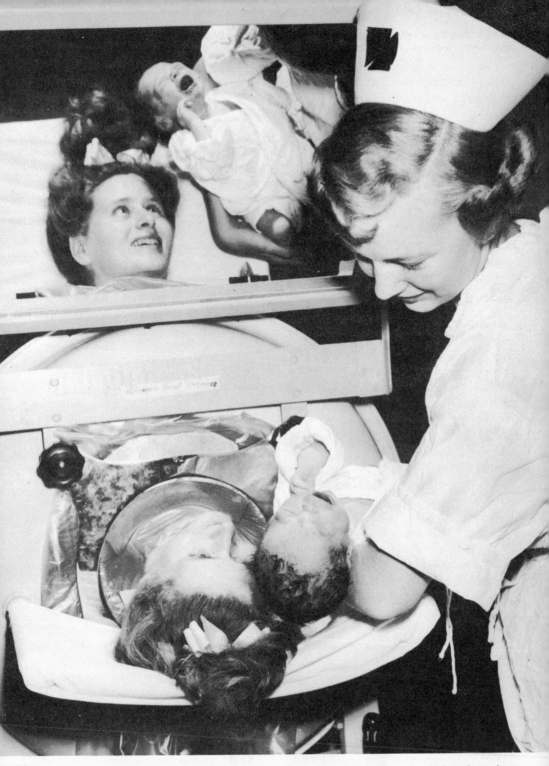

POLIO PATIENT Mrs. Elizabeth Seymour, in iron lung, listens happily to lusty howling of newborn son, Gary. Infant was born in polio ward of Los Angeles hospital

SHEEP'S-EYE VIEW: The eye of a freshly slaughtered sheep was "camera" used to take this portrait, producing animal's view of human face

While he is flying, the electronic brain in the box continually reckons on the aerial acrobatics of the enemy. Silently and rapidly, it also notes more than half a dozen aim-influencing factors. Among the most important are the burning of fuel, which continually lightens the plane; disposal of ammunition; shifting of weight when the rocket tubes reload themselves; and the initial recoil when a rocket is fired.

Even with this auxiliary brain, the fighter pilot is scarcely as secure as a

hunter shooting at sitting ducks. But at least his aim can be as sure as that of a trapshooter standing on solid ground.

On election night, several million television watchers got their first peak at another robot brain in action. By 10:30 (E.S.T.) that evening, political experts were almost unanimously convinced that Eisenhower had been elected. One dissident voice came from a $600,000 room-size calculator named Univac (Universal Automatic Computer), which had made the mistake of being too right much too early.

For six weeks Univac had been in training for its appearance on the C.B.S. network. Its handlers, Remington Rand scientists, had stuffed its magnetic memory with thousands of figures, representing State-by-State returns and trends of the 1944 and 1948 Presidential races. The machine was supposed to spot trends in the 1952 returns by comparing the frag-

EX-G.I. George Jorgensen voluntarily submitted to surgery, hormone injections by Danish doctors, became an attractive female. New name: Christine

mentary results with similar stages of previous elections.

At 9 o'clock, with only 3,400,000 votes reported and the polls still open in some western States, Univac made its first prediction: Eisenhower was a shoo-in. He would receive a total 33,000,000 popular votes, winning 43 States with 438 electoral votes.

When Univac's electric typewriter clattered out this sober estimate—in error, it turned out, by only 4 electoral votes—its human seconds recoiled. Such a landslide might occur, but they refused to believe the machine could detect it so soon.

Hastily they postponed Univac's first scheduled television appearance. By altering one mathematical factor, they purposely reduced Univac's self-confidence. Then they instructed the machine to try again.

This time Univac came up with a more reasonable prediction, which was announced to a nationwide audience at 10 o'clock E.S.T.: Eisenhower winning 28 States and 317 electoral votes.

Still hedging, the scientists further modified the vital factor, so that at 10:30 Univac proclaimed coast-to-coast that the election was virtually a tossup. Not until

TWELVE-HOUR MARATHON OF SURGERY was waged in a Rock Island, Ill., hospital by specialists attempting to separate 15-month-old Brodie Siamese twins, joined at skulls

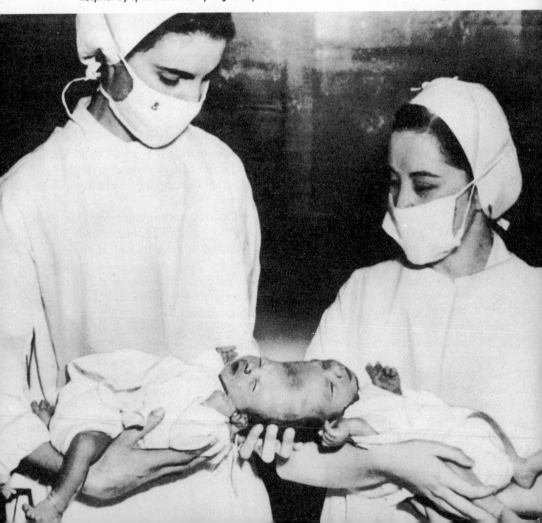

its 11:10 appearance did the bedeviled brain shake off human interference and quote plausible odds of more than 100 to 1 in Eisenhower's favor.

Lamented Arthur Draper, Univac's chief handler: "We went out on a limb and tried to do the most comprehensive mathematical statistical job ever done. The story was in, and we like a bunch of dopes didn't believe it."

C.B.S. commentator Edward R. Murrow offered a simpler explanation: "The trouble with machines is people."

Meanwhile, another robot brain was enjoying triumph on N.B.C. The Monroe Calculating Machine Company's desk-size Monrobot simply tried to do what every human expert does, namely, follow the obvious election trends. Its manager, William Burkhart, told it to assume that "the most you can say about the past [election history] is it's crazy". The Monrobot figured the trends perfectly at every stage. Modest in victory, Burkhart demurred: "The stupider a machine was, the better it could do in this election."

Transistor's Day   Electronics in all its applications began to take on a new look as the transistor came of age. The transistor looks like a primitive radio detector, with a grayish crystal tickled by cat's-whisker wires. Actually, the transistor can take the place of many vacuum tubes. Thanks to the strange electrical properties of its lump of semimetallic germanium, it can change alternating current to direct current and amplify faint, fluctuating signals.

In many ways the transistor is a vast improvement over any vacuum tube. It is no bigger than a thumbnail, rugged in contrast to fragile tubes, and capable of working on tiny amounts of energy.

When Bell Telephone Laboratories scientists invented the transistor in 1948, they predicted its future greatness. Not until 1952, however, was the first transistor product on the market: a hearing aid much smaller than any ever constructed with tubes. Because transistors use so little power, the gadget operated for months on batteries the size of a dime.

The Radio Corporation of America, which had obtained licenses from Bell Labs, exhibited a startling array of experimental transistor machines, all powered by batteries the diameter of a quarter.

One was a portable television receiver, smaller than a standard typewriter and tubeless except for the picture tube. Another was an eight-key toy piano about the size of a child's pencil box, which broadcast eerie notes through a radio loud-speaker. Transistors reduced a phonograph (not including speaker) to less than the size of a cigarette pack. An electronic calculating machine with sixty-six transistors could count to a million in a second. A public-address system with six transistors and a 12-inch speaker was light enough to be carried in one hand.

Out of This World   Real rocket enthusiasts are certain they could build a rocket that would fly to the moon, if they only had the money. But could a passenger survive the ride?

A partial answer came from the rocket proving grounds at White Sands, N.Mex. Three white mice took off in the noses of rockets. Television cameras installed in the pressurized "cabins" watched their reactions as they soared into the upper atmosphere.

When the rockets reached their zeniths, flipped over, and plunged downward through the thin air, the mice became essentially weightless. Experiencing to an exaggerated degree the feeling of descending in a fast elevator, two of the mice thrashed in panic until the rockets hit thicker air and stopped accelerating. The other mouse had had part of the balancing mechanism of his inner ear previously destroyed. Having no sense of equilibrium, he curled up contentedly throughout the flight.

Five monkeys, who similarly took rocket trips, were not so lucky. They were doped with morphine and rested comfortably on sponge-rubber mattresses, while instruments radioed back to earth the changes in their blood circulation and breathing. Apparently the trip caused no ill effects, but all the landings were fatal. Four of the monkey-carrying rockets crashed when their parachutes failed to snap open. The fifth got down safely enough, but the monkey died of heat prostration in the desert.

Other notable space travelers, the flying saucers, got rough treatment from scientists in 1952. People continued to report strange things flitting across the sky.

An air-line pilot spotted a green, tear-shaped glow "going like a bat out of hell" over Indiana. At the atomic laboratory at Los Alamos, N.Mex., observers watched an "apparently metallic" object gyrate on high for half an hour. In Chenango County, N.Y., crowds gathered to watch

ULTRAVIOLET LAMPS sterilize air as "wonder drugs" go into mass production. Operators wear surgical garb; human hands never touch product

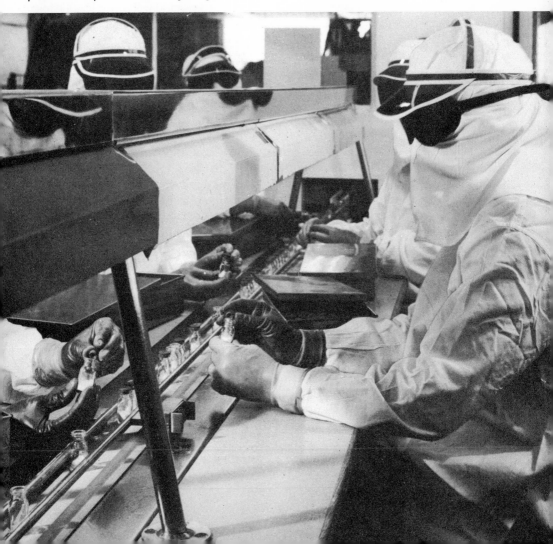

"a whole flotilla of shiny balls". The crew of a Canadian destroyer in Korean waters spotted two shiny disks aloft and picked them up on their radar screen.

Still, scientists remained skeptical about talk of visitors from other planets. And two researchers went so far as to create laboratory illusions which might explain the saucers. Dr. Donald H. Menzel, professor of astrophysics at Harvard, pointed out that a layer of warm air sandwiched between two layers of relatively cold air would act as a mirror. Thus, automobile lights pointed upward as a car came over a hill would be reflected toward earth and would look like gleaming metallic disks. The same sort of freak air layer could create bogus images of the sun during the daytime.

To clinch his theory, he set up laboratory apparatus that produced palpable flying saucers. "Certainly flying saucers are real," Menzel concluded. "And so are rainbows."

Noel W. Scott, a physicist at Fort Belvoir, Va., had a more complicated explanation. He thought that flying saucers were akin to St. Elmo's fire, the will-o'-the-wisp glow that sometimes hovers at the top of a ship's mast or the tip of an airplane's wings. By electrifying a partial vacuum inside a 3-foot-high glass bell jar, Scott created a whole fleet of flying saucers. Some were mushroom-shaped. Others formed umbrellas with conelike handles. The hues ranged from brilliant orange with a purplish exhaust to a lovely green-edged silver. And every so often a string of orange marbles would roll across the bottom of the jar.

To most people, the most heroic peek into space was the first glimpse of the planets by the world's largest telescope. The 200-inch Hale telescope on Mount Palomar had more important jobs to do, and it was not particularly well suited to studying objects close at hand. One as-

tronomer explained: "Using this instrument to observe the nearby planets is like renting a steam shovel to scoop dandruff from your collar."

Nevertheless, Palomar scientists finally gave in to public curiosity and took pictures of the earth's neighbors. The results were disappointing to the public; on Mars, not a Martian was visible.

Astronomer Willem J. Luyten of the University of Minnesota had better luck in his search for small stars, a hobby of his. He found the tiniest one on record, a white-hot blob not much bigger than the moon. But what his star lacks in size it more than makes up for in muscle. It is so dense, Luyten figured, that a cubic inch of its matter would weigh about 1000 tons. And its gravity is so strong that an average man standing on its surface would weigh as much as 75,000 elephants.

The Good Earth   Back on earth, farmers had new hope for heavy soil. The mixture of clay and silt that is sticky as glue when wet, and hard as brick when dry, had always been the agronomist's pet peeve. Then in 1952 the Monsanto Chemical Company came forth with a magic chemical named Krilium.

Charles Allen Thomas, Monsanto's president and a famous chemist, had started research on it before the war. Heavy soils can be lightened with lots of organic matter—manure, peat moss, and green plants plowed under. He tried to find out how the natural organic stuff does its work, and then to create a long-lasting synthetic chemical that would do the same trick.

Starting at $2 a pound, Krilium was the most expensive farm chemical ever marketed. But even at that price it was cheap. For tests showed that 1 pound of Krilium had the same effect as 100 to 1000 pounds of compost. And the effects of Krilium, unlike those of organic mate-

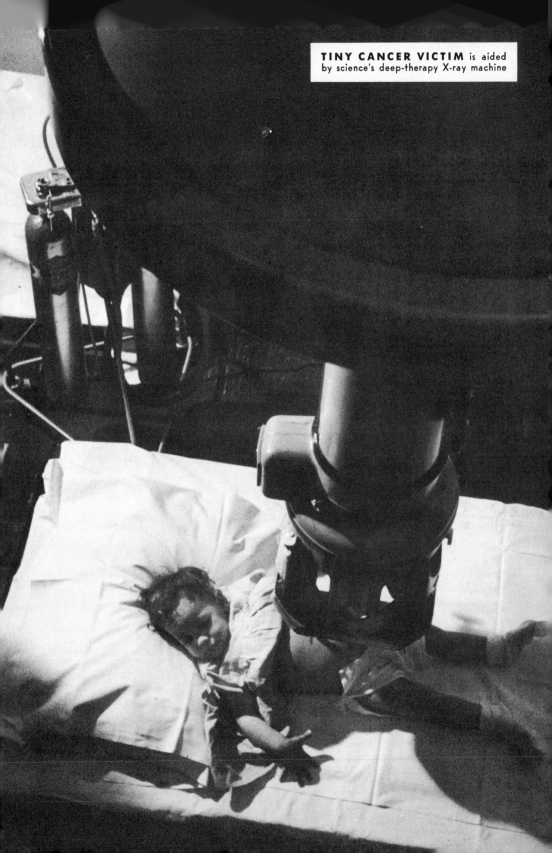

TINY CANCER VICTIM is aided by science's deep-therapy X-ray machine

rials, apparently last indefinitely. By the year's end, test plots which had been treated with the soil conditioner four years earlier were still light and loamy.

Medicine

NEVER BEFORE HAD POLIO STRUCK THE U.S. so savagely. Its victims in 1952 numbered 47,665, and many were left crippled, particularly in the Central States and along the Gulf Coast. Paradoxically, never had the outlook on polio been brighter.

Early one summer morning, more than 200 parents, mostly mothers in sun dresses, stood before the community hall in West University Place, a suburb of Houston, Texas. They shushed the tots clinging to their hands and bowed their heads as a minister prayed. As he finished, the crowd surged into the building to begin one of medical science's most dramatic mass experiments.

First in line was Patricia Ann Burnett, aged 5. "Do you know why you are here?" a radio announcer asked her. "Yes," she mumbled. Her mother elaborated: "I think the effectiveness of gamma globulin is something we should all try to find out in this emergency."

At the door Pat got a card with a number on it. Her mother signed a release, and a nurse weighed the child. Then, buttocks bared, Pat stretched out on a table. With a hypodermic syringe bearing the same number as her card, a doctor gave her a shot of a pale liquid. A lollipop soothed her injured dignity.

No one knew what had been injected into Pat's blood stream, not even the doctor. But through the hot summer months

54,772 children in Provo, Utah, Sioux City, Iowa, and Houston went through the same routine. Half received shots of harmless gelatin. The other half got gamma globulin, a refined part of human blood serum in which disease antibodies are concentrated.

Not until early winter could epidemiologists estimate whether gamma globulin had proved as effective against polio as it is against measles. Following the injections, doctors of the National Foundation for Infantile Paralysis stayed in the

UNDERWATER ATOMIC BLAST shoots millions of tons of water into the air, dwarfing ships at column's base. Bombs that leveled Hiroshima, Nagasaki are obsolete compared to present atomic weapons, but potential hydrogen bomb may have one thousand times power of modern A-bomb

test areas. Each time an injected child came down with polio, they checked its card against a master file that revealed whether that child had received gamma globulin or gelatin.

When the results had been tabulated, Dr. William McDowell Hammond, the University of Pittsburgh epidemiologist who headed the project, issued a hopeful report. Only 26 of the gamma globulin recipients contracted paralytic polio. Of those who received gelatin, 64 suffered some paralysis. It seemed to Hammond that, in most cases, gamma globulin made polio attacks milder and shorter-lived.

Gamma globulin was not the final answer to polio. One injection offers only five weeks' protection. The cost might run to $70 a summer for each child. And if the serum were administered in every county where polio raged, the drain on blood banks would be terrific. But as an emergency stopgap, gamma globulin would serve until researchers perfected one of the long-lasting vaccines that reportedly were on the way.

ARDENT COMMUNIST Frédéric Joliot-Curie, France's foremost nuclear physicist, was removed as director of French atomic-research program

Unvanquished TB

For one golden day in 1952, the world's most lethal germ disease seemed to have been conquered. The news leaked out that 92 tuberculosis patients—all advanced cases—had been cured by a new wonder drug under test at Sea View Hospital in New York. To the delight of news photographers, the supposedly cured men and women danced and cavorted in the wards.

Sound medical caution dampened the first enthusiasm. But all in all, the new drug, isonicotinic hydrazide (a chemical cousin of a B vitamin), still added up to an effective aid against TB.

Of the 92 patients, 44 had fever. In all cases, temperatures dropped to normal within two weeks. Dead appetites revived. Those who had picked at their breakfasts demanded four or five helpings of cereal. One old man started eating eleven eggs a day. All 92 put on weight, some as much as 50 pounds in three months. And many who had been bedridden got up and walked about the wards.

Promising as the new drug was, it quickly developed a weakness. TB bacilli learned to live with it, as they had learned to live with streptomycin. There was hope, however, that streptomycin and isonicotinic acid hydrazide, administered together, might prove to be the doctor's most effective weapon against TB.

Nerve Welder

The first reports of another new drug were made public in more restrained fashion. The chemical, called Pyromen, violated one of physiologists' basic beliefs: that severely damaged spinal cords never heal. At a meeting of the National Institute of Neurological Diseases and Blindness, Dr. William F. Windle, director of research of the Baxter Laboratories and visiting professor at the University of Pennsylvania, told this story of Pyromen's first triumph.

In March, 1950, Charles VanDiviere, a 19-year-old University of Georgia student, was badly hurt in an automobile wreck. Doctors who examined him found that the spinal cord in his neck was severed. If he lived, they predicted, he would be a hopeless paraplegic, unable to feel sensation from his neck down.

Charles faded fast. Within a month his weight dropped from 180 to 85 pounds. Both arms and both legs were limp, and he had no control over body functions. In desperation, his parents appealed to Baxter Laboratories, which had tested Pyromen only on dogs and cats. Forty-three days after the accident the boy began getting shots of the new chemical.

The results were startling. Within two months Charles could control his bladder and move his hands a little. By Thanksgiving Day he took his first step. In Janu-

FATHER OF THE ATOMIC ERA: Albert Einstein's theory of relativity made nuclear fission possible. One of the greatest thinkers in world's history, Einstein, now 74, is associated with Princeton's Institute for Advanced Studies

SCHOOL CHILDREN in Washington, D.C., participate in city-wide mock atomic-bomb drill. Crouching position offers best protection from flying glass

ary, 1951, he was driving a car. Last year he finished college, managing three flights of stairs with the aid of a small brace on his right leg.

Results of early Pyromen treatments were startling in other cases also. At year's end it was being tested on various kinds of paralysis at the Mayo Clinic.

Drug Drawbacks While new drugs were raising fresh hopes, some old ones showed faults.

Chloromycetin, one of the most generally useful antibiotics, turned out to be dangerous. According to the Federal Food and Drug Administration, 88 deaths are "definitely known to have been associated with the use of Chloromycetin", which sometimes prevents the bone marrow from making red and white blood cells. But after long consideration the F.D.A. decided that the drug was much too potent a killer of undulant-fever, typhoid, and tick-fever germs to be banned from prescription lists. As a compromise, the agency told the manufacturer to put on a warning label and advised doctors not to use it indiscriminately.

In Vancouver, British Columbia, a physician admitted defeat when he tried to treat a certain type of baldness with

MISSING LINK: Thought to have been extinct for 75 million years, a coelacanth showed up in fisherman's net. Scientists believe species forms link between ages of fish and land animals. Note armorlike skin on 120-lb. specimen

the hormone ACTH. He gave the drug to three patients who had lost all body hair. After three weeks, all had promising new growths. But when the treatment had to be stopped, because the patients could tolerate ACTH no longer, all the hair fell out again.

In Boston, Mass., under the sedate name "anti-fertility factor", an oral contraceptive created a front-page flurry. Its inventor, Dr. Benjamin F. Sieve, reported giving pills of "phosphorylated hesperidin" to 298 married couples, all of whom had proved their fertility by having at least one child. Over spans of three months to two and a half years, each husband and wife took three pills a day, and none of the wives became pregnant. But, Dr. Sieve reported, when 220 couples eventually stopped the dosage, all wives conceived within three months.

The future of phosphorylated hesperidin seemed unlimited. The basic chemical, hesperidin, comes from orange peel and if made in quantity should cost no more than aspirin.

Yet scientists who investigated Dr. Sieve's new wonder drug had doubts. It seemed incredible that 220 women had conceived so promptly after abandoning the pills. Dr. Sieve had no proof that his human guinea pigs had taken the pills as directed. He had only their word. And most investigators refused to believe that any man would be lucky enough to find 596 people, every one of whom would scrupulously stick to the prescribed medicine.

Medical opinion rated phosphorylated hesperidin not much higher than the vitamin treatment for gray hair which Dr. Sieve had endorsed eleven years earlier and which had since been discarded by the profession. And some doctors pointed out that more women are trying to have children than to prevent them.

More serious was a dispute over krebi-ozen, a drug supposed to fight cancer. Since 1951, Dr. Andrew C. Ivy, head of the University of Illinois medical, pharmaceutical, and dental schools, had been under fire for proclaiming krebiozen's effectiveness. The American Medical Association, the American Cancer Society, and the National Research Institute had all investigated the drug and turned thumbs down. Finally a committee of his own University of Illinois colleagues examined Dr. Ivy's case histories and announced that they could find no proof of krebiozen's worth against cancer.

So far as the university was concerned, this was the last straw. The trustees demoted Dr. Ivy to a professorship and publicly disowned any work he might "do on the outside".

Maggie's Mission A year-long survey of the nation's medical resources sputtered with argument. It started when President Truman appointed as survey director a tall, lanky Minnesota orthopedic surgeon, Paul B. Magnuson, formerly head of the Veterans Administration medical program.

"Maggie", as he is called, drew up a list of prospective commission members. Over the telephone he invited each to join him in the survey. All accepted—all except one.

Dr. Gunnar Gundersen of La Crosse, Wis., a trustee of the American Medical Association, refused and let loose a blast: "The committee is designed . . . as an instrument of practical politics to relieve President Truman from an embarrassing position as an unsuccessful advocate of compulsory health insurance. I certainly cannot subscribe to such a masquerade."

Dr. John W. Cline, president of the A.M.A. but not on Magnuson's invitation list, chimed in: ". . . another flagrant attempt to play politics with the medical welfare of the American people."

Maggie retorted hotly: "If the A.M.A. hierarchy devoted as much time to care of their patients as they do to political maneuvering, we'd all be better off."

In contrast, the survey commission's 252-page preliminary report, which grew from interrogations of 400 witnesses and countless commission meetings, was sweet as could be—on the surface.

Although it praised the A.M.A. for its "exposure of quackery", it nevertheless took several scalpellike cuts at organized medicine.

It blamed chiefly the medical profession for the fact that health insurance covers only 15 percent of the nation's medical expenses. It pointed out that the $180 million invested annually in medical research is far from adequate and is, in fact, "less than the amount spent on monuments and tombstones". It labeled the Veterans Administration medical program a "monstrosity" and suggested that the V.A. cease building so many hospitals in out-of-the-way places and caring for veterans whose ailments are not connected with military service.

Although Magnuson was definitely opposed to compulsory health insurance, the commission recommended that the Federal government set up a $750-million-a-year co-operative health plan with individual States.

Then There Were Two Like all other years, 1952 had its share of medical personalities—people who grasped for their lives while the whole world rooted for them. The plight of Rodney Dee Brodie and Roger Lee Brodie was the personal anxiety of millions.

At 15 months the Brodie twins were in the University of Illinois Hospital in Chicago awaiting an operation. They were handsome and alert little boys, with dark-blue eyes and easy grins. Their favorite game was pat-a-cake, and they could say "mama", "dada", "nite-nite", and "frog".

The Brodie twins differed from normal children in one respect: they were "Siamese", joined awkwardly at the tops of their skulls, so that their trunks and legs pointed in opposite directions. Their mother and father—a farmer from Moline who worked winters as a butcher—agreed with the doctors that the boys had to be separated by surgery. It was better to risk death than to condemn them to hideously unnatural lives.

Guided by X rays, the surgeons had severed the bony connection. There was no way of knowing how the soft tissue was connected. For the final operation, neurosurgeon Oscar Sugar enlisted a corps of fourteen assistants: four surgeons to help with the heads, two more in charge of transfusions, a pair of anesthetists, two pediatricians, and four nurses.

For nearly ten hours, this surgical team cut, retracted, stitched, and transfused Then they learned the bad news. Between them the babies had only one sagittal vein, the big channel through which blood flows from the brain back to the heart.

To which baby should they allot the vital vein? Rodney, the smaller boy, had the best chance to survive; Roger had already been in a state of shock three times. In the hope of saving at least one life, the surgeons gave the vein to Rodney.

After the tops of the skulls were sealed with plastic and aluminum foil, the babies were wheeled from the operating room in separate cribs. Father Brodie said: "It sure looks good to see them apart."

As expected, Roger died, after surviving in a coma for a month and three days. But Rodney slowly gained strength. Gradually the surgeons started closing over the roof of his skull and covering it with skin grafts. Whatever the eventual outcome, the surgeons had earned the year's most spectacular medical victory.

REVOLVING SOUP PLATE: Navy's 600-inch radio telescope is shown to group of visiting Japanese scientists. New science of radio astronomy is greatly widening man's knowledge of universe

SINGING SENSATION Johnny Ray accompanied his ballads with unrestrained emotion. Delighted audiences and record fans helped raise him from obscurity to become one of the nation's highest-paid entertainers

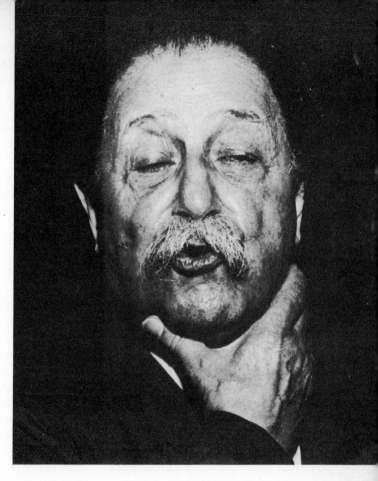

PIERRE MONTEUX was acclaimed for conducting of Stravinsky's "Rite of Spring" at International Exposition of Arts in Paris. Hooting, derision greeted his introduction of piece forty years before

Music and The Dance

AMID THE MELODIC CLATTER SET OFF IN 1952 by the millions of copies of 2868 new popular songs pressed on phonograph records by the seven major record manufacturers, one curious idea emerged.

A man from Morgan City claimed the idea as his own, but another man in Chattanooga, two elderly ladies in Dubuque, and even a few others felt possessive about it. The idea: a phonograph record which, when placed upon a revolving turntable and under a sensitized needle, would emit, throughout its full playing time, something golden called silence.

It would make, it was thought, a fine record. It would be owned and loved by thoughtful and considerate people. It would not, however, make much money.

That is unfortunate, for it is not silence but sound that is golden in the music business. At the year's end there was evidence—called profits—to show that the record manufacturers knew what they were doing. During the year, music lovers loved music enough to pay out more than two hundred million dollars for 7-, 10-, and 12-inch diameter records intended for turning at 45, 78, and 33⅓ revolutions per minute respectively. Each of these sold for at least half a dollar; a few for more than six dollars. But there seemed to be no limit to what the records might have on them.

"Lawdy, Miss Clawdy" was the reproachful title of one hit in the rhythm and blues field. The year's best-selling record among the pops was not really a song; it was a rich and supple instrumental arrangement of Leroy Anderson's "Blue Tango", during which nobody sang a syllable.

In the classical field, Sir Thomas Beecham's performance, with the Royal Philharmonic, one of London's ranking symphony orchestras, of the half-hour-long *Harold in Italy* by the emotionally overcharged 18th-century Frenchman Louis Hector Berlioz was high on the lists of favorites. But it was topped in sales by the late George Bernard Shaw's *Don Juan in Hell,* a more-than-hour-long part of a quarrelsome play read on two 12-inch LP records by Charles Laughton, Agnes Moorehead, Charles Boyer, and Sir Cedric Hardwicke, who called themselves the "First Drama Quartet". *Don Juan* was heavy on epigrams and assorted profundities but it was as short on music as "Blue Tango" was short on words.

If the "Tango" was unsingable because it had no words, a few other big song hits were unsingable despite their words. A case in point was blonde, Kentucky-born Rosemary Clooney's remotely Italian mating call, "Botch-A-Me". And two others, "Little White Cloud that Cried" and a little lament called "Cry", were songs of such abiding melancholy that the words were too much even for their singer, a cadaverous youth named Johnnie Ray.

Whenever Ray, the singer who has worn a hearing aid since childhood, when he was tumbled by some fellow Boy Scouts, went up against either the "Cloud" or "Cry" he opened at the seams and, in about mid-song, went under, wallowing in a heavy wail. Ray cried and everywhere he went his audiences cried too. It started Ray thinking: "I get a pulsation out of a responsive audience that lets me give out and makes me forget I'm in a club or theater and I sing and play like God meant me to. I guess that's why I sometimes break down. That's sincere. It's no act." The case for tears in Ray's life was made public late in the year when the young wife he acquired only some few months before took leave of him. She is the daughter of the owner of the Mocambo, a posh West-coast nitery at which Ray can hardly expect to make any more appearances with or without tears.

Both Johnnie Ray and Rosemary Clooney do their singing for Columbia Records. The man who selects the songs for Columbia to record is a huge, bearded seer named Mitchell Miller. Each Monday when he is in New York, Miller holds open house for song writers. Sometimes as many as a hundred new songs are sung or played for him before the day is over. Miller considers it time well spent if he hears even one worth putting on a record.

While the songs are being played at him, Miller fortifies himself with pastrami sandwiches, quarts of milk, and chocolate sodas, and between bites and drinks delivers pronouncements on things musical.

on records. His name was Jimmy Boyd; he was 12 years old; and his song was "I Saw Mommy Kissing Santa Claus". More than two million copies of his recording were sold before Christmas—and, as a result, probably more than two million mothers of other 12-year-olds hopefully reappraised their sons' vocal endowments.

When his "Mommy" was firmly established as a Columbia best seller, Boyd—a California seventh-grader—made his first visit to New York to run through a few non-Christmas songs and to check on his sales and fame. Admirers gave him a saddle, Columbia Records, Inc. gave him a lot of money, and Boyd headed back West.

In 1952, each of the major companies and most of the two hundred small independent companies made significant additions to the catalogue of serious music pressed on LP records. Four companies

"I don't like songs about songs and I don't like songs that tell me to blow my cares away," he told one song plugger last fall. "Ever since 'Mule Train' all I hear is gimmick songs. Last week one publisher brought in a song that got through a chase, a capture, and a kill all in 32 bars."

"Did you buy it, Mitch?" the plugger asked.

"No," Miller answered, and bit into the pastrami. "But I'm thinking of it."

Eerie and nonmusical songs were the fashion in '52. Toward the year's end an atypical singer put in a single appearance

HIGH PRIEST of popular-recording field, Columbia Records' Mitch Miller is No. 1 target of hopeful song writers trying to interest him in "sure-fire hit"

(Westminster, London, Columbia, and R.C.A.-Victor) released new recorded performances of Beethoven's *Ninth Symphony* for vocal soloists, chorus, and orchestra. The most heralded was the R.C.A.-Victor album, in which the performing artists were Eileen Farrell, Nan Merriman, Jan Peerce, Norman Scott, The Robert Shaw Chorale, the N.B.C. Symphony, and conductor Arturo Toscanini.

From music circles all over the country arose a kind of uncritical exultation over Toscanini's first recorded performance of music's most famed masterpiece. Only the conductor himself seemed able to keep calm and hear the performance for what it was worth.

"This is the closest I can get to Beethoven's *Ninth*," he told one of R.C.A.'s engineers who listened to a playback with the Maestro. "I'm almost satisfied." R.C.A.-Victor's satisfaction was no less impressive. Toscanini, like members of the U.N.'s Security Council, holds veto power over the release of his recordings. He had recorded the *Ninth* a number of times before at a fairly astronomical cost to R.C.A., but each time he found the result to be short of his standards. The cost of the orchestra, chorus, and soloists was R.C.A.'s, but the unpublishable records stayed with Toscanini each time. His approval this time was the signal for considerable rejoicing in that firm's treasurer's office.

Beethoven was also well served by other companies. During the year Columbia Records offered the complete sixteen quartets played by The Budapest String Quartet, and Decca compiled the same composer's thirty-two piano sonatas as performed by pianist Wilhelm Kempff.

Some of the most significant new music was not to be heard on records but only

MOVIE BALLERINA Leslie Caron helped popularize ballet with film audiences. In MGM's "Glory Alley", the French dancing star performed atop bar

in New York's Carnegie Hall or the Sunday afternoon broadcasts emanating therefrom. Dimitri Mitropoulos, the New York Philharmonic-Symphony Orchestra's musical director, continued working at what he describes as his "duty" to put new and worthy music before his audience. His audiences took a mixed view of this missionary work. In the case of his first concert performance in the U.S. of the San Francisco-based French composer Darius Milhaud's rough and muscular opera *Christopher Columbus*, many of the listeners left the hall at intermission. Virgil Thomson, the country's ranking music critic, stayed and described the work as one of Milhaud's best—"a grand and wonderful piece".

An orchestra almost as famed as New York's is Boston's, and under the direction of Charles Münch and Pierre Monteux the Boston Symphony performed with distinction at the International Exposition of the Arts in Paris during the summer. The Exposition brought together artists from the Americas and from all the non-Iron Curtain countries in Europe. It was the free world's answer to a series of "cultural" assemblies inspired by the intellectuals inside the Soviet Union and held within the Soviet sphere of influence. The Exposition's nostalgic high

"THE CAGE": Nora Kaye and Michael Maule, of N.Y.C. Ballet Company, introduce Jerome Robbins' revolutionary ballet of love and violent death. Dance was enthusiastically received in France, but British audiences were not pleased

Music and The Dance 335

"GO! GO! GO!" scream 2500 uninhibited teen-agers who pack Los Angeles auditorium to listen and respond to torrid rhythms of saxophonist "Big Jay" McNeeley

point was Pierre Monteux's conducting of Igor Stravinsky's *Rite of Spring* in the theater where he had conducted its premiere performance almost forty years before. Vegetables and oaths flew at Monteux at that first *Rite*. In the summer of 1952 things were different. Monteux had never heard such acclaim before.

The cast of the Metropolitan Opera Company's production of *Carmen*, featuring the alluring Risë Stevens, was seen in thirty-one theaters throughout the country in a closed-circuit TV performance originating from the stage of the Metropolitan Opera House in New York City. The audience in New York thought it a fine performance. The audiences in the other cities thought it fair but something short of satisfactory. The Met planned to try again in '53 and hoped for better camera work for the outlanders.

In some ways, the foremost musical successes of the year were the Republican campaign songs. Most of the thirty-three million Eisenhower voters were agreed that the "Battle Hymn of the Republic", "Where Oh Where But in America?", and "I Like Ike" were pretty hard to avoid during the campaign months.

During the battle, the Democrats were given to intoning a little 32-bar jingle,

"Don't Let Them Take It Away". They sang it with zeal and earnestness, and often, and loudly. In '56 they may try something different. It didn't work.

Out of the village of Pliatan in faraway Bali came a native orchestra, a company of dancers, and a slight, 12-year-old girl named Ni Gusti Raka who moved through the Balinese rituals with more sinuous grace than had ever before been seen on an American stage. The Indonesian government sponsored the world tour of the troupe of forty-five. John Coast, an Englishman in the Indonesian Foreign Office, supervised the presentation. The Balinese girls were just as delighted to be in the U.S. as this country's dance fans were delighted to have them. Their projected four-week engagement in New York City had to be extended three more weeks because of the demand for tickets.

The Balinese girls, most of them in their early teens, were agreeable to the extension; it gave them that much more time to eat ice cream and sit in hotel

BIG JAY sinks to floor with exhaustion but continues to sound agonized blue notes. The 25-year-old musician has been called America's greatest pied piper since the heyday of Louis Armstrong

bathtubs, wonderful contrivances of Western civilization.

No Balinese dancers performed in Hollywood last year, but there was much choreographic activity. The films *Red Shoes* and *An American in Paris* had incorporated long ballet sequences and film fans seemed pleased by them. Trends start easily in the movie business, and soon Hollywood casting offices were cluttered with the world's best dancers. During 1952, the trend became a pattern and Hollywood's musicals were, in fact, dancing shows.

Roland Petit, Renée Jeanmaire, and

Serge Perrault from France were featured in some of them, as was Moira Shearer, the onetime prima ballerina of England's Sadler's Wells, a ballet troupe which receives some state financial aid and country-wide admiration. Others to show their pirouettes and entrechats before the cameras were Tamara Toumanova, André Eglevsky, and Erik Bruhn from Europe and a pair of lithe American-born stars from the New York City Ballet Company —Maria Tallchief and Melissa Hayden.

Results of this congregation of dancing talent are the dance episodes in the films *Hans Christian Andersen, Tonight We Sing, The Story of Three Loves, One Piece Bathing Suit,* and *Lili,* the last of these a fantasy featuring Leslie Caron, a captivating French import who can dance as well as she can act.

In New York, the five-year-old New York City Ballet was moving well out in front of dance ensembles everywhere, both in the over-all skill of its soloists and corps and in the significance of its choreographers' additions to the ballet repertoire. In Maria Tallchief, the company had, probably, the world's most gifted and hard-working ballerina. In George Balanchine, the company had the most creative and productive of contemporary choreographers.

There was a time, not long gone, when these two were married to each other, but Tallchief has since remarried outside her art (to an air-line pilot) and Balanchine recently remarried within it, to Tanaquil LeClerq, a ballerina who ranks close to Tallchief in the New York company's hierarchy. This was the choreographer's fifth marriage—each to a lady high in his line of work.

In early summer, the New York City Ballet headed for Europe and danced to the acclaim of the French. Balanchine's production of *The Firebird,* with music by the aging and eminent Stravinsky, a set by the lurid-toned modern painter Marc Chagall, and with Tallchief in the lead role, was an unqualified artistic triumph. A 15-minute shocker on the same bill was *The Cage,* conceived by a brash young man from Broadway musicals, Jerome Robbins, one of Balanchine's associates. In *The Cage,* dancer Nora Kaye is a killer, but it is never made clear whether she is a part of the human race or of a civilization of bugs a notch inferior to it. The business she is about has been outlined by Robbins: "There occurs in certain forms of insect and animal life, and even in our own mythology, the phenomenon of the female of the species considering the male as prey."

What that leads to in *The Cage* is a lot of man-killing after the men have helped out in this curious civilization by doing their share of woman-loving. The French were intrigued by this idea for a dance; yet when the company played in London Englishmen weren't—a variance in taste and temperament probably connoting nothing.

Back in New York, Balanchine fashioned four more ballets—two with ex-wife Tallchief in the featured roles, two with his new wife LeClerq. Their titles were *Scotch Symphony, Metamorphoses, Harlequinade,* and *Concertino.* All were found to be agreeable, but none ranked with Balanchine's best work. The male-killer, Nora Kaye, took a temporary leave from the company to do a number in Bette Davis' new Broadway show, a revue titled *Two's Company.*

A few blocks away from the ballet, Mia Slavenska and Frederic Franklin were writhing their way through a somewhat overheated dance portrayal of Tennessee Williams' play, *A Streetcar Named Desire.* Valerie Bettis made the translation from words and action to action only. Few thought she had obscured the play's point.

PRESS

BIG NEWS-STORY WINDS, GUSTY AND LUSTY, blew out of Chicago during 1952. From a dazzling series of journalistic stunts that widened eyes right on through the two major political conventions held in that city, Chicago showed the way—all the way. A town long noted for hard-hitting, tough, and canny newspapermen was never more typical.

The show got off to a fast start in February. Just seven months before, the Chicago *Herald-American,* a Hearst paper, had startled the nation with the banner headline: "Mother Here Expects 5 or 6 Babies".

It sounded like the biggest thing since the Dionne quintuplets. The story had been cloaked in mystery. No names, of parents or doctors, were used. "To protect the parties chiefly involved," the paper had explained. The story was written by the *Herald-American's* respected, 59-year-old science expert, Hugh S. Stewart.

Now, the time limit set for the births just about up, reporters on other Chicago papers began to needle the *Herald-American.* Some phoned in as "curious subscribers"; others wrote letters using aliases. All wanted to know what had happened or was happening to the quintuplets or sextuplets. They got vague answers.

Next, the Chicago *Tribune,* Colonel Robert McCormick's tower of Midwest isolationism, sent reporters out to make a door-to-door check of a neighborhood rumored to be "the" one. All they got were blank stares, slammed doors, and the reaction of one portly matron: "Your newspaper makes me so mad I could have kittens, but never sextuplets."

The Chicago *Daily News* methodically set its reporters to calling, one by one, every obstetrician in the area. Still, there were no clues to the *Herald-American's* heralded blessed events. Hugh Stewart would comment only: "There have been

some delaying actions. Things can't be delayed much longer."

A week later, the whole story blew up. Stewart, after a long "show us" session with his bosses, conceded that he could not produce the names of the persons involved because it was something he had dreamed up. Shamefacedly, the *Herald-American* apologized, hinting that Stewart had been mentally disturbed. He was given his walking papers.

Then another hectic story got under way, no hoax. Edan Wright, a pretty young girl reporter for the Chicago *News,* handled this one.

It started in mid-March when Edan dusted off a 22-year-old Chicago kidnaping mystery—the still unsolved disappearance of the then 2-year-old Mary Agnes Moroney. Every paper in Chicago had brushed up the story, trying to add to it. Edan saw something fresh.

The other children of the Moroney family bore a strong resemblance to one another. Why not, reasoned Edan, just get people looking for a young lady who looked like a Moroney. Her editors liked the idea. So did some editors on the West Coast. The child, it was thought, might have been taken that far away.

The Oakland (Calif.) *Tribune* turned the trick. A photo of the Moroney children run in that paper attracted the attention of a young housewife. She was unsure of her own parentage, having been taken from a foundling home whose records were incomplete. She did, indeed, resemble a Moroney. Edan rode the story for all it was worth.

Scientists from universities across the country were called in for tests to see if the young housewife, Mary McClelland,

UNITED PRESS PHOTOGRAPHER Stanley Tretick gets slugged for taking picture of delegate who had fainted at Republican convention. Tretick announced $250,000 lawsuit against G.O.P.

REPORTERS EAVESDROP on Adlai Stevenson's private conference with Illinois delegation to Democratic convention, hear governor say he does not wish to be nominated for Presidency

mightn't be the Moroney child. Dozens of casts of teeth were made. Blood tests, bone measurements, and skull comparisons were taken. The country waited while the *News* pushed ahead.

The paper arranged a dramatic cross-country flight for Mary McClelland, expecting a heart-tugging "reunion" at which maternal instinct would supply the verification that science couldn't. No scientist would say he could prove, beyond doubt, the family relationship.

The great day came. The girl and the grief-stricken mother met. Next day, other papers reported that nothing had happened. There had been no spark of recognition. After a brief attempt to pump optimism into the story, the *News* quietly backed out.

In August, however, a Chicago paper got, not its woman, but its man. LeRoy ("Buddy") McHugh, a pint-sized, 61-year-old police reporter for the Chicago *Herald-American,* had been the model for one of the characters in the classic play about newspapermen, *The Front Page.* This time, in July, McHugh pulled a stunt worthy of *The Front Page.*

While Chicago police and other law-enforcement officers scoured State and city for a used-car dealer who allegedly had bilked his customers out of about $3 million, McHugh began making friends with the fugitive's friends and family. After a month of cajoling, he got the tip he wanted. If he would go to room 1002 of the Regis Hotel in Omaha, he was told, he would find his man. McHugh went there by plane. He discovered that the Regis is right across the street from the local F.B.I. field office.

At room 1002 he knocked, three quick, two slow, three quick. A big, burly man, familiar to McHugh through photos, opened the door. "Hello Bob!" McHugh said and walked right in for an exclusive interview with Robert Knetzer.

After obtaining an offhand opinion from the U.S. attorney general that the *Herald-American* would not be charged with harboring a fugitive, McHugh stayed with Knetzer for another day, getting a 4000-word affidavit on how the fugitive had been forced into the huge extortion to pay graft demanded of him by public officials.

For two days, while other papers were able only to report that Knetzer was in custody, McHugh and the *Herald-American* ran the story big and loud. It was the biggest capture by a Chicago newsman since 1937, when Robert Irwin, killer of Veronica Gedeon, a New York model, surrendered to reporters on Hearst's old Chicago *Herald and Examiner*.

One of Chicago's merry stunts began to take on national significance when Ray Brennan, star reporter for the Chicago *Sun-Times*, was indicted by a Federal grand jury. His crime, the jury said, was impersonating a Federal officer. It was perpetrated, the jury said, in 1950 when Brennan was assigned to dig loose some secret testimony from the Kefauver crime-investigating committee—testimony that affected Chicago politics.

Brennan flew to Washington. He got the testimony all right. The jurymen thought they knew how. Brennan, their indictment charged, had gone to the stenographic firm that transcribed committee hearings in Washington, identified himself as a "Mr. Whitney" of the committee, and walked out with a full file.

Brennan's paper leaped to his defense. He had, an outraged editorial claimed, "performed an outstanding service to the people . . . in thwarting efforts of a government agency to suppress information vital to the voters". Big question still up to a court to decide at year's end was whether reporters in search of information they consider vital to the public may disregard the law's technicalities.

During all this razzle-dazzle, Chicago and the nation were getting ready for the biggest story of them all, the Presidential election campaign.

President Truman and Adlai Stevenson charged the press with an unfair slant toward Dwight Eisenhower. Nearly two thirds of America's 1700 daily papers—

HUMAN-INTEREST STORY headlined by Chicago papers was possibility that Mrs. Mary McClelland, shown with husband, might prove to be Mary Agnes Moroney, kidnaped 22 years ago. Scientists could neither prove nor disprove alleged identity

though not the 90 percent Truman and Stevenson mentioned—plumped for Ike. About 14 percent backed Stevenson. Others remained uncommitted.

The trade magazine *Editor & Publisher* surveyed some 1300 of the papers for their editorial preference. The grand totals: 933 dailies, with 40 million readers, supported Eisenhower in their editorial columns; 202 dailies, with 5½ million readers, supported Stevenson; 250, with about 4½ million readers, were neutral.

By and large, the news columns of America's daily newspapers were fair, giving equal space to both men, regardless of the choice on the editorial page.

Readers had never taken a more active interest in the opinions of their papers. Millions were spent by prosperous readers who paid to insert ads praising their candidates in daily papers. In Boston, $300,000 went for this purpose.

About $100,000 went to *The New York Times*, pro-Eisenhower. Two New Yorkers paid more than $6000 to print two ads urging *The Times* to switch to Stevenson.

While American editors were digging into the election coverage, the freedom of the press that such coverage made evident was being challenged.

In the United Nations, for instance, U.S. delegates had to reject a proposed code of press-freedom rules because many nations had insisted upon writing restrictive clauses. Russia had insisted that reporters be forced to report the official government line. Thus U.S. reporters might be punished if they peeked behind the facade of peace in Moscow and saw the truth—preparation for war.

In West Germany, a press law was proposed—but then withdrawn—which would have given the government Hitlerian rights to decide who should work on newspapers.

In the U.S., the Pulitzer Prizes for 1952 reflected the fact that newsmen had dug

ROXY

RAY MILLAND
in "THE THIEF"
RITA GAM
ALSO JOHNNY JOHNSTON
PLUS JERRY COLONNA

MARQUEE of New York's Roxy Theater tells the story as policeman trains gun on subdued hold-up man while second thief lies dying of bullet wound. Amateur cameraman chanced on scene, took picture

deep into some governmental "cover-ups". (The prizes are journalism's top awards, given each year by Columbia University.)

In 1952, the top prize went to the St. Louis *Post-Dispatch,* which had started the year-long series of exposures of corruption in the Internal Revenue Bureau and elsewhere in government.

The top cartoon, by Fred Packer of the New York *Mirror,* summed up the troubled relationship of the President and the press. It showed an irate Harry Truman telling reporters: "Your editors ought to have more sense than to print what I say."

The prize of all, for a lot of readers, however, was the whirling, whistling story of the flying saucers, a now well-established item of American journalism.

During the summer a radar operator at the National Airport in Washington spotted something odd on his screen. Newspapers strained to spot something too.

Military headquarters in Washington, a lot of newsmen figured, would be the best place to get the low-down on the high-flying story. Some seventy reporters, the largest press conference at the Pentagon since the end of World War II, fired questions on flying saucers. The military was inclined to favor sunspots.

The Detroit *Free Press* turned up the frothiest saucer of them all after a reader called to report something strange. It turned out to be a blimp with blinking lights advertising a certain beer.

Some readers didn't really trust their papers very far. In Salt Lake City, the *Deseret News* reported a visit by a "suspicious-eyed woman" who felt the press was joined in a gigantic conspiracy to withhold facts about the saucers.

At least one editor proved that boredom, not conspiracy, was responsible for a blackout of saucer news in some papers. For five years, the managing editor

of the Ottawa (Ill.) *Republican-Times* wrote, we have read about deranged disks that flit from one end of the country to the other. From now on, the editor wrote, there would be no more saucer stories in his paper.

One by one, the newspapers of America had been shrinking in size—not in number of pages, but in actual, physical size. By mid-1952, 75 percent were about a half inch narrower than they had been. With paper costs sky high, that little half inch was saving millions of dollars. (*The New York Times* alone would save about $500,000 a year.)

Wages, thanks to a tougher-than-ever attitude in newspaper unions, kept rising. In Tacoma, Wash., the *News Tribune* was closed for four months (one of the longest newspaper strikes in history) by staff members who wanted more money. Business slumped as much as 35 percent because of the blackout of advertising.

In New York, the reverse side of the coin spun into sight. The *World-Telegram and The Sun,* chief paper of the Scripps-Howard chain, entered into wage talks with employees for the first time since a nine-week strike had hit the paper in 1950. The *World-Telegram* talked turkey to its staff. It said that, far from being worried about a wage increase, staffers should be thinking about a possible wage cut. Business was not good enough to allow costs to rise.

But some people were still getting into the newspaper business.

One was 46-year-old John Fox, a self-made multimillionaire who had flown for the marines during World War II, invested wisely in real estate, and reaped tremendous profits which, shortly after he left the service, enabled him to buy a controlling interest in the vast, $265 million Western Union Telegraph Co.

A compact, scrappy Boston Irishman, Fox wanted a voice in his home town. He

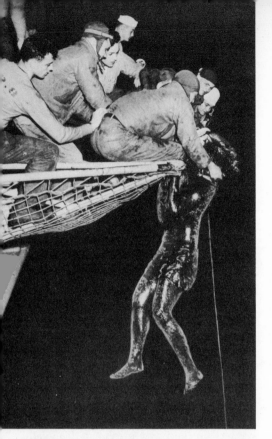

GRIM SEA DRAMA: Oil-soaked survivor is hauled from sea after aircraft carrier "Wasp" collided with destroyer "Hobson". 176 men perished

got it in June when he bought the 121-year-old Boston *Post.*

A man in the business and getting in deeper all the time was Roy Thomson, a Canadian who sails his yacht to Florida every year to escape the winters at home, where he has fifteen newspapers.

In 1952, Thomson got the fidgets under the Florida sun. He plunked down $750,000 and bought the St. Petersburg (Fla.) *Independent.* Thomson took a look around the new property, peering through his thick-lensed glasses and edging his ample 230 pounds between desks. To staffers he explained that there would be no shake-up and that his only reason for getting the paper was "to give me something to do during the winter".

While all this was going on, a mighty figure in American journalism, Roy Howard, was getting ready to relinqush part of his grip on the reins of the Scripps-Howard newspaper chain. After 1952, he revealed, he would let younger men take over the top command posts. He would stand by to edit his pride and joy, the *World-Telegram and The Sun.*

In Cincinnati, a major paper changed hands, but not to a single publisher. The Cincinnati *Enquirer,* a husky, money-making paper that went on the auction block simply because the owning family felt it wanted to invest elsewhere, was sold in June to the paper's employees. Although the *Enquirer's* rival, the *Times-Star* (owned by Ohio's powerful Taft family), bid high and long, the employees finally managed to get backing to put up $7.6 million for their paper.

At the signing ceremonies transferring ownership, James Ratliff, the reporter who had sparked the paper-buying drive, was so emotionally shaken that he could not hold the pen. At the paper itself, a dozen night-long celebrations and a three-column front-page editorial showed how happy the other employee-owners felt. Then the *Enquirer* championed the unsuccessful Presidential-nomination bid of Senator Robert A. Taft, part owner of the paper which had tried to beat the employees to the buy.

Among the magazines, there were some notable accomplishments. *The Saturday Evening Post,* putting out $50,000 and dropping its traditional policy of pictures on its covers, pulled the prize of the year by running serially Whittaker Chambers' haunting account of the trials of the soul that moved him from Communism to the witness stand, where he testified against Alger Hiss.

A magazine in France had a good story to tell about itself. This one began during the war when Didier Rémon, a

French industrial engineer and Resistance fighter, decided to blow up Michel's, his favorite bar, which had been taken over by the Nazis. And he did blow it up.

After the war, when Rémon returned for a nostalgic look at the wreckage of Michel's in the swank Passy section of Paris, he met another man who had loved the bar, Humbert Frèrejean, a junior executive in a steel company.

The two quickly discovered a mutual hobby, the reading of American magazines. Before the evening was over they had decided to put out a magazine of their own. With $2000 they raked up between them, they set out to do just that.

As 1952 rolled on stage, Rémon's and Frèrejean's success was obvious. Their magazine, *Réalités*, a beautifully illustrated, colored, and written publication of general-interest articles, was so good, in fact, that 1952 saw it translated into English and exported to America.

As France contributed one of the happiest success stories of the year, O'Neill, Nebr., claimed the unhappiest story. During the summer, the weekly *O'Neill Frontier* came out with eight rather than its usual twelve pages. The reasons: 1. The office manager had got sick. 2. The paper's only reporter had come down with the flu. 3. The paper's typesetter had to go to bed after a four-tooth extraction. 4. The press operator got pneumonia. 5. The office boy played hookey to go to a basketball game. 6. The furnace blew up.

And, to top it off, just after the harried editor had managed to get the paper out all by himself, his phone rang. Too late for the press run, the caller announced that the village's chief of police had just been murdered—biggest story of the year.

The biggest stories elsewhere followed an expected pattern. The election was tops. The Korean truce talks, government scandals, and world politics all found place on the top-ten lists. One story of personal heroism also made the lists: the epic struggle of Captain Kurt Carlsen to save his sinking freighter, *The Flying Enterprise*. European editors picked the Carlsen story as "the" top story.

In February the army warned correspondents covering the Korean truce talks against fraternizing with enemy newsmen. Reporters from the U.N. side appeared to have become so friendly with reporters from North Korea—including a couple of renegade Britons representing British Red papers—that there was fear of leaks of military information.

American newsmen even dickered with Communists to get cameras and film to an American photographer held captive in North Korea. Even though the stunt enabled him to send back the first pictures of American G.I.'s in Red prison camps, the army feared that it had paved the way for a dangerously close liaison between Red and U.N. forces.

As always, the weather stories got high readership. Chicago provided the gustiest weather story of them all, when Colonel Robert McCormick, the terrible-tempered, venerable owner of the Chicago *Tribune*, got into his reconverted B-17 bomber and flew off for some warmth at Palm Beach, Fla. The colonel, not the temperature, really warmed things up. There was, the colonel discovered, an unseasonable chill in the air.

Next day a front-page announcement in the *Tribune*, "From Our Florida Correspondent", gave the colonel's snappish thoughts on Florida weather. Twenty-four hours later the *Tribune* ran another McCormick blast. This one reported how Floridians had reacted to his first comments:

"Yesterday they formed a mob to lynch me, composed of hotel-keepers, real-estate agents, barbers, bartenders and bathing beauties . . . But they came on skis so I easily skated away from them."

EPIC VIGIL of Captain Kurt Carlsen, shown clinging to rail of doomed freighter "Flying Enterprise", was one of the year's great news stories

DANCING STAR Harold Lang stars as "Pal Joey", all-American heel

THEATER

DURING 1952, SEVENTY-SIX PLAYS OPENED on Broadway. Eighty percent of them closed in short order. Disappointed over the year's slim pickings, New York drama critics called it the worst season in forty years.

But the year had its high lights, which sparkled even more brightly in contrast with the theater's general dreariness. First across the footlights, in January, came a bright, bouncy revival of the musical *Pal Joey*, with music by Richard Rodgers, lyrics by the late, great Lorenz Hart, and book by John O'Hara, master of the hard-boiled story.

Originally presented on Christmas night of 1940, *Pal Joey* was highly sophisticated and vastly different from the typical musical comedy of the day, which usually combined straightforward sentiment with sheer slapstick. Its story of a loose-living woman of wealth who bought

JUDY GARLAND triumphed in record-breaking engagement at New York's Palace Theater

her pleasures with the men she wanted proved distasteful to many theatergoers. One drama critic wrote: "You cannot draw sweet water from a foul well."

Even after such a mixed reception, *Pal Joey* ran 374 performances and its music echoed on down the years, "I Could Write a Book" and "Bewitched, Bothered and Bewildered" taking their places among never-to-be-forgotten show tunes.

For the revival, Vivienne Segal returned to her sultry role as the footloose female and, for company, she had Harold Lang and Helen Gallagher. This time public taste had caught up with it and even 1940's disapproving critic joined in the cheers. Not only did *Pal Joey* surpass its original run, celebrating its first anniversary at press time, but it was happily promising to go on and on.

January also saw a flurry of rekindled interest in the works of Eugene O'Neill, first giant of American playwrights. Ill with Parkinson's disease at his home in Massachusetts, O'Neill has not written anything for Broadway since *The Iceman Cometh,* which was produced six years ago and was not a success by commercial standards. His plays, however, have become native classics, and two of them, *Anna Christie* and *Desire Under the Elms,* were once again brought to life for a generation that had known them only on the printed page.

Desire Under the Elms, a somber and powerful story of the hatreds and desires that rage in the minds of a lustful old New Englander, his new, young wife, and his rebellious son, was splendidly revived under the direction of Harold Clurman.

And *Anna Christie,* the stormy story of a prostitute who returns to her father's barge to find pure love, brought Celeste Holm back to Broadway to try her hand at serious acting—an interesting change of pace for a star most noted for her success in movies and musical comedy. The reviews were mixed but the general opinion was that the undertaking had been very worth-while.

Before the month was out, the theater's brilliant Jack-of-all-trades, writer-producer-director-actor José Ferrer, came up with a new play by Joseph Kramm. Although he didn't write this one, Ferrer was producer, director, and star.

The Shrike told a dramatic story. And author Kramm had a dramatic story of his own. At 44 he had an unenviable history of failure and frustration. He had begun his career as an actor, taken a shot at direction, and, by the time *The Shrike*

IN HER 45-YEAR CAREER
Helen Hayes has had roles ranging from Queen Victoria to a charwoman. In 1952, she was in "Mrs. McThing"

BACK ON BROADWAY after 17 years of movie making, dramatic star Bette Davis sings and dances her way through sprightly revue "Two's Company"

opened, written eight other plays, none of which had ever been produced.

The shrike is a bird of prey. For the play, it symbolized the story of a wife whose vicious possessiveness drives her husband to mental crack-up and attempted suicide.

The play is set in the psychiatric ward of a city hospital to which the husband has been taken after his suicide attempt. Action revolves about his efforts to find release, both from the hospital and from the strangle hold of his marriage.

Ferrer gave a terribly powerful performance. No one who saw it will forget the spine-chilling final scene in which he is discharged from the hospital—into the custody of his wife.

Unfortunately, Ferrer's commitments to other enterprises (particularly the role of stunted artist Toulouse-Lautrec in the film *Moulin Rouge*) made it impossible for him to see the play through the year, even though audiences were still clamoring for tickets. When Ferrer left, the curtain fell on *The Shrike*. But, before it did, Joseph Kramm's ninth play had won him a Pulitzer Prize. And it won solely on its dramatic, tersely written examination of a single situation involving two lives, rather than on the offer of a solution to some great social problem, attempted by so many playwrights at other times during the year, with less success.

February brought back some established talents with new wares to offer. First of these was S. N. Behrman. Our foremost writer of high comedy, and unhappy about it of late because he feels the times are out of joint for frivolity, Behrman contributed a piece called *Jane*, which he had based on a short story by English novelist W. Somerset Maugham. With Edna Best as the star, it told the story of a Liverpool frump who, in a delightful metamorphosis, turned London's smart society upside down with her style, charm, and manners.

Mary Chase, a Denver newspaperwoman who had earlier captured just about everybody's heart with her delightful and successful *Harvey*, brought another charmer to Broadway with *Mrs. McThing*. In this, Helen Hayes played the role of a mother thoroughly determined to turn her little boy (Brandon de Wilde) into a stuffed shirt (j.g.). The youngster, healthy and rambunctious as any normal boy, gets away from it all with the help of a witch who uses a series of magical object-lessons to teach the misguided mama a much better way of bringing up little boys. The play frolicked along through many hilarious escapades, including one in which the queenly Miss Hayes found herself transformed into a scrubwoman.

CRITICS WERE DIVIDED over Katharine Hepburn's performance in "The Millionairess". Co-star Cyril Ritchard goes sprawling during big scene

Originally, the American National Theater and Academy had scheduled *Mrs. McThing* to run for two weeks in New York City. Applauding audiences kicked the schedule off stage and kept the play going through 1952. A long road tour was planned.

February's third contribution came from the Welsh equivalent of José Ferrer —writer-producer-actor Emlyn Williams, long famous for his scalp-tingling *Night Must Fall* and hauntingly sensitive *The Corn Is Green.*

Now the versatile Williams turned up in a one-man show, appearing as Charles Dickens did when he visited America to read from his works. Bearded like Dickens, dressed like Dickens—down to the white carnation in his lapel—and standing behind a copy of the reading desk which Dickens himself had used, Williams gave a remarkably brilliant performance of scenes from the famous novels and stories.

In appearing as he did, Williams continued a trend that had been started not long before by Charles Laughton, and one that saw the return to popularity of old-time reading performances. Before "Dickens", the most successful effort had been the rich-voiced Laughton's appearance with Charles Boyer, Sir Cedric Hardwicke, and Agnes Moorehead in a reading of George Bernard Shaw's *Don Juan in Hell*. Actually, neither presentation was a pure "reading". Although the performers did have stacks of books or scripts in front of them, the lines had really been committed to memory.

March saw another revival—that of Clifford Odet's *Golden Boy*, one of the great, enduring dramas of the 1930's. The "Golden Boy" of the title is a young man who forsakes his dreams of becoming a great violinist to enter the prize-fight ring, where he can earn more money and swifter acclaim. It was played by John Garfield and it was his last role.

Born in the slums of New York City's Lower East Side, the handsome young actor had risen to heights in Hollywood and on Broadway, but the last year of his life was clouded by personal conflicts. In May Garfield died of a heart attack at the age of 39.

March, too, saw the first play by the fiction world's wonder boy, Truman Capote: an adaptation from his novel, *The Grass Harp*. Dean of drama critics, *The New York Times'* Brooks Atkinson went overboard in its favor. He was the only one. *The Grass Harp* closed after thirty-six performances. But it was not an out-and-out failure. Capote had revealed himself as a sensitive and poetic playwright and theater-lovers looked forward with interest to his next offering. Capote

himself made it quite clear that there was going to be a next offering and promptly took off for Europe to start work on it.

The drought of new plays continued through April, there being several bids but no winners. Oddly enough, the laurels went once again to a revival, and a play that had been scheduled for a fortnight's engagement lasted longer than the original run.

The play was *The Male Animal*. The authors were a pair of very funny but very different men—shy, owlish, witty James Thurber, and slick Hollywood writer and party-thrower Elliott Nugent.

Nugent, who had starred in the original 1940 version, came East to take over the role of Tommy Turner, a meek professor of English unwillingly goaded to unfamiliar heroisms. Much credit for the play's success went to Robert Preston, who had also come on from Hollywood to play the role of Professor Turner's pal of undergraduate days, a football hero who for the rest of his life remained devoted to the gridiron.

Everybody in the theater was looking forward to May, and another revival. In 1931, *Of Thee I Sing* had been a resounding success. It had everything—book by George S. Kaufman and Morrie Ryskind, music and lyrics by George and Ira Gershwin. Audiences had roared at its lampooning of the national political scene, gone home whistling and humming its songs, which included "Love is Sweeping the Country" and the rollicking "Wintergreen for President". The show had become part of the theater's glittering memory-book and its rebirth was eagerly awaited.

But for this one, there was to be no second success. That indefinable something which had made it a hit had been lost with time's passing. It was like seeing an old love grown dowdy and a little bedraggled.

SPLASHY MUSICAL: "Wish You Were Here", the show with the built-in swimming pool, stars singer Sheila Bond (standing)

Happily, however, something turned up to give May the shot in the arm it needed. This was the revue *New Faces*.

Its producer, Leonard Sillman, had successfully introduced a revue to bring new talent to Broadway back in the '30's. He had not repeated the idea in years because he knew that a revue is about the most difficult of all theatrical stunts to pull off well. It does not have a story to carry it along, as a musical comedy does. It must depend on the excellence of each of its scenes. Until 1952, Sillman had not felt that he had again found the magic combination. Now his patience and discernment were well rewarded as *New Faces of 1952* sailed strongly into 1953.

Some of the "new faces" were instant hits: Virginia de Luce, a blonde singer as good to look at as to listen to; Alice Ghostley, a pert girl in a droopy sweater, who displayed rare comic genius in her recounting of a sinful week end in sedate Boston; and Eartha Kitt, a brown-skinned bombshell whose hit number, "Monotonous", tells a tale of impossibly far-fetched conquests which, somehow, do not seem impossible when considered in relation to Miss Kitt.

With summer, of course, the theater began its trek to the country resort areas—the so-called barnyard circuit—leaving Broadway to sizzle in heat and humidity. But before this happened, June came up with the splashiest musical of this or any other season—*Wish You Were Here*. For this one, Joshua Logan and Arthur Kober rewrote the latter's successful straight drama *Having A Wonderful Time,* and Harold Rome wrote the music and lyrics.

The first splash took place when director Logan decided to have a real swimming pool built on the stage of the Imperial Theater, at a cost of over $15,000.

GEORGE HOWE starred as "Mr. Pickwick" in comedy based on Dickens' characters

Scene designer Jo Mielziner tried to dissuade him, but he wouldn't budge. True to the tradition of Ziegfeld and Belasco, showman Logan could think only of audience reaction to a bevy of beautiful girls in bathing suits lounging around his pool while someone fully dressed fell in head-first. Logan had his way.

Months before the show opened, the pool was paying off in word-of-mouth publicity. A Broadwayite, returning from a trip abroad, reported that there were people in Europe who knew nothing about the American theater except that there was a show which had a real swimming pool on the stage.

Even so, *Wish You Were Here* had a tough swim. With one exception, the crit-

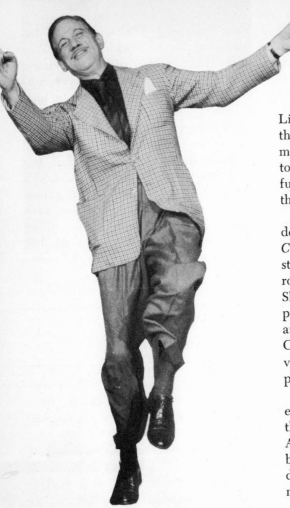

WHEN DAUGHTER scores touchdown for boys' football team in comedy "Time Out for Ginger", Melvyn Douglas, beaming with parental pride, romps around stage

Lillie can make the most toughened theatergoer split his sides with laughter merely by reading the telephone directory to him. Her present show added further luster to her fame as one of the theater's incomparable comediennes.

About the same time, Arthur Laurents delivered his play, *The Time of the Cuckoo,* a half-humorous, half-wistful story of an American woman's search for romance in Italy. In the starring role, Shirley Booth scored another tremendous personal success. No glamour girl, she is an actress in the great, classic tradition of Cornell and Hayes, breathing warm, vivid life into whatever character she portrays.

For all the success of the play, however, there was an air of sadness about the theater in which it was performed. After sixty years of greatness, the much-beloved Empire Theater was to be torn down in the summer of 1953—doomed to make way for an office building.

Meantime, Mary Chase, who wrote *Mrs. McThing,* turned out another comedy, *Bernardine,* a story of teen-age growing pains and passions—Bernardine representing the dream girl of the adolescent male, a curvy and complaisant creature whose vocabulary consists of the one word, "Yes". For a while, with *Mrs. McThing* playing on the same street, Mary Chase had the delightful experience of having two hits running side by side.

October also brought Katharine Hepburn back to Broadway for a limited engagement in *The Millionairess,* one of George Bernard Shaw's last plays. The play had been a smash success in London. Critics ran out of adjectives trying to

ics turned thumbs down. On the morning after opening night, by all the laws of the theater, it was dead as a doornail.

Only Logan didn't know it. Instead of folding his sets, he rolled up his sleeves and went to work rewriting the show. It was a fantastic achievement. By September, *Wish You Were Here* had settled down to a long and solid run.

Not until October, however, did anything else stir up much attention along Broadway. Then Bea Lillie got the ball rolling with *An Evening with Beatrice Lillie.* It is widely believed that Miss

describe Miss Hepburn's flaming vitality in the title role. Toward the end of her London engagement, Miss Hepburn developed a throat ailment. Determined to finish the run, she spoke only on stage—off stage, she used a note pad and pencil.

However, something happened on the transatlantic crossing. Many American critics felt that Shaw's customary bite had been reduced to a nibble by the time he wrote *The Millionairess*. There were, however, enough of those who thought just the opposite to make the limited run a lively one.

COMEDIAN Ronny Graham of "New Faces" was hailed as one of Broadway's best laugh-getters

Meanwhile, S. M. Chartock, a man from Brooklyn who had been carrying the torch for the establishment of a permanent Gilbert & Sullivan Company in America, got his chance. With Martyn Green and Ella Halman cutting ties with London's D'Oyly Carte Opera Company, Chartock promptly signed them up, organized a company of singers, and launched the S. M. Chartock Gilbert & Sullivan Company on Broadway. The reception was moderate, but encouraging. The company, it was agreed, needed more experience, and it set out on tour, hoping that after a year or so it would once again be ready to brave the big city. When last heard from, the troupe had run into trouble and there was talk of reorganization.

With November, Broadway took on a distinctly foreign flavor. The company headed by Madeleine Renaud and Jean-Louis Barrault came over from Paris, and the National Theater of Greece from Athens. Both companies had successful engagements of repertory performances—

TORCH SINGER Eartha Kitt's rendition of "Monotonous" is show-stopping high light of "New Faces"

"I HAVE A BEAUTIFUL EXPRESSION UNDER THIS FAN," warbles the favorite satirist of two continents in one of her all-too-rare Broadway appearances

in which established plays, usually several different ones each week, were given in succession.

In addition to the foreign visitors, two thoroughly American comedies turned up to take their bows. Written by 29-year-old George Axelrod, *The Seven Year Itch* dealt with a husband who has an affair when his wife goes away to the country. Temptation was invitingly portrayed by ex-quiz kid Vanessa Brown, who effectively conceals her I.Q. behind a low-cut neckline.

Time Out for Ginger brought screen star Melvyn Douglas back to Broadway as the harassed head of a delightfully zany

family in which one of three daughters decides to become a football player.

With new plays opening, December is usually a busy month—backers want to cash in on the Christmas-New Year season. This time, there were three new arrivals, but only two were left to celebrate when the holidays did roll around.

Again, one of the successful pair was a revival, Lillian Hellman's *The Children's Hour,* in which the most vicious little brat of the modern theater tells such staggering lies about two of her teachers that their lives are ruined.

Even the second time around, there seemed no doubt that the play was a tri-

WHOOPS! Up goes the fan, and it's none other than the star of "An Evening with Beatrice Lillie"

Many times Russo and Ellis had cause to rue the honor. The revue, *Two's Company*, opened in Detroit. Five minutes after the curtain went up, the star of the show was stretched out on the stage in a dead faint. The curtain went down and first aid was administered. While the audience was still buzzing over the unscheduled excitement, Bette Davis revived, gallantly addressed the house, and brought it down by saying, "Well, nobody can say I didn't fall for you."

The opening performance wound up in a blaze of emotional enthusiasm. But, as it wound its way to New York City, the show was in desperate trouble. New sketches were put in, others yanked out. Lines were polished and repolished. There was trouble inside the cast. Actors left and returned until the stage entrance needed a revolving door. A new director was called in to help rescue what threatened to become a complete flop. But from Boston, last stop before New York, the word was "hopeless".

The producers had sold a number of theater parties big blocks of tickets for the New York run, and announced that they would open on schedule but wanted the critics to stay away until all the changes had had a chance to jell. This was not exactly an endearing gesture and several top reviewers, nettled, let it be known they'd be on hand, welcome or not. The producers thereupon set a new opening date, postponed the theater parties, and prayed. Finally, the curtain came up.

Bette Davis was praised for her courage but not for her abilities as a singer and dancer. Yet, aided by the theater parties, and supported by a loyal following of fans that apparently would string along with her even had she dared to appear in Wagner's *Tristan and Isolde*, *Two's Company* was going well as 1953 dawned.

umph. Many thought that it had gained strength and pertinence for today's audience because it showed the damage that false accusations can do.

Chances are, however, that 1952 will be best remembered for the return to the stage, after some seventeen years in Hollywood, of intense, talented, chain-smoking Bette Davis.

Time and again, top Broadway producers had begged the star to work for them in straight dramatic plays. Instead, she chose a revue, a medium foreign to her training, and she chose James Russo and Michael Ellis, two of the theater world's newer lights, to sponsor her return.

MOVIES

IN 1952 COMPETITION FROM TELEVISION was again Hollywood's biggest headache. Some studios still fought a delaying action, denying TV the use of films and stars. But by and large, people were getting their entertainment in their own living rooms. Weekly movie attendance, estimated at 55 million, was far below wartime peaks and no higher than in 1951.

Late in the year, however, Hollywood had reason to chuckle over the story of the woman movie-goer who snapped impatiently at the man in front of her: "Would you mind moving? You are in the way of the picture."

"Madame," the gentleman replied, "I'm *in* the picture."

The tale might be spurious, but it was

MOST-PUBLICIZED ACTRESS of 1952, Marilyn Monroe helped lure Americans away from their television sets and back into movie houses. Here she poses for calendar artist Earl Moran

certainly timely. And Hollywood laughter was edged with a tone of triumph. For 1952 saw a rebirth of a fascinating illusion, the so-called three-dimensional film. In this technique, promptly dubbed 3-D, moviemakers felt that they had a magnet that again would pull record audiences into their theaters.

Pictures that create an illusion of depth were actually nothing new. Grandma's stereopticon, through which she peered at twin photographs of Niagara Falls, was a primitive example of 3-D familiar to many Americans. When Grandma cupped the stereopticon to her forehead, she saw each of the pictures with a separate eye. This was equivalent to seeing the Falls from two slightly different angles, as a pair of normal eyes would do in nature. The result was an impression of living perspective, and the water almost seemed to flow.

Nor were three-dimensional moving pictures new to Hollywood. As early as 1922, Thomas Alva Edison had tinkered with a stereopticon projector and then had abandoned it. Four years later the audience at a premiere of *Old Ironsides,* a film glorifying the early days of the U.S. Navy, jumped to its feet when the screen suddenly seemed to double its width. The frigate U.S.S. *Constitution,* it appeared, sailed right up to the first row of seats before veering broadside.

This impression was created by a magnifying lens on the projector. By expanding the picture so that it almost filled the audience's field of vision, the lens gave people something to look at with the outside corners of their eyes. And this trick, entirely different from the stereopticon principle, produced an illusion of depth and realism.

Although subsequent and similar giant-

FAVORED to win Oscar for year's best performance by actor is star of "High Noon", Gary Cooper

screen experiments created sensations, all failed artistically. The techniques were fine for panoramas, but when boy met girl, they got lost in the wide open spaces.

In 1936, Metro-Goldwyn-Mayer tried a variant of the stereopticon. Three Pete Smith shorts were filmed with two cameras operating from different angles. One camera took pictures in green; the other in red. The audience was handed spectacles with one green lens and one red lens. When the green and red pictures were projected in overlapping fashion, the spectacles screened the colors so that each eye saw only one picture. The psychological effect was a feeling of depth, although the two-colored view of the world made some people nervous.

Hollywood's most recent fling at three-dimensional movies used both techniques: giant-screen and stereopticon.

The first of the new 3-D movies to appear was Cinerama. New York City movie-goers sat in a Broadway theater almost half surrounded by a huge curved screen. Pictures that had been filmed with a three-lens camera were projected over the entire width of the screen by three synchronized projectors. Meantime, scattered loud-speakers blared six separate sound tracks. In effect, the audience was in the middle of the picture. And the realism of a roller-coaster ride, filmed from the front car, brought shrieks from the fainthearted.

On the heels of Cinerama came Natural Vision with a full-length African jungle yarn called *Bwana Devil*. In order to see the natives spear three-dimensional lions, the audience had to wear special spectacles. These, however, were not the red-and-green-lensed monstrosities of the '30's. The lenses were made of polaroid.

Twin overlapping pictures were projected in polarized light so that each eye seemed to view the scene from a different angle, as with a stereopticon.

Fascinating though they were, both Cinerama and Natural Vision had obvious drawbacks. Cinerama was too expensive for all but a few movie houses. Outfitting a theater with the huge curved screen and multiple projectors and loud-speakers cost from $25,000 to $75,000. And so far as Natural Vision was concerned, people still objected to wearing spectacles.

Late in the year, Twentieth Century-Fox set off on a middle course, Cinemascope. This technique used a wide-angle lens on a single camera, which engulfed a broad view. When this oddly distorted film was projected through a compensating wide-angle projection lens onto a big screen, the panoramic effect was produced. Cinemascope might not give quite so effective an illusion of depth as Cinerama or Natural Vision, but it did away with the costly curved screen, synchro-

DANNY KAYE mimics portrait of himself in London Palladium, scene of personal appearance. Movie-goers saw him in "Hans Christian Andersen"

RITA HAYWORTH'S marital troubles with Aly Khan made many a headline in 1952. Millions saw her return to screen in "Affair in Trinidad"

nized projectors, and bothersome goggles.

By year's end, 3-D was proceeding full steam ahead. Westinghouse, General Electric, the Radio Corporation of America, and many other centers of research were pouring brain power into the development of still better 3-D systems.

No matter what system eventually won out, Hollywood had decided to convert to 3-D swiftly. By 1954, some studios predicted, most films would be made in three dimensions.

Meanwhile, much to Hollywood's collective delight, Americans had taken fondly to the idea of "a lion in your lap, a lover in your arms". In throngs not observed at movie box offices since the war, they were hurrying to see their pictures in three dimensions.

Turning from cinema techniques to personalities, the largest stir of the year must be credited to the rapid rise of Marilyn Monroe, a hip-swinging young blonde of unmistakable raw charm. During the year, Miss Monroe made five pictures, each a success. Earlier pictures in which she had appeared only in bit parts were given top billing on marquees.

Miss Monroe, aided by the unwearying efforts of her press agents, became to some extent the symbol of the industry. And what they failed to accomplish, a romance with Joe DiMaggio, former great Yankee outfielder, achieved with ease.

During an interview, actor Mel Ferrer declared that Miss Monroe's highly touted sex attraction was "nothing more than a certain kind of very obvious high-school physical appeal". Actor Hugh Marlowe promptly counterattacked with the remark that "all men are high-school students, emotionally, to the grave".

Of course Miss Monroe had competition. Rita Hayworth was back making movies. The Gabor sisters, Eva, Magda, and Zsa Zsa, were pointing out that glamour was known in Hungary, too. And in the studio finishing schools other glamour girls were in the process of fabrication, all designed to cut in on the Monroe success and sell their own versions of sex appeal.

It is no coincidence that this trend to

ELIZABETH TAYLOR, seen vacationing on Riviera, was known chiefly for her beauty; then the critics and public discovered her fine acting talents

franker sex coincided with a TV trend away from it: moving pictures were being compelled to sell in areas where TV did not directly compete.

A to-do with far wider implications was provided by one of Hollywood's greatest artists—perhaps the greatest ever to turn his talents to films. For 1952 was the year when Charles Chaplin went to London for the world premiere of his film *Limelight,* and discovered he might never be able to return.

For years he had been a man who stirred debate. His left-of-center politics had been the subject of controversy. He had had his troubles with women—four marriages (to Mildred Harris, Lita Grey, Paulette Goddard, and Oona O'Neill) and a sordid paternity dispute. And although he had spent thirty-two years in the U.S., he had never become an American citizen, a fact which irked many.

Shortly after he left the United States, the Department of Justice announced that he might not be permitted to return, ostensibly because of his left-wing affiliations. Chaplin himself made little protest, and at year's end was living quietly in Switzerland, having reportedly transferred much of his wealth to that country.

But if Chaplin was placid about the affair, the press of Europe was considerably less so, and there the judgment of the U.S. government was widely assailed. Chaplin was feted in London, and received in Paris by the president of France.

As for *Limelight,* it opened in New York City on Oct. 23 to mixed notices. In general, it did well at the box office until various groups, including some local branches of the American Legion, announced their intention of picketing theaters showing the film. The consequences varied with the communities involved—in some areas, notably in California, the film was not shown, in others it was shown but did badly, in still others the attacks upon it had little effect.

The film deals with an English music-hall clown who has lost his ability to amuse his public. Into his life comes a young girl dancer. The story of the film revolves around the clown's pride, loneliness, frustration, and, finally, death.

Chaplin's leading lady was Claire Bloom, a lovely, gentle girl who captured the hearts of the film critics at exactly the moment when she was enchanting London theater-goers with her performance as Juliet in *Romeo and Juliet*.

Another familiar name which managed to make the headlines at regular intervals was that of Rita Hayworth, whose husband, Aly Khan, a bon vivant of international reputation, is the son of a fabulously wealthy Indian spiritual leader, the Aga Khan.

Miss Hayworth spent an undecided year. She had left Aly Khan and announced that she was returning to the films, but later went back to Paris for more talks with her husband while rumors of reconciliation filled the air. In the end, however, a divorce appeared inevitable and Miss Hayworth, having made *Affair in Trinidad* for Columbia, went to work on *Salome*.

Among the year's pictures, two ranked

TIME OUT is taken by Elizabeth Taylor during filming of MGM's "The Girl Who Had Everything" so she can visit with new husband Michael Wilding

JOSE FERRER portrays painter Toulouse-Lautrec in "Moulin Rouge". Lautrec was tragic, deformed genius whose art captured the enchantment of Paris

colleagues in the legitimate theater. Miss Booth won nomination for an Academy Award on the strength of her performance as the wife of an alcoholic, played by Burt Lancaster.

Among the spectacles, *Ivanhoe*, which starred Robert Taylor and Elizabeth Taylor (no relation) and splashed a colorful story of medieval England on the screens of the nation, garnered large box-office receipts for MGM, while Cecil B. De Mille's *Greatest Show on Earth*, with Betty Hutton and Cornel Wilde, did much the same for Paramount.

It should also be mentioned that during the year Bob Hope, Bing Crosby, and Dorothy Lamour teamed up once more for still another "road" picture, this one *The Road to Bali*.

The film capital also got around to making a pair of oddities. One of them, *The Thief*, starred Ray Milland and told the story of an F.B.I. chase. The novelty lay not in the plot but in the fact that no word of dialogue was spoken during the entire picture. The other was *The Four-poster*, with only two characters, Rex Harrison and Lilli Palmer, and one set, a bedroom. Neither film was eminently successful, and no trends seemed to be initiated.

A fair amount of footage continued to be shot overseas, including *Moulin Rouge* in Paris, *Roman Holiday* in Rome, *The Quiet Man* in Ireland, *Mogambo* in Africa, and Orson Welles' *Othello* almost everywhere.

From Europe came several outstanding films. England provided two comedies starring Alec Guinness, as well as *Breaking the Sound Barrier*, a solid hit built around Britain's pioneers in jet aircraft. From France, *Jeux Interdits* (*Forbidden Games*) won the New York Film Critics' Award for foreign films. The first Japanese film to reach the country in fourteen years, *Rashomon*, was well received

as outstanding. One of these, *High Noon*, produced by Stanley Kramer for United Artists, was a classic Western, starring Gary Cooper. An insistent melody, "Do Not Forsake Me", which made the hit parade, added to the strength of the film.

A Paramount release, *Come Back, Little Sheba,* marked the screen debut of Sh─── Booth, for years one of Broad─── least appreciated stars—least ───ted, that is, except among her

JOHN WAYNE, one of filmdom's top box-office draws, starred in highly praised "The Quiet Man"

in New York. Italy provided nothing to match its entries of earlier years.

During the year, one of Hollywood's better-known stars tried the New York stage, and another prepared to invade Broadway early in 1953. Abandoning serious drama for the moment, Bette Davis starred in the revue *Two's Company*, which opened late in December to somewhat unfavorable notices.

Danny Kaye worked his way east via San Francisco and Dallas, preparing for an early January opening of his one-man vaudeville show at the Palace Theater, where Judy Garland had scored a sensational success a year earlier. There was little doubt that Kaye would be welcome

at the Palace just as long as he cared to stay.

Hollywood took note, too, of the fact that Lucille Ball, who had never quite reached the top in movies, had done exactly that on television. Her filmed comedy *I Love Lucy* was the hottest thing on the air, capturing stupendous audiences when she had her pregnancy written into the script.

Lucy was filmed in Hollywood, and studio after studio, among the independents, turned its facilities over to TV shows. It became fairly certain that Hollywood's wide background in making films would guarantee it the lion's share of television programming, and TV's move from New York City to Hollywood took on added speed during the year. For the most part, the quality of Hollywood's television product was low.

BEAUTIFUL Zsa Zsa Gabor was featured in "Moulin Rouge" as Jane Avril, one of Lautrec's models

Other movie stars besides Lucille Ball made the jump into television and must now be considered primarily as TV stars. Both Groucho Marx and Dinah Shore became staple TV fare, and the termination of Joan Crawford's contract with Warner Brothers also appeared to have TV overtones.

Less directly, Bing Crosby became an important participant in TV programming when a subsidiary of his corporation, Bing Crosby Enterprises, signed a $4,000,000 contract to make television films. It calls for 208 half-hour films, and makes Crosby's firm the country's largest producer of TV film footage.

Within the industry, Howard Hughes, wealthy industrialist and film mogul, made news.

When the year began, Hughes was firmly in control of R.K.O. Radio Pictures, a $50,000,000 corporation which was having rather tough sledding. Abruptly, he closed the studios. His reason: he wished to weed out the Communist element at R.K.O. Others believed that Hughes was trying to cut the corporation's losses.

In September, Hughes suddenly sold his interest in R.K.O. to a five-man syndicate, which made a down payment of $1,250,000 on a deal totaling $7,345,950. The syndicate took over a corporation which had piled up an operating loss of nearly $4,000,000 during the first six months of the year. Ned Depinet, president of R.K.O., submitted his resignation, and other veterans found themselves suddenly without jobs.

Then the entire deal came toppling down. Three men resigned as directors, and the two who remained could make no progress in reorganizing the company. By the end of the year it was clear that Hughes was back in the saddle at R.K.O.

At year's end, the anticipated merger between United Paramount Pictures, Inc. and the American Broadcasting Company was still awaiting government approval, although that approval seemed a foregone conclusion. When it came into being, it would unite a powerful film corporation with a potentially mighty television network.

Paramount was also investing considerable time and effort in a color-tele-

NEW IDOL OF THE BOBBY SOXERS, actor Tony Curtis keeps smiling as he is mobbed by two thousand screaming teen-agers. Before he reached safety of waiting automobile, his coat was torn to shreds. Curtis recently costarred with Jan Sterling in "Flesh and Fury"

vision system—invented by Nobel Prize winner Ernest Lawrence of the University of California—and in a pay-as-you-watch television system. Either or both of these innovations may well bring about immense changes in Hollywood.

Finally, no survey of 1952 would be complete without mention of a quiet young woman named Lillian Ross, who appeared in Hollywood during 1951 with the modest announcement that she was to write a story for the *New Yorker*. By 1952 she was more or less part of the Hollywood scene. When her story began to appear in the *New Yorker*, Hollywood considered it devastating.

Miss Ross had performed that most deadly of all journalistic tricks: she had encouraged her victims to talk, then callously set down exactly what they said.

Writing about the making of a motion picture, she had selected *The Red Badge of Courage*, and her story took it from its inception to its New York opening. No one who had any share in the making of the picture was left with his skin whole, from the director down to the extras.

The account appeared week after week while Hollywood sputtered, arguing that Miss Ross had been meticulously honest, but not entirely fair. She had selected her material with bias, and had set down the answers to questions without pointing out that they *were* answers—thus suggesting that the odd items of information had been spontaneously offered. But she had, on the other hand, arresting material for her notebook.

Miss Ross made no friends, but it may be that her articles, which later appeared as a book, *Picture*, were the best description available of Hollywood in 1952.

It was not, all in all, a vintage year. It contained more promise than performance. And in the battle against television —the overriding consideration in the movie industry today—it lost ground.

JANE RUSSELL made box offices hum when she appeared in "Las Vegas Story" and "Son of Paleface"

DRAMATIC BEDLAM of political conventions was brought to 20 million TV-equipped homes

RADIO-TV

IN NOVEMBER, 1952, SOME THIRTY-FOUR million Republican voters went up against an insufficient twenty-seven million Democrats—the largest vote in the history of the U.S.—and indicated that it was time for a change in the nation's administration. It was no coincidence that the record balloting occurred in the same year that candidates turned to a new campaigning technique—television. With its political oratory, television had made whistle stops of some twenty million living rooms from coast to coast. By merely flicking a dial, viewers and voters looked right into the eyes of the candidates, listened to the issues, and were inspired to head for the polls. It was an event that marked television's coming of age; from then on, TV was no longer just a medium of entertainment—it was a nationwide force.

The year's big television story was the coverage of the national political conventions and the Presidential campaign. Both Democrats and Republicans convened in Chicago's International Amphitheater near the stockyards—an inconvenient location but, significantly, one that provided plenty of room for TV equipment.

The major TV and radio networks dispatched a thousand workers and 30 tons of equipment to the Amphitheater. Networks and sponsors spent $10 million to carry convention doings into twenty million television and forty-five million radio homes. Sixty cameras covered the proceedings. They were located not only in the hall but in hotel lobbies and corridors, forcing each candidate to act as if he were under a spotlight that never dimmed.

At times, television was unwelcome. Network executives fumed when their cameras were barred from a preconvention meeting of the G.O.P. National Committee. (The meeting was called to unsnarl the hotly controversial issue of seating the contested Southern delegations.) When the committee decided that TV equipment would interfere with its deliberations, the networks set up their cameras outside the conference room—a crafty move which gave the viewer all the pleasures of proximity and also the frustrations of exclusion. One radio reporter was clever enough to smuggle a

microphone into the conference room and record some of the testimony, which he later got on the air. Another succeeded in lowering a microphone from a projection booth, then came a cropper. The mike hit a committee member on the head and the reporter was thrown out.

In the comfort of his home, the TV viewer had a front-row seat at the conventions and, in some ways, could follow proceedings more closely than delegates at Convention Hall. For example, the TV audience, but not the delegates, saw Mrs. Charles P. Howard, Republican National Committee secretary, slipping off her shoes on the rostrum as she stood up to speak. It was not an event of any political magnitude but it was a memorable human touch.

During the Democratic convention, TV producers gave an excellent demonstra-

"I DON'T DARE GO HOME TONIGHT," quipped Margaret Truman after innocently spelling out "I Like Ike" in TV comedy skit with Jimmy Durante. The Schnoz praised President's daughter for being such a good sport

tion of their creative technical ability through use of the split-screen technique and rare timing. At one point, viewers were able to see Thomas Gavin of Missouri, President Truman's alternate, casting his pro-Stevenson vote at the convention at the same moment as Mr. Truman was seen waving good-by at Washington Airport before leaving for Chicago. A few hours later, viewers simultaneously watched some frantic maneuverings on the convention floor and the arrival of the Presidential plane at the Chicago airport. Truman, who had a television set in the plane, commented: "This is the first time that a President has been able to see himself get into an airplane, take off and then land."

Gavel-to-gavel coverage of the Republican convention filled seventy hours of air time. For the Democrats, the total was seventy-seven hours. Viewers in the East followed one night session until 4 A.M., as delegate after delegate, red-eyed and exhausted, rose to shout: "Mr. Chairman, I demand that the delegation be polled."

Prior to the conventions, neither of the men who won the Presidential nominations had been on television much.

When the Presidential campaign got under way, Eisenhower advisers emphasized whistle-stop campaigning so that the folksy charm of their hero could be brought to bear on the voters in person. Most television campaigning was left to other Republicans.

The Democrats, forced to "sell" Stevenson in a hurry, emphasized TV. A brilliant speaker, Stevenson was able to put his message and personality across within the time limits of TV broadcasts, and made twice-a-week appearances.

Television also helped to rescue the Republicans from a desperate situation in September, when their Vice-Presidential candidate, Richard M. Nixon of California, was accused of having used, while U.S. senator, an $18,235 personal-expense fund contributed by friends.

Senator Nixon accounted for the fund in a television broadcast, even told the TV audience about a puppy which a Texas admirer had given his two little girls. His wife sat nearby, her eyes rigidly fixed on him, not a muscle moving. One rumor held that it was not Mrs. Nixon at all, but a cardboard model of her!

Some thought the senator's speech a masterpiece. Others considered it cheap theatrics. *Variety,* the show-business weekly, referred to it as "in the best tradition of the American soap opera" but "a brilliant feat in political journalism."

The greatest political television show on earth had its moments of unintended humor too. In Indianapolis, Eisenhower had trouble with the Teleprompter, a device on which a copy of a speech is slowly wound as the speaker reads. It is operated by a man hidden under the rostrum. When the local audience applauded during the speech, the Teleprompter halted. "Go ahead! Go ahead! Go ahead!" shouted the general. "Yah, damn it," he complained to startled technicians nearby, "I want him to move up."

On a TV station in Des Moines, Iowa, Republican Senator Joseph McCarthy got mixed up one night with the "Life with Luigi" program which stars J. Carrol Naish as an Italian immigrant. As the senator opened an attack on Governor Stevenson, the Iowa station carried the senator's picture, but the voice came from the network's Luigi. "Thees is a greata country," McCarthy seemed to say. The senator's picture remained on the screen and he was heard, it seemed, urging his audience to buy a particular brand of coffee. Then came organ music. The confusion lasted for seven minutes.

The high cost of television campaigning, with an hour of air time running as high as $50,000, stunned politicians.

Expenditures for other kinds of advertising were curtailed. The Democrats beat the bushes for $5 donations. Networks demanded cash before a speech went on the air, and on one occasion the Democrats rounded up $50,000 only minutes before the deadline.

1952's most talked-about newcomer to television was a religious leader—the Most Reverend Fulton J. Sheen, Auxiliary Bishop of the Archdiocese of New York and National Director of the Society for the Propagation of the Faith. The Du Mont network gave him a half hour of free time on Tuesday evenings, a time period long dominated by Milton Berle on the rival N.B.C. network.

Bishop Sheen began with a hookup of three stations, soon expanded to include twenty-five. His program, "Life is Worth Living", was presented in front of an audience, from a studio stage made up to represent his study. The bishop wore the vestments of his office, moved slowly around the stage, and used a blackboard to illustrate his points. While his views naturally reflected the doctrines of the Roman Catholic Church, many members of the Protestant and Jewish faiths drew inspiration from his talks, which were lightened with occasional quips.

In addition to his jokes, Bishop Sheen made some entertainment-industry news in 1952. The Admiral Corporation, manufacturers of radio and television sets and household appliances, signed to sponsor his program, putting up $1 million for a 26-week period. The bishop's fee, unrevealed, would go to Mission Humanity, Inc., a voluntary agency of the United Nations.

Meanwhile, Milton Berle's show surrendered its No. 1 popularity rating, though it still attracted millions. Some critics objected that Berle was crashing into every guest act on his show and berating the studio audience when it did not laugh at his jokes. During the summer months, "Uncle Miltie" decided that what the public needed was a new Berle and proceeded forthwith to conceive one.

When he came back to the air in the fall, he had a new format. Six new writers had been hired to write a musical-comedy type of show. No longer was he the all-knowing, ever-present master of ceremonies; the show had none. On his first appearance as the new Berle, everyone in the cast kicked him around unmercifully. But it was a matter of opinion as to whether he had become a more sympathetic character. Berle, modestly, was positive that he had.

The TV show that ruled the roost in 1952 was "I Love Lucy", a situation comedy about a married couple, starring Lucille Ball and her real-life husband, Desi Arnaz. It was the first regularly scheduled show to be tuned in by ten million homes, according to the American Research Bureau. By October, an estimated thirty-four million viewers were watching Lucy.

What made it click? Basically, it allowed husbands and wives to laugh at irritations in their own marriages. Even little Junior could join in the fun, watching Lucy and Ricky, played by Desi, but seeing his own mama and papa fumbling through life together—basically congenial, but with many conflicting desires and viewpoints. The situations rang true. When Lucille Ball dived into the world of farce, the viewer went along with her because the basic situation was believable. Arnaz, a former band leader, developed into an engaging foil for Lucy's comic escapades. The "I Love Lucy" show, filmed in Hollywood, started a new trend in programming. Film producers rushed to turn out imitations, but none

HOMEY, RASPY-VOICED Arthur Godfrey is one of radio-TV's hardiest performers. C.B.S. star is on radio 8½ hours a week, on television 5½ hours

achieved anything like the success of the original.

In the fall, Tallulah Bankhead brought her supercharged personality to TV and the show's opening chorus hailed the new era of "Tallulahvision". The era, however, was without staying power. Despite a heavy advance build-up, the show was considered pretty sluggish except for one sketch in which she tried to reserve a drawing room on a New York City subway train and pay her fare to 181st Street by check. Miss Bankhead was experimenting in a new medium and apparently it frightened her. Radio had done the same thing two years earlier, but she had finally won out. She must have been confident that she could repeat her radio success in TV, for she agreed to do five more shows during the season.

During the year, the nation's most famous piano player—Harry S. Truman—turned in two bang-up television performances, both loaded with surprises.

On March 29, at a Jefferson-Jackson Day Dinner in Washington, he rambled jovially through a half-hour speech. With his television time about to run out, he calmly exploded a bombshell. Said the President: "I shall not be a candidate for re-election."

On May 3, TV viewers got an hour-long tour of the White House, personally conducted by Truman, who proved himself not only a good guide but a capable historian, humorist, and pianist, with a poised television manner.

The show was unusually intimate and personalized. The President recalled being alone in the barnlike White House and noticing a baseball game being played along the Potomac. He stole down the hill to watch. But the only thing he managed to do, he said, was to break up the ball game.

In the East Room of the White House, Truman ran a finger across the keyboard of a Steinway grand piano, then played a portion of Mozart's *Ninth Sonata*. Then he crossed the room to another piano and played that one. This, said he—wise in the ways of commercials—was a Baldwin, also a fine instrument.

Another performer in the Truman family, the President's daughter Margaret, had been put under contract by N.B.C. in 1951 for a number of guest appearances on radio and TV. In 1952, N.B.C. renewed Margaret's contract for another year—*after* her father had said he would not again be a candidate. Miss Truman, a soprano, has a charming television personality and has shown skill in clowning with such comedians as Jimmy Durante. Originally, she was tailor-made for jokes about politics: now her writers may have to work harder.

To C.B.S. in 1952 went the honor, if it can be called that, of introducing the world's first electronically presented wooer, weary-looking Renzo Cesana, billed as "The Continental". His job, aside from selling stockings made by his sponsor, was to woo the American housewife with sweet nothings. With organ music in the background, "The Continental" would light two cigarettes and hand one toward the camera. He would pour two glasses of champagne and extend one (to a stage hand unseen by the audience). He offered a rose, a quivering smile, an elegant accent, and heavy breathing. "Ah," he began, "alone at night in a man's apartment!" "The Continental" was not retained after his first thirteen weeks on the air, but at year's end he was back on a local New York station.

Dagmar, big and busty portrayer of the traditional dumb blonde, tried a comeback early in the year. She had started in 1950 over N.B.C. in Jerry Lester's "Broadway Open House", in a bit role which made her nationally known. After being off the air for some time, she finally got

MILTON BERLE changed his program's format from variety to situation comedy. Millions continued to regard "Uncle Miltie" as Tuesday night must

her own show in March, 1952. In "Dagmar's Canteen" she played the hostess in a club for servicemen, but the show didn't click and the comeback was not a success.

Stranger yet in the history of 1952 TV was the case of comedian Ken Murray who, in effect, was paid $2000 a week for doing nothing. Murray had been on TV for several seasons, hired by a sponsor, but in June, 1952, he signed a long-term contract directly with C.B.S. It was a pay-or-play contract—the artist being guaranteed a specified weekly fee whether or not the network puts him on the air. Came the new fall season and C.B.S. was unable to sell Murray to a sponsor. If he went on the air unsponsored, the network would have to foot production costs that could easily run to $15,000 or $20,000 weekly. It was a lot cheaper for C.B.S. to let Murray stay home and await the postman bringing his weekly $2000 check.

One of the commentators did better than Murray. Walter Winchell made his TV debut in October, doing a Sunday evening newscast over A.B.C., a few hours before his regular radio broadcast. Winchell considered several formats for television, but decided to let folks see the old radio Walter—tie loosened at the collar, hat on, and reading his script.

"We bought a photographed version of your radio program," said his sponsor.

Biggest man to hit television in 1952 was Herman Hickman, who weighs upward of 300 pounds. Hickman quit his football-coaching job at Yale to do a fifteen-minute weekly show for a cigar sponsor. Actually, he was already a TV

DAGMAR soared to fame soon after first TV appearance. She got her own show, and her picture adorned cover of "Life". But stardom proved brief

personality, having won fame as a panel member on "Celebrity Time" while still coaching. In the fall, he also reported Saturday football scores after each game televised by N.B.C.

"Television is less strenuous than coaching college football," said Hickman. "It's pretty rugged when you're depending on a 19-year-old quarterback to keep your room and board paid up."

Joe DiMaggio, baseball's immortal Yankee Clipper, switched to a television career in April, doing a show before and after each baseball game televised from Yankee Stadium. Joe, clearly a better man with a bat than with an English sentence, suffered from early mike fright, didn't hesitate to describe his first TV show as "a real stomach jumper". He improved, however, as the season went along. He was also more relaxed on another weekly show, filmed for television, in which he told tots and tykes how to play baseball. It was, everyone agreed, more in DiMaggio's line.

In 1952, the professional partnership between Jack Benny and Phil Harris ended after sixteen years. Bob Crosby became the new band leader on Jack's radio show and also appeared on his television program.

Benny denied personal friction between Harris and himself, but admitted business conflict. Benny was under contract to C.B.S., while Phil's radio program, on which he costars with his wife, Alice Faye, was heard over N.B.C. It was impossible for Phil to appear on Jack's TV show at 7:30 on Sunday evenings, then make his own radio show at 8.

Benny, a real master of dead-pan comedy, increased the frequency of his television appearances from once every six weeks to once a month. He said he would never do a weekly TV show, but might eventually appear twice a month. If so, he added, he would quit radio.

Unlike the new Berle, Benny refused to use a regular format for his show. "I want it casual," he said. "I don't want the audience to know what's coming next. Just a monologue to start with, and then maybe have a few people drop by for a chat. But I don't ever want a regular cast on my show."

A pioneer puppet show on TV, "Kukla, Fran and Ollie", took some hard knocks in 1952. In television's early days, the show ran for a half hour each weekday evening and picked up a loyal following. When N.B.C. cut the show to fifteen minutes, fans howled. Toward the end of the 1951-52 season, N.B.C. considered dropping the show entirely. But a compromise was made and the puppets were scheduled for once a week on Sundays at 6:30 P.M. Then along came an N.B.C. sponsor who wanted that time and "Kukla, Fran and Ollie" was switched again, to Sunday afternoons.

Bing Crosby made his television debut during the year, doing a 14½-hour marathon with Bob Hope to raise money for the United States Olympic Fund. The "telethon" ran all Saturday night and into Sunday afternoon. As entertainment, it was disappointing: during a 10-hour stretch, "Der Bingle" did only one complete song.

Over $1 million was pledged to the Olympic Fund, but only about $300,000 was forthcoming. However, this proportion between "pledges" and "receipts" is customary for "telethons", which are magnets for practical jokers and egotists who never intend to pay off but love to hear their names read over the air.

One person telephoned Bob and Bing, identified himself as Thomas J. Watson, head of International Business Machines, and said he was pledging $150,000. Even zillionaires Hope and Crosby were astounded at the sum. Verification seemed in order and the caller, not surprisingly, turned out to be an impostor. The real Mr. Watson said that he knows of no one who can afford to peel off $150,000 in these days of high taxes.

One of the year's most surprising innovations was Dave Garroway's "Today" program of news and news features which N.B.C. put on from 7 to 9 A.M. Garroway himself got up at 4 A.M. to reach the studio and put his show together. "All you have to do to get up at 4," he commented, "is to go to bed at 8 o'clock at night."

Late-rising newspaper critics asked who would look at television at 7 A.M. The answer: millions. Why? Partly, perhaps, because they are fascinated by the communications gadgets used on the show: banks of teletype machines, rows of TV monitors, microphones, earphones, and clocks giving the time all over the world.

And Dave thought his show might be helping marital bliss through a crucial hour. "Goodness knows," he said, "that a lot of husbands watching the show aren't arguing with their wives."

Every television show gets an award at some time or another—most awards are cooked up by press agents and promoters —but in 1952 Arthur Godfrey and Eddie Cantor got unique accolades.

According to the *Toronto Globe and Mail,* a farmer in Ontario installed a TV set in his barn to amuse the hired hands. But the cows watched television too—and liked it so well that they gave an extra 15 gallons of milk daily. Judging from their variations of output, they liked Godfrey and Cantor best.

The televising of the atomic-bomb explosion at Yucca Flat, Nev., on April 22, was doubly dramatic because electronic gremlins almost jinxed the picture. There was transmission trouble with relay facilities set up on mountain peaks. Minutes before the bomb was dropped from a plane, viewers were puzzled by a wavy and wobbly video screen. When the an-

nouncer yelled "Bomb away", the screen showed blobs of black and white.

The announcer counted off the seconds, indicating the number to go before the bomb blew up. Millions of viewers sat on the edge of their seats, wondering if they'd be able to see the explosion. Three seconds before the bomb went off, the picture cleared up.

Suddenly there was a tiny white spot in the middle of a large black oval. For a second, the whole screen was dark—a TV phenomenon caused by the intense light of the explosion. The brilliance was more than the electronic camera could absorb.

Not much of the mushroom effect immediately following the blast was visible to the home audience, for gremlins interfered again. But when the picture quality improved, there was the pillar of dust and, atop it, a cloud that resembled a huge doughnut. After all the excitement was over, the picture came in perfectly.

Reaction to the telecast varied. Some thought it sensational; others said it fizzled. Whatever the audience thought of the show, tremendous credit was due TV engineers who fought against great odds in making it possible.

The American Telephone and Telegraph Company had been asked to set up relay facilities from Yucca Flat to Los Angeles, but declined because its policy prohibited the installation of temporary TV facilities. So all Los Angeles video stations got together to accomplish the feat. The Marine Corps provided a helicopter that dropped microwave relay equipment on mountain peaks—including Mount Baldy, which is 10,080 feet high. And technical crews camped out for several days in snowdrifts atop the peaks while they hooked up the equipment.

Theater Network Television, wherein shows are piped by a closed circuit onto the regular screens of movie houses, made big strides during the year. The heavy-

"I LOVE LUCY", with audience estimated at 30 million people, became nation's No. 1 TV show. It quickly attracted host of imitators. Situation comedy stars Lucille Ball and Desi Arnaz

weight-championship fight between Jersey Joe Walcott and Rocky Marciano in Philadelphia on Sept. 23 was fed to fifty theaters in thirty-one cities—the first time theater TV went coast-to-coast. The bout was not telecast for home consumption, nor broadcast by radio.

It was a sellout in the theaters. Most houses charged from $3 to $5 admission, with the International Boxing Club, the fight promoters, being paid about $1 for each theater ticket sold. A drive-in theater in Rutherford, N.J., carried the fight, first drive-in ever to carry theater TV. It charged $10 per carload and had 1300 of them, besides 6000 "walk-ins" at $3 a head—an estimated 16,000 crowded into a space normally holding 3500.

A regular performance of *Carmen* on the stage of New York's Metropolitan Opera House was televised in thirty-one theaters in twenty-seven cities on Dec. 11. It was a success, but not the success the Walcott-Marciano fight was. Said a sales-girl at a theater popcorn counter in Fort Lee, N.J.: "We've only sold two bags. Usually, by this time, we're all sold out."

Television poked its nose into hospitals during the year—once to watch the birth of a baby and again to view doctors removing part of a man's stomach. The nation's tiniest television star—weight 5 pounds, 7 ounces—made his debut in the delivery room of Colorado General Hospital in Denver on the night of Dec. 2.

The TV audience saw the doctors preparing for the delivery, but not the delivery itself. Viewers did hear the magnified rumblings of the unborn baby's heartbeat as a doctor held a stethoscope. Then the camera switched to another scene, and when it returned there was Gordon

Kerr, the third child of Army Sergeant and Mrs. Kerr, being lifted by a doctor.

On June 10, the general public was "allowed" into an operating room in Chicago's Wesley Memorial Hospital to view eight crucial minutes of a stomach operation. The vital operation had been in progress for two hours before the TV audience was let in.

During the telecast a doctor described the progress of the operation to viewers, who saw masked doctors and nurses standing around a patient whose head was not visible. They saw the operating surgeon's gloved fingers as he worked. But only those familiar with anatomy could have known what was going on. Especially vivid, however, was the sight of the retractors holding open the wound, and the sterile pads used to keep the incision dry.

Several outstanding high-level programs—none originally designed to sell goods—were put on during the year. One was "Omnibus", the TV series produced by the Ford Foundation's TV-Radio Workshop, and for which the foundation put up $2 million.

Alistair Cooke, the program's host, described "Omnibus" as "a vaudeville show of the arts and skills of man". In its debut, it presented a play entitled *The Trial of Anne Boleyn,* written by Maxwell Anderson and starring Rex Harrison and Lilli Palmer; excerpts from Gilbert and Sullivan's *The Mikado,* starring Martyn Green; *The Witch Doctor,* a short film of a Haitian voodoo dance; and a play, *The Bad Men,* written especially for television by William Saroyan.

In its weekly ninety minutes of running time, "Omnibus" was not always outstanding; in fact, sometimes it was downright boring. But it was free of the curse of format. None of its sequences, for instance, was timed to end on the quarter hour or half hour, except for the closing

JACK BENNY'S TV SHOW won critics' acclaim. Veteran showman continues radio program

portion. Two months after it went on the air, "Omnibus" was sold to sponsors.

Victory at Sea, a filmed history of naval operations in World War II, televised by N.B.C., gave fresh perspective and meaning to the recent past. Produced by Henry Salomon, Jr., with a musical score by Richard Rodgers, the program was winnowed from over 60,000,000 feet of film from both Allied and enemy sources.

The National Collegiate Athletic Association again restricted the televising of college football to one game on eleven successive Saturdays. Its argument was that uncontrolled TV hurt gate receipts, particularly for smaller colleges. Notre Dame and the University of Pennsylvania were among the major dissenters, with Notre Dame arguing that "the plan is illegal and unfairly restricts an institution's right to televise". If it had been allowed to sign a contract with a TV network, Notre Dame might have received $300,-000 for its schedule of home games.

The merger of two unions representing performers in radio and television was approved by the Associated Actors and Artistes of America (A.F.L.), parent organization of all performer unions. The unions merged were the American Federation of Radio Artists and Television Authority. They represented twenty thousand performers. The newly formed union is known as the American Federation of Television and Radio Artists.

This first step toward a full merger of all performer unions may ultimately enable an artist to carry a single card, pay dues to a single union, and work in any branch of entertainment—an ideal long sought in show business.

In 1952, the four major radio networks made a 25 percent cut in nighttime rates to most advertisers, the second reduction within a year. The obvious reason was the growing loss of the radio audience to TV. And TV, of course, continued to take

giant strides. During the year, it acquired two Pulitzer Prize winning writers. Robert E. Sherwood signed with N.B.C. to write nine original one-hour plays for the highest fee (unrevealed) ever paid in television. And Ben Hecht, coauthor of *The Front Page,* agreed to write two half-hour plays a month for C.B.S. and to be supervising editor of a new dramatic series.

Both C.B.S. and N.B.C. opened huge new television studios in the Hollywood area. The C.B.S. studios, known as Television City, represented an investment of $12 million, and the company's long-range program for additional studios there would increase the outlay to $35 million.

Perhaps the most important TV news of the year came in April when the Federal Communications Commission lifted its 3½-year-old "freeze" on the construction of new television stations. The new plan provided for the opening of no less than 2053 new stations in 1291 communities.

With the expanding number of stations came two big problems. The first was how to find sufficient program material. The average television station presents as many hours of programming a week as Hollywood picture companies turn out a year. No other entertainment medium has ever gobbled up material so rapidly. How its ever-expanding appetite can be satisfied is a question that hasn't yet been satisfactorily answered.

The second problem was a real poser. How long can the same actors be seen again and again without boring the public? Never before has a performer been called upon to walk out in front of the same audience and be seen week after week. How soon will the audience consider him stale?

To learn the answer, tune in at this same hour five or ten years from now.

MADCAP COMICS Sid Caesar and Imogene Coca star in television extravaganza "Your Show of Shows"

YANKEES' JOHNNY SAIN is ruled out by umpire Art Passarella, but camera proves Sain safe. Bad call occurred during tenth inning of Series' fifth game

SPORTS

IN '52, TV MADE ALL EARLIER SPORTS AT-tendance figures seem puny. According to the Advertising Research Bureau, fifty million persons saw the 1952 World Series. Football attracted one hundred million. Wrestling, tennis, boxing, horse racing, and roller derbies lured millions more.

Yet, paradoxically, attendance at the year's greatest athletic carnival, the 15th Olympiad, was only about one million. Staged in Helsinki, Finland, on the rim of the Arctic Circle, it was beyond TV eye-range. With the U.S.S.R. competing for the first time, 5780 athletes—more than ever before—gathered from 67 nations.

Opening ceremonies, however, were delayed briefly by an overzealous stadium employee. Paavo Nurmi, famed former Finnish track star, carried the Olympic torch on its final lap from Mount Olympus in Greece. As part of the pomp and ritual, the torch was to light a symbolic flame in a towering dome atop the stadium. A bedraggled raincoat covered Nurmi's suit. At the stadium, a skeptical

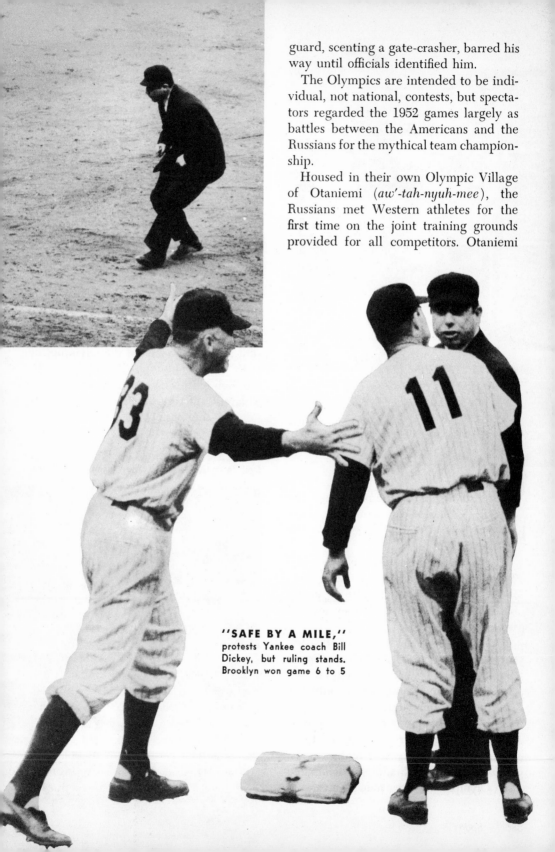

guard, scenting a gate-crasher, barred his way until officials identified him.

The Olympics are intended to be individual, not national, contests, but spectators regarded the 1952 games largely as battles between the Americans and the Russians for the mythical team championship.

Housed in their own Olympic Village of Otaniemi (*aw'-tah-nyuh-mee*), the Russians met Western athletes for the first time on the joint training grounds provided for all competitors. Otaniemi

"SAFE BY A MILE," protests Yankee coach Bill Dickey, but ruling stands. Brooklyn won game 6 to 5

BOB MATHIAS again won Olympic Decathlon title. Many consider him world's greatest athlete

field. Compact New Yorker Lindy Remigino won the closest 100-meter race in Olympic history. The U.S. swept the shot put with mammoth Parry O'Brien setting a new Olympic record. Cornell's 400-meter hurdling specialist Charlie Moore beat Russia's surprising Jurii Lituev. And the long-striding Negro, Jersey City whippet Andy Stanfield, led American sprinters to a sweep in the 200 meters. Harrison ("Bones") Dillard, a 100-meter-dash man in the '48 international clash in London, broke the Olympic record in the 110-meter hurdles.

Of all Olympic events, however, the decathlon is the most thorough test of skill and endurance. In the Olympics of 1948, held at London's Wembley Stadium, Bob Mathias, husky 17-year-old from Tulare, Calif., outran, outthrew, and outjumped the best. In 1952, the poised,

JUBILANT CZECH Dana Zatopek, wife of Emil Zatopek, cartwheels after winning javelin toss

was off-limits to Westerners until the friendly U.S. rowing committee chairman, Clifford ("Tippy") Goes, broke the Russian ice.

"I expected to get my ears chewed off," Tippy said. "Instead, they couldn't have been nicer . . . They had three single sculls. We needed one and they insisted we take one of theirs."

Communist village Otaniemi boasted carpeted floors, upholstered furniture, a permanent dining hall, and dancers, actors, and singers to entertain the athletes. At capitalist camp Käpylä (*kah'-poo-lay*), where Western athletes were housed, there were concrete floors, bare stools, and meals in a drafty field tent.

From the first, U.S. athletes dominated the Olympic feature, men's track and

OLYMPIC official scurries out of path of G-man Horace Ashenfelter, 3000-meter steeplechase winner

handsome giant (6 ft. 3 in., 200 lbs.), a veteran of eight decathlon meets, four times national champion, established himself as the modern world's greatest all-around athlete.

That took stamina, muscle, speed, and nerves. A rival once said that Mathias "relaxes so completely between events you think he's asleep". This nerveless self-control was demonstrated on the chilly, overcast second day of competition. With only three events to go, the weary Mathias, bandages covering a painful leg injury, lagged 99 points behind the world mark he had set a month earlier in the trials at Tulare. A new record seemed impossible.

In the gathering darkness, with the electric scoreboard casting shadows across the track, he vaulted 13 ft. 1½ in. (his best by 0.72 in.). Then he surpassed

HUMAN MACHINE Emil Zatopek, winner of 26-mile marathon, is rewarded with kiss from wife

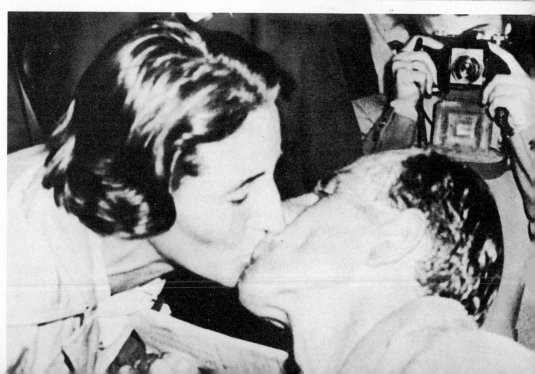

AQUATIC STARS Jimmy McLane (nearest camera) of Yale and Ford Konno of Ohio State warm up before pacing U. S. swimmers to Olympic victory. Konno won 1500-meter race by 20 yards

his Tulare javelin heave. After that, calling on his amazing reserve, he sliced 4.5 seconds off his best time in the 1500 meters. After twelve grueling hours of competition, Mathias had scored 7887 points to beat the world mark he set at Tulare by 62 points.

While the U.S. dominated the shorter races and field events, American distance runners, as was expected, were blanked. In forty-four years, no American had ever won an Olympic race longer than 800 meters. Little hope was held for American 3000-meter steeplechaser Horace Ashenfelter, the Penn State graduate and F.B.I. agent. Neither he nor any other American had ever broken 9 minutes. European and Russian champions rarely ran over 9 minutes.

It was wiry Vladimir Kazantsev, the Russian champion, the crowd watched as the race began. At the fourth lap, the stringy (145 lbs., 5 ft. 10 in.) American champion took the lead, his Russian shadow on his heels. At the turn of the last bend, Kazantsev pulled even as both runners poured on speed. They took the final water jump together. Faltering from weariness, the Russian stumbled into the water. Ashenfelter leaped the barrier cleanly and the race was decided. Horace sprinted down the homestretch to win in the Olympic record time of 8:45.4.

Although the crowds cheered just a little louder whenever a Russian was beaten, a new high in good feeling between American and Soviet athletes was

reached when Bob Richards, an ordained (Church of the Brethren) minister, won the pole vault. Russian fourth-place winner Peter Denisenko, with a bear hug, lifted the vaulting vicar off the ground. His display of good sportsmanship was applauded.

Meanwhile the Soviets piled up points (nearly 200 in gymnastics) and dominated the women's field events. And at the halfway mark, the Associated Press showed the Russians leading by 100 points in the unofficial team standings.

On the twelfth day, a Soviet spokesman predicted victory. He said the Rus-

ONE-MAN STEAM ROLLER Pat Harder, Detroit Lions back, eludes three Los Angeles Rams tacklers to cross goal line in professional National Conference play-off game. Detroit won 31 to 21

sians attached "great importance" to their "official system of reckoning sporting virtues".

In the next two days, the U.S. picked up 34 points while Russia failed to score. David ("Skippy") Browning, red-haired University of Texas junior, led the U.S. 3-meter divers to a sweep. The lithe Texan, first or second in every national springboard-diving meet since 1948, gave an almost perfect performance. He gained tremendous height off the board and his nearly splashless entry into the water impressed the judges.

Off the high board, diminutive (5 ft. 1¾ in.) Samuel ("Sammy") Lee, Army Medical Corps major, matched Browning's grace and perfect co-ordination.

In one event after another, U.S. swimmers and divers closed the gap in the team scores, but it was left to Ford

RED-HOT MAMA Sophie Tucker shows some red-hot enthusiasm as she whoops it up for favorites

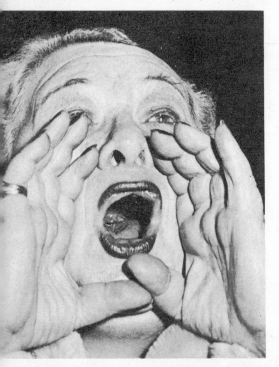

Konno, a young Hawaiian Nisei, to supply the clincher in the 1500-meter race. With a smooth, gliding motion and a six-beat kick in which his feet scarcely broke water, the slight Ohio State freshman rippled across the pool to win by 20 yds. His time? An amazing 18:30. His Olympic-record victory moved the U.S. into the team lead.

The winning surge continued in basketball and boxing. Five American boxers, all Negroes, entered the finals. All five won gold medals representing first places.

It remained for a loose-jointed Czech with thinning blond hair to become the top Olympic hero and running phenomenon of modern times with a triple win. Tireless Emil Zatopek, Czechoslovak army major, with an agonized running style, facial contortions, and a wobbling head, broke his own 1948 10,000-meter Olympic record on opening day. A week later, he electrified the crowd with a burst of speed to win the 5000-meter.

Three days thereafter, he entered the marathon (26 m. 285 yds.), though he had never before run the full distance. Multilingual (he speaks French, German, Russian, English, Czech), the star joked with spectators lining the roads but set an incredibly fast pace. At one point, he dropped back to exchange pleasantries with Britain's favorite, Jim Peters—was he setting too fast a pace? Grimly, the Englishman shook his head, but, 20 miles out, seized with a cramp, Peters gave up. "The pace," he said, "killed me."

When Zatopek came through the tunnel into the stadium, 2½ minutes ahead of his nearest rival, the stands roared. His time, 2:23:03.2, was 6 minutes, 16 seconds faster than the record for an Olympic marathon. Someone shouted to Americans in the Press box: "Lucky for you Zatopek didn't run in the sprints."

After sixteen days of competition, the

LIKE A BIRD: Dick Groat tries to hurdle N.Y.U. guard Ted Elsberg in field-goal attempt

Olympic flame atop the tower of Helsinki Stadium flickered out. The U.S. had won more gold medals (40 to Russia's 23) than any other nation in Olympic annals. The test of athletic strength between East and West was over.

On the U.S. national scene, the Brooklyn Dodgers and New York Yankees staged exciting drives for the National and American League baseball pennants.

In 1951, tense, jittery Brooklyn blew a 13½-game August lead, wound up in a tie with the New York Giants, then lost the League pennant on Giant Bobby Thomson's ninth-inning homer. In 1952, Brooklyn Manager Charlie Dressen promised fans "The Dodgers won't blow it again!"

They almost did. A fighting Giant team whittled Brooklyn's 10-game lead to a 3-game lead.

But Brooklyn finally clinched it, thanks largely to Most Valuable Rookie of the Year Joe Black, giant (6 ft. 2 in., 225 lb.), intelligent, right-handed Negro relief pitcher.

At season's start with the Dodgers, Black warmed the bench. After the first month passed, Brooklyn's pitching staff was in bad shape. Don Newcombe was in the army. Clem Labine, Ralph Branca, and Johnny Rutherford nursed sore arms. Preacher Roe suffered the miseries of an aching back.

Finally Dressen gave Black his first assignment. Asked to pitch one inning, he struck out two men and retired the side. Ten days later, he blanked the Phils for three innings. By year's end, he had appeared in 56 games, more than a third of the total played. He had won 15, lost 4, saved 15 others, and had even started 2 games to prove he could go the route.

Though the Giants also had a fine rookie reliefer in knuckle-ball artist Hoyt Wilhelm (15-3), their hopes for the National League pennant diminished when

cleanup hitter Monte Irvin splintered his ankle in an exhibition game and the army drafted star defensive outfielder Willie Mays.

To scrappy Giant Manager Durocher, Brooklyn fans offered consolation with a thorn in it: "Wait till last year."

Meantime, in the American League, the pennant race proved to be the hottest in years. With three great pitchers working in rotation (Mike Garcia 22-11; Bob Lemon 22-11; Early Wynn 23-12), favored Cleveland won practically everything statistically (runs batted-in, runs scored, homers); but it lost the League championship.

So, to shrewd, oil-rich, 62-year-old Yankee Pilot Casey Stengel went his fourth straight American League pennant. To win, Stengel had shifted players all over the diamond and used 99 different batting orders. His reward: a new two-year contract at an estimated $100,-000 a year.

The seesaw Yankee-Dodger struggle in the 49th World Series probably generated more excitement than any other Series in history. Though there were sixteen homers—oddly enough, play was highlighted by spectacular outfield catches, puncture-proof infield defense, and brilliant pitching.

Three heroes of the 7-game Series were Yankee centerfielder, switch-hitting Mickey Mantle (at 20, potentially one of the game's great), and Dodgers Duke Snider and Peewee Reese.

Each batted .345, and outfielder Snider hit four home runs to tie World Series records set by Babe Ruth and Lou Gehrig. Mantle won 2 games with four-baggers. But top Series star was veteran (39) Johnny Mize. In 5 games, imperturbable Mize batted .400; he pinch-hit a home run, and slammed two more on successive days.

The inevitable Series "goat" was an

umpire, whose bad call at first base was exposed by a photographer. It proved what fans had suspected—umpires are human.

In 1952, the Series went the full seven contests, and throughout the first six of these there was a nice symmetry. The Dodgers won the first, third, and fifth games by scores of 4–2, 5–3, and 6–5. The Yanks took the second, fourth, and sixth contests, 7–1, 2–0, and 3–2. And then there was the seventh, and that settled it. The Dodgers, trailing by two runs, loaded the bases in the seventh inning. Casey Stengel reached into his bull-pen grab bag, came up with Bob Kuzava, a left-hander who had stopped the Giants in the '51 series finale. Kuzava did it again. Score: Yankees 4, Brooklyn 2.

The Flatbush Faithful shuffled home sadly.

In 1952, the cold hand of war touched baseball as it touched so many other American activities.

Recalled to active duty by the U.S. Marine Corps were Boston Red Sox outfielder Ted Williams and Yankee second-baseman Jerry Coleman. Williams, twice winner of the Most Valuable Player Award (1946 and 1949), gave up a yearly $125,000. An individualist, the 33-year-old slugger had always refused to acknowledge the crowd's plaudits. In his final game, he homered. The fans yelled. At the plate, Ted turned awkwardly and, for the first time, tipped his cap. The Red Sox, with a rookie-studded lineup, finished sixth.

At year's end, baseball writers tabbed the Philadelphia A's tiny (5 ft. 6 in., 139 lbs.) control pitcher Robert Clayton Shantz as the American League's Most Valuable Player because his curves and knucklers were elusive enough to win 24 games, or almost a third of the A's total during the entire season. Top winning pitcher was another Philadelphian, Na-tional Leaguer Robin Roberts, a chunky, 25-year-old right-hander who won 28 games, 6 of them from the pennant-winning Dodgers.

The National League's Most Valuable Player of the Year was Chicago Cub outfielder Hank Sauer, who hit 37 circuit swats during the season to tie Pittsburgh Pirate outfielder Ralph Kiner for the home-run leadership.

In the midst of the pennant fight in New York, another kind of sports battle was staged in Philadelphia. When it was over, it took fourteen stitches to patch up the battered face of Rocky Marciano, new World Heavyweight Champion, who had kayoed aging Jersey Joe Walcott.

Knocked down for the first time in his professional career, outmaneuvered, outfought for twelve rounds, Marciano ended the contest with a mighty right to Walcott's chin.

The new Champ, undefeated as a professional, had won 38 of 43 fights by knockouts. Ungraceful, with thick torso and short arms, he is light (184 lbs.) by heavyweight standards. But he has two tremendous assets. He can take punishment and he can punch explosively with either hand.

Born in Brockton, Mass., son of an Italian immigrant shoemaker, Marciano outside the ring is soft-spoken, modest, puppy-dog friendly. He has limpid brown eyes and a boyish grin. He does not drink or smoke and he relishes the boring rigors of training. His goal in life?

"Maybe someday," he said, "they'll talk of Dempsey, Louis, and Marciano."

A more complicated personality is Middleweight (160 lbs.) Champion Sugar Ray Robinson, a stylist with light, dancing feet and raw punching power. The tall (5 ft. 11 in.), handsome Negro, formerly Welterweight (147 lbs.) Champion, wanted a third title to cap a great career and challenged Light-heavyweight King Joey Maxim, who outweighed him 15 lbs.

Yankee Stadium on fight night was an oven. At first, Robby's fists flashed with oiled precision, bang-banging the slow-moving Maxim, who seemed mainly concerned with saving his strength. In the tenth round, Referee Ruby Goldstein collapsed from heat prostration. By round thirteen, Robinson was exhausted in the stifling heat. His spent legs staggered in a Chaplinesque jig. With seconds remaining in the thirteenth round, Robby missed

MURDEROUS HAYMAKER from the fist of challenger Rocky Marciano sends Jersey Joe Walcott to canvas, beaten and unconscious. 13th-round knockout made Marciano heavyweight champion of world

Maxim with a roundhouse right and sprawled to the canvas. The bell rang, and the fight, Robinson's dream of a triple crown, and Maxim's dogged wait were over.

Before the year ended, fighting-machine Sugar Ray turned tap dancer, opening at New York's French Casino night club. A perfectionist in the ring, he was sweating to become one behind the footlights as well.

Summer crowds had hardly shuffled out of the big outdoor arenas when football slammed in. The Michigan State Spartans, led by Clarence ("Biggie") Munn, swept through their second unbeaten season, ran their victory streak to 24, and were crowned mythical champions. Chunky, 44-year-old Munn stressed fundamentals and speed, with his players moving out of deceptive multiple variations of the T, winged-T, and single- and double-wing formations.

Former All-American guard from Minnesota, Munn is not a coach of the grim-grind school, believes that "without laughs, the game isn't worth playing". But the pressure of big-time football takes its toll and its trade-mark is ulcers even for genial "Biggie".

Other winners were Georgia Tech (rated number two in the nation) 24, Mississippi 7 in the Sugar Bowl; and Southern California 7, Wisconsin 0 in the Rose Bowl.

In the bread-and-butter pro game, the have-not Detroit Lions (last title 1935) beat the championship-rich Cleveland

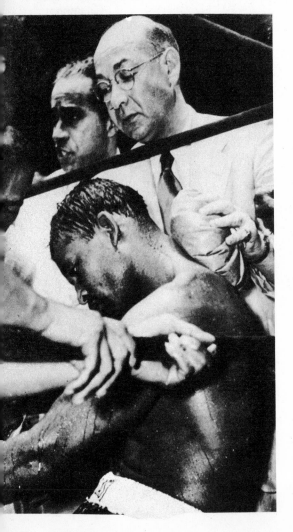

KAYOED BY HEAT, Sugar Ray Robinson can't get up for 14th round in title bout with Joey Maxim

Browns (six straight titles) for first place. After a dismal early-season start (lost 2 out of first 3 games), it was an uphill battle for Coach Buddy Parker's Lions.

More than fifty thousand shivering fans turned out in Detroit to watch the bitterly fought battle with Cleveland on the frozen turf. Score: Lions 17, Browns 7.

In the 1951–52 season, basketball suffered growing pains with the disclosure of wholesale bribery, dumped games, and shaved points. Further repercussions in the 1952–53 season resulted in Kentucky's one-year suspension by the

FLYING HOOFS: Barefoot Boy rounds the final turn at Florida's Hialeah race track and wins race

N.C.A.A. for disregard of the collegiate code of ethics. Late in the year, scandal-tainted basketball players were barred from playing pro ball by New York's General Sessions Judge Saul Streit.

"An athlete," said Judge Streit, "who has been convicted . . . of receiving a bribe . . . has forfeited all rights . . . to participate in any public sport, amateur or professional."

By Christmas, however, badly shaken basketball was getting into high gear once more. Kansas State, Seton Hall, and Illinois moved into top rankings. In the pro National Basketball Association, the 1951–52 champion Minneapolis Lakers, sparked by giant George Mikan, led the Western Division at year's end, while the New York Knickerbockers held a precarious lead in the East.

In 1952, Australian Davis Cup winners demonstrated their stroking power and depth in the U.S. Tennis Championships at Forest Hills, N.Y. Along with three of the best amateurs in the world (Frank Sedgman, Ken McGregor, Mervyn Rose), Australia displayed the talents of two beardless 17-year-olds.

In the quarter finals, slim, baby-faced Kenneth Rosewall (5 ft. 7 in., 150 lbs.) dazzled the gallery with his all-court game and blazing smashes to topple top U.S. player Vic Seixas in five sets. On the same day, chunky Lewis Hoad trimmed 1950 U.S. titleholder and No. 3 U.S. player Art Larsen.

In the semifinals, aging (38) Gardnar Mulloy, only remaining U.S. entry, outmaneuvered the inexperienced Rosewall to face 24-year-old Sedgman. It took the Australian only three sets and 47 minutes to whip Mulloy.

U.S. women did better. In the all-U.S. final, pert, 17-year-old Maureen ("Little Mo") Connolly of San Diego beat former Wimbledon Champ Doris Hart to win her second U.S. title. She joined a select group (Helen Wills, Alice Marble, Pauline Betz) who have won both U.S. and Wimbledon crowns in one year.

Maureen, grimly serious on court, finds tennis an ideal solution for one womanly problem. "Thank heaven I'm getting thinner," she said. "Tennis is a perfect recipe."

Nancy Chaffee Kiner, beautiful tennis-playing wife of Pittsburgh home-run slugger Ralph Kiner, was outclassed in tournament play. She announced philosophically, "I'm going home now and have some babies—four boys!"

In golf, Toledo millionaire bar-bell enthusiast Frank Stranahan flexed his mus-

JOCKEY Tony DeSpirito, 18, shown with mother, broke record set in 1906 by bringing in 390 winners

cles to try for his third British Amateur title. In the all-U.S. final, Stranahan was 2 up over Harvie Ward, easy-going stockbroker from Tarboro, N.C. Both golfers suffered finalitis jitters on the wind-swept Scottish fairways. They flubbed irons, banged into bunkers and traps, blew pushover putts. Ward finally pulled his game together to shoot four under even fours for the next 14 holes. Winner: 26-year-old Harvie Ward, on his first try, 6 and 5.

Youth is often served in sport, but not always. At the West Coast's Seattle Country Club, gray-haired oldster (47) Jack Westland became the oldest golfer ever to become U.S. National Amateur Champion. A part-time player, Westland took a vacation from politicking as Republican candidate for Congress to whip through a field of youngsters. Westland also won on Election Day.

Play-for-pay golfers came up with a new name: Julius Boros. In his two previous years of professional golf, the stocky Boros earned less than $7000. This year's U.S. Open Champion and top money winner (more than $37,000), Julius Boros was named Professional Golfer of 1952 in the annual Professional Golfers' Association poll.

Big money in golf is chicken feed in horse racing. Jockey Eddie Arcaro has pocketed a quarter of a million dollars while winning purses totaling more than two million. One July day in Chicago, on a horse named Ascent, the little man with the big, sensitive hands won his 3000th race to set a record for American-born jockeys.

Atop Calumet Farm's Hill Gail, Eddie won the Kentucky Derby ($96,300). Arcaro missed his chance for a triple crown when Hill Gail was injured and scratched from the Preakness. It was Blue Man who won that one, going away. But in the $82,400 Belmont Stakes, money-rider Arcaro, mounted on 13–1 long shot One Count, upset favored Blue Man by 2½ lengths.

While Arcaro's victories were impressive, it took 18-year-old Tony DeSpirito, an apprentice jockey from Lawrence, Mass., to climax one of the year's most exciting sports stories. The tiny (5 ft. 2 in., 107 lbs.) DeSpirito smashed a 46-year-old record—most winners for jockeys in one year. The record (388) was set by Walter Miller in 1906 and equaled by Willie Shoemaker and Joe Culmone in 1950.

Ruled off the track for incompetence in his first race, Tony was told to find less hazardous work. But DeSpirito wouldn't quit. Injured and out of action in November, suspended ten days for rough riding in early December, he hustled from one race track to another up and down the Eastern seaboard, flew to Havana, and closed the year with a terrific rush in his personal race against the calendar. He rode fifteen winners in six days, added four more on December 30th to break the record, and breezed home another winner on the last day of the year, to run his total to a record 390.

Two-dollar betters calculated Arcaro's thousands and totaled DeSpirito's wins, but turf experts centered their interest on Alfred Gwynne Vanderbilt's 2-year-old Native Dancer, gray son of Polynesian.

For the skeptical who wondered whether this colt, as big as a 3-year-old, could stay for distance, Native Dancer, at odds 1 to 5, breezed home in the East View Stakes over a mile and a sixteenth. He won his ninth straight race with flowing ease and at year's end was being touted as a new Man o' War.

LITTLE MO: 17-year-old Maureen Connolly was outstanding women's singles tennis star of 1952. She won both U.S. and Wimbledon championships

"MOTHER AND CHILD" by William Zorach was acquired by N.Y.'s Metropolitan Museum

U.N. HEADQUARTERS were planned by ten leading architects, constructed at cost of $67½ million. Though architectural genius Frank Lloyd Wright voiced criticism, structure received general approval

Art and Architecture

IT SEEMED BEST LAST YEAR TO BELIEVE THAT architecture need not be symbolic and that art does not imitate nature, particularly the nature of man. Among men the signs of disunity mounted steadily in what is still called the world's family of nations. But on a slender plot of real estate fronting Manhattan's East River men of many nations joined in building a bold and hopeful home for an organization called, as bravely as possible, the United Nations.

Its cost was $67.5 million. Its business was justice and peace. These should be well housed, the member nations agreed, and therefore much was expected architecturally of the U.N. buildings. They were planned by a team of ten leading world architects, headed by an American —Wallace K. Harrison, coplanner of Rockefeller Center. Then came the appraisals.

America's greatest architectural genius, towering and crusty Frank Lloyd Wright, was pointedly critical, called it: "A perfect symbol of division." Paul Rudolph, a leader in the young generation of architects, wrote, in *Architectural Forum:*

"The sloping walls of the General Assembly surrounding the timid dome seem to unwittingly symbolize a world which has indeed gone a long way toward crashing upon itself." So much for the exterior.

Inside the buildings there was trouble too. A pair of extremely abstract murals designed by the noted French painter Fernand Léger was installed in the General Assembly hall. Here, ironically, the gripping realities of peace and war will be debated, making this assembly hall the most meaningful room in the world. Someone in it asked, "What does this mural mean?", and a New York art critic replied, "A mural does not have to mean anything." *Life* magazine reported that the mural's abstract gray, white, and orange swirls provoked critics to cry "fried eggs". President-elect Eisenhower's comment was, "You don't have to be nuts to be modern." Defeated Presidential candidate Stevenson did not go on record.

Chief architect Harrison, commenting on the ruckus, replied: "We were not trying to make a monument. We were building a workshop . . . the best damn workshop we could." Some architects and statesmen agreed that he had accomplished his purpose. Some disagreed.

Meanwhile, in France, building plans for one of the U.N.'s most important agencies, U.N.E.S.C.O. (United Nations Economic, Social and Cultural Organization), were bogged down in a Parisian comedy of errors. U.N.E.S.C.O. commissioned Eugene Beaudouin to draw the plans and then rejected his work: "We believe this plan lacks clarity . . . it does not offer, on a spiritual plane, the high significance expected of it." The French government then diplomatically suggested a new site and U.N.E.S.C.O. diplomatically appointed a new team of distinguished architects (Breuer, U.S.A.; Zehrfuss, France; Nervi, Italy). The Paris Building Committee rejected the new plan, called it "a Notre Dame built of radiators", and told U.N.E.S.C.O. to come back again when it had plans for a "more esthetic" building. However, an international panel of architects appointed as an advisory group called the three-man team's new plan "not only practical, but inspired". Net result: controversy, but no workshop for U.N.E.S.C.O.

Out of World War II came not only the U.N. buildings and hope for a peaceful world, but also the inevitable battle monuments and cemeteries of war. General of the Army George C. Marshall has made it his special duty to see that these commemorative monuments are built with dignity and without delay. Representing the American Battle Monuments Commission, he toured Europe to inspect their sites. Published reproductions of the models and plans for cemeteries in Europe, Africa, and the Pacific indicate varying styles. A special monument to the six million Jews murdered by Hitler's Nazis in concentration camps and crematoriums was under way at Riverside Park in New York City. It was designed by the German-born architect Eric Mendelsohn working with Yugoslav-American Ivan Meštrović, first sculptor to see his work the subject of a one-man show at New York City's Metropolitan Museum of Art.

But plans for averting another war and plans for remembering the last one were not the only considerations last year. The building of schools was an important part of the year's architectural achievement. Postwar design can mean a lot of things, many of them comic, but in schools it means improvement — unequivocally That the mind may be enlightened, the eyes need light, and most postwar schools are buildings in which window space and wall space are about evenly matched.

One of the biggest, most comprehensive building projects of modern times is Mexico's new University City. Not since the Renaissance has there been so vast an integration of the arts of painting, sculpture, and architecture into one whole. Former President Miguel Alemán rushed the project to completion before leaving office so that it would be a proud memorial to his administration. Its student capacity: 26,000. Its planners: 140 architects, sculptors, and mural painters, all of whom worked together, literally, from under the ground up. Intermixing modern international style and ancient native tradition with purely functional form, University City still manages to be one place, not just many buildings. In design, it is a part of the surrounding Mexican landscape, embodying a principle of placement and construction practiced and preached by Frank Lloyd Wright.

Wright's own Florida Southern College is a completely "organic" campus—a blend of buildings, bushes, and topography which makes it hard to decide which came first, schoolrooms or scenery. 1952 saw more new buildings fitted into his master plan for this college built into the contour of the earth. It also saw the dawn of an age when architecture took a new and practical place in academic circles. The attractiveness of the Florida campus has been credited with an increase of enrollment, and even of donations.

Prominent among the year's other architectural showpieces was the new Creative Arts Center at Sarah Lawrence College, the cautiously avant-garde girls' school in Bronxville, New York. The Center was designed by Marcel Breuer, the crew-cut Harvard professor who in 1937 came to this country from Germany, where he had been a designer of metal furniture until that nation's politics became unbearable to him. Breuer's Center is unusually flexible because its stage can be converted into a theater-in-the-round or even into a theater-in-the-wide-open-spaces that parks its audience on the tennis court beside the Center.

Of the many religious edifices built during the year, the one that stands out for sheer originality is Frank Lloyd Wright's Meeting House of the First Unitarian Society of Madison, Wisc. Its central triangular shape of glass, stone, and wood is as appropriate as it is striking. Wright is a "reasoning" architect, and his triangle has a reason for being. In his own words: "As the square has always signified integrity and the sphere universality, the triangle stands for aspiration . . . Here is a church where the whole edifice is in the attitude of prayer."

In '52 the skyscraper found new clothing to cover its steel skeleton. In New York City the Lever Brothers Building, designed by Skidmore, Owings and Merrill, was almost completely walled with glass, but had no movable windows. The building was air-conditioned and its glass was for visibility, not ventilation.

In Pittsburgh the Alcoa (Aluminum Corporation of America) building, designed by the U.N.'s Harrison and his partner Max Abramovitz, wore an all-aluminum covering. 1952's most expensive skyscraper office building was being built in Chicago by the Prudential Insurance Company. It featured neither glass nor aluminum—just limestone and stainless steel and $40 million. Atop the 600-foot-high building, 16-foot letters spelling *Prudential* will be visible 35 miles away in Gary, Ind. What this may mean architecturally is unclear. It is hoped it will not hamper insurance sales.

In the field of home building, over 1,100,000 family dwelling units, public and private, were built in 1952. By Christmas the new Levittown in Bucks County, Pa., accounted for 3250 of these units, each of them priced at $10,500. Levittown, Pa., is a large-scale, planned community, built by private capital to service

PRO-COMMUNIST MURAL in Mexico's Palace of Fine Arts portrays Joseph Stalin as kindly and peace-loving. Villains are gun-toting Uncle Sam and brass-knuckled John Bull

the new industrial site of the United States Steel Fairless Works. It sought to prevent the growth of slums, which characterize many industrial dwelling areas.

In the French port of Marseilles there was housing construction too—a $6-million apartment project designed by the noted modern architect Le Corbusier (*kor-beeoo-zeeay'*). It was completed in 1952. The architect calls it "Radiant City"; traditionalists, including most of the citizens of that Mediterranean town, call it "Madman's House". The huge glass-and-concrete structure is raised off the ground and rests on concrete supports. In Marseille, The Society for the Protection of Esthetic Beauty sued Le Corbusier on the esthetic ground that the building marred the city's water front and on the patriotic ground that "Radiant City" harmed the individualistic tradition of French housing. The French courts favored Le Corbusier, who said he was merely "writing sunlight into the lease". Moreover, at the official dedication of the building held in the noonday sun, the French government made him a commander of the Legion of Honor.

In the field of hospital architecture in the United States, the estimated expenditure for 1952 was $866 million. With such a sum spent and still more needed, the necessity for clear thinking in hospital planning was apparent. One of the clearest thinkers in this field was Isadore Rosenfield, who had been planning or consulting architect for sixty-six hospitals in his lifetime. And Rosenfield had a good eye for the difference between the elegant and the essential. Very wisely, he commented that "It is far better to have a good hospital to go to . . . even if you have to rest in a large ward, than to sleep in a private room in a hospital that has an X-ray bottleneck or an unsafe nursery."

It was, on the whole, a fruitful year in the world of art and architecture, but it

DIEGO RIVERA, whom many consider world's foremost muralist, painted work on opposite page

could not be called a golden one. It was a year of confusion and controversy, yet there were a number of creative achievements. Art galleries, art schools, museums, and architectural firms could report increased activity, but artists reported that it was still difficult to earn a living. Some important artists died and some, undoubtedly, were born.

In the arts of painting and sculpture in 1952, the one personality who managed to rise above the cold war and be acclaimed by both sides of the Iron Curtain was Leonardo da Vinci, whose birth five hundred years ago on April 15, 1452, was celebrated this year. A tug of war took place for the soul of this universal genius who, of course, could not be consulted as to his preference.

In the field of sculpture, the year began with a heated controversy raging around awards given at the American Sculpture show in·New York City's Metropolitan Museum of Art. It was touched off by the

New York art critics, who unanimously turned thumbs down on the show. It blazed when the National Sculpture Society sent a letter to 4000 prominent American citizens protesting awards to work "not only of extreme modernistic and negative tendencies but mediocre work at that". In the name of "democratic tolerance", the letter asked that "sound, normal American people" do something about "a serious cancer in the culture of our nation", and it went on to name New York City's Metropolitan, Whitney, and Modern museums as co-conspirators.

That, however, wasn't all. An influential group within the same National Sculpture Society, including past presidents, publicly disavowed the letter as "discourteous, and harmful to the best interests of American sculpture" and moreover denied having a hand in it in the first place. The art critics who originally blasted the exhibit on esthetic grounds now turned their guns on the National Sculpture Society for indulging in totalitarian tactics. A sizable number of art organizations throughout the country also condemned the offending letter. Like all other troubles, it finally worked its way to Washington. In Congress, modern art was subjected to an attack which mirrored all the confusion and frustration of the first letter. The affairs of state had to wait.

The outcome of the controversy was a two-jury system, one modern, one traditional, for the later Metropolitan Museum National Drawing and Water Color Show —a contest which went off without incident except for a minor skirmish with a group of unreconstructed abstract painters who refused to show.

At the Philadelphia Museum of Art, October crowds closed in to consider modern art in a show called "Sculpture of the 20th Century". Planned as a traveling exhibit, it was the largest and most varied collection of its kind ever assembled in this country.

At the Tate Gallery in London, which had once rejected the bronze statue "Lucifer" by Jacob Epstein, this American-born sculptor tasted triumph with a comprehensive exhibition of his work. After years of disparaging publicity marked by one furor after another, Epstein came into deserved esteem.

In New York, on Jan. 5, fire consumed a large part of the lifework of noted sculptor Jacques Lipchitz. One of his pieces, "Prometheus" (the Titan who first brought fire to mankind), was spared by being on exhibition at the Pennsylvania Academy, where it won the George D. Widener medal. "There is a lesson for me somewhere in these ruins," the sculptor said. "I must find what the fire was saying to me."

The two large international exhibitions held this year in Venice, Italy, and Pittsburgh, U.S.A., offered interesting contrast. At Pittsburgh's Carnegie International exhibit the assemblage of canvases was overwhelmingly abstract and nonobjective, while reports from Venice indicated that the less abstract paintings from Mexico aroused more interest there.

In New York City, the Metropolitan Museum cleaned and restored its Rembrandt collection of paintings, all about three hundred years old, and held a Rembrandt exhibition. The cleaning revealed hidden beauties of color and brushwork. The Metropolitan also exhibited the French impressionist painter Paul Cézanne, dead since 1906. Although considered the source of contemporary painting styles, Cézanne is the object of as much reverent esteem as Raphael.

The Museum of Modern Art presented an exhibition called simply "Fifteen Americans", which showed diverse styles in contemporary American painting. Later in the year, the same museum held an exhibition of the "Fauves"—a group of free-spirited French painters who were considered the wild men of early-20th-century painting, but who are, today, safely behind museum walls.

This year Boston's Institute of Contemporary Art organized retrospective exhibitions of three important artists, the late Mexican muralist José Orozco, the late Russian-born Vasili Kandinski, and the American Jack Levine.

As the year drew to a close, the Metropolitan Museum of Art announced the acquisition of William Zorach's lovely statue "Mother and Child". It was completed in 1930 and had its first major showing in 1931 at the Art Institute of Chicago, where it won the Logan Medal. Since then "Mother and Child" has wandered from one major museum to another.

It was exhibited for many years at the Museum of Modern Art, then at the Cleveland Museum, and later at the Metropolitan in New York. Lovers of the beautiful were glad to know that "Mother and Child" had found a permanent home.

All mankind could share in Director Taylor's explanation for wanting the statue. "We fell in love with it," he said.

"RADIANT CITY", Le Corbusier called his apartment project in Marseille, France. He explained design as "writing sunlight into lease". But to traditionalists, it was "Madman's House"

RELIGION

IF JOHANN GUTENBERG COULD HAVE VISITED the United States in 1952, he would have been astounded.

Gutenberg, who invented movable type five hundred years ago, had been largely responsible for a Bible which could be mass produced and brought into the home rather than chained to the church pulpit. In 1952, he would have found (1) his Bible memorialized on an American 3-cent stamp; (2) a new Protestant Bible, known as the Revised Standard Version, appearing as the biggest single publishing venture of all time; (3) that Bible being publicized by one of the largest advertising firms in the U.S.; and (4) a new Roman Catholic Bible, the Confraternity, in process of translation from the original Latin of St. Jerome (Vulgate).

The Revised Standard Version was easily the most important Protestant Bible to be published since the King James version appeared 341 years before. For fifteen years, ninety-one scholars of forty denominations had worked to clear up the language and correct errors (5000 came to

light in the King James New Testament alone). Original sources had increased vastly with archeological discoveries of fragments, particularly the Isaiah scrolls, found in caves near the Dead Sea in 1947.

The R.S.V. Bible got a mixed—and in some places hot—reception. Some praised the fact that 40 percent of the Old Testament was now in blank verse and congratulated the owners, the National Council of Churches of Christ in the U.S.A., huge interdenominational agency which represents thirty Protestant and Eastern Orthodox bodies in such fields as evangelism, missions, research, education, and charity.

But in Akron, Ohio, a fundamentalist minister of the Furnace Street Mission applied a blowtorch to the book ("It's like the Devil; it's hard to burn."). Similar Bible burnings took place in Rocky Point, N.C., Phoenix, Ariz., and Crestview, Fla.

BISHOP FULTON J. SHEEN attracted large following among members of all denominations with weekly television show "Life Is Worth Living"

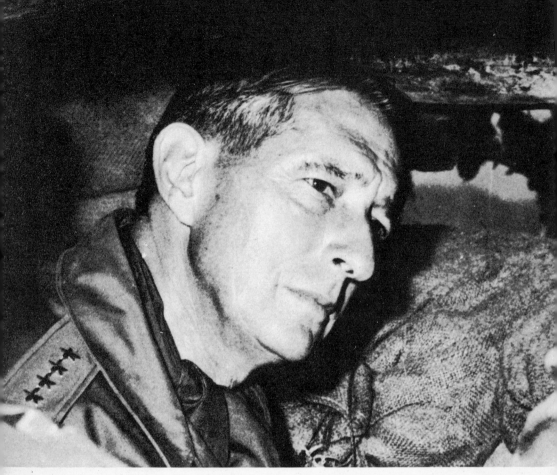

SLATED FOR AMBASSADORSHIP to Vatican was General Mark W. Clark

A Miami minister publicly dropped the book into a tubful of lye and water. The fundamentalists felt the new Bible cast doubt on the virgin birth of Christ and His divinity because the word "virgin" was changed to "young woman" in Isaiah 7:14 ("Behold, a virgin shall conceive, and bear a son, and shall call his name Immanuel"). The R.S.V. scholars replied that the Hebrew word meant "young woman", not "virgin".

In spite of controversy, the R.S.V. had sold 1,600,000 copies by the end of the year. One New York department store was advertising it as "hard-to-find . . . limited to three to a customer".

The record Bible sales were only one indication of the fact that the American people were experiencing a surge of religious feeling. Their wave of church-joining was perhaps best exemplified by the nation's President-elect, Dwight D. Eisenhower.

Brought up in the small Mennonite Brethren in Christ Church, he called himself simply a "Protestant" during his Presidential campaign. After his election, he announced he would join the National Presbyterian Church in Washington, where eight other Presidents had worshiped before him. Its pastor is the Reverend Edward L. R. Elson, a military man for a military President.

Dr. Elson, 46, had known Ike during

World War II when he was chaplain of the 75th Division in Europe. The general had sent him as "emissary" to Germany's Protestant churches. He went to National Presbyterian in 1946 with nine decorations—including the French *Croix de Guerre*—which he likes to sport on his vestments. Dr. Elson preaches straight from the shoulder. A sample: "We jazz our music and syncopate our thinking, we philosophize with boogiewoogie and esthetically cavort in jitterbug . . . Too many live by a philosophy of a leer, a jeer, and a jug of gin."

In 1952 approximately 89,000,000 Americans belonged to a church. It was the largest number of church members ever recorded in the United States—58 percent of the population, as contrasted with 49 percent in 1949.

Protestants, who numbered roughly 52,000,000, were almost twice as numerous as Roman Catholics (some 29,000,-000). There were about 5,000,000 Jews. Orthodox and smaller sects made up the balance.

The churches were intensifying their efforts to win people to God. For example, in 1951-52 the National Council of Churches, which represents more than two thirds of American Protestant and Orthodox believers, sent 175 preachers to military bases and 250 to college campuses.

There was also the pull of the personally appealing evangelist. He could be the new star of television, Bishop Fulton J. Sheen. He might be the Reverend Loyd Corder, putting across his message with a dummy called Joe the Baptist, who looks like Charlie McCarthy. He might be the Prophet Jones, "the rich man's Father Divine".

The 45-year-old Right Reverend Dr. James Francis Jones, Negro minister, has founded a church called "The Universal

STORM OF PROTEST erupted at President Truman's proposal to resume formal diplomatic relations with Vatican. President quietly abandoned plan

Triumph, the Dominion of God", and claims a world membership of 6,000,000. In 1952 he finally got his own huge church in Detroit. It was the old Oriole Theater, dressed up with 2000 plush seats, heavily tufted white chenille carpeting in the main aisle, a $35,000 organ, and a $5300 throne. Prophet Jones tells his people that when they are sick or in trouble they should "call my name eight times and God will bring you out of all snares". He believes that after 2000 A.D. souls will remain in bodies—and he expects to live to see that day.

Or the powerful evangelist might be the Reverend Billy Graham, the Southern Baptist fireball who reminds many of the late Billy Sunday. Striding around on a platform wired for sound (he uses a lapel microphone), Billy Graham calls down the wrath of God on the sinner and urges him to renounce his ways. General Douglas MacArthur finds him "one of the most inspiring men I ever met". At 33, Billy is now America's No. 1 revival preacher.

Billy Graham tries to follow up on his converts. A worker inquires the church of their choice, then urges local pastors to invite them to services in their own communities.

During 1952, Billy Graham stormed Washington, D.C., with the cry "Repent!" In nine weeks, 500,000 people attended his rallies—nearly two thirds of the capital's population. Each night some 25 to 40 representatives and about 5 senators came, but, to Billy's disappointment, Baptist Harry Truman didn't. Billy warned Washingtonians that some were following the debauchery of Belshazzar's Feast, which he dubbed "the greatest cocktail party in history".

And Americans were supporting their churches enthusiastically in 1952. A National Council of Churches survey revealed that 47 Protestant and Orthodox denominations contributed more than $1.2 billion in a year. The average gift was

STANDEES at revival meeting listen intently as Billy Graham calls for religious campaign with slogan "The Christian Army should march to war under the banner of God."

about $34, but the Free Methodists and
the Seventh-Day Adventists gave almost
$200 and $160, respectively, per man per
year.

With building restrictions off, a boom
in church building was on and six times
as much construction was going up as in
1946. A billion dollars' worth of Protestant church plans was on architects' drawing boards. The Roman Catholic Church
planned to spend $1 billion a year from
1945 to 1955, erecting 150 to 200 churches
a year. New temples and synagogues
were rising in many cities.

In Los Angeles, the new Greek Orthodox cathedral, *Hagia Sophia* ("Holy Wis-
dom"), was completed after ten years of
work, at a cost of $2 million. Patterned
after the St. Sophia Cathedral built in
Constantinople (now Istanbul) in the 6th
century, it is air-conditioned, earthquake-

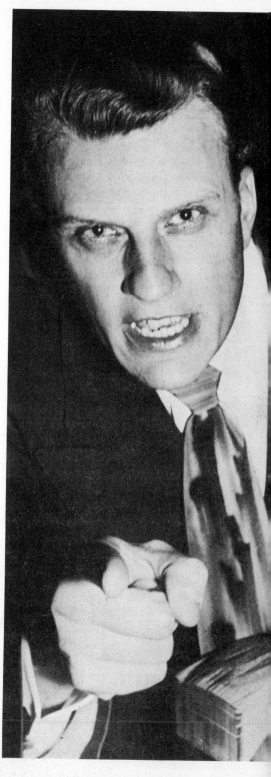

proof, and ornamented inside with 24-carat gold leaf.

Even at the United Nations building in New York City, there was a place to pray. Called the "Meditation Room", it had no altar, but merely an upright section of a 250-year-old mahogany tree from the Belgian Congo, designed to "go back to nature itself, like almost all religions".

But while American churches flourished, on the other side of the Iron Curtain a Red vise was squeezing religion to death. In 1905, Lenin wrote: "Religion is a sort of spiritual gin in which the slaves of capital drown their human figures, their demands for any sort of worthy human life." The statement echoed in 1952 when Red Czech Minister of Information Václav Kopecky warned that "people who go to church demonstrate their opposition to the People's Democracy . . . In the struggle against such enemies, we stop at nothing."

The words might have been said in Poland, Hungary, Russia, Lithuania, Estonia, Latvia, Romania, Bulgaria, Albania, or China. There the hammer and sickle were mowing down the cross and crosier. In China, during 1952, many non-Chinese Catholic and Protestant missionaries were killed, imprisoned, or expelled.

Sorrowful over Catholics who suffered such persecution, Pope Pius XII sought to strengthen his church by the creation of new cardinals. Ever since thirty-two dignitaries from all over the world were raised to the purple in 1946, Catholics had been waiting for another consistory. The full strength of the Sacred College of Cardinals in Rome is seventy, but by 1952 deaths had reduced its number to forty-six. In November, the pope announced the names of twenty-four new cardinals, including one from the United States, Archbishop James Francis Aloysius McIntyre of Los Angeles.

With Francis Cardinal Spellman of New York, Samuel Cardinal Stritch of Chicago, and Edward Cardinal Mooney of Detroit, he makes the fourth American cardinal now in the College.

Defying Communist pressure, the pope also elevated Polish Archbishop Stephen Wyszynski of Gniezno and Warsaw (a distant relative of the Russian Andrei Y. Vishinsky) and Archbishop Aloysius Stepinac of Zagreb, the Yugoslav prelate whom Tito imprisoned in 1946 and released in December, 1951, but who is not allowed to practice his archiepiscopal functions.

Religious books invaded the best-seller lists in 1952—from the Revised Standard Version of the Bible to Norman Beasley's *The Cross and the Crown,* a history of the Christian Science movement and its founder Mary Baker Eddy. (The Vatican, incidentally, put two new authors on the Index of Forbidden Books, the late Andre Gide of France, winner of the Nobel Prize, because of his "taste for profanity" and "feeling of lasciviousness", and the Italian novelist Alberto Moravia, author of *The Woman of Rome* and *Conjugal Love,* because he "describes in detail obscene and immoral things".)

An estimated 200 religious films were produced in 1952 alone, and many were shown on TV.

Despite the upsurge in religious life, Dr. Norman Vincent Peale, pastor of the Marble Collegiate Church in New York City, found that Americans now are "probably the most nervous generation" ever. For this generation he picked an American patron saint. "The patron saint of the Irish," he said, "is St. Patrick; of the English, St. George; and the patron saint of Americans is St. Vitus."

CHURCH MEMBERSHIP rose in 1952, with almost 89 million Americans belonging to a church or synagogue. Here, converts enter Baptist faith

YEAR'S MOST CONTROVERSIAL book idea was advanced by publisher Ian Ballantine
in simultaneous printing of hard- and soft-cover editions. So far, idea has proved successful

BOOKS

NINETEEN FIFTY-TWO LEFT NO BIG MARK on American writing. But book business was good and the official samplers of literature—the critics—found much to recommend.

Readers, too, found much to read. There were more books published in 1952 than in any other year in our history—11,840 titles, a total made possible by the increasing demand for biography, memoirs, and books of personal adventure, inspiration, and politics.

The President of the United States, for instance, picked up a copy of Tallulah

Bankhead's autobiography, *Tallulah,* and declared: "This is the most interesting book I have had in my hands since I became President." (Tallulah is a good Democrat.) Perhaps he was simply being modest, for a book about Truman himself, by Washington correspondent William Hillman, had captured the public imagination earlier in the year with its revealing details of how a President performs his job. The book, *Mr. President,* was a history-making work, for never before had a President published his state papers while still in office.

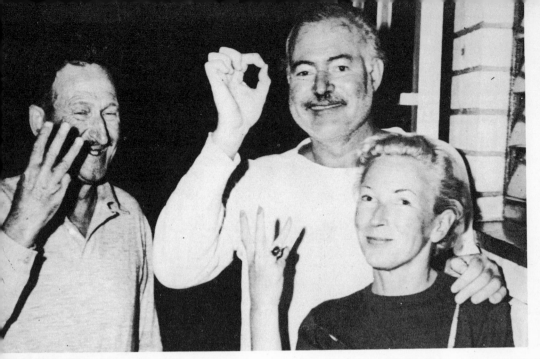

ERNEST HEMINGWAY (center) wrote a best-selling fishing novel, "The Old Man and the Sea", but as a fisherman, author Hemingway must concede his limitations. On recent angling expedition, wife and friend caught three marlin; Hemingway, none

In one way, the most unusual achievement of the year was a book written by a convict in the Ohio State Penitentiary, Robert E. Preyor, Jr. In the fall of 1952 the Boston publishers, Little, Brown & Co., received a partially completed manuscript from Preyor entitled *Position Unknown.* They liked it, advanced him $500 to finish the book, and waited. At regular intervals came neatly typed 3500-word installments. Finally, in December, the last chapters arrived. For a first novel, it required remarkably little editing and the publishers congratulated themselves on their discovery. The book was set in type and advance copies were mailed to critics and others in the trade.

Only one thing was wrong with *Position Unknown.* It had been written once before. The sleuth who spotted the plagiarism was a middle-aged, gray-haired woman who had probably read more books than any one per~ ~United

States. Her name is Virginia Kirkus and she reads about eight hundred books a year, two or three months in advance of publication. Her findings are reported to bookstores and libraries that subscribe to her service. Reading *Position Unknown,* Miss Kirkus smelled a rat—or rather, a hauntingly familiar plot. Digging back in her files, she found that she had reported on exactly the same story in 1944. That time it was a novel called *Island in the Sky,* by Ernest K. Gann. A check of the two books bore out her hunch, and Little, Brown canceled publication before copies were sent to the bookstores. But they did not bring action against the author. He was already in jail.

Quite a few of 1952's most widely read books came from government leaders, past and present. While ruddy-cheeked Herbert Hoover was telling the story of his administration, in Volumes 2 and 3 of his *Memoirs,* William O. Douglas, an as-

EDNA FERBER'S "Giant" was about Texas, but Texans weren't pleased. One critic suggested Miss Ferber be made "guest of honor" at lynching party

but for the maritime-minded there were fictional compensations; novelist C. S. Forester brought his famous Horatio Hornblower, who began his career many years ago as an admiral, down to the rank of lieutenant in his latest novel, *Lieutenant Hornblower.*

Among the not-so-gentle sex, Tallulah Bankhead's autobiography led all the rest —in sales, at least. The famous actress, whose flair for the dramatic has put her into the headlines as often as it has put her on the stage, found a new audience— the book-buying public. But the nation also bought, in great numbers, two radically different books by women—*A Man Called Peter,* by Catherine Marshall, an inspirational biography of Peter Marshall, chaplain of the Senate, and Rachel Carson's fabulous account of the marine world, *The Sea Around Us.*

Both were holdovers from the year before, and took endurance prizes on the best-seller lists. But the surprise best seller of the year was *Anne Frank: The Diary of a Young Girl,* a remarkably sen-

sociate justice of the Supreme Court, was riding horseback through the Himalayan mountains. His book, *Beyond the High Himalayas,* was the record of his journey.

Fleet Admiral Ernest J. King, who retired in 1945 as the highest-ranking naval officer in the country, was the only member of the top brass to publish his memoirs during the year (*A Naval Record*),

JOHN STEINBECK, shown with wife Elaine, returned to best-seller lists with 250,000-word "East of Eden", saga of California's Salinas Valley

sitive account, by a 16-year-old Jewish girl, of privation and danger under the Nazis.

If 1952 introduced no new writers of outstanding promise, it did bring forth one of the most ambitious—a 59-year-old Waco, Texas, wholesale-grocery merchant named Madison Cooper.

For eleven years, Cooper secretly spun the story of a small Southern city he calls Sironia, Texas. Page by page the novel grew, until at last it became somewhat longer than the Old and New Testaments combined. Then Cooper shipped it off to a Boston publisher, Houghton Mifflin, winning the company's Literary Fellowship prize for 1952.

The novel, *Sironia, Texas,* is the longest ever published (1731 pages). At the almost unheard-of price of $10, it sold surprisingly well—about 23,000 copies, in fact, by year's end, for a gross "take" of almost a quarter of a million dollars. In the book business, that ain't hay.

But it wasn't all a matter of money. (Madison Cooper was well off to begin with.) Critically, his book seemed to justify his labors. By and large, reviewers liked it, especially in the North. For Southern critics, its scenes of violence, its lynchings and rapes and decadence, seemed unfairly directed at Southern society. But Cooper denied such intention. Sironia, he said, was typical and true.

Cooper was not the only amateur to gain literary fame during the year. In New York City, a policeman suddenly bobbed up as an authority on Shakespearean puns. The patrolman, Redmond O'Hanlon, wrote a letter to *The New York Times Book Review* in March, asking for unusual examples of the Bard's word-play. By midsummer he had acquired a file in his home on Staten Island of 3500 puns from Shakespeare's plays. After years of pu‗‗‗‗‗ ‗‗‗‗‗ hobby quietly, O'Hanlon sud‗‗‗

national reputation. Then the inevitable happened: a professor at Yale University, Helge Kökeritz, incorporated many of the puns in a scholarly work on Shakespearean language to be published in 1953. Meanwhile, O'Hanlon retains his job as a policeman in Chinatown. "I am just a cop who was arrested by Shakespeare," he says.

The most successful book of the year, as in every year, was the Bible. But it was not the well-known King James version— the Bible that grandfather kept on his parlor table. The new Bible was called the Revised Standard Version and it was newly translated from the Hebrew language by a group of divinity scholars, at a cost of $500,000.

Its public reception was controversial. In Rocky Mount, N.C., the pastor of one church burned it in public with a blowtorch. Others denounced it from their pulpits. Their complaint: the translation, which turned such well-known passages as "I am become as a sounding brass" into "I am a noisy gong."

Despite such literal translation, the new Bible had sold 1,600,000 copies between publication (Nov. 1) and year's end. So heavy was the demand that the publishers, Thomas P. Nelson, were forced to subcontract about half their orders to a rival publisher—of King James Bibles. All told, the Revised Standard Version rang up $10 million in sales.

Most of the authors who made big news during the year were old-timers, suddenly back in the limelight. Three made remarkable comebacks: California-born John Steinbeck, who earned his reputation with *The Grapes of Wrath,* returned to the scenes of his earlier triumph in a new novel called *East of Eden,* a three-generation story that provides the framework for a three-decker book. Many critics called it Steinbeck's ‗‗‗‗ impressive achievement.

Edna Ferber, whose novels (*Cimarron, Saratoga Trunk, Come and Get It*) have depicted different regions of the country, set her latest in Texas. She called it *Giant,* and it was frankly designed to irritate Texans and please everybody else.

In this she succeeded. Texas reviewers jumped on the book because of what they called its grossly exaggerated picture of cattle ranchers and millionaires. Miss Ferber had one character flying his own DC-6. Not only is there no privately owned DC-6 in Texas, pointed out the critics, but none at all in the United States outside of the air force.

Another reviewer and newspaper columnist, Carl Victor Little of the Dallas *News,* devoted eleven separate columns to attacking the book. He dared Miss Ferber to come to Texas for an autographing party and warned her that it might turn into a lynching party.

But even in Texas the book sold briskly, and over the country as a whole it was one of the year's best-selling novels. *Giant* might be overdrawn, but it was exciting and provocative and besides— readers were saying—it was about time someone took Texas and the Texas myth to task.

The third big comeback of 1952 was Ernest Hemingway. And comeback it was: the critics had clobbered his earlier novel, *Across the River and into the Trees,* published in 1950. But the new one, *The Old Man and the Sea,* earned nationwide applause. It is a brief, beautifully written novel that is short on words and long on symbolism.

Hemingway's book achieved added significance when it was printed, in its entirety, in *Life* magazine a week before the book itself went on sale. In a sense, this was a very risky trial balloon for the publisher. If people could read the book for 20 cents, would they also buy it for $3?

Although *Life* sold more copies of its "Hemingway" issue than any other in its history, *The Old Man and the Sea* did very well in the bookstores. Many argued that millions of persons who read the novel in the magazine were being introduced to Hemingway for the first time. Some of these people undoubtedly wanted the story in more permanent, book form. In any event, the experiment seemed to indicate that magazine publication did not seriously impair the normal sale of the book.

Other books, too, were noteworthy for one reason or another. Whittaker Chambers' *Witness*—the personal story of an ex-Communist—topped the year's confession literature, summing up the mood of guilt and disillusionment shared by so many who confused social reform with Communism.

For one of the few times in history, a Presidential candidate collected his campaign speeches and sold them. They were *The Speeches of Adlai Stevenson,* and it was clear from reading them that whatever else the Democratic nominee might be, he was well versed in the world of books. The speeches were magnificent.

Few were the ones in which Stevenson did not manage to work in a quotation from a well-known author. He quoted the great 19th-century poet Walt Whitman to the farmers of Minnesota. He cited—to an audience in Richmond, Va.— the late (*Gone with the Wind*) Margaret Mitchell. He talked about another Southern novelist—William Faulkner. Sometimes he fell back on Plato. Stevenson won the literary vote almost unopposed.

The most written-about man in 1952 was Abraham Lincoln. Altogether nine books dealing with Lincoln came off the presses. One of them—Benjamin Thomas' biography *Abraham Lincoln*—became a best seller. It was the first authoritative one-volume life of the great President

"TALLULAH": Actress Bankhead's frank autobiography topped best-seller list for months. Opening paragraph: "Despite all you may have heard to the contrary, I have never had a ride in a patrol wagon."

be remembered longest—was by a man who had been dead seventy-seven years. His name was George Templeton Strong, a New York City lawyer who lived from 1820 to 1875. From the age of fifteen until his death this man kept a diary. In it he recorded the social and political changes that came over New York. He knew the famous people of his time. He attended the theater, the opera, concerts, and museums. He was active in the church. This incredible man committed to his diary, every night before going to bed, the happenings of the day. It is by all odds the most detailed account of life in New York City during that period, outside of the newspapers.

The Diary of George Templeton Strong, although it waited three quarters of a century to see the light of day, is one of the publishing achievements of 1952. It contains more than four million words and was sold in four volumes totaling 2254 pages, at a price of $35.

The year also saw a Congressional investigation of obscenity in books. Publishers were uncertain whether to be flattered or insulted. The book business is seldom spotlighted by anything as newsworthy as a full-scale Congressional investigation. This one, headed by Arkansas Congressman Ezekiel Gathings, centered its fire on the paper-bound reprints, which were described by the committee as "media for the dissemination of artful appeals to sensuality, immorality, filth, perversion and degeneracy".

The growth of the "paperbacks" in 1952 was the most important development of the year. An industry that began cautiously in 1939 with the founding of Pocket Books, it now numbers sixteen

since Lord Charnwood's *Abraham Lincoln* appeared in 1916. The importance of this book is that it includes information based on the material recently made available from the Robert Todd Lincoln collection in the Library of Congress.

1952 saw two books on the late Wendell Willkie and a reissue of General Ulysses S. Grant's *Memoirs.* The American painter Grandma Moses—an uneducated farm woman who once worked as a hired girl and did not begin painting until she was in her sixties—wrote *My Life's History.* John Masefield, the English poet laureate, began his autobiography with the publication of a book about his early days as a writer—*So Long to Learn.*

One of the most remarkable books of the year—the book for which 1952 may

firms and last year published a grand total of 257,000,000 books.

About 1000 titles were represented in this output, most of them reprints—at 25 cents and 35 cents—of books originally published in hard covers. Only a small fraction of these could accurately be described as "sensual, immoral, filthy, perverted or degenerate".

True, a great many reprints carried lurid covers; it is one of the paradoxes of the industry that good books were being sold as bad books or, to put it another way, that people were reading the right books for the wrong reasons.

Moreover, at least 100 titles published in 1952 were either standard classics or works of established merit. They ranged from such religious books as *The Confessions of St. Augustine* and such philosophical works as *The Dialogues of Plato* to such old favorites as Sir Walter Scott's *Ivanhoe*. They included such excellent contemporary novels as A. B. Guthrie Jr.'s *The Way West* and Jessamyn West's *The Witch Diggers*, such forbiddingly titled books as *The Greek Way to Civilization*, by Edith Hamilton, and Margaret Mead's work on anthropology, *Sex and Temperament in Three Primitive Societies*.

Moreover, some of the world's greatest living writers were being sold cheek by jowl with mysteries and westerns. The eminent German author and Nobel Prize winner, Thomas Mann, went into paper covers in 1952 with an early novel, *Buddenbrooks*. So did the author of *Point Counter Point* and *Antic Hay*, Aldous Huxley.

These are men who have usually been considered "difficult" to read, and their sales, in hard covers, have never been spectacular. Yet in paper covers they racked up sales of 250,000 to 300,000 each. William Faulkner, another frequently honored but seldom read author in hard-

LIFE IN AN IMPERIAL PALACE was described in "Windows for the Crown Prince" by Elizabeth Gray Vining, tutor to Japan's Prince Akihito

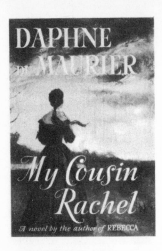

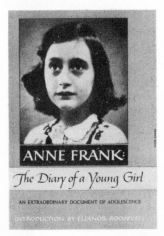

JACKETS AND AUTHORS of some of 1952's best sellers. Authors are: Top: M. Cooper—"Sironia, Texas"; Middle: B. Berenson—"Rumor and Reflection"; D. S. Freeman—"George Washington"; Bottom: W. O. Douglas—"Beyond the High Himalayas"

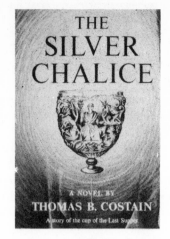

Top: Herbert Hoover—"The Memoirs of Herbert Hoover", Vol. 2; Taylor Caldwell —"The Devil's Advocate"; Middle: Herman Wouk—"The Caine Mutiny"; Bottom: Rachel Carson—"The Sea Around Us"; Mickey Spillane—Mike Hammer series

cover editions, experienced a sale of one million copies with a single reprint title— *The Wild Palms*. Although *The Wild Palms* is not easy reading, it has a large measure of violence—involving, as it does, the flight of two escaped convicts. Faulkner's realism, his emphasis on sensationalism and degeneracy, seem to appeal to many readers in the reprint audience.

It became evident, by 1952, that the paper-bound book was profoundly altering the structure of the publishing industry. Books, as never before, were becoming an agency of mass culture, in competition with the movies, radio, and television.

Against a price of $3 or more for a hard-bound book, the paperbacks were selling at 25, 35, and 50 cents. Against 2000 outlets for trade books, there were 100,000 for the reprints. The effect of this was healthy. It brought books within reach of men and women to whom a book is ordinarily a luxury.

By 1952, Pocket Books could report that some 66 of its titles had sold, through the years, more than a million copies each. Other reprint publishers were reporting comparable sales—books by John Steinbeck, James Michener, Ernest Hemingway, and Norman Mailer, for example, have all passed the million-copy mark.

As a result, authors who had always looked condescendingly upon paper books were now showing their manuscripts to the reprint publishers first. Soft-cover methods were developing a whole new audience for books—some estimates placed this at ten million regular buyers.

By all odds the boy wonder of the field was a soft-spoken young man who, in his free time, is a lay preacher for a religious sect called Jehovah's Witnesses. His name, five years ago, was unknown to anyone. Today, he is the most widely read author in America—Mickey Spillane. To date, his reprint publishers, The New American Library, have sold more than sixteen million copies of his books. It is no exaggeration to say that the country has gone "Spillane crazy", although it must be said, too, that his reputation leans toward literary notoriety.

Spillane took the mystery novel and vividly intensified two elements: sex and brutality. His books—*My Gun Is Quick; I, the Jury; Kiss Me, Deadly* are some of the titles—compound the sensationalism of the torture chamber with the salaciousness of the brothel. But he sells, and already imitators are moving into the field.

Another highly popular novelist, although on a much more serious level, startled the publishing world late in 1952 with the statement that she would write directly for the soft-cover market. This was Miss Taylor Caldwell, whose fourteen novels have nearly all found their way onto the best-seller lists. Her new publisher, Gold Medal Books, had already become the third largest in the paper-book field solely by publishing original novels at 25 cents.

A much more important experiment was the formation of a new firm, Ballantine Books, to publish hard- and soft-cover editions of a book at the same time. This was certainly the most discussed and controversial book idea of the year. The originator of the plan is a young man, Ian Ballantine, who introduced the British paper-cover "Penguin" line into the United States in the late 1930's. He has spent all his adult life in the paper-book field. His decision to publish the "original" and the "reprint" edition of a book at the same time has been called "moonshine" by at least one competing reprint house, but Ballantine is firmly in business and his books are selling.

The advantage of the plan is that authors receive 8 percent royalties, instead of the 4 percent which is customary in the paper-book field. At the same time he has brought the price of his hard-cover books down to $1.50. At year's end, the whole idea was still experimental and no one was willing to say that a new day had dawned for author or customer.

Book clubs held their own during the year, although membership was down from the immediate postwar years. The Literary Guild remained the largest, while the Book-of-the-Month Club retained its position in terms of prestige. A number of new clubs invaded the field, notably the Atlantic Monthly Book Club. Altogether, there were sixty-seven adult and seven juvenile clubs by the end of 1952—a record total for this country.

Like all years, 1952 in books had its troubles. Most of them centered around a book by two men from the New York *Daily Mirror*—editor Jack Lait and columnist Lee Mortimer. The book was *U.S.A. Confidential*, which, claimed to "expose" crime conditions and political shenanigans in many cities throughout the country. The critics panned it as highly inaccurate, insulting, and probably libelous. Many newspapers refused to advertise it. Moreover, upward of $10 million in libel suits were filed by individuals, labor unions, and the fashionable Nieman-Marcus department store in Dallas, Texas. Some of the suits were settled out of court, but most of them were dropped after the excitement blew over. Although *U.S.A. Confidential* was the rage in midsummer, by the end of the year it was practically forgotten.

"U.S.A. CONFIDENTIAL", an exposé of just about everything, attracted $10 million in libel suits. Some grievances against coauthor Lee Mortimer were settled out of court

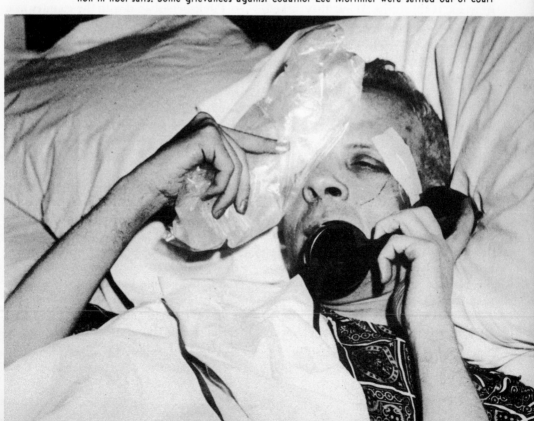

There were the usual number of literary awards. The most valued are the Pulitzer Prizes, established in 1920 by the great newspaper publisher Joseph Pulitzer. In 1952, the anonymous jury gave the fiction award to Herman Wouk for *The Caine Mutiny*. The biography prize was won by a Washington, D.C., newspaperman, Merlo Pusey, for his book on the late chief justice of the Supreme Court, Charles Evans Hughes. The history award went to Harvard professor Oscar Handlin for a study of immigrants in American history; it was called *The Uprooted*. The elderly and little-known poet, Marianne Moore, was awarded the poetry prize for *Collected Poems*. Each award is worth $1500 in cash.

For several years past there has been dissatisfaction with the Pulitzer awards in the field of literature. Critics of the Pulitzer jury have accused it of choosing books that tend to romanticize American life, rather than books which deal with America realistically. Why, they asked, had Ernest Hemingway or John Dos Passos never received a prize? Both of these men are acknowledged masters of prose.

Partly as a result of this dissatisfaction, new awards were set up three years ago by the publishers, the book manufacturers, and the booksellers. They are called the National Book Awards, and are given each year for fiction, nonfiction, and poetry.

In 1952 they went to James Jones for his sensational novel about army life, *From Here to Eternity*, and to Rachel Carson for *The Sea Around Us*. But the new judges and the Pulitzer jury saw eye to eye on poetry. Marianne Moore won the National Book Award, too, for the same book, *Collected Poems*.

No great literary controversies arose in 1952, but political overtones had their influence on writers. Graham Greene, the English novelist who had been a member of the Communist Party for six weeks in his youth, was denied a visa to come to the United States. Ironically, the purpose of his visit was to receive the Catholic Literary Award for 1952. The ban was later revoked and Greene was offered a short-term visa, which he refused.

The American writer was free to say just about anything he wanted to say. However, the man with an unpopular idea was finding it harder to get a publisher. Textbooks were being scrutinized —by Congressional committees, patriotic societies, and State legislatures—for possible subversion. The State of Georgia, finding undesirable passages in a history text that it had bought but not yet distributed to its schools, cheerfully offered to sell the books to some other State. A Congressman from Illinois, Harold H. Velde, introduced a bill making it mandatory for libraries to label all books containing Communist propaganda. The bill was not reported out of committee.

Publishers shared with the country as a whole a goodly measure of prosperity. Sales were up significantly over 1951. More and more books were being exported abroad, both as part of the government's overseas information program and through private export channels.

Television—the great bugbear of the book industry—seemingly had not hurt the sale of books, despite the inroads it had made on people's time. In fact, some publishers were finding it a valuable advertising medium (Doubleday & Co., for example, spent $1 million on radio and television time), and others maintained that, by making people more interested in more things, television was enlarging the book-reading public.

Whatever the reasons, between the 25-cent reprint and George Templeton Strong's $35 *Diary*, American publishing in 1952 proved that it could grow in both directions.

EX-COMMUNIST Whittaker Chambers (seated, foreground) described association with Alger Hiss (arrow) and flight from Red pursuers in "Witness"

TO KINGS' TASTE:
When Samia wiggled, Faruk goggled; so did U.S. oil heir Sheppard King who wooed and wed her

PEOPLE

TO SOME FUTURE READER OF HISTORY, THE year 1952 will appear clear-cut. Its achievements, its disasters, its great debates and stormy disagreements will have been recorded.

To know a year in a history book is one thing. To know its flavor is another. The mood of a year comes as much from its small happenings as from its major events, and takes depth from its losses as well as its gains.

It is made up of countless ingredients, each of them adding an individual touch to the whole.

Here, then, is 1952.

January A big-election year began with a lot of little elections. A poll of the governors of the forty-eight States, conducted by the Columbia Broadcasting System, named General Douglas MacArthur as "The Man" of 1951, with General Eisenhower a runner-up. For the second time in a row, John Wayne, poker-faced star of Western movies, was tagged most popular actor of the year by the *Motion Picture Herald*. For the first time, Britain's Princess Margaret got on the New York Dress Institute list of "ten best-dressed women". An in-law, the Duchess of Windsor, topped the list.

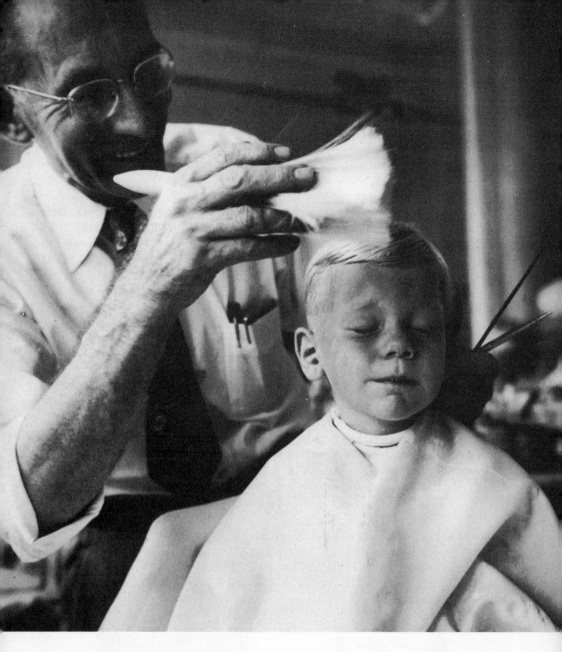

★ At her villa on the Isle of Capri, famous comedienne Gracie Fields announced that she was going to marry a 48-year-old Romanian whom she'd met when he came to repair her radio.

★ When John McCloy, U.S. High Commissioner for Germany, parked illegally in Garmisch-Partenkirchen, a whimsical traffic cop scrawled a notation on his parking ticket. It read: "To a cow, traffic's only a lark, but you must learn how to properly park."

★ The audience in a Hollywood theater was treated to the spectacle of actor James Mason getting up, walking down the aisle, and slapping a man who had been talking during the movie. As the slap resounded, Mason recognized his target:

playwright William Saroyan. "Oh, hello, Bill," said Mason. "Shut up, will you."

★ While most people in Cairo were getting ready to go to work one morning, a 101-gun salute roared over the city. The occasion: King Faruk's 18-year-old bride, Narriman, had just given birth to a son, Prince Ahmed Fuad, heir to the throne.

★ Egypt's king seemed to have been responsible for "discovering" Samia Gamal, a dancer whose ability to wiggle like a bowl of jelly apparently pleased the monarch's taste. Next, young Sheppard King, heir to a Texas oil fortune, discovered her in a Cairo night club. He wooed her, he said, on camel-back, became a Moslem, changed his name to Abdullah, was cut off by his family, then married the girl. Finally, a lot more Americans discovered her when she arrived in this country with her bridegroom and a series of night-club contracts. As she disembarked, Samia told reporters that "American women use too much soap". Her own secret of success, she said, was to bathe twice a week and sponge herself with a little olive oil in between times. "A woman," she opined, "should shine a little."

DEATHS: Jo DAVIDSON. One of the best-known sculptors of his time, Davidson died just after arriving in France from Israel where he had been working on busts of the new nation's leaders. He called himself a "plastic historian" and among his subjects were such differing personalities as Frank Sinatra, Albert Einstein, and Gandhi.

February Senator Willis Smith, Democrat of North Carolina, chided his staff for its spelling. Inadvertently, someone in his office had typed Attorney General Mc-Grath's name as "McGraft".

★ In Cincinnati, a hearse-and-ambulance company got busy on a quarter-million-dollar order for a fleet of twenty remodeled Cadillacs. Each car would have six doors, two full rear seats, electric fans, and one-way mirror glass in the windows. The passengers: as many of the 120 wives of King Ibn-Saud of Saudi Arabia as might want to take a ride.

★ The season for sniffles found a group of doctors gathered in Chicago at a meeting sponsored by the Common Cold Foundation. Dr. Thomas G. Ward, of Johns Hopkins University, brought the

LITTLE FALA, after lifetime of romping with the great, lies again at F.D.R.'s feet

discussion down to earth with this comment: "If I were to ask the fifty doctors in this room what was the best treatment for the common cold, I'd get fifty different answers. Personally, my favorite treatment is old Maryland rock and rye."

★ For 19-year-old film beauty Elizabeth Taylor and 39-year-old actor Michael Wilding, both recently divorced from former mates, there was a nick-of-time break that permitted a London wedding, after it was found that she had forgotten her divorce papers. The day was saved when an American news agency had them radio-photoed across the Atlantic.

★ Glamorous grandmother Gloria Swanson, 52, announced she would marry her 44-year-old manager, Branden Brent. It would be her sixth trip to the altar.

DEATHS: GEORGE VI, by the Grace of God, of Great Britain, Ireland, and of the British Dominions beyond the Seas, King, Defender of the Faith.

HAROLD ICKES. They called him "the old curmudgeon", and he seemed to like it. From the day his political star began to rise in the early days of the Roosevelt administration, Ickes built a reputation for honesty and bitingly frank commentary. Franklin Roosevelt chose him as first secretary of the interior and he lasted until 1945, when he got fed up with President Truman's administration and turned in a blistering 2000-word resignation. Some of his other blistering comments: he once said Huey Long had "halitosis of the intellect". He called Wendell Willkie "the barefoot boy from Wall Street", and when Governor Dewey became a Presidential candidate in 1944, Ickes said "he has thrown in his diaper".

KNUT HAMSUN. In 1920 his novel *Growth of the Soil* won a Nobel Prize. Later he won the bitterness of his Norwegian countrymen because of his pro-Nazi viewpoint. When he died at 92, Oslo papers ignored his passing.

March After a nationwide chase by police and the F.B.I., Hollywood bank robber John Richard Bayless was captured as he stepped off a plane at La Guardia airport in New York. He turned his loot over willingly but begged arresting officers "don't take my cookbook", which contained recipes he had compiled during a twelve-year stretch in Alcatraz.

★ For all his titles (King of Kings and Conquering Lion of the Tribe of Judah), Emperor Haile Selassie of Ethiopia didn't have a throne. The Italians, who had invaded his homeland years before, still held that item of royal furniture as a war trophy. Now, the emperor said, they should return it. His wish was granted. And he got a bonus. Along with the gilt-and-golden throne came his scepter, two oil paintings, two rifles, and a brass bed.

★ The Presidential primaries gave Virginia's Governor John S. Battle a bad moment. A headline in the *Roanoke* (Va.) *Times,* referring only to the close race in New Hampshire, boldly said, "Battle Gets Tight in New Hampshire".

★ Customs agents at a New York pier felt they had stumbled on a big find, probably dope, when they tapped a suitcase belonging to John Bohling, a traveling ironworker just back from a trip to Germany. Yes, Bohling admitted, his suitcase had a false bottom. When the agents ripped it open their triumph turned to amazement as they surveyed a pungent 8 pounds of Bohling's favorite salami.

★ On the stage of New York's Metropolitan Opera House, a great star set. Just seventeen years after her debut on the same stage, soprano Kirsten Flagstad said she was retiring. Her last audience gave her one of the greatest ovations ever heard in the Metropolitan.

★ Entertaining troops in Korea, Betty Hutton got the honorary title of sergeant major of "Los Angeles' Own" 106th Infantry Regiment, then a resounding kiss from

UNDERWORLD TYCOON Frank Costello shells out while jury is deciding he must go to prison

a real sergeant to seal the deal. As soon as she got back to the States she got something else—her second husband, dance director Charles O'Curran.

★ In the Carnaval Room of New York's Sherry-Netherland Hotel, W. Stuart Symington, former secretary of the air force, watched a 24-year-old "discovery" make his debut as a singer. The lad in the limelight was James W. Symington, his son.

★ Marilyn Monroe, Hollywood's flashiest new star, gave her studio a good case of jitters by candidly admitting to reporters that she *was* the model who posed for a notable nude calendar back in 1949 when she needed rent money. Very promptly a brisk business in calendars, both reprints of the original and close imitations, was noticed across the nation.

★ Another confused participant in the political primaries was the harried woman in New Brighton, Minn., who begged to be allowed to change her ballot. When she heard she couldn't, she groaned, "Oh my, I just voted for myself for President."

★ In Hackney, England, Joseph Cowley, a dock worker who had beaten up a friend, heard a judge give him an admonition. The assault, said the judge, was "anti-social, anti-British, anti-everything".

★ Top birthday of the month was the 85th celebrated by Arturo Toscanini, world-famous symphony conductor.

★ Divorces romped through Hollywood. Severed during March: Barbara Stanwyck and Robert Taylor; Linda Darnell and Peverell Marley; Gene Tierney and Oleg Cassini; Hedy Lamarr and Ted Stauffer.

DEATHS: HUGH HERBERT. In more than forty films in the '30's, Herbert's trade-mark, a loony cry of "Woo-Woo!", became one of the most familiar sounds on the American screen. He was 66 when he died of a heart attack in Hollywood. JOHN FLANAGAN. Few who read his obituaries recognized his name, yet everyone in the country would recognize his work. Flanagan, one of the foremost medalists of the time, was the man who designed the George Washington quarter. When he died at 87, in a New York City charity ward, he was penniless.

April A few weeks after a battle-area reunion with his pilot son, and a joking remark that "I tried like the devil to bring Jim up with the doughboys", General James Van Fleet, commander of the troops in Korea, got word that his flying son had failed to return from his third night-bombing mission over Red lines.

★ For the first time in British history, a British ruler officially continued a dynastic name when the new queen Elizabeth decreed that Windsor would be the name of her house through all her descendants. Until her decree it would have been possible for the name to be changed back to Saxe-Coburg-Gotha, name of the ruling house prior to a World War I decision to drop the German-sounding designation.

★ Three-year-old Prince Charles, heir to the British throne, was unregally propelled from his first public church attendance when his family's efforts failed to quiet his chattering and his grandmother had to remove his royal presence.

★ The biggest settlement ever granted in a patent case went to Harry Ferguson, a farm-machinery inventor, when the Ford Motor Company forked over $9¼ million for infringement of Ferguson's patents on a device for linking tractors and other farm equipment.

★ In Brighton, England, Joseph Griffin drew a fine for exceeding the local 20-miles-per-hour speed limit in what was undoubtedly the strangest hot rod in history: a motorized wheel chair.

★ General Douglas MacArthur tasted the brevity of fame when a Japanese committee trying to raise funds for a memorial in his honor sadly reported that it had collected only $222.

DEATHS: FERENC MOLNAR. A Hungarian playwright with the gift of pleasing playgoers, Molnar's best-known works include *Liliom* (which became the musical *Carousel*), *The Red Mill*, and *The Guardsman*. He had authored forty plays and more than sixty novels before his death at 74.

SIR STAFFORD CRIPPS. Once one of the wealthiest lawyers in England, Sir Stafford gave up law for politics, eventually became one of the Socialist leaders. When he joined Britain's wartime cabinet, Winston Churchill glanced at the spare, zealous advocate of austerity and commented, "There, but for the grace of God, goes God." As British ambassador to Moscow, Cripps had drawn a complaint from Joseph Stalin, who said he'd prefer a dip-

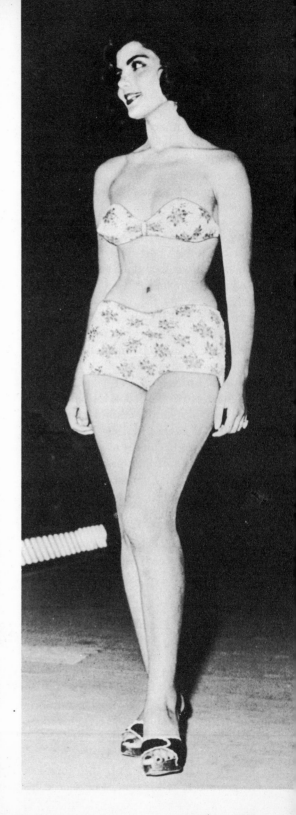

CHALLENGE ACCEPTED: Miss Europe bares almost all, silences meows from runner-up critics

lomat who could drink and that Cripps "insists on arguing Communism with me all the time". Sir Stafford was just three days short of his 63rd birthday when he died in a Swiss clinic.

FALA. No other black Scottie has ever rated front-page obituaries. Fala did when after 12 years he was laid to rest in the rose garden at the foot of the grave of his former master, Franklin Delano Roosevelt.

May Somehow, the rumor got around that Senator Robert Taft favored a six-day school week, and 12-year-old Carole Collina of Omaha heard about it. Naturally, she wrote the senator a troubled note. When he answered, assuring her it wasn't so and asking if she'd help squash the rumor, Carole commented with political sagacity that "after all, a thing like that could ruin him".

★ A lot of people felt a lot older when they opened their papers and learned that a little girl named Shirley Temple, now 23, had again become a mother, this time of a 6-pound son. The proud father: her second husband, Lieutenant Commander Charles Black.

★ The woman who arranged a store-window book display in Communist-dominated Czechoslovakia had been imprisoned, but she became a heroine when the story of her "crime" leaked out from behind the Iron Curtain. She had arranged the books so that their titles read: "We Want to Live" "Far from Moscow" "In the Shadows of the Skyscrapers" "Under a Foreign Flag".

DEATHS: WILLIAM FOX. A film producer who once headed a $300 million empire, Fox began creating the film fare that bore his name in 1913. He lost much of his fortune in the crash of '29. He was 73 when he died in New York City.

CANADA LEE. One of the foremost Negro actors of his time, Lee scored his greatest success in the title role of the play *Native Son,* and shortly before his death at 45 had starred in the film version of *Cry, the Beloved Country.*

ROLLIN KIRBY. Cartoonist for the New York *World* and winner of a Pulitzer Prize, Kirby, who died at 76, was best known for the gaunt, long-nosed character "Mr. Dry" whom he created to represent Prohibition.

FULTON OURSLER. Of all the millions of words that Oursler wrote in a long and distinguished career as a journalist (he edited the old *Liberty* from 1931 to 1942, then went to the *Reader's Digest*), one book, *The Greatest Story Ever Told,* based on the life of Christ, was the work for which most people would remember him after his death at 59.

June Queen Mother Elizabeth showed that she was keeping up with the air age when she revealed that she had piloted a Comet jet airliner at better than 500 miles per hour during a flight over Western Europe. She said she had thought of the passengers during the flight but "what the other passengers thought I really would not care to say". One passenger might have told her: her daughter, Princess Margaret.

★ In El Paso, Texas, Carl Weiss, retiring after forty-seven years as a master brewer, explained that the secret of his good health and spirits was "my daily breakfast of beer and pickled herrings".

★ The forthcoming political conventions inspired the Reverend James C. Hester, pastor of a church in Guymon, Okla., to entitle a sermon "Will Hell Be as Hot as the Republican Convention?"

★ After a lot of critics had reached the same conclusion, a tax-court judge ruled that Kathleen Winsor, author of *Forever Amber,* was due a refund on her taxes because she was not really a professional writer.

★ Of all the month's college graduates, John Robert Sarr, 23-year-old ex-G.I., seemed to deserve a special place of honor. While holding jobs to support his wife and two children, he had motorcycled back and forth between two colleges in Tennessee to get his sheepskin.

★ In Great Britain, a 19-year-old named Anthony Rose was sent back to the army after an audacious attempt to get out. He had mailed his commanding officer a death certificate saying that Anthony Rose had died of "prolonged apoplexy, conjectural degeneration, and final insensibility".

★ In Los Angeles Superior Court, the 13-year-old daughter of film star Ingrid Bergman and Dr. Peter Lindstrom calmly told a judge "I don't love my mother." She wanted, she said, to stay with her father and not go to her mother, who had eloped with and was now expecting the second child of Italian film director Roberto Rossellini.

★ To prove to his ten cowboy-conscious children that there was something else of excitement in the world, Max Conrad, a 48-year-old flying enthusiast from Hopkins, Minn., took up a tiny Piper Cub and soloed it right across the Atlantic Ocean from Washington to Norway.

★ In Los Angeles, little 10-year-old Kenneth Wright, Jr., explained how he had been able to survive a fall off a 200-foot cliff, then a slide down a 1000-foot rock face, and another 300-foot fall. "I bounced pretty often," he grinned.

★ At Long Beach, Calif., beauty lovers got a look at some real women of the world when judges finally picked a winner in the Miss Universe beauty contest. With entrants from thirty countries, Armi Kuusela, a blonde from Finland, won the title, then posed with the runners-up (the Misses Hong Kong, Hawaii, Germany, and Greece) for one of the most striking beauty-contest photos of all time.

★ The white man's burden, the dinner jacket, was doffed for a tempestuous time in Singapore when Malcolm MacDonald, British commissioner general for Southeast Asia, showed up for a concert in shirt sleeves but wearing a black tie. A British tailoring magazine described his action as a "terrifying precedent".

DEATHS: DR. JOHN DEWEY. In his 92 years, Dr. Dewey had done more to stir up educational controversies than any other man of his time. A champion of progressive education and of learning by doing, he was bitterly attacked for sowing the seeds of a materialist philosophy in public education. A free-wheeling free thinker, he had been a professor and then professor emeritus at New York's Columbia University for forty-eight years before his death.

ADOLPH BUSCH. German-born Busch was the musical father of the famed Busch Chamber Music Players and world-famed as a violinist. His death, at 60, came in Vermont.

IRVING WEXLER. At 63, Wexler was hardly known by his real name or remembered for his past infamy. The man who had been called "Waxey" Gordon when he was a kingpin underworld boss during Prohibition died in Alcatraz prison.

July The Republican National Convention ended and Dwight D. Eisenhower's trip to the White House began. A sign painter, Malcolm Hale, felt it was all right now to tell about the signs he had made for the Minnesota delegation. They read "Minnesota Wants Stassen", but when a paper strip was ripped off they read "Minnesota Wants Ike".

★ A New Hampshire delegate to the convention cannily gathered up all the old Warren buttons he could find around Convention Hall. They would, he explained, help him in his own campaigning. His name was John D. Warren.

SCREEN STAR Anne Baxter, now a blonde, retains charm and femininity even while smoking cigar

★ At their summer home in Italy, Ingrid Bergman and Roberto Rossellini, the man for whose love she had left her old home and husband, proudly posed with the latest additions to their family—twin girls. Watching was their 2-year-old son, Renato.

★ In England, the jazziest wedding of the year was also one of the swankiest—the marriage of the Honorable Gerald David Lascelles, 27, a cousin of Queen Elizabeth II and the country's top collector of jazz records, to former actress Angela Dowding. When it was over, the bride did a little quickstep for photographers that made her look plenty hep herself.

★ A 34-year-old Egyptian named Leon Cabili achieved a notable but grim "first" when he became the first man in the 4850-year existence of the Great Pyramid of Cheops to commit suicide by leaping from its 451-foot-high apex.

★ When police in Tucson, Ariz., asked Henry Arreala how come he was driving his car "round and round" a school athletic track, he gave what probably seemed a reasonable reply after the few beers he admitted he had taken aboard. "I'm on my way home," Arreala said, "but I can't get off this street. I'm supposed to turn off here pretty soon."

★ When the Democratic convention rolled around toward the end of the month, it managed to produce just as many offbeat sidelights as the Republican. Perle Mesta, American minister to Luxembourg, phoned Harry Truman to say that until she arrived in Chicago she had never heard of this man Adlai Stevenson. "Don't worry," Truman told her, "you'll be hearing plenty about him."

★ Hopping mad after Radio Moscow charged that Jersey City was crime-ridden, Mayor John V. Kenny replied: "I'll admit that by Red standards our city is ridden by crime—crimes such as freedom of speech, freedom of assembly, freedom of religion, and freedom to vote as one pleases."

DEATHS: SENATOR BRIEN McMAHON. A Connecticut Democrat and a pacifist, McMahon nevertheless led the fight to bolster America's production of atomic weapons. Elected senator in 1944, he became chairman of the Atomic Energy Commission. A few months before his death at 48, his failing health forced him to withdraw as a candidate for the Presidency.

LAMMOT DU PONT. Between 1936 and 1940, when president of the vast chemical empire that bears his family's name, Du Pont would hoist his tall, stooped frame on a bike and wheel off to a day's work. Part of that work was making his company first in world production of synthetics. He was buried near the original site of the powder mill on the Brandywine Creek where the Du Pont fortune had been founded in 1802.

August General Douglas MacArthur, who, upon his return from Korea, had told Congress that "old soldiers . . . just fade away", faded into the board chairmanship of Remington Rand Inc., at a salary reported to be $100,000 a year.

★ When a Los Angeles minister cast about for a likely person to answer his questions about flying saucers or whatever it was that people said they saw, he chose Albert Einstein. Back from the famed mathematician came a direct answer: "Dear Sir: Those people have seen something. What it is I do not know and am not curious to know."

★ When Frank Hayostak was sailing back from war in 1945, he wrote his name and address on a slip of paper, stuffed it in an aspirin bottle, and tossed it overboard. Eight months later an Irish milkmaid named Breda O'Sullivan found the bottle and wrote to Hayostak. In August, they finally got together when Hayostak took a trip to Ireland. Breda's neighbors sensed romance. She herself had other ideas. "There will be no wedding," she said, "but we will remain good pen pals."

★ Frank Costello, flashily dressed prime minister of the New York underworld, swapped his pin stripes for prison stripes to begin serving an eighteen-month contempt sentence arising from his refusal to co-operate at the Kefauver crime hearings. As he entered prison he breezily told reporters to "tell the boys I've come in to do my bit. Tell them I don't want no favors from nobody. Tell them I expect to be treated like anybody else without no special requests."

★ When Gunzeli Basar, Miss Turkey, walked away with the Miss Europe beauty title, she received plaudits from an appreciative audience and criticism from some of her rivals. Both Miss France and Miss Germany had challenged her to wear a Bikini bathing suit. Her refusal to do so, meowed Miss France, was because "her thighs are not well modeled". A photo of Miss Turkey in the bathing suit she *did* wear, however, made the criticism seem pretty carping.

★ Dagmar, bosomy blonde of TV fame, came near to tragedy when a spark from a barbecue pit set fire to a bow on her blouse. Her husband extinguished the flames, then sighed with relief and commented: "That almost put Dagmar out of show business."

★ For the fourth time in five years, Hubert Scully of Erie, Pa., hustled off to the hospital, heard a maternity-ward nurse announce that his wife had given birth to twins.

DEATHS: MARK SULLIVAN. Dean of American columnists, Sullivan was also one of the distinguished historians of his time. His six-volume history of the first decades of the century, *Our Times,* had become a standard reference work long before he died at 77.

HEYWOOD PATTERSON. He was serving time for manslaughter in a Michigan prison when he died of cancer at 38.

LIGHT ON HER FEET and thrilling to see was beloved actress Gertrude Lawrence, dead at 50

Earlier, another crime had drawn him into the web of American history. Patterson was one of the nine Scottsboro boys whose trial on charges of raping two white women made headlines in the '30's.

September Apparently nobody in the world could celebrate birthdays with the verve of Bernarr Macfadden, publisher and health faddist. For his 84th, while 1000 French police cordoned the banks of the Seine, Macfadden parachuted into a vacant lot, a half mile from his target in the river. The birthday before, he pulled the same stunt over the Hudson River in New York City.

★ One family that managed a well-rounded impartiality in political matters was that of Ben R. Isenhower in Chatsworth, Ga. With one son named Dwight David, they christened their newborn Adlai Stevenson Isenhower.

★ While Senator Wayne Morse stood on the Asian side and cheered them on, U.S. Ambassador to Turkey George McGhee and Senator Russell B. Long of Louisiana swam the half-mile stretch across the Bosporus Strait, the link between the Black Sea and the Sea of Marmara that separates Europe and Asia.

★ In the Aberdeen, Scotland, *Press and Journal* a small ad noted a most unusual occurrence. "Dr. E. Forbes-Sempill," it said, "wishes to intimate that in future he will be known as Dr. Ewan Forbes-Sempill. All legal formalities have been completed." The reason: only a few days before, the good doctor had been a woman. Now, he explained, he had completed a long medical treatment that meant "I have been biologically as well as socially a man for several months." A little while later he proved it all by getting married.

★ Clad in heavy jackets, strenuously marching, and munching hamburgers, a rooting corps of young girls trooped into their seats at the Natchez, Miss., football field and promptly began fainting. By the time the shouting and the ambulance sirens died down, nearly two hundred had passed out from "overheating, overeating, and mass hysteria".

★ In New York City, Mrs. Jolie Gabor, Hungarian mother of the three glamorous Gabor sisters, revealed the secret of her success in raising children. "Beauty—to capture; brains—to hold the man. That's what I've taught my daughters. And I think I'm a success. Is not so?"

★ After setting fire to a church in White Castle, La., and watching it burn down, a supposedly cured 48-year-old mental patient named Marcel Nicet told the sheriff he had set the fire because "I got married there and never had luck since."

★ A mistaken estimate of the appetite of small boys proved costly for a Richmond ice-cream-store company. To reward C. G. Winston, who had thwarted a holdup of the store, the company offered his 5-, 7-, and 8-year-old sons all the ice cream they could eat for a year. In September, the store totted up its figures on the deal. Cones consumed to date: 2197, worth $203. Cash that would have been lost if Winston hadn't intervened: $40.

DEATHS: GERTRUDE LAWRENCE. She once summed herself up by saying: "I am not what you would call a wonderful dancer, but I am light on my feet and make the best of things. I know that I am not a great singer . . . but I do know how to sell a song." She first appeared on the New York stage in 1924 and took the city by storm, one critic writing, "Every man in town is, or will be, in love with her." Her untimely death came when she was only 50.

HAROLD TUCKER WEBSTER. His craft was cartooning but he added a phrase to the language when he created Caspar Milquetoast, "The Timid Soul". He died at 67 in Stamford, Conn., so far ahead on his famous cartoons that they continued

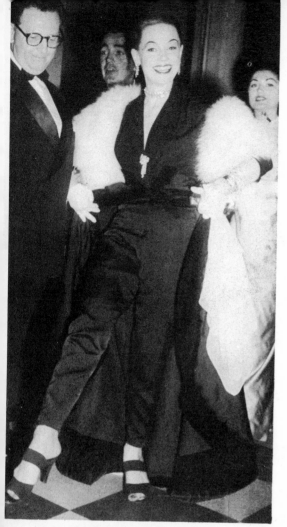

THE LADY WORE PANTS to the opera.
Juliana Larson sets opening's most exotic style note

to run without interruption throughout
the year.

JOHN COBB.   Still trying for the speed
records he had sought and set on both
land and sea, Cobb, one of the world's
greatest racing drivers, was killed at 52
when his jet-propelled boat exploded on
Loch Ness in Scotland.

COUNT CARLO SFORZA.   A pioneer in
the movement toward a unified Europe,
and an early foe of Fascism, he resigned
his Italian government post the day Mussolini came to power. After the war he
became Italy's foreign minister. He died
in Rome at 78.

JOSEPH HUDSON SHORT, JR.   As White
House correspondent for *The Baltimore
Sun*, Joe Short had come to know Harry
Truman well and, when Truman needed
a press secretary after the death of veteran Charles Ross, Short was the man.
He served as the buffer between Truman
and an increasingly hostile press until a
sudden heart attack, at 48, brought his
full and able life to an end.

October   *Tailor and Cutter*, outstanding British magazine of men's fashions,
turned in a forecast on the American
election. The magazine felt that Stevenson might lose votes because he is better
dressed than Eisenhower. His clothes,
said the magazine, smack of the British
Foreign Office and "the man in the American street is traditionally suspicious of
apparent Limey tendencies in his public
figures". Eisenhower, however, was
bound to be popular because he looks
like "a kind of military Will Rogers".

★   When Vice-President Alben Barkley's
nephew got sick in Paducah, Ky., the
Veep fortunately was on hand to help out
with the boy's paper route. He greeted
one housewife subscriber with an offer to
take orders in advance. "But," she told
him, "I'm paid up until January 1."
"That's fine," the Veep cracked, "I'll be
back then. I'm going to be out of a job
the first of the year anyway."

★   Even if it was a press agent's stunt,
movie star Vanessa Brown's startling request for a "nice, happily married Hollywood photographer" before whom she
could pose in the nude, got attention
everywhere. Her reason, she said, was
that she wanted to prepare for a forthcoming Broadway role by learning how
it feels to be stared at with nothing on.

★   Anne Baxter, usually a conservative
sort of Hollywood star, decided to do

something about it. She blossomed out with a blonde dye job for her hair, a rhinestone in her navel (for a film role), and took to smoking cigars. "They are," she said, "very soothing on the nerves."

★ Freeman F. Gosden and Charles J. Correll, better known as Amos 'n' Andy, announced they would retire from radio after twenty-five years and ten thousand broadcasts.

★ In Memphis, Tenn., 7-year-old Elisabeth Hamblin dropped a quarter in a church collection plate, then added a penny with the whispered comment: "For taxes."

DEATHS: HATTIE McDANIEL. Creator of the role of "Beulah" on radio and TV, winner of an Academy Award for acting, Hattie McDaniel was one of the best loved of Negro actresses. She was 57. SUSAN PETERS. After astounding Hollywood by courageously returning to the screen after a spinal injury left her paralyzed seven years ago, Susan Peters climbed all the way back to stardom, but then, her doctor said, she "lost the will to live" and died at 31.

DAVID A. SMART. His magazine, *Esquire*, which he began to publish in 1933, brought a new slant to men's fashions in both clothes and pin-up girls. Also publisher of *Coronet*, he was 60 when he died in Chicago.

ALVIN ANTHONY KELLY. Better known as "Shipwreck" Kelly, he was the best-known stunt man and flagpole sitter of the '20's. When he died, at 61, after collapsing on a New York City sidewalk, he was clutching a scrapbook of his press clippings.

November One hundred and six years old but still anxious to vote, Agatha Hamill of Seattle, Wash., got her son to help her fill out an absentee ballot and, when told that Adlai Stevenson and Dwight Eisenhower were the nominees, sharply asked: "They don't think they can beat Franklin D. Roosevelt, do they?"

★ Sugar Ray Robinson, who, as middleweight boxing champion, made quite a name for himself with his fists, set out to make another name with his feet—as a $15,000-a-week dancer in a New York City night club.

★ Out of the election whirl came the first mother-son team in the history of the American Congress. Elected by the Republican voters in two Ohio districts were Representative Frances P. Bolton, who had been in the House since 1940, and her 35-year-old son Oliver, who went in for his first term.

★ The usual rash of election-bet payoffs brought, among others, the drinking of the front page of a newspaper (burned and its ashes put into coffee) by Mrs. Carolyn Howard in Montgomery, Ala.

★ Kay Summersby, the pretty, 43-year-old, Irish-born W.A.C. who was General Eisenhower's wartime secretary-chauffeur (and wrote an account of it called *Eisenhower Was My Boss*) got a new boss when she married New York stockbroker Reginald H. Morgan.

★ After twenty years of searching for Detroit gangster Leonard Moceri, wanted for a killing, Los Angeles police checked the fingerprints of a man who had been caught dropping slugs in pay phones—despite a roll of $1800 in his pocket—and discovered he was none other than Leonard Moceri.

DEATHS: WILLIAM GREEN. Starting his career as a coal miner in Coshocton, Ohio, Green had become $25,000-a-year president of the 8,000,000-member American Federation of Labor by the time he died at 82. Originally he had wanted to be a Baptist minister.

BENEDETTO CROCE. So secure was he in his world-wide reputation as writer and philosopher that when Mussolini came to power in his native Italy Croce spoke openly against the regime but was never forced to flee the country. When he died, at 86, in Naples, both houses of the Italian Parliament closed for an hour in mourning.

DIXIE LEE CROSBY.   A singer and actress, she gave up her career in 1930 to marry Bing Crosby and become the mother of his four sons. She died of cancer at the age of 40.

REPRESENTATIVE ADOLPH J. SABATH.   At 86, his forty-five years in Congress (as a Democrat from Illinois) was the greatest stretch of service ever recorded there. When he died he had just won election to his twenty-fourth term.

December   When an irate Chicagoan reported that a "wicked-looking" parrot at the Brookfield zoo had been extremely profane, the zoo's boss, Robert Bean, soberly defended his feathered charges by saying that "I've interviewed them exhaustively and the strongest words any of them said were 'Oh fudge.'"

★   During General Eisenhower's trip to Korea, the G.I. driver of a car assigned to the general's party had eyes only for a steep hill up which he was supposed to drive Charles E. Wilson, president of General Motors and defense secretary-designate. At the foot of the hill he asked Wilson to transfer from the Chevrolet in which they were driving to a jeep. The hill was too steep for the G.M. car, explained the soldier. "Are you sure?" asked the justifiably concerned Wilson. "I'm damned sure, sir," was the answer.

FANCY FOOTWORK takes Champ Sugar Ray Robinson from the boxing ring to a ring of show beauties as he makes debut as hoofer in New York night club—at $15,000 a week

★ A House committee investigating off-color books and magazines was chagrined when it found that novelist Margaret Culkin Banning, who had been called in to put the finger on some bad examples, was the author of an article entitled "Is Virginity Old-Fashioned?" which appeared in a magazine whose index also listed such provocative titles as "Betrayed by Sex".

★ In Korea, marine lieutenant Allen Dulles momentarily outshone two newsworthy relatives (his father, Allen Dulles, deputy chief of the Central Intelligence Agency, and his uncle, John Foster Dulles, secretary of state-designate). While attacking enemy machine-gun emplacements he was wounded three times, then recommended for the navy's highest decoration, the Navy Cross.

★ One of the happiest endings of any story came when former naval lieutenant Sam Byrd, 44, announced that he and 18-year-old Patricia Ann Bolam had been secretly married for a year. Byrd first met her when serving as a beach officer during a rehearsal for the Normandy invasion being staged near Plymouth, England. Pat, then 10, had been watching and got so excited that she fell off a cliff. Byrd carried her home, later brought her to America, tried first to adopt her, then fell in love with her.

★ As a finishing touch to his London music-hall act, a comedian tossed a bottle of champagne into the audience, where it was caught by a charmer in the sixth row. She was Princess Margaret, who had slipped in unnoticed.

★ When Dr. Selman Waksman, codiscoverer of the miracle drug streptomycin, arrived in Stockholm to receive the Nobel Prize in medicine, he was approached by a man and his small daughter. The daughter, it was explained, had been saved from death by Dr. Waksman's he meeting, said Dr. Waksman,

was "a greater honor even than receiving the Nobel Prize".

★ James M. Lambie, Jr., business manager of General Eisenhower's New York City campaign headquarters, had one little chore to attend to before closing the office doors. It concerned fifty-two portable radios that had been lent to the staff for use during the campaign. As discreetly as possible, he circulated a memo that said: "To date, eight of the radios have been returned. It is requested that the staff members concerned examine their effects and their consciences and drop off at the business office any product of such examination."

★ Los Angeles police finally caught the gray-haired little old lady who had been going around town sticking up banks and getting away with it. Somewhat to their surprise, she turned out to be Mrs. Ethel Arata, 52, four-time divorcee and daughter of the late Robert M. Catts, a real-estate operator once worth $20 million. Mrs. Arata's only explanation for her robbery spree: "I did it . . . for others. I gave them the money because they needed it and kept nothing for myself."

DEATHS: QUEEN MOTHER ALEXANDRINE. Widow of King Christian X of Denmark, the queen mother died, at 73, in Copenhagen.

VITTORIO EMANUELE ORLANDO.   An Italian statesman of genuine stature, he was, at 92, the last survivor of the "Big Four" (Lloyd George, Clemenceau, Wilson) who drafted the Versailles Treaty.

SISTER ELIZABETH KENNY.   After years of uphill battling that had taken her from Australia around the world, Sister Kenny finally received support for her polio treatments from such respected institutions as the Mayo Clinic. When she died, at 66, she was back home in Australia.

MRS. DAVID W. WALLACE.   Mother-in-law of Harry Truman, Mrs. Wallace was 90 when she died in the White House.

JUGGLING cups and saucers, circus star Dietar Tasso seemed to symbolize civilization. As 1953 dawned, mankind waited and wondered

PICTURE SOURCES

SLIM AARONS: 356.

ZINN ARTHUR: 351.

FRANK H. BAUER: 317.

BLACK STAR: Manning 134, Robert Cohen 162(bot) and 188(lt, cn), Paul Pietzsch 198, René Groebli 237, Meldolisi 250, Guzman 264 and 406, Francis Sully 300, Ruohomaa 360 and 361, ABC 409, Farabola 426(cn-lt), Arthur Davey 441.

PHILIP BLOOM: 335.

CBS: 382, 383.

COLUMBIA PICTURES: 365.

COLUMBIA RECORDS: 333(lt, rt).

COMBINE: 149, 197, 210(t, bot), 211(t, bot), 213, 222-3, 226(t), 227(lt), 232(lt, rt), 233, 246.

EUROPEAN: Endpapers, 92, 204, 234(t), 253, 276, 277, 283, 291, 292, 293(rt), 294, 364, 389(bot), 412, 443.

FRED FEHL: 352, 357, 358, 359(lt, rt).

HARRISON FORMAN: 270(t, bot), 278, 279.

FREEPORT SULPHUR CO.: 137.

GLOBE: 337(bot).

BOB GOLBY: 350(bot), 353.

GRAPHIC HOUSE: 336(lt, rt), 337(t).

HARRIS & EWING: 17.

JIM HERVEY: 379(bot).

INTERNATIONAL: 10, 19, 20, 39, 51, 55, 56, 61, 71, 73, 81, 82(t), 91, 93, 98, 99(t, bot), 100, 114, 127, 130, 145, 150, 151, 154, 157, 169, 186, 191, 193, 194(lt), 195(bot), 200, 201, 207, 219, 221, 239, 248, 255, 274, 275, 281, 290(lt, rt), 298, 299(lt, rt), 307, 311, 314(rt), 322, 324-5, 389(t), 392, 396, 415, 421(bot), 429, 431, 432, 436, 437, 445.

KEYSTONE: 205, 217(t, bot), 240, 247, 323.

LIFE PHOTOS: Mark Kauffman 339, Peter Stackpole 350(t), Eliot Elisofon 354.

LOOK: 30, 68, 104, 107, 235, 303, 319, 330, 362, 411, 414, 417, 424, Robert Capa 368 and 369(lt).

METROPOLITAN MUSEUM OF ART: 402.

MGM: 334, 367.

NBC: Sidney Desfor 372, 373, 379(t).

NEW YORK TIMES: 181.

PARAMOUNT PICTURES: 371.

PARIS MATCH: 147(t), 158, 366.

PHOTOGRAPHY MAGAZINE: W. H. den Exter Blokland 139, Joern Gerdts 433.

P.I.P.: Werner Braun 234(cn).

PIX: 189, 220, 426(bot-cn), 447.

PROVIDENCE JOURNAL BULLETIN: 94, 96-7.

RAPHO-GUILLUMETTE: Ormond Gigli 112, Pabel 184, Belzeau 310, Sabine Weiss 331.

RKO: 369(rt).

SOVFOTO: 142-3, 170, 171, 172, 176, 178, 265, 267, 268-9.

OZZIE SWEET: 377.

UNITED ARTISTS: 363.

UNITED NATIONS: 288.

UNITED PRESS: 22-3, 24(t), 33, 34, 35(lt), 38, 77, 82(bot), 85, 86-7, 88, 89, 106, 124, 131, 144, 146, 147(bot), 159, 162(t), 163, 192, 196, 203, 215, 228, 254, 257, 258, 259, 284, 289, 296, 313, 341, 343, 349, 374, 398, 403, 420, 427(t-lt).

U.S. AIR FORCE: 161.

U.S. ARMY: 79(t), 80.

WIDE WORLD: 12-3, 14, 15, 16, 24(cn, bot), 25, 26, 27, 31, 32, 35(rt), 36, 37, 41, 42, 43, 44, 45, 46, 47, 49, 50, 52, 57(t, bot), 60, 63, 64, 65, 66, 67, 69, 72, 78, 79(bot), 83, 84, 95, 102, 103, 105, 108, 109, 110, 111, 113, 115, 120, 121, 128, 148, 152, 153, 155, 166, 173, 179, 183, 188(rt), 194(rt), 195(t), 199(t, bot), 202, 206, 209, 216, 225, 226(bot), 227(rt), 229(t, bot), 234(bot), 241, 242, 243(t, bot), 245, 252, 261, 273, 280, 282(t, bot), 285, 286, 287, 293(lt), 295, 304(lt, rt), 305, 314(lt), 315, 321, 326, 329, 342, 345, 347, 370, 378, 385, 386, 387, 388(t, bot), 390, 391, 393, 397, 399, 401, 407, 413, 421(t), 427(t-rt, bot-rt), 434, 440.